A HARVEST OF RUSSIAN CHILDREN'S LITERATURE

TO:
Greg + Chris - HAVE
A MERRY SPINGTIME +
A HAPPY SUMMER
FROM,
Dan
Dudson

A HARVEST OF
RUSSIAN
CHILDREN'S
LITERATURE

EDITED, WITH INTRODUCTION AND COMMENTARY, BY

MIRIAM MORTON

FOREWORD BY RUTH HILL VIGUERS

UNIVERSITY OF CALIFORNIA PRESS

Berkeley   Los Angeles   London 1970

UNIVERSITY OF CALIFORNIA PRESS
BERKELEY AND LOS ANGELES, CALIFORNIA

CAMBRIDGE UNIVERSITY PRESS
LONDON, ENGLAND

© 1967 BY MIRIAM MORTON
SECOND PRINTING, 1967
THIRD PRINTING, 1968
FOURTH PRINTING, 1970
ISBN: 0–520–01745–5
LIBRARY OF CONGRESS CATALOG CARD NUMBER: 67–21384
DESIGNED BY HARLEAN RICHARDSON
PRINTED IN THE UNITED STATES OF AMERICA

THIS BOOK IS DEDICATED

to the memory of those Russian
children who were forever deprived
of the joys and wisdom of
their native literature by the
merciless Nazi invaders at whose
hands they perished

and

to my two American daughters who
enriched their foreign-born mother
with their childhood love of
American literature for the young.

FOREWORD

In the "world republic of childhood," of which Paul Hazard has written, children's books keep alive the sense not only of nationality but of humanity. If Miriam Morton had done no more than extend acquaintance with the books in this world republic, she would have performed a signal service by giving to English-speaking boys and girls glimpses of other ways and attitudes of a land we have known all too little. One has only to read at random in this remarkable compilation of stories from Russian writers to realize how much more she has done.

Most book lovers, whether they realize it or not, read as much for communion with the personality behind the words of a book as for the words themselves. Mrs. Morton has introduced to young people some of the personalities of Russian letters who know the way along that often obscure, wonderfully serendipitous path that leads directly to the minds and imaginations of children.

In every national literature for children the books, stories, and poems that live long are those that were written by people whose greatness grew from able intellects and lively fancies, but most of all from informed hearts. The selections here give bountiful evidence of the third source. Because of it, great literature for children not only reflects but transcends the time and environment in which it was written.

Such writers as Maxim Gorky, Ivan Krylov, Ivan Turgenev, and Anton Chekhov, whose stories and poems are included here, are familiar to English-speaking young people. Here, however, they are recognized as authors of work that has special meaning to boys and girls. Leo Tolstoy, knowing how lastingly important are children's first impressions, believed that the books he had created for children were among his most significant, and could say, ". . . having written these books, I can now die in peace."

In the first section—for young children—one is impressed by the extravagance of the nonsense; the highly imaginative, even fantastical, qualities of almost all the stories and rhymes; and the skill with which, in some stories, fairy-tale style and feeling are combined with scientific truth without any sacrifice of dignity. In later sections the shadings of humor, the unusual characters, and the emotional power of the stories stimulate a desire to explore Russian children's literature far beyond this inviting anthology.

I cannot forget Vladimir Korolenko's "Children of the Vaults"—little ghosts who will, I expect, forever haunt me; nor can I cease to smile at the intrepid explorer Chechevitsin of Chekhov's "The Boys," who to the family of his friend Volodya seemed only an incorrigible troublemaker. All too few young people have met the deaf-mute giant serf of Turgenev's "Mumu," yet surely the humanity of the writer of so moving a tale should reach readers whose minds are fresh and whose hearts are receptive.

Almost every story reminds me of another reason for being thankful for this *Harvest of Russian Literature for Children*. May seeds from the harvest take root in the lives of American boys and girls.

Ruth Hill Viguers

ACKNOWLEDGMENTS

I want to thank all those good people who made this book possible. First among them is Robert Zachary, an erudite and imaginative editor, an innovator whose eclectic vision of books and readers encompassed even a foreign children's literature. I am also greatly indebted to James Kubeck, an editor with a keen sense of how the physical embodiment of a book can enhance it. I valued, too, his sensitivity to an author's occasional need for an extra bit of attention and a pat on the back. Very special thanks are due to Mrs. Frances Clarke Sayers, a professor of children's literature and librarianship who inspired, encouraged, and advised me in this effort. The interest and help of Donnarae MacCann, Chief Librarian of the University Elementary School Library at the University of California, Los Angeles, was also invaluable. I extend my thanks and affection to her and to the children of the school who came to their library to listen so intelligently and feelingly to my readings of some of the stories and poems translated for this anthology. I am also most grateful to Wilbur J. Smith, Head of the Department of Special Collections, University Library, University of California, Los Angeles, for his generous coöperation in affording me access to the Russian children's books in his care.

I want to express my gratitude to all the kind people in the Soviet Union who helped me pursue sources and obtain material that has greatly enriched this volume. My special thanks go to the children's authors, particularly to Kornei Chukovsky, Vera Smirnova, Boris Polevoy, and Leo Kassil, who helped me gain important insights into the literature to which they have so richly contributed. I also want to thank the Soviet children who shared with me their opinions about the books they loved best.

Special gratitude is due to Grace Stimson and Frederick Guilford for their expert editorial assistance.

M. M.

CONTENTS

PART II: A FEAST OF FOLK TALES
for all ages

PART III: STORIES, VERSE, AND FABLES

for boys and girls from eight to eleven

PART IV: SHORT STORIES, SELECTIONS FROM NOVELS, PROSE POEMS

for more mature young readers— ages twelve to fifteen and up

INTRODUCTION

Of all the arts, it is literature that has always played the star role in Russian culture. It was Russia's novelists, playwrights, and poets who first put their country on the cultural map of Europe. Sovietologists speak of Russia's cultural nationalism, pointing out that her greatest pride has been in her literature, in its unflinching and compassionate humanism, and in the recognition her writers have received throughout the civilized world.

The Russians have also taken an enormous pride in their literature for children, in its goals and achievements.

Authorities on comparative children's literature contend that a country's writings for its young readers reflect the essence of its vision of itself and of the world. Frances Clarke Sayers * was their spokesman when she said:

> The literature of childhood, in any country, is indicative of the social and ethical goals of the time and the place which produced it, and in addition, it is the one area which also invites the highest creative imagination of the artists and writers, so that the whole spectrum of accomplishment and expectation is to be discovered in books for children.

It is within the purview of this anthology to reveal the social and ethical directions of Russia in the past and in the present, while it fulfills other objectives as well.

The purpose of this anthology is threefold:

First, to make available to American children from five to fifteen a substantial sampling of Russian children's literature for approximately equivalent ages.

Second, to give American adults who work with children and books, and those teaching comparative literature and librarianship, an acquaintance with a significant portion of this significant literature for the young.

Third, to offer those interested professionally or as concerned laymen an insight into an important aspect of Russian child culture—its literature—and to show how it reflects modern Russia's ideas and ideals.

The hundred selections represent material published in children's editions from 1825 to the present. As all these inclusions are currently in print in the Soviet Union, the anthology offers a substantial sampling of what *today's* Soviet child reads.

The volume has been planned as a family book and as a book to be acquired by children's libraries. Because of the difficulties of translating and

---

* Frances Clarke Sayers is an American professor of children's literature and librarianship; formerly she was for many years in charge of work with children in the New York City public library system. She is an anthologist and an author of children's books and books about children and literature.

publishing from a children's literature so esoteric as the Russian, an anthology is virtually the only practical and plausible way of making certain that this interesting and beguiling literature does not remain indefinitely unavailable.

To make the selections meaningful and enjoyable for the young reader, only complete works or excerpts of sufficient length and substance are reproduced. For the excerpts, summaries of or comments on the whole story are provided so that the reader's curiosity and response are not frustrated. Full versions are given of all the twenty folktales.

My approach to the material has limited the diversity of genres drawn from, but I hope that it has resulted in a more readable and less unwieldy book, especially for the children. For the adult specialist or the student of children's literature, the longer selections and the occasional multiple representations from different works of the same author offer not only more satisfying reading, but fuller insight into the genres chosen. This approach also helps avoid extreme fragmentation of masterpieces and violation of artistic integrity.

There is a separate section in this volume for each of three different age groups: from 5 to 7, from 8 to 11, and from 12 to approximately 15. The first two sections begin with material for the youngest *within* each group and progress to that for the oldest. The three main groupings are useful merely as guidelines, for books for young people should not—indeed, cannot—be rigidly classified according to chronological ages or grades in school. Rather, the child's reading ability, sensitivity, and mental development should be the guide to his reading choice in an anthology. Thus, essentially, only a half-title page stands between the child reader and his exploration of this book.

The genres from which the majority of selections have been taken are:

For the youngest group: nursery rhymes, animal tales in verse, simple fables and parables, short folktales, short modern stories, and story poems.

For the middle group: stories and excerpts from longer works with the proper content level. Here are also modern stories revealing the life and preoccupations of the Soviet schoolboy and schoolgirl. Nearly the full version of the famous verse tale by Pyotr Ershov, *The Little Humpbacked Horse,* is also given in this section, as well as three of the less difficult fables of Krylov.

For the oldest group: classical and modern stories, excerpts from novels, prose poems.

Twenty folktales, a number of them of interest to the more mature young reader, are given in a separate section.

Selections from the abundance of Russian children's books of biography, exploration, adventure, and science fiction, as well as a representation of Russian children's literature of the theater arts, will have to be accommodated in a second anthology. The material in these fields is too extensive to permit its inclusion in this first anthology. Russian children from the age of about twelve read and study the poetry of such outstanding writers as Pushkin, Lermontov, Nekrassov, Koltzov, Tiutchev, Fet, Essenin, and others. Unfortunately, the available translations of these poets do not measure up to the excellence of the original works. I have therefore decided, with great reluctance and regret, to omit such poetry from this book.

In dividing the material into age categories, I gave only casual attention to vocabulary readiness, especially in the selections for the two older groups. A child's enthusiasm for reading is seldom permanently impaired by having to look up a few words in the dictionary or to gauge the meaning of a word from its context in the sentence.

The selection of material presented other problems, however—problems that were both challenging and bewildering. Because both the adult and the child who will use this book are unfamiliar with the parent literature, with the ramifications of the political and social history of Russia, and with most Soviet mores, much thought had to be given to nearly every selection. Only those works that would be understandable and enjoyable without involved commentary or footnotes were chosen. Nearly five hundred Russian books for children, as well as several bibliographies, were used in making the selections.

The undeniable evidence that basic Soviet ideology is generally unaccepted in America gave rise to many quandaries in choosing material. Ideology, however, is pervasive in almost all Russian literature and, in fact, has been part of its strength and inspiration. The Russian people have never known a time without extreme social stress, without turbulent political events and disturbing currents and undercurrents of protest. As Russians have also traditionally ascribed to literature a guiding and teaching role, it is not surprising that their leading authors reflect in their work the social as well as the human condition of the people.

Russian children's literature, for the child of about nine and up, has shared not only the superior quality of its adult counterpart, but also its concern with the social problem—with the woes of the underprivileged and their strivings for a better life and a new social order. Great care has therefore been taken to strike an objective balance: to include among the selections some that reflect universal values and measure up to acknowledged literary criteria, as well as some that elucidate evolving Russian social and political ideals.

Another challenging aspect of the preparation of this anthology was translation from the Russian. The limited availability of usable translations made it necessary for me to translate a disproportionate number of the selections—nearly half—from both prose and poetry. Most of the rest of the translations are attributable to Soviet translators, but many of these had to be changed to give them more of an American style. (Soviet translators, even those who are originally from the United States, use the British idiom.)

Translation of the verse for younger children proved to be a demanding, yet gratifying, task. A conscientious effort was made to transform the original into a poem pleasant to read in English. The rhythm and the rhyme scheme of the original were usually retained, but not at the cost of irritating and incongruous inversions, forced rhyming, cuteness, or Victorianisms of syntax, and not at the cost of losing the original intent or spirit. Yet some of the alchemy of the poem was inevitably lost.

The volume contains nearly a hundred reproductions of graphic works from children's books published in the Soviet Union. All these illustrations are by Soviet artists. In addition to introducing the reader to Russian book illustrators, they help to illuminate the material. A list of the illustrations and their artists is given in the back of the book.

Book illustration, regarded as an important applied art in the Soviet Union, is given serious attention, especially in books for the preschool child. Yet it is the word and not the picture that is supreme—the writer and the artist do not vie for the reader's attention. Nor is the child's private world of vision invaded and overpowered by the artist's own conception of the images evoked by the words.

This anthology is a pioneering effort. There is no anthology in English of *any* foreign children's literature. All that we have, even from other Western literatures, is a sprinkling of translated modern stories published individually and a few collections of folktales. Of Russian literature for children, we have only a few books of fables, several small collections of folktales, and an occasional story. Practically nothing of the wealth of Russian poetry and prose of the nineteenth century, a substantial portion of which has since become an integral part of Russian reading material for the young, or of nineteenth-century works written expressly for children, has been translated and published in English. There was a flurry of translated modern stories for the young, published during World War II years and soon after the war ended, when the Soviet Union was considered an ally against a common enemy. These few books have long since been out of print. As recently as 1963, only five Russian children's stories, translated and published in America, were still in print (*Translated Children's Books* [New York: Storybooks, International, 1963]). This anthology, then, is the first attempt to present a sizable collection of Russian stories, folktales, fables, poems, and excerpts from longer works, for children of all ages.

A number of the unique features of Russian children's literature are reflected in the works chosen for this volume:

The pervasive humanist tradition and the basically optimistic realism of Russia's nineteenth-century literature, so richly endowed by Russia's master writers, are also present in the works of the same period written expressly for the young. This tradition has been carried over in large measure to books written and published for children in the Russia of the twentieth century, including, of course, Soviet Russia.

The Soviet child, especially the schoolchild and the adolescent, has been doubly fortunate. He has inherited his country's nineteenth-century masterpieces, and he has had enlightened and courageous Soviet children's authors —men and women of artistic conscience and unusual creative abilities—write expressly for him. Some Soviet writers have safeguarded children's literature from the limiting and corroding effects of the excesses of socialist didacticism of the Stalin era. Notable among these crusaders have been Kornei Chukovsky and Samuel Marshak, champions of the child's need and right to experience the whole range of literary genres from nonsense verse and fantasy, folktales and fairy tales, to social satire. The careers of these two poets for the very young have spanned five of the six decades of the twentieth century. Marshak began to write for children in the 1920's, and died in 1964. Chukovsky published his first animal tale in verse in 1916; he is now eighty-six.

These two poets and literary critics, together with Sergei Mikhalkov and Agnya Barto, founded an excellent literature in verse for the preschool child. (In the Soviet Union, this means the child from three to seven, for kindergarten begins at the age of three and ends at the age of seven. The age categories used in classifying children's books are somewhat different in Russia; in addition to the more extended preschool age, young people are considered as children through the age of seventeen. In America, the child over fourteen is now considered a young adult, at least in the libraries and by publishers.)

Little attention was given to the literary needs of the very young prior to the 1920's. A "Great Literature for Little Folk" was developed by the energetic quartet named above. Maxim Gorky, though noted for his realistically grim novels and plays, an important part of Russia's "literature of accusation" against the oppressive czarist autocracy, was paradoxically also the leading spirit in establishing the principle that the very young need happy as well as artistically sound verse, and jolly stories and folk literature for their mental and emotional growth. He exerted much effort and influence, over a period of years following the Revolution of 1917, in founding in the new Soviet Republic a uniquely felicitous literature for the very young. English nursery literature served as a model for Chukovsky, Marshak, Mikhalkov, and Barto. Chukovsky and Marshak have provided excellent translations of English nursery rhymes.

In Russia, to a greater degree than perhaps in any other country, literary masters have written deliberately for the older child reader. More masterpieces have been adopted by the young. There has been a coherent and purposeful effort since the 1860's to enrich children's reading with the works of the great Russian writers. Important stories and novels have often been published in children's editions at the same time or soon after they appeared for grown-ups. These gifts from the masters have been made fully available to the Soviet child, for Soviet publishers issue them constantly and in mammoth editions, with helpful and appropriate commentary by educators, critics, and even academicians. Soviet children thus have in their libraries and on their bookshelves at home works by writers who have immeasurably enriched world literature: the poets Zhukovsky, Ershov, Pushkin, Lermontov, Nekrassov, Tuitchev, Fet, Blok, Essenin, Mayakovsky, and others, and the prose writers Pushkin, Leskov, Aksakov, Turgenev, Leo Tolstoy, Korolenko, Chekhov, Gorky, Paustovsky, Aleksei Tolstoy, Sholokhov, Kataev, Fadeev, and more.

The genre of the short story has been highly respected and developed in the whole body of Russian literature. Many short stories by the past masters of the medium and by more recent writers of great talent are part of the literature for Russian children. This is a happy circumstance for the anthologist.

The earnestness and the serious goals of Russian writings for children are another unique feature of this literature; such goals are stressed more than similarly serious goals in children's literature of Western countries. Russian works, particularly for the older child, do not merely or primarily seek to entertain him. The bitter past of Russian life is not sweetened or hidden from him in what he reads. The following words of Maxim Gorky are therefore often quoted in connection with reading material for the young: "Lead them into the future by teaching them to know and value the past." Professor Marc Slonim, literary historian and critic, in the introduction to his book, *The Epic of Russian Literature* (New York: Oxford University Press, 1950), touches upon the same theme: "For centuries the search for truth, the ideological controversies, the political longings of the Russian people found expression in the literature. It would be futile to attempt to separate Russian writers from the spirit of their times and the various trends of national thought." Those in Russia who have concerned themselves with literature for the young have deemed attempted separation of writers from the spirit of their times not only futile, but also undesirable. Such a separation would diminish the enlightening and inspiring force of their literature and would render the young less prepared when they become adults to enjoy and value their literary heritage.

The serious intent of Russian children's literature has been expressed in writing of excellent quality, encompassing a wide spectrum of human aspirations and experience. The child can enjoy, understand, respond to, and identify with the people and events in his books. The recurring themes have been the moods and delights of nature, the love of country, issues of social justice, love of one's fellowman, love of work, peace, adventure and discovery, faith in the goodness of man, hope for the future, courage, the importance of knowledge, and the fascinations of science. These themes are treated with perspective and with careful regard for the child's nature. Humor, satire, and optimism lighten the solemnity. Sensationalism and excitement for their own sake are conscientiously avoided.

Because of the long tradition of viewing literature as enlightenment, and because of the noncommercialized methods of Soviet publishing, Russia's literature for children, despite its diversity, is exceptionally coherent in standards and purpose. It constitutes an integral part of the child's education. Moreover, it is common practice to refrain from abridging important works, distorting classics, softening folktales and fairy tales, or in other ways violating the integrity of artistic literary works.

Most of the fare for preschool children and young schoolchildren is free from solemnity; it is remarkably gay and full of fantasy, humor, and light satire. The wealth of folk literature is also made amply available to these children. It now includes the folktales of many peoples of non-European Russia. There are 167 distinct nations and ethnic groups in Russia, and 60 different languages. The esoteric and exotic folk literature of these peoples, who since the Revolution of 1917 have gradually acquired cultural identity, is translated and published for Russian-speaking children. The folktales in this anthology include examples from some of these folk literatures. Violence and grimness are not a basic characteristic of these folktales; shrewdness, tenacity, kindness, forgiveness, and courage, as well as a healthy and unequivocal condemnation of evil, put violence and grimness in their proper place.

Books read by the older child, however, often reveal life in the raw. The harshness of Russian life in the past is not glossed over. Reality is not expurgated, although it is leavened with optimism and faith in human nature.

The Russian youth finds in his reading no sharp transition from a romanticized view of human existence to an extremely pessimistic one—a transition that the young reader in the West has to make and still manage not to feel a deep disillusionment in his world. The alienated youth of the West is suffering, among other things, from a letdown induced by the nihilism and negation of contemporary literature.

The Russian thinking behind the unexpurgated realism offered to the older child reader is not new. It goes back to the middle of the nineteenth century when the intelligentsia, seeking to lead the people to a better life, affirmed that the young have to know and understand the evils of their society to be spurred on to a dedicated resolve to improve it. This approach was well expressed in Professor O. F. Miller's introduction to a collection of Dostoyevsky's stories published for children in 1896, *Dostoyevsky for School Children* (St. Petersburg: Enlightenment Publishers):

> I could have foregone a foreword were it not for those who insist that "Dostoyevsky is not for children." Of course, not all of his works are suitable for children. There isn't a single author for adults whose entire literary output can be offered to the young. But children's literatures would be impoverished if they were deprived of all the writings of the best artists of the word. It is not to be allowed that the child should not be introduced to the works of a great writer until he is old enough to read all of his books. Why keep from the young reader so precious a part of the realm of creative art—an opportunity to learn about life in the images drawn by the masters of the written word. Caution should be exercised in the manner in which such work is presented to children, so that they do not receive a distorted conception of the great writers. They cannot be shown all pictures of life, but those that they are shown must remain in their original form, with all their excellence. . . .

> I suppose I will now be told that all this will not change a grim picture to a bright one. Firstly, the general impression will be less grim when the more extreme episodes are omitted . . . ; secondly, not everything is grim in the works of any writer—including Dostoyevsky; thirdly, we must clarify what we mean by "grim"; to say nothing of the inadvisability of nurturing the young reader only on bright images.

> I insist that the "grimness" in Dostoyevsky is not dangerous to children, but, on the contrary, it is beneficial, that many of his pages are understandable by children of twelve and above, of course mentally developed ones. When reading Dostoyevsky, children will seldom laugh, but must every book stimulate laughter? Laughter is salutary, but it doesn't hurt the child to weep occasionally with those good, sacred tears that are good for his spirit, as spring rain is good for the field. Not such tears make the child "nervous"— believe me—not such!

> There are, of course, disturbed, nervous children who cannot bear anything sad. But these children are not well. Perhaps they are sickened by being surrounded by fathers and mothers who do not know how to weep with good tears but shed tears of self-pity and hatred. . . . The tears of the young reader may drop onto the book, but they will not be tears of despair and hostility but of compassion and love for the "degraded and the insulted" [the

words in quotation marks are the title of a novel by Dostoyevsky]. These tears will not poison their hearts, but will touch the most sensitive strings and will enhance their ability to love. The writer who evokes love is undoubtedly good for children. . . . But the reading of Dostoyevsky should be alternated with the reading of other writers.

An omnipresent aspect of unexpurgated realism in contemporary Soviet children's literature is the political and social theme, the truth about war. When I asked Leo Kassil, a prominent Soviet children's author, how Soviet educators and cultural leaders justify exposing children to these realities, he repeated to me his reply to a similar question put to him by a group of American educators: "How is it that in the West you expose children from practically nursery school age to the complexities of religion and the tragic story of Christ and the Christian Martyrs?"

I asked another children's author, Boris Polevoy, how the theme of possible nuclear warfare is dealt with in Soviet literature for the young. His answer was that the children are assured that nuclear war is an impossibility because of the basic sanity of humanity. The subject is not stressed, but the theme of victory over the Germans in the last war, the defeat of such formidable past invaders as the Mongolians of the Golden Horde and as Napoleon, and the legendary courage of the Russian people in times of war are everywhere emphasized. Mr. Polevoy pointed out that 73 million Russians lived in the territory invaded by the Nazis in World War II. Children's books celebrate, in fiction and biography, the many adult and child heroes of those years.

Other heroes in Russian works for children are the political leaders, foremost among them Lenin; but there is also the writer hero who faced persecution, exile, and at times the firing squad or the hangman's noose for the sake of writing the truth; or the revolutionary, the great scientist, the scholar, the dedicated physician, the poet, the explorer, the naturalist, the outstanding musician or painter. But the victim of social injustice is the greatest hero of all.

There is a trend now, after the discrediting of the personality cult, to bring a new type of hero into literature for the child—the boy, girl, or adult who tries, against great odds, to cope with a personal or a family problem. A new villain is the adult who is inflexible, authoritarian, and self-seeking, particularly in his attitude toward youth.

The Russians have been characterized as moody and somber people, and their literature has been prejudged as depressing. Such judgments are made largely by those who lack knowledge of the Russian temperament and of the diversity of Russian letters. Wright Miller, in *The Russians as People* (New York: E. P. Dutton, 1961), makes this comment: "To characterize the Russians as a people addicted to melancholy seems to me no more or no less true than to call them a people addicted to optimism. They are capable of abandoning themselves to either; what is striking is the sincerity and wholeheartedness of their abandonment." And John Cournos, in his introduction to *A Treasury of Russian Life and Humor* (New York: Coward-McCann, 1943), speaks of the variety of humor found in the works of different Russian authors: the "crystalline humor" of the fabulist Krylov, the "nuanced humor" of the novelist Goncharov, the "quiet folk humor" of Leskov, the "gentle laughter-through-tears humor" of the playwright and short story writer Chekhov, the "exuberant humor" of the early Soviet satirists Ilf and Petrov, and the "sheer farcical" humor of the Ukranian writer Zoschenko. Several of these writers are represented in this anthology. To this list should be added the Soviet children's authors, Kornei Chukovsky and Samuel Marshak, for the rollicking humor in their verse stories for the very young, and Leo Kassil, the spinner of comedy-fantasies for the "middle-aged" child.

Humorists have not considered their calling less of a responsibility and an art than have serious writers. They are confirmed believers in the persuasive force of humor and the child's need for laughter. Their work is highly valued by both the cultural specialist and the child. The quality of their work, too, is evaluated in accordance with strict criteria.

The older child in Russia, for whom so much serious literature is created and republished, is also offered a full measure of the lighter genres. There is for him an abundance of nature writing, satire, exploration and adventure stories, science fiction, and highly inspiring works of biography and reminiscence.

The young reader's acceptance of, admiration for, and response to his literature are enhanced in the Soviet Union by the unusual and diverse means of communication between the author and the child. Many books have a prologue or an epilogue in which the author tells something important and interesting about the story, about his experiences as an author or as a growing and maturing human being. In the same spirit, many children's authors have published autobiographies of their childhood and youth. Bibliographies with commentaries by the authors on their own books are published as reference material for children and are distributed to all children's libraries. This direct communication with the reader, as well as the lively correspondence between writers and children's clubs and literary circles, and the personal appearance of authors before audiences of children at a variety of functions, bring the writer, the child, and the book into close communion.

In a foreword to a collection of his early stories published for young readers, Mikhail Sholokhov (1965 winner of the Nobel Prize in Literature), speaks about the noble record of the Russian masters of the past who continued to write despite constant harassment, persecution, and exile, which many of them had faced. He says to his young reader, "I hope you will never forget that in order to open the doors to the world and to knowledge to all of you without exception, and in order to keep these doors forever open, many writers gave all of their strength, and much blood was shed by your ancestors. . . . Go forward with courage into the world and love your books with all your soul."

Kornei Chukovsky, the "Pied Piper of Peredelkino," * communicates with his preschool audience in many unusual ways. For example, he appears as the

---

* See article under this title in *The Horn Book Magazine* (Oct., 1962).

main character in "At Home with Chukovsky," a program at the world-famous Obraztsov Puppet Theater in Moscow.

Authors are as popular with Soviet children as movie stars are with American children. On October 23 (1965) I was present at an appearance of Leo Kassil before a thousand Moscow schoolchildren, who had gathered to celebrate the writer's sixtieth birthday. Mr. Kassil had been in demand for similar gatherings ever since July 10, his real birthday, and he was "booked up" well into January.

There was an air of festivity and excitement in the Palace of Pioneers that afternoon. The attendance was to be limited to eight hundred children, the capacity of the auditorium; the most enthusiastic readers were to be chosen by their teachers from among the schoolchildren of the district. Their teachers told me that the extra two hundred were so anxious to attend the celebration that they quickly gobbled up several Kassil books and wrote reports on them. The overflow audience was accommodated on the stage, the children standing up throughout the hour's proceedings.

The author's arrival was marked by the release of a rocket with his name on it. The rocket, genuine though small, had been built by the boys of an interest club at the Pioneer Palace. The master of ceremonies was another children's author, a newcomer to the fold. The program had been arranged by the House of the Children's Book (Dom detskoi knigi), a complex of publishing enterprises and functions having to do with many phases of the educational use of children's literature and with children's books in general.

During the program Mr. Kassil was greeted on the stage by small groups of two or three children, each representing its own class. These children came up to the author with flowers or models of planes, ships, and cars, and delivered their gifts with congratulatory speeches. Each time one or more of the group came forward, faced the audience, and recited by heart long passages from Leo Kassil's books. As Kassil is a humorist and a lover of fantasy with humor, there was much laughter and recognition of the funny episodes. Kassil writes only in prose; the recitations were well prepared and full of histrionics. Most of the participants had excellent speaking voices. To me they sounded like potential talent for the Moscow Art Theater.

The bouquets filled a whole table. In his speech, Kassil told, to the delight of his audience, of his first misadventures as an inexperienced imaginative writer. One of the anecdotes was about the author's invention of a name that he wanted to be as piquant as Dickens' "Pickwick"; his character ended up with the name Kissmequick, for the author was at that time completely innocent of any knowledge of the English language. His amusing speech over, Kassil announced that on his way home he would lay the flowers presented him on the monument of the poet Vladimir Mayakovsky. The children heard this announcement with exclamations of awe and approval.

When I had entered the auditorium to attend the program, my companion from the House of the Children's Book asked the child who happened to be occupying the best seat—in the front row on the center aisle—to take another and give his to "the auntie from America." How this auntie wished at the end of this afternoon and on other such occasions that she could relive her childhood and enjoy the cultural opportunities Russian children now had; her own childhood in czarist Russia had little resemblance to that of these youngsters, although she too had loved books, music, and the ballet.

Indeed, I made a number of surprising discoveries regarding children and books in my travels in the Soviet Union. One of the most unexpected was the extent to which American children's literature has been made available in Russian translations. The diversity of authors and titles, and the size of the editions, are overwhelming. For example, *Uncle Tom's Cabin* has been issued in ten different cities, by as many publishing enterprises; the total number of copies put out from 1926 to 1960 was 1,298,000. There have been six editions of a six-volume collection of the works of James Fenimore Cooper, totaling 1,800,000 sets; and seven individual titles have come out in editions of from 10,000 to 300,000. Five different collections of O. Henry stories have been issued in a total of 310,000 copies. Three works of Bret Harte have appeared in a total of 225,000 copies. *Hiawatha* has had several editions, totaling a quarter of a million copies. Mark Twain is a great favorite: *The Adventures of Huckleberry Finn* has appeared in ten separate editions, in five different cities, and in a total of 500,000 copies; *Tom Sawyer* has had fourteen editions, in six cities, with a total of 1,700,000 volumes. Ernest Hemingway's *The Old Man and the Sea* was published in a young readers' edition before it came out for adults. Esther Forbes's *Johnny Tremain* was published in an edition of 85,000 copies. Dorothy Sterling's *Mary Jane* has come out in an edition of 100,000 copies. And many more titles could be added to the list.

At the Research Library of the House of the Children's Book, in Moscow, there are several hundred titles of more recent American children's books, including picture books, some translated and some untranslated. They are used for research, or as textbooks of the English language, or as a reservoir of titles to be translated into Russian and widely circulated in children's libraries. Parents at the American Embassy in Moscow often borrow these books for their children.

In a sense, this anthology constitutes an unofficial "exchange." Russian children have benefited from some of the best that American children's literature has to offer. It is hoped that this book will be the beginning of a continuing process of making the best in Russian literature for the young available to American children.

PART I

VERSES AND TALES
with sugar and spice ...

for boys and girls from five to seven

a gift
of rhymes and rhythms
from Russian poets
for the very young

Kornei Chukovsky, the dean of Soviet poets for the very young, is a Russian Dr. Seuss and Santa Claus rolled into one six-foot-five-inch-tall octogenarian. He speaks for himself and for the group of dedicated writers of verse for the preschool and primary school child of Russia when he discusses in the remarks below some of the distinctive aspects of Soviet poetry for young children. After pointing out that Edward Lear and Lewis Carroll, whom he greatly admires, were not brought into contact with more than the few children they knew personally, but that millions have enjoyed their work, he goes on to say:

As for us who write for Soviet children, we could not seclude ourselves even if we wanted to, for we are surrounded by a whole sea of youngsters all our lives, a great sea that stretches from the Artek Pioneer Camp in the Crimea to the Arctic Circle. In the depths of this sea we look for and find ourselves as writers.

We read our verses or fairy tales, as soon as we get them written, to large audiences in kindergartens, schools, children's homes, libraries, sanatoriums, Houses of Culture, summer camps.

Of course, we could read our books to a few children, to those growing up in the family. . . . But the entire style of the verses and stories, their rhymes and rhythms, are arranged so that they can be grasped easily by large audiences of children. I know that when I write my fairy tales, I always imagine myself standing on a stage in front of a great assembly of curious, impatient, and restless listeners. Hence the "scenic" quality of my tales. The plot unfolds like a play—opening scene, the clash between good and evil, the climax. All of it has to move along at the very fast tempo child psychology demands.

The verse in this section is by five noted poets. Alexander Blok and Samuel Marshak have also distinguished themselves with their poetry for adults. Kornei Chukovsky, Samuel Marshak, Agnya Barto, and Sergei Mikhalkov have been for the past several decades the favorite poets of the preschoolers.

It is hoped that parents and others who read to children will take Kornei Chukovsky's advice and enliven their presentations to their audiences, small or large, with the proper histrionics. "The language," says Chukovsky, "must be melodic, lilting, and the phrases and sentences so orchestrated that children love them not only for the story they tell but also for the mood their music creates."

In discussing his own verse, Mr. Chukovsky has pointed out that the action, or mood, of each episode—sometimes of individual couplets—calls for its own distinctive meter.

The Silly Little Mouse

SAMUEL MARSHAK

Mother Mousie sang one night:
"Sleep, my darling, sleep in peace,
And when you wake in morning bright,
You shall have some candle grease."

Little Mouse, half asleep,
Gave a fretful little peep:
"Stop your squeaking, Mommie dear,
Find a nurse and bring her here."

Mother Mousie ran to get
The Duck to nurse her little pet:
"Please to move into our house
And be a nanny to my mouse."

Ducky came and sang her song:
"Quack, quack, grow big and strong,
I shall find a worm for you,
A fat and juicy worm to chew."

Silly Mousie, half asleep,
Gave a fretful little peep:
"Go away, you horrid nurse—
Mommie's bad, but you are worse."

Mother Mousie ran to get
The Toad to nurse her little pet:
"Please to move into our house
And be a nanny to my mouse."

Toady came and croaked with pride:
"I am sitting by your side,
If you're good and do not cry,
You shall have a big fat fly."

Silly Mousie, half asleep,
Gave a fretful little peep:
"Go away, you horrid nurse—
Ducky's bad, but you are worse."

Mother Mousie ran to get
The Mare to nurse her little pet:
"Please to move into our house
And be a nanny to my mouse."

The Mare sang out with all her might:
"Close your eyes and close them tight.
Cats are nasty, so are goats;
But mice are nice, I feed them oats."

Silly Mousie, half asleep,
Gave a fretful little peep:
"Go away, you horrid nurse—
Toady's bad, but you are worse."

Mother Mousie ran to get
The Pig to nurse her little pet:
"Please to move into our house
To be a nanny to my mouse."

"Umph, umph," was Piggy's song.
"Umph, umph, the night is long.
Go to sleep, and if you do,
You shall have a beet or two."

Silly Mousie, half asleep,
Gave a fretful little peep:
"Go away and let me be—
Your voice is much too rough for me."

17

Mother Mousie went to get
The Hen to nurse her little pet:
"Please to move into our house
And be a nanny to my mouse."

"Cluck-cluck-cluck," the Henny said,
"You're very restless in your bed;
Tuck-tuck-tuck your little head
Beneath my speckled wing instead."

Silly Mousie, half asleep,
Gave a fretful little peep:
"Go away, you horrid nurse—
Piggy's bad, but you are worse."

Mother Mousie ran to get
The Fish to nurse her little pet:
"Please to move into our house
And be a nanny to my mouse."

18

The Fish began to sing away,
But what it sang was hard to say:
It moved its mouth, no doubt of it,
But not a sound came out of it.

Silly Mousie, half asleep,
Gave a fretful little peep:
"Go away and let me be,
Your voice is much too soft for me."

Mother Mousie ran to get
The Cat to nurse her little pet:
"Please to move into our house
And be a nanny to my mouse."

Pussy's voice was full of joy:
"Meow, meow, sleep, my boy;
Meow, meow, I'll lay my head
Here beside you on the bed."

Silly Mousie, half asleep,
Gave a happy little peep:
"I *adore* the way you sing—
It's just too sweet for anything!"

In came Mother at a bound,
Searched the bed, searched all around,
Searched the house for Silly Mouse,
But Silly Mouse could not be found . . .

Henny Penny and the Ten Ducklings

SAMUEL MARSHAK

Do you know the tale of the old man and his wife
and the hen that lived with them all of her life?

You may have heard it told by your mother.
If you have, then listen—I'll tell you another.

Now this *other* old man and his *other* old wife
had a hen that lived with them all of her life.

This hen, Henny Penny, was black and gray,
and she laid a remarkable egg one day.

It was round,
And sound,
Without a single flaw—
The prettiest egg you ever saw.

A mouse ran past,
Its tail went—swish!
The egg went—crash!
And was smashed!

How Henny Penny did cry!
And the wife had a tear in her eye.
She went out to the hen coop. What luck!
There she found ten eggs—of a duck!
She took them and said: "Henny Penny,
I have brought you some eggs—see how many!"

Henny Penny accepted them gladly.
There was nothing she wanted so badly.
She sat on the eggs night and day,
And nothing could drive her away.
She hardly took time off to drink,
Or eat, or even to think.

And then, on a bright sunny morn,
The ducklings began to be born.
They pecked and they scratched,
And at last they were hatched,
And they cried, when they stood on their feet:
"Tweet! Tweet!
Give us something to eat!"

They were not like chickens at all;
They were darker and much too tall,
And each wore a web on its toes,
And each had a long, flat nose.

Henny Penny went out with her brood,
To teach them to look for their food.
She scratched in the dirt with her claw,
In search of a seed or a straw.

When she found one, she gave a low cluck:
"Here's a nice juicy seed for a duck!"
But the ducks would have none of her seeds.
They ate nothing but grasses and weeds.

Now the beak of a chick never grows
To the size of a duckling's nose;
Grass is easy for ducklings to pick,
But it's hard, very hard, for a chick.

The weather was sunny and still.
They walked to the top of a hill,
Saw some birch trees below, and beyond?—
Beyond they discovered a pond.

Down the hillside the ducklings dashed,
And into the water they splashed.
They swam in the liveliest way,
But their mother cried out in dismay:
"Cackle-cack! Get back
On the ground!
Cackle-cack! Come back,
You'll be drowned!"

(Henny's mother had carefully taught her
Never, *never* to enter the water.)

But the ducks weren't frightened a bit.
They were quite contented to sit
On the ripples and rock, or to race,
Splashing water all over the place.
Henny Penny was simply distraught;
Was *this* what her mother had taught?
"Cluck-cluck-cluck, are you crazy?" she said,
"The water is over your head!"

She would gladly have pulled her babes out,
But then *she* would have drowned without doubt.

Nine of the ducklings at last
Came waddling out very fast.

But the tenth didn't want to come out,
It kept swimming and darting about,
And it suddenly dived out of sight.
Henny Penny was frantic with fright.
"Help! To the rescue!" she cried.
"Help! My youngest has died!"

But soon this babe reappeared.
(There was nothing, of course, to have feared);
And the nine were joined by their brother,
And they all trailed off with their mother.

They were suddenly spied by a cat.
There on the hillside it sat,
Without moving a hair of its fur,
Without uttering even a purr.
It just narrowed its eyes on the brood,
Very sure it had found itself food.

But it didn't escape Henny's eye.
The mother let out a wild cry,
And her feathers stood up all around,
And she rose right up off the ground,
And she opened her claws, and she flew
At the cat to tear it in two.

The cat was frightened to death.
It fled without stopping for breath.
But hard on its heels went the hen—
Down the road,
Through a field,
To a glen,
Where the hen chased the cat up a tree.
What a brave Henny Penny was she!

Snooks

SAMUEL MARSHAK

A lady sent by train freight:
A bag,
A box,
A crate,
A basket,
A picture,
Some books,
And a wee little doggy named Snooks.

When the luggage was brought to the train,
It was counted all over again,
And packed away in the freight car:
A bag,
A box,
A crate,
A basket,
A picture,
Some books,
And the wee little doggy named Snooks.

But off the wee doggy ran
As soon as the journey began.
And only on reaching to Don *
Was it found that the doggy was gone!
All the luggage was safe on the train:
The bag,
The box,
The crate,
The basket,
The picture,
The books,
But—where was the doggy named Snooks?

Just then an enormous black hound
Came across the rails at a bound.
It was caught and put on the train
Along with the bag and the box,
The basket,
The picture,
The books,
Instead of the doggy named Snooks.

The lady got out of the train
At a station in southern Ukraine.**

---

* The *Don* is an important river in Russia.
** The *Ukraine* is the name of one of the fifteen Soviet Republics; it is in the south-western part of the Soviet Union.

She called to a porter who came
To bring her the things:
The bag,
The box,
The crate,
The basket,
The picture,
The books,
And the dog—that was *not* named Snooks.

The hound gave a terrible growl,
The lady emitted a howl.
"You robbers, you rascals!" cried she,
"This isn't my dog, can't you see?!"

She tore at the handles and locks,
She kicked at the bag and the box,
The basket,
The picture,
The books:
"I *will* have my doggy named Snooks!"

"Just a minute, dear madam, don't shout,
And don't throw your luggage about.
It seems that you sent by freight:
A bag,
A box,
A crate,
A basket,
A picture,
Some books,
And a wee little doggy named Snooks.

"But the smallest of dogs, as you know,
In the course of a journey may grow."

Two Cats

SAMUEL MARSHAK

2 cats?—
Why! that's
8 paws,
2 tails and
40 claws.

2 pets that purr? 2 balls of fur?
Yes—till trouble started.
Soon they were one single blur;
None could get them parted.

Furry furies, equal-matched,
How they clawed and bit and scratched!

Neither cat would cry "Enough!"
What was left?—2 specks of fluff!

So you see, my dear young friends,
How all catty squabbling ends!

The Cockroach

KORNEI CHUKOVSKY

Part 1

Here comes a pike
Riding a bike.

Followed by a cat—all black—
On a scooter front-to-back.

Next, five mosquitoes come into sight,
Flying along on a yellow kite.

Then arrives Mousie Mollie
On a limping, smiling collie.

And a stork astride a mare,
And a bear in a wheel-chair.

Little rabbits, soft and huggy,
Come riding in a baby buggy.

A frog does a funny trick,
Diving down from a broomstick.

Camels, horses, and donkeys
Come carrying monkeys.

A white unicorn
Trots, blowing a horn.

Slowly along the road
Hasten a turtle and a toad.

"Be careful! Don't crush the ants,"
A hippo warns the elephants.

To the picnic they all come,
Munching candy and cake,

In a very merry mood,
For a day at the lake.

Then suddenly they grow numb and still!
Who's that coming round that hill?!

A fierce and dreadful Roach!
A mean cock-cock-*Cockroach!*

"Don't you dare to approach!"
He roars, he rages:

"I'll lock you in cages!
And swallow you ALL
Like one tiny meatball!

"Or with a twitch of my mustache,
I'll turn you all to succotash!"

The birds—they shudder!
The beasts—they flutter!

The poor crocodile
Forgets how to smile!

The hungry wolves, in their alarm,
Though meaning no evil or harm,
Right then and there they sup,
Gobbling one another up!

And a terrified lady dog,
Falls into a faint
On a prickly hedgehog!

Alas! Not one dares to fight,
Every bird and beast takes flight!

The Lobster, backing up a mile,
Murmurs with a bitter smile:

"I, too, have a long mustache,
I, too, can make succotash. . . ."

The Cockroach continues to roar,
The Lobster backs up some more.

Now the Lion climbs a hill;
From there he speaks his royal will:

"We must regain our happy land!
Against the brute we'll take a stand!

"And to the warrior who fears not this
     foe,
Who this monster will overthrow,
To him I'll give a juicy bone
And the finest pine cone!"

The creatures in one eager crowd,
Surge forth and cry out loud:

"We do not fear this nasty foe,
With tooth and claw
We'll lay him low!"

And they all rush to do battle—
Birds, fish, fowl, and cattle.

But the Roach moves his mustache
And bellows: "SUCCOTASH!"

One and all they beat a retreat.
The enemy they don't defeat!

Into the fields and woods they dash—
Terrorized by the Roach's mustache!

The Lion shouts: "What a disgrace!
Come back! Come out and show your
    face!
Pin the enemy with your horns—
Bulls, rhinoceros, unicorns!"

But each in his hiding place stays,
And wails: "Horns aren't cheap these
    days. . . .
And our skin is precious too—
What you ask of us, we cannot do!"

Caught in nettles the crocodiles twitch,
And the elephants get stuck in a ditch.

Lo! All that's heard now
Is the flow of their tears;
All that's seen now
Is the trembling of their ears!

And the shark, scared and pale,
With a flail of his tail,
Slithers into the lake—
Not like a shark, like a snake!

While the cunning little skunk
Already packs his trunk.

Part 2

To the Cockroach they all yield—
He's now lord o'er wood and field.
He struts about among them,

Rubbing his big tummy,
Looks at their young ones
And thinks: "How very yummy!"

Gazes at the little ones with greed,
Orders supper to be brought him with
    speed!

"I want no beans or corn,
But flesh of baby unicorn;
Other youngsters as well—
Those with a savory smell."

The poor, poor parents
Are in distress.
Their dear babes
They hug and caress:

For what mother could give up her child,
Her baby tame or her baby wild?!
So that the monster could devour
Her precious crumb, her little flower!

So mommies and daddies moan and cry
As they bid their infants good-bye!

And the monster is secretly cursed:
"May the glutton blow up!
May he burst!"

But now we see another picture:
The Kangaroo, that nimble creature—
Leaps, leaps—she's at the Roach's hill,
And for a moment all are mute
As she points to the mustached brute:

"A monster?! Where?!
A Giant?! There?!

"It's a roach, a roach, a wee-bit roach,
A wee-little beetle you fear to approach.
Look! It's a midge, a mite,
A bug that can't even bite!

"For our trouble *we're* to blame!
What a shame!
What a shame!"

The Hippo then comes forth
With slow pace and worried face,
Muttering in an anxious way:

"Please go away, go away!
Your words will make him very mad,
He may think of something very bad!
Go, Kangaroo, Kangaroo,
Go, go back to your zoo!"

Then the Hippo falls still,
Surprised by a sudden trill . . .
  "Cheek-chee-reek, cheeky-reeky,
  Cheek-chee-reek."
And from behind a bush
They see it peek.

Hop-hop-hop—comes the reckless
  fellow,
A gay and carefree little Sparrow.
And right there, on the Roach's hill,
With his cheeky-reeky trill,
Peck, peck, peck—
NO MORE ROACH!
Not a smidgen, not a speck!

He's swallowed in a flash,
All of him and his mustache!

Part 3

What joy! What glee!
All the creatures again are free!

The Sparrow is praised and
On loving paws it's raised—
There's a parade,
A celebration,
A masquerade!

The mules bray a song,
Hippo strikes his gong.

To honor the Sparrow, a path is cleared:
The goat sweeps it with his beard.

The sheepish sheep
Don't sing but hum,
The bold baboon
Beats a drum.

And from the roof the joyous bats,
Wave their hankies and their hats.

But when the elephants start to prance,
To clap and stomp a happy dance,
The orange moon shakes loose—
And falls right on big Moose!

Like a pinwheel it falls from the sky,
Now all is dark—save the firefly!

The Monkeys who are no fools,
With hammers, nails, and other tools,

In a row make a trek,
Up the Giraffe's long, long neck.

To the sky the moon is nailed,
The Monkeys bow as they're hailed.

Again the moon sheds its light,
Again the world is friendly, bright.

The Magic Tree

KORNEI CHUKOVSKY

Look at the bold blue jay
On the nose of Uncle Matvei!

In the tree, see four poodles
Building nests out of noodles!

A large ram in a tiny boat,
Over the green lawn is afloat!

And in the orchard,
Near and handy,
Grows delicious
Chocolate candy!

But most wonderful to see
Is our Magic Tree!

Not a leaf grows on this tree,
Not a blossom can you see—
Only shoes, socks, and boots,
Like so many colored fruits!

They grow in pairs,
They grow in clumps.
Also pretty little pumps!

So all that Mommie needs to do,
Daddy, grandpa, grandma too—
Is pluck some hose, booties, shoes.
Isn't *that* good news?!

There are
Galoshes for Masha,
Satin pumps for little Nina,
Dancing shoes for Irina!

Yes, most wonderful to see
Is our Magic Tree!

Come children!
If your shoes are worn,
Stockings full of holes,
Boots tattered and torn,
Come, come to the Magic Tree—
Get new ones!
They are free!

They are ripe, done, and ready.
Come one, come all!
It's shoe-harvest time!
It's Fall!

Never again need you
Shoeless go,
Or with holes at your toe
Walk over ice or snow!

*What Murochka Did after She
Heard the Tale of the Magic
Tree.*

Murochka took her shoe,
Picked some toys,
And planted them with
Rake and hoe—
    "Grow shoe,
    Grow toys,
    Grow!

    "I'll water you,
    My dears,
    Till a Magic Tree
    Appears,
    For all poor
    Girls and boys,
    Without shoes,
    Without toys."

Another Magic Tree
Did grow!
What do you know!
What do you know!

Children came in a
Noisy crowd,
Picking and plucking,
And laughing aloud.
Dancing about,
They started to shout:

    "Where is Murochka?
    Thank you, Murochka!
    Come out and play!"

The No-Water Boy

KORNEI CHUKOVSKY

The quilt
Ran away!
Away flew the sheet!

And the pillow,
Like a frog,
Leaped down the street!

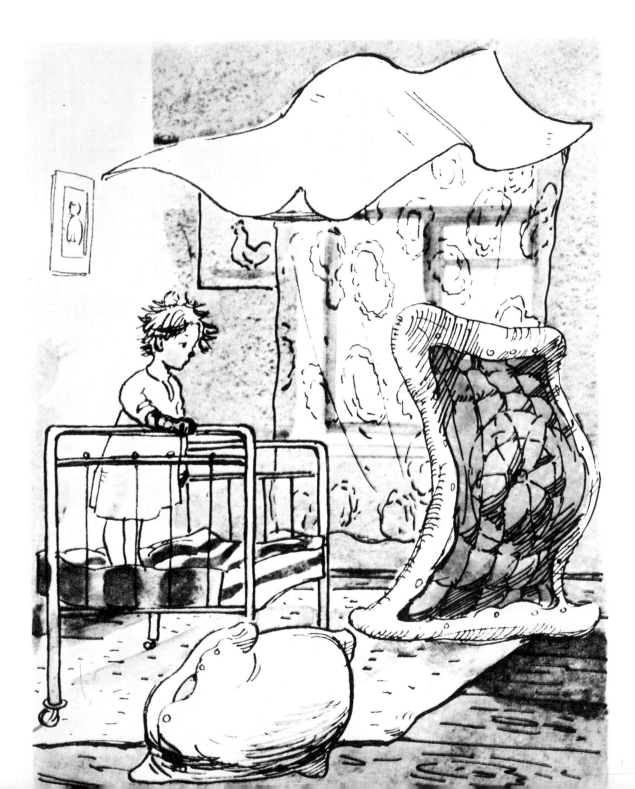

I reached for the light—
The light, too,
Took flight!

And my book
'Bout Duck Ned
Shuddered,
And sped
Way under my bed!

I went to pour some tea—
But the samovar
Fled from me!

It dashed
Down the hall,
Potbelly and all!

What was wrong?!
What was the matter?!
Why did all things
Run and scatter?!
Whirling,
Turning
In the air,
As if wishing
I weren't there!!

All things rose
From the floor,
To somersault
Out the door!

Suddenly,
From Mommie's room,
With a grump, grumble
And boom!
Bowlegged and lame,
Mr. Washstand came!

And he scolded as he came:
    "Oh, you unwashed
    Little pig!
    In what dirt
    Did you dig?!

    "The filth on you
    Is inches deep!
    You look . . .
    A chimneysweep!

    "Little kittens,
    Ducklings, mice,
    Even flies!
    Wash themselves
    As best they can,
    Having neither
    Soap or pan!

"Only you hate
To wash—
In water never splash!
That's why
Your socks and shoes,
Ran from you
With hoots and boos!

"I, Mighty Washstand
You now command
In this lake
A bath to take!"

The water was frigid,
Cold as ice!
I was out of there
In a trice!

I ran and ran
Till I reached
The tub,
There to rub, rub
And scrub!

Soap clung to my hair,
Suds filled my eyes.
Did that soap care?!

And like a wasp
The sponge
Did sting!
More salty tears
To my eyes to bring!

To get away from that
Mean old sponge,
Into the ocean

I meant to plunge;
But it would not
Let me be—
Everywhere it followed me!

And I quickly jumped a rail
With the sponge
Right on my tail!

On the way I met
Kind Uncle Croc,
With his twins
Out for a walk.

On his right
Was Totosha,
On his left
Was Kokosha.

"Help! Help! Uncle Crocodile!
Save me! At least for a while!"
And that mean sponge
By whom I was followed,
Like a pea, Croc swallowed!

Uncle Croc then stared at me,
Stamped his foot, and glared at me:
    "Home! At once!" he cried.
    "Wash your face and hands," he
        cried.

    "If you don't!
    I'll swallow YOU!"

Like lightning I went,
To the Mighty Washstand,
And I washed,
And I rubbed,

34

And I washed,
And I scrubbed!

Till off came the polish,
Off came the ink,
My face was, at last,
Spotless and pink!

And, behold!
Back came my pants,
Leaping right into my hands!

A pie spun through the air!
"Eat me, pal—down the hatch!"
The pie went down,
Without a scratch!

My things returned
In a gay band,
Each shaking me
By the hand:
Objects small,
Objects big—
As my schoolbooks
Danced a jig!

Then Mighty Washstand
Ran to me,
Hugged me,
Kissed me,
And said as he smiled:
    "Now you look a decent child!"

So, let's wash!
Let's splash!

Let's swim and dive,
Look clean,
Look alive!

Let's wash,
Let's splash
In water hot,
In water cool,
In washtub, bathtub,
Ocean or pool!

For water then,
Let's give a cheer!
Very loud, very clear!
So it's heard
From here,
To faraway Tangier!

Zakaliaka

KORNEI CHUKOVSKY

My little girl
Liked to draw
And drew
Everything she saw:

A bird pecking food,
A doll made of wood,
A butterfly's pretty wings—
All kinds of things!

"Murochka," I said,
"What's that you just drew?
A thing never seen,
A thing that's quite new:
With ten horns and ten feet!
And twenty sharp teeth!"

"This is horrid Zakaliaka,"
Murochka replied,
"A dangerous elf;
I thought it up myself."

"Stay, Murochka, stay!
Why are you running away?"

"It scares me!" she said,
And fled.

I'm a Big Girl Now

AGNYA BARTO

Now with toys I cannot bother:
I'm learning how to read!
I'll give them to my little brother:
He shall have them—yes, indeed!

Not my wooden tea things though—
No, not yet, they're new, you know.
And although my Bunny is lame,
I will keep him just the same.

Teddy Bear? His coat's too greasy.
He won't have my Dolly, for
He'll pull her all to pieces
Or he'll drop her on the floor.

Let him have my choo-choo, maybe?
It's too old to give away.
Then, although I am no baby,
Even I must sometimes play.

Now with toys I cannot bother:
I am learning how to read.
But I shall not let my brother
Have a single one, indeed!

My Seashell

AGNYA BARTO

My pretty little seashell—
I keep it safe and dry.
Yet once down at the seashore,
In water it used to lie.

My Granddad
From the Black Sea
Has brought it to me;

And if you listen closely,
You'll hear in it the sea.

You'll hear in it the breakers,
The hissing of the foam,
And you will think the Black Sea
Has come into your home.

Cradle Song

ALEXANDER BLOK

In the sky little stars burn,
In the river ripples turn,

In the window the Moon peeks,
And to little ones it speaks:

"Sleep, sleep till the break of day,
When Sister Sun comes out to play—

"Sister dressed in warm gold;
I in silver bright, but cold.

"When She dozes off toward night,
I, in moonlight quiet, recite

"A sleepy fairy tale or two,
As I keep watch over you . . .

"Sweet slumber I bring,
A hushed song I sing. . . .

"Sleep, sleep, sleep,
Children, chipmunks, chicks,
And sheep. . . ."

The Rabbit

ALEXANDER BLOK

In summertime the rabbit
Feasted his eyes
On white flowers,
Garden bowers,
And blue skies.

Now, in autumn,
He rests his chilly paws
On wet yellow leaves,
And shakes with fears
Of the hungry wolf's claws!

All the cabbages
Have been dug up!
Where is rabbit a juicy meal—
A cabbage leaf or two to steal?
Where is he to sup?!

Of summer he thinks,
And with sad, sad eye
Looks up, and blinks—
The heavy rain has hid the sky,
Poor rabbit tries hard not to cry!

Summer Rain

APOLLON MAIKOV

"Gold, gold is falling from heaven"—
The children shout as they chase the rain . . .
Wait, my darlings, we'll gather that gold
In our fields of golden grain!

The Cricket

AGNYA BARTO

Daddy was working,
So I sat quite still.
Just then,
A cricket
Chirped under the sill.

I searched near the window,
And looked on the floor,
But then heard the cricket
Chirp hard by the door.

He's near and he's far,
But where?—who can say!
At times he is silent,
At times chirps away.

Does he fly? Does he jump?
Does he crawl like a snail?
Perhaps he has whiskers,
And also a tail?

Or maybe he's fuzzy,
And frightful to see?

And when he crawls out,
How surprised all will be!

And then Mommie said,
"He makes noise all day.
I think we should drive
This lodger away."

We searched high and low,
And we searched all around:
A long-lost umbrella
Was all that we found.

And under the couch,
Dad's glasses found we,
But never a sign
Of the cricket did see.

Unseen little cricket,
You come and you go,
But what you may look like,
I still do not know.

THE MILLER, THE BOY, AND THE ASS

An old folktale retold in verse by Samuel Marshak

An old man,
A miller,
Was riding
An ass.
His grandson
Was walking
Behind
On the grass.

"Look!
A disgrace!"
Was the villagers'
Talk.
"Grandad
Is riding,
But grandson
Must walk!"

Quickly
The miller
Dismounted,
And put—
The boy
In the saddle,
While he
Went on foot.

"Goodness,
No manners!"
An old woman
Said.
"Age
Walks behind,
While Youth
Rides ahead!

"Who ever
Heard of it?
There is no
Word for it!
Age walks behind,
While Youth
Rides ahead!"

Grandad
And grandson
Both mounted
And rode.
They came
To a man
Who was hauling
A load.

"Ugh!"
Said the man,
"No shame,
Not the least!
Two men
On the back
Of that poor
Little beast!

"Who ever
Heard of it?
There is no
Word for it!
Two men
On the back
Of that poor
Little beast!"

Grandad
And grandson
Both went
On foot.
On grandfather's
Shoulders
The donkey
Was put.

"Ha, ha, ha!
Ho, ho, ho!"
Roared a man
With a sack.
"An old ass
Has put
A young ass
On his back!

"Who ever
Heard of it?
There is no
Word for it!
An old ass
Has put
A young ass
On his back!"

My Best Friend and I

SERGEI MIKHALKOV

My best friend and I—why we
Live as happily as can be!
We are faithful friends and true:
Where he goes,
There I go, too.

And we carry in our pockets
Lots of interesting things:
We've a couple of bottle stoppers;
In a matchbox, two grasshoppers;
Two big coins, and two brass rings.

Both of us live in one flat
(Anyone can tell you that);
Ring four times if you want me,
While for him, ring only three.

And we keep two prickly hedgehogs,
Two grass snakes that love to play;

In a cage we have two finches,
Who just sing the livelong day.

And about each snake and bird
And each hedgehog, all have heard—
All the folks on all the floors
From the first to the twenty-third.

My best friend and I each day
After breakfast make our way
To our school, which isn't far—
Often leaving doors ajar.

And those pets of ours would stray
Through the neighbors' flats all day.
Our grass snakes just love to creep
Into draughtsmen's hats to sleep.

Our house-manager, in terror,
Jumped from bed the other night,
When he found two hedgehogs sleeping
Underneath his bed sheets white.

Our two finches love to sing—
All day long their voices ring;
When our neighbor turns on his TV,
He can't hear a single thing.

To the manager, the draughtsmen
Drag the snakes. What can they do?
And they see him, with two hedgehogs,
Puzzled by that question, too.

Soon the neighbors all complain,
"When shall we have peace again?"
And the man next door suggests
That the only thing to do,
Is to send those nasty pests
For safe keeping to the Zoo.

When we came back from the park,
No one met us in the dark;

Sadly we put on the light—
There was not a pet in sight!

Hedgehogs, finches, and grass snakes—
Where, oh where, are you tonight?!

My best friend and I next day
After breakfast made our way,

With misgivings, to the Zoo—
Feeling very mad and blue.

All our thoughts have one refrain:
"Shall we get them back again?"

We walk slowly past the cages,
Past the keepers watching there,
While at least a hundred finches
Sing and flutter in the air.

But our finches, which are they?
Who can tell us? Who can say?
And which hedgehog, and which snake
Is our own without mistake?

For a hundred snakes or more
Hiss and wriggle on the floor;
Of the hedgehogs in the Zoo,
There must be a hundred, too.

But our birds and beasts, somehow,
Do not recognize us now.
When it's near the end of day,
We are asked to go away.

"Let's go home, this is the end!"
Very sadly says my friend.
We are faithful friends and true:
Where he goes,
There I go, too.

The Song of the Merry Friends

SERGEI MIKHALKOV

We'll go riding, riding, riding,
To where the rainbow ends,
We are the best of neighbors,
The happiest of friends.
We love the life we're living,
We'll sing a jolly song,
And in the song we'll be singing
Of how gaily we roll along.

All aboard! Don't delay!
We will take along our jay,
Our cat, our dog, a carrot
To feed our little parrot,
Our fighting cock, and monkeys two—
Now, that's the company for you!

We sing while we are riding,
Our jolly song, and then,
Together as we started,
We all ride home again.
The gentle breeze kisses us,
The sunbeams say, "Good day!"
And we all sing in chorus,
As we speed on our way.

All aboard! Don't delay!
We did take along our jay,
Our cat, our dog, a carrot
To feed our little parrot,
Our fighting cock, and monkeys two—
Now, that's company for you!

Uncle Steeple

SERGEI MIKHALKOV

In our street, at eight-dash-one,
Known to all the local people,
Lived a man who was so tall,
He was nicknamed "Uncle Steeple."

Now, his surname was Stepanov
And his given name Stepan;
Of the giants in the district,
He was quite the tallest man.

Stepan Stepanov, so tall,
Was well-loved by one and all;
Coming home at close of day,
He'd be seen when miles away.

You could hear his footsteps beat
When Stepan stomped down the street,
The boots were at least size twenty
That he wore upon his feet.

He would search each shop and fair,
To find shoes that he could wear;
He would look for coats so wide,
You and I could hide inside.

After searching long, he'd hit
On a suit that seemed to fit.
While he stood, the suit was perfect;
When he'd bend, the suit would split!

Over any fence or wall,
He could see, he was so tall;
Dogs would loudly bark in warning,
Thinking thieves had paid a call.

In the restaurant he'd eat
Like a giant, as a rule,
And at night he'd stretch his feet
From the bed on to a stool.

He could reach the bookshelf seated.
At the movies folks would frown,
And he'd often be entreated:
"Comrade, won't you please sit down?"

But at games, believe you me,
They would let him enter free,
For they thought that Uncle Steeple
Was a champion, don't you see?

And the neighbors near and far,
Every grownup, every kid—
All could tell you where he lived,
Where he worked, and what he did.

For when kites would catch and dangle
High above from wires or trees,
Who but he could disentangle
Them so quickly, with such ease?

And he lifted at parades
Little boys and little maids,
So that from his shoulders high
They could see our troops pass by.

All about loved Uncle Steeple,
All were fond of Uncle Steeple,
For he was the friend of children—
Of the kids in every yard.

Very early Steeple rises,
Opens up his window wide,
Does his daily exercises,
Takes a cold shower, besides,
And the brushing of his teeth,
Steeple never puts aside.

Once Steeple rode on a donkey,
Feet a-dragging far behind;
People split their sides with laughter,
But he didn't really mind.
They all shouted to Stepan,
"Try a camel, little man!"

So a camel Steeple tried;
People laughed until they cried.
Someone made a merry crack,
"You will break the camel's back!
Camels, friend will never do—
Elephants were made for you!"

Into shooting galleries,
Uncle Steeple'd barely squeeze;
To the keeper he would say,
"Let me have a rifle, please."

But the keeper would reply,
"You don't need a rifle—why,
Surely you can reach the targets
With your hand, if you but try."

In the park this Saturday,
It will be so bright and gay;
There'll be music all night long—
Dancing, laughter, merry song.

At the entrance Steeple asks,
"Will you, please, show me some masks?

I want one that will disguise me,
So that none will recognize me."

"What's the use?" they say in jest,
"Even though you do your best,
Anyone will recognize you:
You're much taller than the rest."

What's the matter? What has happened?
"Schoolboy's drowning!" people shout.
"He has fallen in the river,
Hurry up and pull him out!"

While the people raised a din,
Uncle Steeple waded in.

Frightened, wet, but safe and sound,
Stands the schoolboy on the ground;
Uncle Steeple rescued him,
For the youngster couldn't swim.

All the people, for this deed,
Wish to shake him by the hand;
"Ask for anything you need,"
He is made to understand.

"I don't need a single thing,"
Steeple answered, coloring.

Whistling loud, the engine sped,
While the driver stared ahead;
When they thundered past a station,
To the fireman he said:

"On this line from end to end,
I've seen every semaphore,
Yet I'll make a bet, my friend,
That one was not there before."

And they hear Stepan explain:
"Look, the track is spoiled by rain;
And I raised my hand on purpose,
So that you would stop the train."

Why the smoke and all the clatter?
What has happened? What's the matter?
There's a neighbor's house ablaze,
Crowds of idlers stand and gaze;
Firemen ply the flames with water,
As the tall ladders they raise.

Soon the attic's all in flames,
Birds dash at the windowpanes.
In the yard the youngsters crowd,
To Stepanov they all turn
And in anguish cry aloud,
"Please, don't let our pigeons burn!"

Steeple reaches to the attic
Standing tiptoe on the ground,
And his hand goes to the window
Through the flames that lap around.

When he opens up the shutter,
From the window small and narrow
Fly the pigeons, all a-flutter—
Eighteen pigeons and a sparrow.

Children praised and worshipped him,
For he set the pigeons free,
And the grownups all advised him
That a fireman he should be.

"I don't want to be a fireman,"
Was his answer to them all.
"I would rather join the Navy—
If I do not prove too tall."

In the corridor there's laughter,
Jokes and merry conversation.
In the doctors' office, Steeple
Strips for his examination.

The Army doctors, all in chorus,
Say to him, "Sit down, please, do.
You are quite a problem for us:
We aren't half as tall as you."

"We'll examine," said the doctors,
"Both your hearing and your sight.
Is you liver quite in order?
Are your heart and lungs all right?"

They examined him and weighed him
And he passed in every test;
And they said. "Your heart beats
    soundly
And your lungs are of the best.

"You're quite tall, we must confess,
But we'll pass you nonetheless.

"As a tankman, you won't do,
Tanks are far too small for you.
As an infantryman?—No.
From the foxholes you will show.

"Now, if you become a flyer,
We're afraid your legs would tire:
Planes don't have much room to spare—
You'd be very cramped in there.

"And for men who are so tall,
Any horse would be too small.
You can serve your country, though,
In the Navy—that we know."

"I'm prepared to serve my people.
Fire and flood for them I'll dare,"
Proudly answered Uncle Steeple,
"Send me where and when you care."

Winter, spring, and summer pass.
Once again it's snowing hard.
Uncle Steeple, where is he?
There's no answer from the sea—
Not a letter, not a card.

Then the little kids, one day,
Had a wonderful surprise,
For a sailor came their way
Who was Uncle Steeple's size.

As he walked along the street,
Snowflakes crunched beneath his feet.
Maybe *you* can tell me who
Was that man in navy blue?

He wore neatly ironed trousers,
Sailor hat without a brim,

Woolen gloves, a big brass buckle;
Anchors shone all over him.

When he got to eight-dash-one,
He was recognized by none.
Children asked him, by the door,
"Whom may you be looking for?"

Uncle Steeple turned their way,
Gave a cordial salute,
And the children heard him say,
"I've come home on leave today.

"Haven't slept the night, what's more,
Walking seems so hard on shore.

"Let me change and rest my feet,
Have some tea, a cup or two;
Then come in—you'll get a treat
And some tales I'll tell to you.

"Of the war and cannonade,
Of the Leningrad * blockade,
Of how, serving on the cruiser,
I was wounded in a raid."

Prouder children you won't meet
Than the children of our street.
For their friend's a Soviet sailor
Serving in the Baltic Fleet.

Now when they see Stepanov coming,
All the small children run out,
But instead of "Uncle Steeple,"
"Lighthouse" is the name they shout.

---

* *Leningrad*, the second-largest city in the USSR, was under siege by the Germans for 900 days in World War II.

"We Have Made a Wish"

We have made a wish this day:
May the whole world with us say,
"Peace is forever!
War will come never!"

To learn to read and count we try;
Up to the moon we want to fly!
We are good friends and true to all;
We serve our country though we're small.

May there be peace!

This little poem appears on the last page of
the primer used by first-year pupils in schools
throughout the Soviet Union. It is learned
by heart and sung by millions of Russian
children.

very
short tales
for very young
folk

The two little tales, "Sunrays" and "Mitya's Four Wishes," were written by Konstantin Ushinsky (1824–1870), one of the dedicated Russian educators of the previous century. He was a teacher who championed the cause of the poor and was instrumental in persuading the government to open several schools for the children of destitute families. In his miniature stories—many of them included in school readers—Ushinsky wrote about the world surrounding the peasant child—about nature, animals, and the family. These tales continue to be published in modern Russia.

SUNRAYS

At dawn the red sun rose in the sky. The sun sent its golden rays in all directions to wake up the world.

The first ray beamed on a skylark. The bird fluttered its wings, left its nest, and flew about singing a silvery song: "Oh, how good it is to fly in the sky, so high, so high! How pure is the air!"

The second ray fell on a rabbit. The rabbit twitched his ears and hopped gaily over the dewy meadow. Then he ran off to find some juicy grass for his breakfast.

The third ray peeked through the chink in the wall of the chicken coup. The rooster beat his wings and cried: "Cock-a-doodle-doo!" The hens flew down from their perches, cackled, and began to dig for worms.

A fourth ray shone on the beehive. A tiny bee crawled out of the honeycomb, rested on a window pane, opened its wings, and—zim-zim-zim—flew away to gather honey from fragrant flowers.

A fifth ray entered the children's room, hopped on the bed of a lazy boy and tickled his eyelids. But the lazy boy turned over and fell asleep again.

MITYA'S FOUR WISHES

It was a sunny day in winter. Mitya went outside and took his sled with him. He carried it up the hill. He had lots of fun sledding down the hill. Then he skated on the frozen river. When the sun went down, Mitya ran home feeling happy, his cheeks rosy with cold. When he came into the house he said to his father:

"It's so nice in the wintertime! I wish it were always winter."

"Write down your wish in this little book," his father said, taking one out of his pocket. Mitya wrote down the wish he had just made.

Spring came. Mitya chased bright butterflies over the green meadow, picked flowers, looked for tadpoles, waded in the pond, and ran here and there. Then he came to his father and said:

"What a wonderful time spring is! I wish it were always spring."

Again his father took out the little book and told Mitya to write down his wish.

Summer arrived. Mitya and his father went to the haymowing. Mitya enjoyed himself all day long. He gathered berries, rolled down the haystacks, and played with the pony. In the evening he said to his father:

"Today I had the best time. I wish summer would never end." This wish, too, Mitya wrote down in his father's little book.

Autumn began. Fruit was gathered in the orchards—red apples, yellow pears, purple plums. The air smelled of ripened grain. The leaves turned gold, orange, and red. The breeze whirled them in the air like small colored balloons.

"Autumn is the very best time of the year!" Mitya said.

His father took out his little book and showed Mitya that he had said the same about winter, about spring, and about summer.

"The whole year is the best time of the year," Mitya then said.

TALES FOR ALYONUSHKA

DMITRI MAMIN-SIBIRYAK

The Little Tale Before The Big Tale

Rock-a-bye, little one, rock-a-bye.

One of Alyonushka's little eyes sleeps, and the other is awake; one of her little ears sleeps, and the other listens.

Sleep, Alyonushka, sleep, my pretty one. Your Daddy will tell you a nice, long fairy tale.

They all come, they all want to hear: Vas'ka the Cat, Shaggy the village Dog, Crunch-Munch the little gray Mouse, the cricket on the hearth, the bright-feathered starling in its cage, and Petya the proud Cock.

Sleep, Alyonushka. The tale is just beginning.

From its seat high in the sky the new moon is peeping in at your window. A cross-eyed rabbit has just hobbled by in his soft boots. The eyes of a gray wolf gleam like two yellow lights. Mishka the Bear sucks at his paw. An old sparrow has just flown up to the window, tapped at the glass with its beak, and asked how soon we would begin. They are all here, and they are all waiting for our fairy tale.

One of Alyonushka's little eyes sleeps, and the other is awake; one of her little ears sleeps, and the other listens.

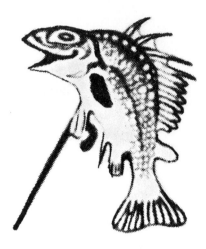

Quicky-Tricky the Sparrow,
Handy-Dandy the Perch,
and Yasha
the Gay Chimney Sweep

Quicky-Tricky the Sparrow and Handy-Dandy the Perch were great friends. Every summer day Quicky-Tricky would fly to the river to speak to his friend.

"Hello there, Handy-Dandy!" he would call. "How are you?"

"Fine! Thank you," the perch would reply. "Come and pay me a visit. It's really very nice here. The river is so deep and cool and quiet. There are more water plants than anyone could wish for. And I'll treat you to some delicious frogs' eggs and worms and water bugs."

"Thank you very much, Handy-Dandy! I'd be glad to come, but I'm afraid of the water. Why don't you fly up to the roof and pay me a visit yourself? I'll give you some of my berries, I have a whole garden of them, and then we might be able to get us a crust of bread and a few oats and a bit of sugar and a mosquito. You do like sugar, don't you?"

"What does it look like?"

"Oh, it's white and small and . . ."

"Like the pebbles in the river?"

"Yes, only you can't eat pebbles, but sugar is sweet and melts in your mouth. Let's fly up to the roof now, shall we?"

"No, I can't fly and I can't breathe out of the water. You'd better come swimming with me. I'll take you all over the river."

Quicky-Tricky the Sparrow would go into the water; he'd wade in up to his tiny knees, but he would go no farther. He didn't in the least want to drown. He would just take a drink of the clean river water and on hot days splash around in a shallow spot, and then he'd clean his feathers and go back to his roof again. But he and Handy-Dandy the Perch were good friends just the same and liked to talk about all sorts of things.

"Don't you ever get tired of being in the water?" Quicky-Tricky wondered. "It's wet—you might catch cold."

But the perch could not understand his friend's way of life any more than the sparrow could his.

"Don't you ever get tired of flying, Quicky-Tricky?" he would ask. "It's so hot in the sun; I don't see how you can breathe. Now the river's always cool, and you can swim all you want. Why, everyone goes bathing in the river in summer. But catch anyone going up to your roof!"

"Oh, but they do, Handy-Dandy, they do! There's Yasha the Chimney Sweep. He's a very good friend of mine. He comes to see me often. He's such a merry fellow, too, he sings all the time. He sweeps the chimneys and he hums songs. And sometimes he sits down for a rest on the very top of the roof and takes out a piece of bread and eats it while I pick up the crumbs. We enjoy being together, Yasha and I. I'm a merry fellow myself."

There was much in common between Quicky-Tricky and Handy-Dandy. Even their troubles were much the same. Winter was one. How raw the days sometimes were, and how cold poor Quicky-Tricky the Sparrow was! It got so cold his heart nearly froze in him. He would ruffle his feathers, tuck his legs in under him, and sit there without moving. He could only get warm by wriggling into a chimney and lying there, pressed close to its wall. But this was dangerous.

Once Quicky-Tricky nearly came to grief, and all because of his good friend the Chimney Sweep. He was snuggling in a chimney when Yasha came and dropped his brush and iron weight into it—nearly cracking Quicky-Tricky's skull. Out he jumped, all covered with soot and as black as a chimney sweep. Quicky-Tricky was in a terrible huff.

"What do you think you're doing, Yasha?" he said, very crossly indeed. "Why, you might have killed me!"

"How could I tell you were inside the chimney?" Yasha replied. "You'd better be careful from now on. I dare say I might have hit you with the weight, and that would not have been good at all, would it?"

Now Handy-Dandy the Perch wasn't having an easy time of it in winter, either. He would slip into some deep pool and sleep for days and days. It was dark and cold, and Handy-Dandy would stay without moving for hours. He would only swim out to the ice hole in the rare moments when Quicky-Tricky came for a drink of water and called to him:

"Hello there! Are you all right?" the sparrow would call.

"I'm all right," Handy-Dandy would answer in a sleepy voice, "only I'm so sleepy all the time. Winter's awful. Everyone here is asleep."

"It's the same with us, Handy-Dandy. Oh well, it can't be helped! But how bitter the wind can be! There's no sleeping when it blows. I keep hopping on one foot to get warm. And people see me and say: 'Look what a gay little sparrow he is!' Ah, if only it would get warm soon! Are you asleep again, Handy-Dandy?"

But summer brought troubles of its own. A hawk once flew after Quicky-Tricky for nearly a mile and only gave up the chase when he hid in the reeds in the river.

"I only got away by the skin of my teeth," he complained to Handy-Dandy afterward, gasping for breath. "The villain! If he had caught me, it would have been the end of me."

"He sounds like the pike in our river," Handy-Dandy said, trying to comfort his friend. "He nearly caught me, too, a few days ago. He went after me like lightning. I had just swum out with some of my friends and thought that was a log floating in the water, when suddenly the log rushed after me. Why do pikes exist at all! I just can't understand it."

"Neither can I. You know, I think the hawk must once have been a pike, and the pike a hawk. Bandits both of them."

And so that was how the two friends lived: they shivered in winter and were fairly happy in summer. And Yasha the merry Chimney Sweep swept chimneys and sang songs. Each of them had his own joys and his own troubles.

One summer day Yasha finished work and went to the river to wash off the soot. He was walking along and whistling a tune when suddenly he heard the most fearful noise. It came from the river, and he was wondering what it was when he saw flocks of birds circling over the water—there were ducks and geese, and swallows and snipe, and crows and pigeons. They were screeching and calling and laughing, and Yasha could not make out what it was all about.

"Hello there! What's happened?" he called to them.

"Something has, you may be sure!" a pert little titmouse chirped up. "It's so funny! Look at Quicky-Tricky over there. I do believe he's taken leave of his senses." And the titmouse gave a little laugh in its squeaky little voice, whisked its tail, and flew high up over the river.

When Yasha came to the riverbank, Quicky-Tricky fairly rushed at him. He looked very fierce—his beak was wide open, his eyes burned like two coals and all his feathers stood on end.

"Come now, Quicky-Tricky, what are you making such a fuss for?" Yasha asked him.

"I'll show him! I'll show Handy-Dandy!" Quicky-Tricky the Sparrow screeched, nearly choking with rage. "He doesn't know me! I'll show him! I'll give him something to remember me by, the rascal!"

"Don't listen to him!" Handy-Dandy the Perch called to Yasha from the water. "He's lying!"

"What? I'm lying, am I?" Quicky-Tricky screamed. "Who found the worm, tell me that? I'm lying, huh? Such a nice fat worm, too! *I* dug him up and don't think it was easy, either. But I got him at last and was dragging him off to my nest; I have a family, you know, and they've got to be fed. Well, I had just flown up over the river when Handy-Dandy—may a pike swallow him—called loud as anything: 'A hawk!' I screamed, the worm fell into the water, and Handy-Dandy got him. I'm lying, am I? There was no hawk anywhere in sight. He had made it up on purpose, to trick me."

"I was only joking," Handy-Dandy said, trying to justify himself. "As for the worm, it was very good, I must say."

"I hope Handy-Dandy chokes on my worm!" Quicky-Tricky shouted. "I'll dig up another one for myself. But it really is too bad that he has the nerve to laugh at me now, after cheating me out of my worm. To think that I used to invite him to my roof for a visit. A fine friend he turned out to be! Yasha will agree with me, I know. He and I are good pals; we even take our meals together now and then. He eats and I pick up the crumbs!"

"Just a minute, friends. Let's talk it over," Yasha said. "Let me wash up first, and then I'll find out who's right and who's wrong. Meanwhile, Quicky-Tricky, you calm down a bit."

"But I am calm! I haven't done anything wrong!" the sparrow shrieked. "I'll show Handy-Dandy how to play tricks on me! I'll teach him!"

Yasha the Chimney Sweep sat down on the river bank, placed the small package with his dinner beside him on a rock, washed his hands and face, and said:

"Well, friends, now we'll see who's right. You, Handy-Dandy, are a fish, and you, Quicky-Tricky, a bird. Right?"

"Yes, yes!" the birds and the fishes cried.

"Well, then let's go on. A fish lives in the water, and a bird in the air. Right? Now then, a worm lives in the ground. Very well. Now look!"

Yasha unwrapped his package. There was only a piece of dark bread inside, and that was his whole dinner. He put the bread on the rock and said:

"Look! Do you know what this is? Bread. I worked and earned it, and I'll be the one to eat it. I'll eat it, and then I'll have some water. And no one will be the loser. Now fishes and birds if they want their dinners, they must work for them, too. What's the good of quarreling? Quicky-Tricky the Sparrow dug up the worm, that means it's his."

"Just a minute, Yasha," a tiny little voice piped out in the crowd of birds. The birds stood aside and made way for a small sandpiper who hopped up to Yasha on his spindly little legs.

"It's not true, Yasha," he chirped.

"What's not true?"

"It was *I* who found the worm. Ask the ducks—they saw me. I found it, and Quicky-Tricky the Sparrow grabbed it."

Yasha didn't know what to say. Something was wrong.

"How can that be?" he muttered. "Have you really been lying to us all along, Quicky-Tricky?"

"No, I haven't. The sandpiper's lying. He's got the ducks to back him up and . . ."

"I don't think you're being honest. Hm! Of course, the worm is not very important, but it's wrong to steal. Stealing leads to lying. Don't you think so?"

"Yes! Yes!" they all cried again. "But you settle Handy-Dandy's and Quicky-Tricky's quarrel. Which of them is right? They were the ones that started this. They screamed and fought and disturbed everyone!"

"Which of them is right? Neither is. You're both mischief-makers—

you, Handy-Dandy, and you, Quicky-Tricky. You are, indeed! Shake hands and make up at once, do you hear?"

"Yes! Yes!" the fishes and birds cried. "Let them make up!"

"As for the little sandpiper who worked so hard to get the worm, I'll give him some bread crumbs to make him feel better," Yasha went on. "That should please everyone."

"Yes! Yes!" they all cried again.

Yasha reached for the bread, but—it was gone! While they had all been so busy talking, Quicky-Tricky had flown off with it.

"The robber! The cheat!" the fishes and birds cried angrily.

And they all rushed after the thief. The piece of bread was large and heavy, and Quicky-Tricky could not fly very far with it. He was caught just over the river, the big and little birds rushing and pecking at him. It was an awful scramble. The birds pulled so hard at the bread that crumbs kept dropping into the water, and the piece, or what was left of it, soon followed. The fish rushed after it, and they began to fight with the birds. They pulled and pecked till the piece of bread was all crumbled up, and then they ate the crumbs. So finally nothing was left of the bread at all. It was then that they realized what they had done and were ashamed of themselves. They had eaten up the stolen bread!

As for Yasha the merry Chimney Sweep, he sat on the bank, watching and laughing. It was really quite funny. They had all run away from him, all but the sandpiper.

"Why don't you fly after the rest?" Yasha asked him.

"I would if I weren't so small. Why, the big birds might peck me to death."

"Well, that's the way things are, little sandpiper. We're both left without our dinner."

It was just about then that Alyonushka came to the river. She asked Yasha the Chimney Sweep to tell her what had happened, and when he did she laughed very hard, too.

"Oh, how silly the fishes and birds are!" she cried. "I would have divided everything up equally, the worm and the bread, and then there'd be nothing to quarrel about. Why, the other day Daddy brought me four apples and told me to divide them among Liza and him and me. And I did. I divided them into three parts. I gave one apple to Daddy, another to Liza, and I took two for myself."

Long Ears-Squint Eyes-Stub Tail, the Bravest Rabbit of Them All

A little rabbit was born in the forest and was afraid of everything. A twig had only to snap, a bird to flutter a wing, a clump of snow to fall from a tree, and the rabbit's heart was in his mouth.

The little rabbit was afraid for a day, he was afraid for two days, he was afraid for a week, he was afraid for a year, and then he was all grown up and quite tired of being afraid.

"I'm not afraid of anyone!" he shouted for the whole forest to hear. "Not the least bit afraid, and that's all there is to it!"

At this the papa rabbits gathered near, and the little bunnies came running, and the mama rabbits came too. They all listened to Long Ears-Squint Eyes-Stub Tail boast. They listened and they couldn't believe their ears. There never lived a rabbit who wasn't afraid of something!

"Look here, Long Ears-Squint Eyes-Stub Tail, aren't you even afraid of the wolf?" someone asked.

"No, I'm not—not of the wolf or the fox or the bear—I'm not afraid of anyone!"

Now this was really beginning to be funny. The young bunnies giggled, covering their fuzzy muzzles with their paws; the kindly old mama rabbits burst out laughing; and even the old papa rabbits who had been in a fox's paws and had felt a wolf's teeth on them, smiled. Here was a funny rabbit, indeed—too funny for words. He made them feel quite jolly.

They began to skip about and cut capers and turn somersaults and chase one another's tails just as though they had all suddenly lost their senses.

"What's the use of all this talk!" Long Ears-Squint Eyes-Stub Tail cried, feeling quite brave and sure of himself. "If ever I come across a wolf—why, I'll eat him up myself!"

"Oh, what a funny rabbit Long Ears-Squint Eyes-Stub Tail is! What a silly rabbit!" They laughed and laughed at him.

So there were the rabbits laughing their heads off about the wolf, and there was the wolf right beside them. He had been prowling about the forest and attending to his affairs, and he was very hungry. He was just thinking how nice it would be to have a tender young rabbit for dinner when what did he hear but many rabbits all shouting at once and all talking about him, Gray Wolf. So he stopped and sniffed the air and began to steal up to them.

He crept quite close to them. But they were making such a racket they never heard him. They were laughing at Gray Wolf; and the little braggart Long Ears-Squint Eyes-Stub Tail, laughed louder than any of them.

"Hm, brother rabbit, you wait, you're the one I'm goint to eat!" said Gray Wolf to himself.

But the rabbits never saw him. They were laughing and shouting and enjoying themselves more than ever. Finally, Long Ears-Squint Eyes-Stub Tail clambered up on a tree stump, sat down, and said:

"Listen to me, you cowards! Look at me and listen. I'm going to show you something you've never seen before. I . . . I . . . I . . ."

But he couldn't say another word. It was as if the little boaster had swallowed his tongue. For Long Ears-Squint Eyes-Stub Tail had seen Gray Wolf staring at him! The other rabbits had not seen Gray Wolf, but Long Ears-Squint Eyes-Stub Tail had, and he was so frightened he could not breathe.

Then something quite remarkable happened.

Long Ears-Squint Eyes-Stub Tail bounced up like a ball, and—in his fright, fell straight on Gray Wolf's muzzle, rolled head over heels down his back, turned a somersault in the air, and bounded away so fast that he all but jumped out of his own skin!

He ran and he ran till he could run no more. He thought Gray Wolf was at his heels and about to catch him between his teeth.

But at last the poor little boaster was so tired that he closed his eyes and dropped down in a heap under a bush.

As for Gray Wolf, he went lolloping off in a different direction and never looked back. When Long Ears-Squint Eyes-Stub Tail had tumbled on top of him, he had thought at first that someone had shot him Then he saw Long Ears-Squint Eyes-Stub Tail and decided that there were many rabbits in the forest and no reason in the world to bother about this one—who was quite mad, as anyone could see!

It took the rabbits a long time to come to themselves. Some of them had hidden behind bushes, some had ducked behind a stump, and some had scrambled down holes in the ground and kept very, very still.

But at last they were all tired of hiding, and those of them who were the braver of the lot began to peep out one by one from their hiding places.

"Long Ears-Squint Eyes-Stub Tail gave Gray Wolf quite a scare. Wasn't it wonderful of him?" they said. "If not for him, we'd never have got away alive. Where is he, though?"

They began to look for him; they looked and they looked but Long Ears-Squint Eyes-Stub Tail was nowhere to be seen. Had another wolf eaten him up? But no, they found him at last. He was lying in a hole under a bush, half dead with fright.

"Three cheers for Long Ears!" the rabbits all cried together. "Three cheers for you! How you frightened that bad old wolf! Thank you, Long Ears! And we thought you had been boasting."

Hearing them, Long Ears-Squint Eyes-Stub Tail took heart at once. He climbed out of his hole, shook himself, screwed up one eye, and said: "Who, me? Boasting? Don't be funny!"

And from that day on Long Ears-Squint Eyes-Stub Tail really believed that he feared nothing in all the world.

Rock-a-bye, little one, rock-a-bye Alyonushka.

One of Alyonushka's little eyes sleeps, and the other is awake; one of her little ears sleeps, and the other listens. Everyone has gathered around Alyonushka's bed: the brave Rabbit, the Gray Wolf, the Sparrow, the Perch, and the teeniest weeniest little bug that ever lived. They are all here, at Alyonushka's bedside.

"Daddy, I love them all," Alyonushka whispers. "I love them all, Daddy."

64

Alyonushka's other little eye closes, and her other little ear falls asleep.

Alyonushka sleeps, and the spring grass gayly pushes up its green blades right by her bed, and the flowers smile at her. There are many flowers—blue and pink and yellow and violet and red. A slender little birch tree bends over Alyonushka and whispers something very tender into her ear. The sun shines brightly, the yellow sand gleams, and the blue sea waves call to Alyonushka.

Sleep, Alyonushka, sleep tight and grow big and strong.

Hush-a-bye, little one, hush-a-bye.

CONSCIENCE

ALEXANDER SOKOLOVSKY

Egorka's mother had left strict orders that he was not to touch the jar of honey on the pantry shelf. Egorka disobeyed. He pushed a chair over to the wall, stood on it tiptoe, and reached for the jar. The jar slipped out of his hand and crashed to the floor, breaking into many pieces.

When Egorka's mother came home she scolded him:

"You naughty boy! I told you not to touch the honey!"

"I didn't touch it," Egorka said.

"What do you mean, you didn't touch it? Did the jar drop itself to the floor?"

"Yes, it did."

Egorka's mother shook her head in disappointment, saying:

"Egorka, you have lost your conscience."

Egorka thought about that and was puzzled.

"Where did I lose it?" he asked.

"How would *I* know?" answered his mother. "Go look for it. Maybe you'll find it. But don't expect to have honey with your tea this evening."

Egorka felt sad. He walked off along the path that led to the woods, and before he knew it he was there walking along a green glade. He lay down on the grass and looked up at the white clouds. The clouds were swimming in the sky like large fish in a blue sea.

Over his head Egorka saw some birch trees. They were making a slight noise in the breeze, whispering something. He couldn't make out what they were saying. But their voices, Egorka noticed, were not gay.

A crow flew over. It sat down on a tree stump, stared at him with her shiny black eyes, and crowed:

"You lied! You lied!"

Egorka felt unhappy.

"Scat!" he shouted at the crow.

The crow fanned out its wings and flew away. But the birch trees continued their whispering. And it seemed to Egorka that they were saying to him:

"That wasn't nice. . . . No, that wasn't nice. . . ."

Then another bird landed on a tree branch, turned its head toward Egorka and chirped:

"Con . . . science? Con . . . science?"

Egorka felt quite ashamed by now. He jumped to his feet and hurried home. He threw the door wide open and ran into the house.

"Mother!" he cried, "I broke the honey jar!"

His mother smiled. "Where did you find your conscience, Egorka?"

Egorka lowered his head.

"In the woods," he answered. "In the glade where the birch trees grow."

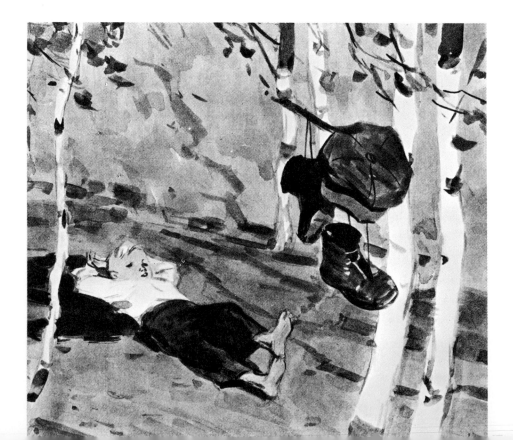

SHORT STORIES FOR YOUNG CHILDREN by LEO TOLSTOY

It is not generally known that the great master of the Russian novel and the foremost humanitarian and moral teacher of our times, Count Leo Tolstoy (1828–1910), author of the monumental *War and Peace,* was also a major children's author.

Tolstoy wrote 629 stories, fables, realistic animal tales, and sketches for children. Most of these were written for his series of four graded readers, published in the last quarter of the nineteenth century under the general title of *The New Alphabet.* The miniature works offered here were selected from these readers. Most of the tales have been published and republished in Russia and are, to this day, a staple in young children's reading fare.

There is considerable evidence that the great Tolstoy regarded his writings for the very young as a significant part of his literary achievements. When he was completing the readers, to which he had devoted fourteen years, he wrote:

These are my proud thoughts about my "Azbuka" [Alphabet]: they are the only readers that will be used to teach generations of all Russian children, from the czar's to the peasant's, and from these readers they will receive their first poetic impressions, and having written these books, I can now die in peace.

By "poetic impressions" Tolstoy meant the lyrical and the exalting in life, revealed artistically and truthfully, together with the tragic and the deplorable.

Leo Tolstoy wrote these miniature stories with deep artistic concern, applying his immense talent to making them works of art. They are illumined in their simplicity and economy of words with strong incident and emotion.

TWO FRIENDS

One day two friends were walking in the woods, when a big bear jumped out at them. One of the two men started to run, climbed up a tree, and hid himself in its thick branches. The other man remained where he was. There was nothing else he could do but throw himself to the ground and pretend to be dead.

The bear came closer and started to smell him. The man stopped breathing.

The bear smelled his face, thought he was dead, and went away.

When the beast was out of sight, the man in the tree came down and started to laugh.

"Well," he said, "what did the bear whisper in your ear?"

"He told me that it is an evil person who runs away when a friend is in danger."

THE OLD MAN AND
THE APPLE TREES

A very old man was planting apple trees. Someone said to him:

"What for are you planting apple trees? It will be a long time before they bear fruit, and you will not live to eat a single little apple."

The old man replied:

"I'll not eat them, but others will, and they will thank me."

THE DUCK AND THE MOON

Once a duck was swimming in the river, looking for fish. The day passed without her finding a single one.

In the evening the duck saw the moon mirrored in the water. Thinking it was a fish, she dived down to catch it. The other ducks saw her and they laughed at her.

From that day the duck was so ashamed and so shy that even when she did see a fish under water she would not try to catch it, and before long she died of hunger.

THE SQUIRREL AND
THE WOLF

A squirrel in a tree was skipping from branch to branch and fell down on a sleeping wolf. The wolf jumped up and was about to eat up the squirrel.

"Let me go," begged the squirrel.

"All right," the wolf then said, "I'll let you go if you tell me what makes you squirrels so happy. I always feel sad, but whenever I look at you up there in the tree you always hop and play."

"First let me go back to my tree," the squirrel replied. "I'll tell you from up there, for I'm afraid of you."

The wolf let the squirrel go. It scampered up the tree and when it reached the very top it said to the wolf:

"You are always sad because you are mean. Your meanness hardens your heart. We are happy because we are kind and never do harm to anyone."

THE GRANDFATHER AND
HIS LITTLE GRANDSON

The grandfather had become very old. His legs would not carry him, his eyes could not see, his ears could not hear, and he was toothless. And when he ate, he was untidy. His son and the son's wife no longer allowed him to eat with them at the table and had him take his meals near the stove. They gave him his food in a cup. Once he tried to move the cup closer to him and it fell to the floor and broke. The daughter-in-law scolded the old man, saying that he damaged everything around the house and broke their cups, and she warned him that from that day on she would give him his food in a wooden dish. The old man sighed and said nothing.

One day the old man's son and his wife were sitting in their hut, resting. Their little son was playing on the floor. He was putting together something out of small bits of wood. His father asked him: "What are you making, Misha?" And Misha said: "I'm making a wooden bucket. When you and Mommie get old, I'll feed you out of this wooden bucket."

The young peasant and his wife looked at each other and tears appeared in their eyes. They were ashamed to have treated the old man so unkindly, and from that day they again ate with him at the table and took better care of him.

THE WOLF AND THE DOG

A lean and hungry wolf was walking past a village and met a fat dog.

The wolf asked the dog: "Tell me, dog, where do you get your food?"

"People give it to me," the dog answered.

"That means you work hard for these people," said the wolf.

"No, we dogs don't work hard. All we do is guard the yard at night," the dog said.

"And for doing only this service they feed you so well?" wondered the wolf. "I would accept this kind of job at once. It is hard for us wolves to find food."

"Well, go ahead," said the dog. "My master will feed you then as well as he feeds me."

The wolf was glad and went with the dog to work for people. As the dog was entering his yard, the wolf noticed that some of the fur on his neck had been rubbed away.

"How did this happen to you, dog?" he said.

"Oh, it just happened," answered the dog.

"What do you mean 'it just happened'?" asked the wolf.

"It just happened . . . from the chain. They chain me during the day and the chain rubs away the fur on my neck."

"Well," said the wolf, "if that is so, then good-bye, dog. I will not live with people. I would rather be hungry, but free."

THE CZAR AND THE FALCON

A czar once went hunting. He let loose from his arm his favorite falcon to have him catch a hare.

The falcon caught the hare. The czar took it from him and then began to look for water to quench his thirst. He found water coming, drop by drop, from a weeping rock. He took a cup and placed it under the rock. When the cup was full, the czar raised it to his mouth and was about to drink from it when the falcon became agitated, flapped his wings against the czar's hand causing all the water to spill from the cup. Again the czar placed the cup under the rock. He waited a long time for it to fill up. And when he raised it to his mouth, the falcon once more spilled the water.

When the czar filled the cup for the third time and raised it to his mouth, the falcon spilled the water for the third time. The czar grew very angry. With all his strength he dashed the falcon against a stone and killed him. At that moment the czar's servants rode up to him. One of them climbed up the hill to the spring that fed the weeping rock and where there was more water, so that a cup could be filled more quickly. But the servant came back with the empty cup and said: "You must not drink this water; there is a serpent in the spring. It poured its poison into the water. It was lucky that the falcon spilled the water. If you had drunk it, you would have died."

The czar then said: "Badly have I repaid the falcon. He saved my life and I killed him."

THE LION AND THE PUPPY

Some wild beasts were on view in a London zoo. As payment for seeing them either money was accepted or dogs and cats which were used to feed the animals.

A man wanted to see the beasts. He picked up a puppy in the street and brought it to the zoo. They let him in, took the puppy from him, and threw it into the lion's cage for him to eat.

The little dog drew in its tail and pushed himself against the corner of the cage. The lion approached it and smelled it.

The puppy turned on its back, raised its little paws, and began to wave its little tail.

The lion touched it lightly and turned it over.

The puppy jumped up and stood before the lion on its hind legs.

The lion kept looking at the little dog but did not harm it.

When the keeper threw some meat to the lion, he tore off a piece and left it for the puppy.

In the evening, when the lion lay down to sleep, the puppy lay down against his side and put its head on the lion's paw.

From that day on the little dog lived in the cage with the lion. The lion never hurt it, but slept near it, and at times played with it.

One day a gentleman came to the zoo, noticed the little dog and claimed that it was his. He asked the keeper to give it to him. The keeper wanted to do it, but as soon as they began to call to the puppy, the lion bristled and roared.

The lion and the little dog continued to live together in the same cage for a whole year. At the end of the year the little dog got sick and died. The lion stopped eating, kept smelling the puppy and touching it gently with his paw.

When the lion understood that the puppy was dead, he suddenly jumped up, bristled, began to whip his sides with his tail, threw himself at the bars of the cage, and tore at them.

For a whole day he rushed about the cage and roared. Then he lay down near the dead little dog, embraced it with his paws, and remained there for the next five days.

On the sixth day the lion died.

THE FROG WENT A-TRAVELING

VSEVOLOD GARSHIN

Once upon a time there lived a frog. She inhabited a swamp, went after mosquitoes and other tiny creatures, and in the spring she croaked loudly together with her frog friends. And this is the way she would have peacefully lived on and on if, of course, a stork hadn't gobbled her up in the meantime. But something unusual happened.

One day she was sitting on a knot of a tree stump that jutted out of the water, enjoying a warm drizzle.

"My, what lovely wet weather we're having today!" she thought. "What a delight it is to be alive in this fine world!"

The drizzle fell gently on the frog's shiny little back, the drops ran down her tummy and her fat little legs and this was wonderfully pleasant, so pleasant that she almost croaked. But, fortunately, she remembered that it was already fall and that in the fall frogs did not croak— this was done only in the spring. To croak in the wrong season of the year would be most undignified. So she kept quiet and continued to enjoy herself.

Suddenly the frog heard a thin whistling sound. There is a certain breed of ducks who make this kind of sound when they are in flight. As their wings cut the air they make the sound of a whistled song. Few-few-few-few, one hears as a flock of these ducks soars high in the sky—they fly so high that you can't even see them. This time, flying in a semicircle, the ducks came down and sat in the very same swamp where the frog made her home.

"Quack-quack!" one of them said. "We still have far to go. We had better stop and eat."

The frog hid herself at once. She knew that the ducks would not make a meal out of her, for she was too large and too fat for that; but to be quite safe, she dived under the tree stump. But, after giving the matter a little more thought, she decided to raise her head out of the water and watch the ducks. She was very curious to know where the ducks were going.

"Quack-quack!" another duck said. "Br-r-r-r, it's getting cold! Let's hurry south! Let's hurry south!"

And all the other ducks quacked in agreement.

"Pardon me, ladies and gentlemen ducks," the frog made bold to say, "but what is this south whereto you are flying? Please forgive me for this interruption."

The ducks surrounded the frog. At first they felt like eating her up, but each duck decided that the frog was too big and would stick in the throat. Then they began to quack loudly, flapping their wings.

"It's good in the south! It's warm there now. There are such warm swamps! And what worms! It's perfectly lovely in the south!"

They quacked so loudly that the frog thought she'd get deaf from it. When she finally got them to quiet down, she asked one of them, a duck who was fatter than the others and seemed more wise, what was "south." And when the frog heard all about it she was enchanted, but asked just the same, because she was a careful frog:

"But are there many mosquitoes and other insects there?"

"Oh, clouds of them!" the wise fat duck answered.

"Croak!" the frog croaked and looked around at once to make sure that none of the other frogs heard her do this out of season. She just couldn't resist croaking at least once.

"Take me with you!" she said to the ducks.

"You surprise me!" exclaimed the wise fat duck. "How can we take you with us? You have no wings."

"When are you starting out again?" the frog asked.

"Soon, soon!" the ducks screamed. "Quack-quack! Quack-quack! It's cold here! To the south! To the south!"

"Allow me to think for just five minutes," said the frog. "I'll be back very soon. I'm sure I can think of something."

The frog leaped into the water from the stump onto which she had climbed again, and dived to the bottom of the swamp, there to think undisturbed. Five minutes passed and the ducks were about to fly off, when the frog appeared again. Her face was beaming as only a frog's face can beam.

"I thought of something! I have an idea!" she announced. "Let two of you hold the end of a twig in your beaks; I'll hang on to it in the middle with my mouth. You'll fly and I'll ride. If you don't quack and I don't croak, all will go well."

The ducks saw little pleasure in dragging a heavy frog for three thousand miles in complete silence, but they were so impressed with the frog's cleverness that they all agreed to take her along. They decided to take turns and change conductors every two hours. And since there were ducks in this flock almost without count, and only one frog to transport, it wasn't going to be too much work for any single duck.

So they found a strong twig, two of the ducks raised it in their beaks, the frog leaped up and grabbed the middle of it with her mouth, and off they went. The frog almost lost her breath from fright as they flew higher and higher, especially since the ducks didn't fly smoothly and jerked the twig. The poor frog swayed in the air like a clown on a trapeze. She clamped the twig as tightly as she could in her jaw so as not to lose hold of it and be hurled to the ground. However, she soon got used to it all and even began to look around. Fields, meadows, rivers, and mountains sped by under her. It was hard for her to get a good look at these places because she was facing forward. But she managed to see some of the landscape, and was happy and proud that she was taking such an unusual journey.

"That was pretty clever of me," she thought.

And the other ducks followed the pair in front who were carrying the frog, and they screamed and praised her.

"What a clever one is our frog!" they said. "There are few who are that clever even among us ducks."

The frog could barely resist thanking them, but remembering that if she opened her mouth to speak she would drop from the terrible height, she held on to the twig even more tightly and decided to be patient and silent.

All day long the frog hung on this way. The ducks took turns carrying her, changing drivers in mid-air. This was very scary for the frog, and she nearly screamed with fright several times.

In the evening they would stop for a rest in some swamp and at dawn they would continue their journey. After the first day the frog rode facing backward in order to see better the places they flew over. They passed harvested fields, golden forests, and meadows full of haystacks. From the villages they could hear the sound of people's voices and the noise of threshing.

The peasants looked up at the flock of ducks and, noticing that they were carrying something, pointed and made some remarks. The frog wished they were flying nearer to the ground so that she could show off and hear what the villagers were saying about her. Next time they stopped for a rest she said:

"Couldn't we fly a little lower? I get so dizzy from flying so high, and I'm afraid that I'll fall if I get sick to my stomach."

And the kind ducks promised that they would fly lower. Next day they flew so low that they could hear every word the villagers were saying.

"Look, look!" some peasant children cried in one village, "the ducks are carrying a frog."

The frog heard this and her heart leaped with pride.

"Look, look!" some grown-ups cried in another village. "What a miracle!"

"I wonder if they realize that it was *I* who thought of it and not the ducks." the frog thought.

"Look, look!" the people cried in a third village. "What a sight! Who could have thought of such a clever trick?!"

The frog now lost all self-control and, forgetting to be careful, cried with all her might:

"I did! I did!"

And saying this she lost hold of the twig and somersaulted down toward the earth. The ducks yelled loudly. One of them tried to catch the falling frog in mid-air, but missed. The frog was coming down fast. Luckily she fell into a muddy pond on the edge of the village.

The frog quickly came up to the surface and again screamed as loudly as she could:

"I did! I thought of it!"

But there was no one there to hear her. Frightened by the sudden splash when the frog fell into the water, the other frogs hid beneath it. When they came up again they stared at the newcomer, wondering who she was.

And the frog told them the amazing story of how all her life she tried to think of a new way of traveling and how she at last invented "travel by ducks." She told them that she had her own ducks who carried her wherever and whenever she wished to go and that she had traveled this way to the south where it was very pleasant and where there were wonderful warm swamps and lots of insects of all kinds.

"I came here to see how *you* live," she added. "I think I might stay with you until the spring, when my ducks—to whom I gave a vacation —will return."

But, of course, the ducks never came back. They thought that the frog had been killed in the fall, and they felt very sorry for her.

DO YOU KNOW?

M. ILYIN, E. SEGAL

The Soviet authors of this book which answers "a thousand 'how's?' and 'why's?' " explain its purpose to the young reader:

This is a book about the things you can find all around you.

Many of them are old friends of yours: a notebook and a pencil, a teacup and a knife, a shirt and a pair of shoes, a saw and a hammer, a watch and an electric bulb, the house you live in and the car that speeds down the street, past your house.

You've known all these things for a long time, and yet you don't really know them well.

You would probably be surprised if you were told that your notebook grew up in a forest and your shirt in a field, that your rubber boots are made of sawdust and your buttons of cottage cheese, that a small hailstone can tell us which wind is blowing high up in the sky.

Here are three tales from this big book giving the answers to three "how's?" and three "why's?" They are true stories although they sound like fairly tales.

M. Ilyin is the leading Soviet writer of children's science tales. He is the brother of the famous children's poet Samuel Marshak.

SNOWFLAKES

Once upon a time, there lived some snowflakes. They were born in a snow-cloud high above the earth and began growing the minute they were born. They became more dainty and beautiful with every passing hour, and although they all looked alike, as sisters do, each one had its own lovely dress. One looked like a star with six points, another like a flower with six petals, and a third sparkled like a six-sided precious stone.

The snowflakes grew up and drifted down to earth in a white flock. There were so many of them, that it was impossible to count them. They floated very close to the earth, but the wind didn't want them to lie down. It kept whirling them around in the air, in a mad dance. Yet they managed to reach the ground, where they settled down like fine ladies taking care not to crush their lovely gowns.

Some snowflakes came to rest on a stubble field, others on the branches and underneath the trees in the forest, some rested on the roofs. Others settled down in the middle of country roads or city streets, and their fate was sad indeed, for with the morning came people, wagons, and trucks. The snow-flowers and snow-stars melted under the many feet and the many wheels that trampled them.

The farmers welcomed the snow. The slush and mud of autumn were a thing of the past; they were now able to change their wagon wheels for sledge runners and fly along the smooth white roads. Children made snowballs from the snowflakes and shaped thousands of the delicate snow-flowers and snow-stars into fat snowmen. Such gifts don't often drop from the sky, and the children had to hurry, for it was quite possible that the white blanket presently covering their world would soon melt.

The snowflakes were saved by the evening frost. It shooed all the children home to their warm beds, and when they awoke the next morning everything was still white. It was nice to hear the snow crunching underfoot and the sledge runners moving along the roads. No one realized that the crunching was the cracking and the splitting of the petals of snow-flowers and the rays of snow-stars.

The snowflakes that had gone to sleep in the field rested more peacefully, and no one bothered with them for a long time. The farmers knew that the snow would cover and protect the green shoots of winter wheat from the frost. The snowflakes would have remained in the same spot all winter, just like little sleeping beauties, if the wandering wind had not come upon them. It tore across the field and started to scatter them, blowing them from their beds and whisking them away. They might have circled over the field endlessly, but at one end of it there was a ditch. They hid there away from the wind and were happy to have found a quiet place again.

But, alas! They were much worse off in the ditch than they had been in the field. At least they hadn't been cramped when they had been out in the field. There in the ditch they were packed in hard. They and their lovely petals and rays broke in the crush. No one could tell them apart any more, for they had become a solid mass of broken snow pieces.

It was then that the farmers decided to take a hand in the matter. They didn't want the wind to blow all the snow off the field. With the coming of spring the field would need the snow-water, but all the snow was now in the ditch. That's why they wanted to stop the wind from robbing the field. You've perhaps already read the story of how the farmers put up all kinds of barriers to keep the snow on the fields.

The snowflakes that settled in the forest were most fortunate of all, because the trees there held back the wind and prevented it from disturbing their sleep. It is quiet in a forest. From time to time an animal would scamper by and leave its tracks in the snow. The soft, fluffy snowdrifts kept growing higher and higher between the trees. The snow was only knee-high in the fields, but you'd fall into a snowbank up to your waist if you ventured into the forest without skis.

But even in the forest the poor snowflakes could not find peace or save their gowns forever. What happened to them? You'll have to wait till spring to find the answer.

A HAILSTONE WENT VISITING

A little hailstone fell on the ground and bounced along the path like a ball.

Where did it fall from?

From the sky.

How could it grow so big and heavy in the sky? What held it up there?

It will tell you its story itself. But you had better be quick with your questions, before it melts away. Look under that bush! Do you see the hailstones that have rolled there? Pick up the biggest one and get out your penknife. Now, cut the hailstone in half. It's as transparent as glass on the outside and as white as porcelain inside. Of course, it's not porcelain, for porcelain doesn't melt. It's snow. And the glass is not glass at all. It is ice.

Now we have found out the hailstone's secret: it's made of snow, like the fairy-tale Snow Maiden, and its dress is made of pure ice. This was not the prettiest hailstone, however. Some of them wear as many as three or five petticoats. First there's a transparent ice petticoat, then a white snow petticoat on top, and finally an ice dress on top of the last snow petticoat. Where do they get into all these petticoats when they decide to go visiting? Why, at home, of course, high up in the sky.

A hailstone has a hard little white nut in the center. This little snow-nut was born in a snow cloud and started falling down to earth, but it had a very long way to go. There are many clouds in the sky, and the snow clouds are higher up than the rain clouds. On its way down the hailstone met a rain-cloud, which gave it a water petticoat. The dress froze on it and became an ice petticoat. But how did it get a white snow petticoat on top of its ice petticoat? When it came out of the rain cloud it didn't fall toward the earth, but climbed up to the Kingdom of Snow again. Where else could it have found a snow petticoat? But our hailstone had more than two petticoats. And this means that it had been flying up and down, putting on a new petticoat at each stop: a snow one upstairs and an ice one on the level below.

How could it go up again once it had found itself on a lower level? Surely, it had no wings?

Well, it was tossed upward by the wind, the only thing powerful enough to lift it up.

Now you know the hailstone's story, and you know it because you found out what it was wearing. It took a long time for it to dress up and get ready to go visiting, but when it finally arrived, all its lovely petticoats started melting. However, it still had enough time to tell you where it had been and what it had seen.

THE INVISIBLE ONE

Do you think that invisible creatures exist only in fairy tales? Then look up at the sky. See the clouds floating way up there? What is pushing them? The Invisible One. When he crosses a field, the wheat bows low to him; when he passes through a forest, the trees bend their heads. This morning he tore the linen off a clothesline, knocked off a boy's cap, snatched a newspaper from the table and sent it flying to the floor; he asked no one's permission before he came into the house, and didn't even bother to knock. In fact, he didn't come in by the door at all, but through the window.

In autumn the Invisible One whirls the dry leaves down the street. In summer he stirs up the dust and tosses it into people's eyes. He has so many adventures in his journey across the plains, over the forests and seas! The Invisible One brings the cold from the north and the heat from the south, rain from the seas and dust from the deserts. And he billows out the sails of boats and turns the windmill sails to grind the corn.

You've surely guessed who he is by now. It's the wind that cannot be seen as it moves over the earth.

The story you're going to read now will tell you about the wind's adventures.

Far in the north, in the Kingdom of Ice, the Invisible One is known as Northern Air. There he often blew across the ice fields, sweeping up the snow in his path. Sometimes he raised clouds of snow-dust, and then chased after the dust across the fields of ice. What other playmate could he have had in this snow kingdom?

Oh, how cold it was in the Kingdom of Ice! There the sun never rose very high, nor did it shine for very long, and the Invisible One never had enough time to warm up during the short day. At night things got still worse. He hardly ever had a chance to snuggle under a fluffy cloud-blanket. The nights were usually cloudless and starry, and by morning the Invisible One would be quite frozen.

There came a day when he managed to escape from the Kingdom of Ice and start out on a long journey southward.

His way lay over an ocean. The water in the ocean was warmer than the northern ice, and as the Invisible One sped over the warm water, he began to thaw out. There were many things he could play with there. He pulled the water up into waves, and the faster he went, the higher the waves rose. As they moved along in rows, the Invisible One tore off their caps and beat them into white foam. Sometimes he came across ships and played with the smoke that streamed out of the stacks. He found other work too, and washed and rewashed the decks with ocean spray, although the sailors had swabbed them down already. He nearly washed a sailor overboard, and it was the sailor's good luck that he managed to catch hold of the rail.

The Invisible One went on his way, rocking the ships and fishing boats with all his might. When he left the Kingdom of Ice, he had been frozen through and through, but as he passed over the ocean he thawed out and stored up some of the water that rose from the ocean in a mist. The mist became tiny drops of fog, which the Invisible One carried off and spread low over the water, blotting out the sun.

Somewhere over the ocean the Invisible One blew straight into an airplane. He was very pleased to find such a toy and started tossing it around, wrapping it in a white blanket of fog. The pilot's first thought was to get out of the trap, and he made the plane climb higher and

84

higher until the snow-white fog was left far below, and the sun's rays had found their way into the cockpit.

The Invisible One sped along very fast, but he still had far to go. It took him a long time to reach the shore, where he filled the streets of the coastal cities with a thick pea-soup fog; the street lights in the coastal cities flickered dimly through it; drivers kept honking their horns in warning, for the cars could not be seen in the fog. The Invisible One went on his way traveling farther inland. No one could see him, but everyone saw what he was carrying with him from the sea; the little drops of water he carried gathered into big drops, and heavy clouds hung low over the earth.

Suddenly, there was a flash of lightning and a loud clap of thunder. The children who were swimming in the stream heard the thunderous voice of the invisible traveler and scrambled out of the water, for they wanted to get home before the rain storm. The Invisible One poured the ocean water on the fields and forests and continued farther south.

There was another invisible one in the south, called Southern Air.

The two Invisible Ones had argued many times before, as neither would give the other the right of way. And they argued this time, too. The battle between the two giants began. When two giants are fighting it out, the best thing to do is to keep as far away from them as possible. When they are whirling around, the cyclone they create can pull a tree up by its roots, sink a ship at sea, or smash up an airplane in flight. As soon as people find out that such a storm is approaching, they start preparing for it, and no matter how fast the Invisible Ones travel, the radio and telegraph wires carry their messages still faster.

The battle between the two giants called Northern and Southern Air was about to start, but the people had already been warned. The farmers were hurrying to stack the hay before it got wet; the pilots were hurrying their planes into the hangars; the fishermen had called off all fishing until the storm blew over.

The battle was on. It started when the Southern Air climbed on to his enemy's back. Light banks of fleecy clouds appeared high in the sky, covering it with a white film. Then the clouds got darker. Far off in the distance a gray wall of rain appeared. It was coming closer, and soon moved over the woods and the fields and the village. "Tap-tap-tap!" the first drops spattered on the windowpane. They were followed by others, which spattered the roofs, the leaves, and the park benches. It looked like a long rainy spell, but gradually the clouds parted, the sky cleared, and it became hot. The Southern Air had won. How long would the victory last?

The Northern Air would not accept defeat. He circled around to the enemy's rear, and an avalanche of cold descended on the Southern Air and tossed him high up; the sky was suddenly filled with mountains of clouds. A terrible storm ripped across the earth, breaking branches off the trees, raising pillars of dust, and whirling the leaves on the ground. Luckily though, the people had again been warned of the oncoming storm and were prepared to meet it.

And so the Invisible Ones roam the earth and bring rain, storms, snow and frost with them.

Meteorologists keep a sharp lookout for the Invisible Ones in order to warn farmers of a coming frost, pilots of fog, and railwaymen of snowdrifts on the tracks.

TALL TALES

NIKOLAI NOSOV

Mishutka and Stasik were sitting on a bench in the garden, talking. But they were not simply talking, they were telling each other tall tales. Each was trying to tell bigger fibs than the other.

"How old are you?" Mishutka asked.

"Ninety-five. And you?"

"I am one hundred and forty. You know," added Mishutka, "I used to be very, very big, like Uncle Boris, but then I got little."

"And I," said Stasik, "I used to be little, but then grew big, and then I got little again. Now I'll soon be big again."

"And when I was big I could swim the whole river," Mishutka said.

"I could swim across the sea!" said Stasik.

"That's nothing! I used to swim across the ocean!" Mishutka said.

"And I, I used to know how to fly!" This from Stasik.

"Let me see you fly now! Go ahead!" Mishutka challenged his friend.

"Now I can't any more. I've unlearned how."

"Once, when I was swimming in the sea," Mishutka said, "a shark came right at me. I hit it with my fist and it bit off my head."

"You're lying!"

"No, I'm not!"

"Then how come you didn't die?"

"Why should I have died?" Mishutka said. "I swam to the shore and went home."

"Without a head?"

"Of course, without a head. What did I want a head for?"

"But how did you walk without a head?"

"I just walked. Why can't one walk without a head!"

"How come you have a head now?"

"I grew a new head."

"That's a clever fib," Staik thought with envy. He wanted to tell even a better one, so he said: "That's nothing! I was in Africa once and a crocodile swallowed all of me."

"There's a good lie!" Mishutka laughed.

"No, it's true!" Stasik assured him.

"Then how come you're still alive?"

"Because the crocodile spit me out later."

Mishutka thought hard. He wanted to think of a still better story than Stasik's. He thought for quite some time, then he said: "Once I was walking down the street. There were buses, cars, and trucks everywhere."

"I know, I know!" Stasik cried. "Now you're going to say that you got run over. You've already fibbed about that."

"I wasn't even thinking about that."

"All right. Go on."

"So, I was walking along minding my own business. Suddenly a bus came toward me. I didn't notice it until I stepped on it. Cr-rack! I just flattened it out."

"Ha-ha-ha! That's some fib!"

"No, it's not a fib at all!"

"How could you crush a real bus?"

"It was just a very little one. It was a toy bus. A small boy was pulling it on a string."

Just then Igor, a neighbor's boy, came over and sat down on the bench beside Mishutka and Stasik. He listened to them for a while, then said: "Just listen to them lying! Aren't you ashamed?"

"We are not fooling anybody," Stasik said. "We're only thinking things up, we're making up fairy tales."

"Fairy tales!" Igor sneered. "Have you nothing better to do?!"

"Do you think it's so easy to make up stories?" asked Mishutka.

"What could be easier!" said Igor.

"All right, you think up something." Stasik said.

"Just a minute. Let me think." Igor said.

Mishutka and Stasik were glad there was someone else to play their game with them, and they sat back and waited.

"Wait a second," Igor said again. "Uhh . . . Mmmm . . . Umm. . . ."

"Why do you keep saying 'uhh' and 'mm'?!" Mishutka asked.

"Wait, give me a chance to think."

"Then go ahead and think."

"Uhh . . . ," Igor said again and looked up at the sky. "Wait! Ummm. . . ."

"Well?? You said that it was easy—that nothing could be easier."

"Wait! Ah, I know! Once I teased a dog and it bit me. Look, you can still see the scar on my leg," Igor finally told them.

"But what did you think up about it?" the other boys asked.

"Nothing. I told you everything as it really happened."

"And you say you're good at making up stories!"

"Yes, I am, but not at making up stories like yours. You tell lies for no reason. But I—I told a lie yesterday and got something out of it. And how!" boasted Igor.

"Really? What did you get out of it?"

"Yesterday evening my mother and father went out. My sister Ira and I stayed home. Ira went to bed, but I helped myself to half a jar of jam. Then I thought: I'll catch it from my parents! So I smeared some of the jam on Ira's face while she was asleep. When they came home Mom said: 'Who ate the jam?' and I said, 'Ira.' Mom went over to her and saw that her face was covered with jam, and this morning Ira got it from Mom! But she gave me some jam with my breakfast. That lie was of some use!"

"Someone got punished because of you, and you're glad?!!" Mishutka said.

"What do *you* care?" Igor said.

"You are a *real* liar! That's what!" answered Mishutka.

"You two are liars yourselves!"

"Oh, go away. We don't want to play with you."

"I don't care," Igor said and got up and went away.

Mishutka and Stasik soon went home. On the way they bought one ice cream cone because they didn't have enough money for two.

"Let's buy one cone and divide it into equal parts," Stasik had suggested. "Let's take it home and cut it with a knife. That way we can divide it exactly in half."

"OK. Let's go," Mishutka had agreed.

On the stairs they later met Ira. Her eyes were red from crying.

"What were you crying about?" Mishutka asked.

"My mother wouldn't let me go outside to play."

"Why not?"

"Because of the jam. I didn't eat it. Igor said that I did. He must have eaten it and then blamed it on me," she explained through her tears.

"Sure, he ate it. He even boasted about it. Don't cry. Come on up to my house, and I'll give you half of the ice cream," Mishutka said.

"And I'll give you my half. I'll have just one lick and then I'll give the rest to you," Stasik promised.

"Don't you want it?" asked Ira.

"Nope. We've already had ten ice cream cones today," Stasik answered.

"Let's cut it into three pieces," Ira said.

"All right," the boys agreed willingly. And Stasik added, "If you eat the whole cone you'll probably get a sore throat anyway."

So they went to Mishutka's and cut the ice cream into three parts.

"Yummy! I love ice cream!" Mishutka said. "You know, once I ate a whole pail of ice cream!"

RAINBOW FLOWER

VALENTIN KATAYEV

There was once a girl named Zhenya. One day her mother sent her to the bakery for some bread rings. Zhenya bought seven bread rings: two with caraway seeds for her father, two with poppy seeds for her mother, two with sugar coating for herself, and a little pink one for her brother Pavlik. The bread rings were on a string, just like beads. Zhenya started back for home with the string of bread rings. She walked along looking up and down, reading the signs on the way, just passing the time of day.

Meanwhile, a strange dog came up to her from behind and began eating the bread rings. First it ate the ones for her father with caraway seeds, then the ones for her mother with poppy seeds, then her own two that had sugar coating on them. Zhenya suddenly felt that the string of bread rings was very light. She turned around, but it was too late. There was nothing but the string left in her hand, and the dog was just swallowing the last piece of Pavlik's little pink bread ring and licking its chops.

"Oh, you horrid dog!" Zhenya cried and ran after it. She ran and ran, but couldn't catch it. Finally, she got lost. When she stopped, she saw that she was in a strange place. There were no big houses there, just very little ones. Zhenya began to cry. Suddenly an old woman appeared.

"Why are you crying little girl?" she asked.

Zhenya told the old woman what had happened.

The old woman was sorry for Zhenya. She led her to her little garden and said: "Don't cry. I will help you. I don't have any bread rings and I don't have any money either, but there is a very special flower growing in my garden. It is a rainbow flower and it can do anything you ask it to. I can see that you are a good girl, even though you are absent-minded. I will give you the rainbow flower, and it will help you."

With these words the old woman picked a very pretty flower from one of the flower beds. It looked like a daisy. It had seven petals, but each one was of a different color. One was yellow, one red, one blue, one green, one orange, one violet, and one light blue.

"This is not an ordinary flower," the old woman said. "It can make

any wish come true. All you have to do is tear off a petal, throw it up in the air, and say:

> Fly, petal, oh—
> East to West you go.
> Then North to South
> And turn about.
> Touch the ground, do,
> Make my wish come true.

Then you say your wish, and it will come true."

Zhenya thanked the old woman. She went out of the garden gate and suddenly remembered that she was lost and didn't know how to get home. She wanted to turn around and ask the old woman to take her to the nearest policeman, but both the little garden and the old woman had disappeared. What should she do? Zhenya was just about to start crying, as usual—she even crinkled up her nose—and then, suddenly, she remembered about the magic flower.

Zhenya tore off the yellow petal, threw it up, and said:

> Fly, petal, oh—
> East to West you go.

Then North to South
~~And turn about.~~
Touch the ground, do,
Make my wish come true.

Make me be back home again with the bread rings!

No sooner were the words out of her mouth than she was back in her own house, holding a string of bread rings!

Zhenya gave them to her mother and thought: "This is really a wonderful flower. I'll put it in the prettiest vase we have."

Zhenya was only a little girl; so she climbed up on a chair and stretched her hand toward her mother's favorite vase that stood on the top shelf. Just then some crows flew by the window. And of course Zhenya had to know exactly how many of them there were—seven or eight? She opened her mouth and began to count on her fingers when—bang!—the vase toppled off the shelf and crashed into a thousand pieces.

"My goodness, what a child!" her mother called angrily from the kitchen. "What have you broken this time? I hope it's not my favorite vase!"

"Oh, no, Mommie! I didn't break anything!" Zhenya called back. She quickly tore off the red petal, threw it up, and whispered:

Fly, petal, oh—
East to West you go.
Then North to South
And turn about.
Touch the ground, do,
Make my wish come true.

Make Mommie's best vase whole again!

No sooner were the words out of her mouth than the tiny pieces began moving toward each other and fitting themselves together.

Her mother came in from the kitchen—and there was her favorite vase sitting prettily on the top shelf as always. Zhenya's mother shook her finger at her—just in case, you know—and sent her out to play in the yard.

When Zhenya went outside she saw that the boys in the yard were playing, making believe they were Arctic explorers. They were sitting on a pile of old boards and had a stick stuck into the sand nearby.

"Can I play, too?" she asked.

"Of course not. Can't you see this is the North Pole! We don't take girls along to the North Pole!"

"That's not the North Pole, it's only a pile of boards."

"It's not boards, it's ice floes. Go away and don't bother us! Can't you see the ice is beginning to crack?"

"Come, let me play!"

"No. Go away!"

"Think I care? I can get to the North Pole without any of you. Only it won't be this awful pile of boards, it'll be the *real* North Pole. So there!"

Zhenya went off into a corner of the yard, took the rainbow flower from her pocket, tore off the blue petal, threw it up, and said:

> Fly, petal, oh—
> East to West you go.
> Then North to South
> And turn about.
> Touch the ground, do,
> Make my wish come true.

Make me be at the North Pole this minute!

No sooner were the words out of her mouth than suddenly a terrible blizzard was howling all around, the sun disappeared, everything became black, and the earth spun around under her feet like a top.

Zhenya found herself all alone at the North Pole, in her little summer dress and nothing on her bare feet but sandals. And the frost was just terrible there!

"Oh, Mommie, I'm freezing!" she wailed, but her tears turned into icicles and hung from the tip of her nose.

Meanwhile seven polar bears had suddenly appeared from behind an ice hill and started toward her. One was more horrible than the next: the first was jumpy, the second was mean, the third was grumpy, the fourth was lean, the fifth had a cap, the sixth liked to scrap, and the seventh was the biggest of all.

Zhenya was scared to death. With frozen fingers she tore off the green petal, threw it up, and shouted at the top of her voice:

> Fly, petal, oh—
> East to West you go.

Then North to South
~~And turn about.~~
Touch the ground, do,
Make my wish come true.

Take me back to our yard right now!

No sooner were the words out of her mouth than she was back in the yard. And the boys made fun of her.

"Where's your North Pole, smarty?"

"I was just there."

"Well, we didn't see you there. Prove it!"

"See, I still have an icicle here."

"That's no icicle, it's a piece of fuzz, silly!"

Zhenya decided that the boys were horrid and she'd never play with them again. So she went into the next yard to play with the girls.

There she saw that the girls had a lot of toys. One had a doll carriage, one had a ball, one had a skipping rope, one had a tricycle, and one had a big talking doll with a doll's hat on and a pair of doll's boots. Zhenya was terribly unhappy. Her eyes turned as green as a cat's from envy.

"Hm! I'll show *you* who has the best toys!" she thought.

She pulled the rainbow flower from her pocket and tore off the orange petal. She threw it up and said:

Fly, petal, oh—
East to West you go.
Then North to South
And turn about.
Touch the ground, do,
Make my wish come true.

Make all the toys in the world mine!

No sooner were the words out of her mouth than toys began rushing toward her from all sides.

The first to come, of course, were the dolls. They blinked their eyes and said "Ma-ma, Ma-ma," over and over again. At first Zhenya was very pleased. But in a few minutes there were so many dolls that they filled up the yard, the little street, two big avenues, and half the square. No one could move without stepping on a doll. No one could hear anything except the dolls' chattering, "Ma-ma, Ma-ma!" Can you imagine the noise five million talking dolls can make? And there were at least

96

that many. And these were only dolls from Moscow. The dolls from Leningrad, Kharkov, Kiev, Lvov, and other cities had not yet arrived. They were squawking like parrots on every road of the Soviet Union. Zhenya was getting worried. But this was only the beginning. After the dolls came rubber balls, rolling along by themselves. Then came the marbles and scooters, tricycles, toy tractors, and cars. Skipping ropes were crawling along the ground like snakes; they got tangled underfoot and made the nervous dolls squeak louder still.

Millions of toy airplanes, blimps, and gliders were flying through the air. Paper parachutes were coming down from the sky like snow and got caught in the telephone wires and the trees. All traffic in the city stopped. The policemen at the crossings climbed the nearest lamp posts and didn't know what to do.

"Stop, stop!" Zhenya screamed. "That's enough! I don't want any more! I don't need so many toys! I was only fooling. I'm scared. . . ."

Ah, but who would listen to her? The toys kept pouring in. When all the Soviet toys had come, American toys started arriving. The whole city was filled with toys. Zhenya ran upstairs—the toys followed her. Zhenya rushed out on her balcony—the toys followed her. Zhenya ran up to the attic—the toys followed her there, too. Zhenya climbed up on the roof and hurriedly tore off the violet petal. She threw it up and quickly said:

> Fly, petal, oh—
> East to West you go.
> Then North to South
> And turn about.
> Touch the ground, do,
> Make my wish come true.

> *Make all the toys go back to the toy shops!*

No sooner were the words out of her mouth than all the toys disappeared.

Then Zhenya looked at the rainbow flower and saw there was only one petal left.

"Oh dear!" she said. "I've used up six petals already and I've had no fun from any of them. Well, I'll be smarter next time."

Zhenya walked along the street, thinking.

"What else should I wish for? I know, I'll wish for a pound of chocolate candy. No, I think I'd rather have a pound of peppermints. No, I'll have half a pound of chocolates, half a pound of peppermints, a bag of nuts, and I might as well get a pink bread ring for Pavlik. But what's the use? What if I get all that candy? I'll eat it up and have nothing left. No, I better wish for a tricycle. No, that's no good. I'll have a couple of rides on it and then the boys will probably take it away. I think I'll buy myself a ticket to the movies or the circus. That's a lot of fun. But maybe I'd better ask for a new pair of sandals? That's also nice. But then, what's the use of a new pair of sandals? I can ask for something much better than that. The main thing is not to be in a hurry."

This was what Zhenya was thinking about as she walked along. Suddenly she saw a boy sitting quietly on a bench. He had big blue eyes that looked good-natured. The boy was really nice; you could see he wasn't a bully. Zhenya decided to make friends with him. She came up close, so close that she could see her own face mirrored in his eyes; there were her braids touching her shoulders.

"Hello. What's your name?" she asked.

"Vitya. What's yours?"

"Zhenya. Let's play tag."

"I can't. I'm crippled."

And then Zhenya saw that he had on a big ugly shoe with a very thick sole.

"Oh, that's too bad!" she said. "I like you and it would have been a lot of fun to play tag."

"I like you too, and I know it would have been a lot of fun to play tag with you. But I can't. I'll never be able to. I'm crippled for life."

"Don't be silly, Vitya!" Zhenya said and took the precious rainbow flower from her pocket. "Look!"

She carefully tore off the last petal, the light-blue one, and held it up to her eyes for a second. Then she opened her fingers, let it fly off, and sang in a high, happy voice:

> Fly, petal, oh—
> East to West you go.
> Then North to South
> And turn about.
> Touch the ground, do,

Make my wish come true.

Make Vitya well again!

No sooner were the words out of her mouth than Vitya jumped up from the bench and began playing tag with her. He ran so fast that Zhenya could not catch him, no matter how hard she tried.

THE NEW YEAR'S TREE
IN THE SOKOLNIKI SCHOOL

ALEXANDER KONONOV

Vladimir Ilytch Lenin, the founder of the Soviet Republic, is the George Washington of the new Russia. Understandably, he has been celebrated in every art form, not the least, of course, in Soviet literature. Every known detail of his life has been recorded in biographies, plays, stories, poems, legends—and even myths. The books about Lenin for young readers are without number.

Here is an early "classic," a true story about a New Year's Eve celebration in 1919, in a school for young orphans in a forest in Moscow's outskirts. Lenin was the children's special guest at this celebration.

Much of the writing for the young about Lenin emphasizes his simplicity and his humanity.

It was not necessary to go far for the New Year's tree. Right there in the woods of Sokolniki grew many fir trees. The nicest one was chosen, thick and curly branched, and it was carried inside the little schoolhouse in the woods.

The children watched the tree being fastened with nails to a wooden cross so that it would stand firmly on the floor. Then the electrician Volodya connected a string of lights to it.

Next day, from early morning the children awaited impatiently the arrival of Vladimir Ilytch Lenin. It was still light when they began to ask the school custodian: "What if Lenin doesn't come?" or, "If there is another blizzard, will he come anyway, or won't he?"

The custodian was an old laborer from Petrograd. He had known Lenin even before the Revolution. That is why the children were asking him those questions. And he kept assuring them:

"If Lenin said he would come, then he will."

Finally it was evening. A blizzard began to rage. The wind whistled in the pine trees, drifts of dry snow whirled and swept over the ground like thin, white snakes. Then white tufts of it began to fall from the sky.

The fir tree had been trimmed, and the toys waited under the gleaming branches. The children had made the toys themselves. There were bears, rabbits, and elephants. But the best toy of all was Grandfather Frost, with his long silver beard; he now sat on the topmost branch of the tree.

Time passed, but Lenin did not come.

And when the children overheard some grownup whispering: "In such weather, of course he will not come," they again ran to the custodian, and he spoke to them sternly:

"Don't pester me! I said, 'If he promised to come, he will come!' "

Again they waited. The wind whistled louder, the dry snow beat against the windowpanes. Because of all the noise of the storm, no one heard the car stop at the schoolhouse. From the car stepped out Vladimir Ilytch.

He came up the stairs, took off his coat, wiped his face wet with snow with his handkerchief, and went straight to the Big Room to join the children.

They recognized him at once. Many times had they seen his portrait! But just the same, they felt very shy at first—they just stood there like little statues, and stared at him.

But Lenin did not wait long for them to greet him. He winked at the children and said:

"Is there any one here who knows how to play cat-and-mouse?"

Vera, the oldest of the girls, was the first to speak.

"I know how!"

"And I!" cried Lyosha, one of the boys.

"Then you can be the cat," Vladimir Ilytch said to him.

The children formed a circle around the New Year's tree.

Lyosha chased after Vera, and she hid behind the tree. Lyosha ran to the left, Vera escaped to the right. Then Lyosha pounced on little Katya. She grabbed at Lenin for protection. Lenin lifted her high above his head, saying:

"We won't let the cat have her!"

Lyosha tried and tried to catch a "mouse," but did not succeed. Finally he caught the boy, Senya. Lyosha then became the mouse and Senya the cat.

The game continued for a long time. Everyone began to feel very warm.

Then the door opened and a large, gray elephant entered the room. The children shrieked in chorus. It is true that many of them recognized at once the gray piano cover. But who was under the cover? The elephant moved and his long trunk swayed back and forth. He had gray felt boots on his front legs but his rear feet were in shoes. Anyone not too fussy would regard him as quite a respectable elephant. This elephant went around the New Year's tree, waved his trunk in farewell, and moved toward the door. Outside the room, behind the door, the electrician Volodya and the custodian, both old hands at practical jokes, threw off the piano cover and emerged into the room. The children laughed so hard that Grandfather Frost shook on top of the tree.

Although the children had recognized the gray skin of the elephant for what it really was, and had wanted to hold on to him and not let him leave the room so soon, they had been a little afraid to touch him. What if it was a real elephant after all, they thought.

There was other fun that evening.

One of the children yelled: "Now let's play hide-and-seek! Hide-and-seek!"

Lenin then took his handkerchief from his pocket and tied it around his eyes. The electrician quickly moved the New Year's tree into a corner to make more room for the game.

His arms outstretched, Lenin went around on tiptoe in search of the children, who had scattered and hidden. One by one, they came out of their hiding places and stole up to Vladimir Ilytch, touched him, and ran off shouting:

"You're hot! You're hot!"

And when Lenin was very close to someone, they all shouted:

"Watch out, you'll get burnt!"

The children were quick and tricky. They would get down on their haunches right under Lenin's outstretched arms, and he would pass without touching them.

Then they would shout:

"You're cold, watch out, you'll freeze!"

Lenin realized that the children were too fast for him and that he would have to go around with his eyes covered for a long time before he caught one of them. So he pretended to go in one direction, turned around suddenly on his heel, and grabbed the nearest one behind his back.

The children shouted, as was required by the rules of the game: "Guess who it is! Guess who it is!"

Vladimir Ilytch felt the captive's hair, ran his fingers over his forehead and cheeks.

"Senya!" he announced.

Senya was sorry that he was caught, but glad that Lenin remembered him.

Then little Katya recited a poem. She forgot the words in the middle of it and began to cry.

Lenin consoled her. She stopped crying, wiped her tears, and said:

"Vladimir Ilytch, please don't go away. Live here with us."

Lenin laughed. "I live very near here, we're neighbors."

Soon a circle was formed and everyone began to run around the New Year's tree, holding hands. Little Katya was next to Vladimir Ilytch. She liked having her hand nestled in his large warm one.

Just then Lenin's wife and his sister came into the room carrying a large basket of gifts that Lenin had brought for the children. There were balls, drums, bugles. Katya got a doll.

While the children were noisily examining and comparing their toys, Vladimir Ilytch slipped out and drove away.

That's how it was on New Year's Eve in the year 1919, in the little schoolhouse in the Sokolniki woods.

THE ADVENTURES OF DUNNO AND HIS FRIENDS

NIKOLAI NOSOV

If there were in the Soviet Union such a thing as a best-seller list of children's books, *The Adventures of Dunno and His Friends* would most certainly be perpetually on it. It is the book most loyally loved and read by younger schoolchildren. And its hero, the blundering, mentally lazy but physically overactive lilliputian ignoramus, *Neznaika* ["Don't Know"—"Dunno" for short], is one of their most favorite characters.

This mite and his adventures have not only been immortalized in a series of books, but have also been staged, filmed, and turned into a puppet play. And Neznaika has been singularly honored by having a restaurant named after him in Tokyo; the books about him have been translated into Japanese.

Neznaika was born into the world of Russian children's books in 1954. His "father," the author Nikolai *Nosov* ["The Nose"] is gifted in writing the best kind of humor, the kind that is spiced with satire and wit.

THE MITES OF FLOWER TOWN

Once upon a time, in a town in fairyland, lived some people called the Mites. They were called Mites because they were very tiny. The biggest of them was no bigger than a pine cone. Their town was very pretty. Around every house grew daisies, dandelions, and honeysuckle, and the streets were all named after flowers: Bluebell Street, Daisy Lane, and Primrose Avenue. That is why the town was called Flower Town. It stood on the bank of a little brook. The Mites called it Cucumber River because so many cucumbers grew on its banks.

On the other side of the brook was a forest. The Mites made boats out of birch bark and crossed the brook in them when they went to the forest to gather nuts, berries, and mushrooms. It was hard for the Mites to pick berries because they were so small. When they picked nuts they had to climb the bushes and take saws with them to cut off the stems, for the Mites could not pick the nuts by hand. They sawed off mushrooms, too—sawed them off at the very ground, then cut them into pieces and carried them home on their shoulders like logs.

There were two kinds of Mites—boy-Mites and girl-Mites. The boy-Mites wore long trousers or shorts held up by straps, and the girl-Mites wore dresses made out of brightly colored cloth. The boy-Mites couldn't be bothered to comb their hair, so they cut it short; but all the girl-Mites wore their hair long. They loved to comb it in all sorts of pretty ways. Some wore it in long braids with ribbons woven into them. Others wore it hanging about their shoulders with big bows on top.

The boy-Mites were so proud of being boys that they would have nothing to do with the girl-Mites. And the girl-Mites were so proud of being girls that they would not make friends with the boy-Mites. If a girl-Mite caught sight of a boy-Mite coming down the street, she would cross to the other side. And she was quite right, for some of the boy-Mites were so nasty they would be sure to give her a shove or pull her hair. They were not *all* like this, of course; but you couldn't tell what they were like by looking at them, and so the girl-Mites decided to cross the street every time, just in case. Sometimes you could hear a boy-Mite call a girl-Mite "Stuck-up!" and the girl-Mite would call back "Bully!" or something else just as rude.

Perhaps you don't believe this. Perhaps you think such things don't happen in real life. Well, nobody says they do. Real life is one thing, and fairly-tale life is another. Anything can happen in fairy tales.

In one of the houses on Bluebell Street lived sixteen boy-Mites. The most important of them was Doono. He was named Doono because he *did* know everything, and he knew everything because he was always reading books. There were books on his bed and under his bed. You could hardly find a spot in his room without a book on it. He learned all sorts of things from these books, and so everybody admired him and did whatever he said. He always dressed in black, and when he sat down at his desk with his glasses on and began reading a book, he looked like a professor.

In this same house lived Dr. Pillman, who looked after the Mites when they were ill. He always wore a white coat and a white cap with a tassel on it. Here, too, lived the famous tinker Bendum and his helper Twistum. And here lived Treacly-Sweeter who, as everyone knew, had a great weakness for sodas with lots of syrup in them. He was very polite. He liked to have people call him Treacly-Sweeter and was very unhappy when they called him simply Sweeter.

Besides these there was a hunter named Shot. He had a little dog he called Dot and a gun that shot corks. There was also an artist named

Blobs, and a musician named Trills. The others were called Swifty, Grumps, Mums, Roly-Poly, Scatterbrain, and—two brothers—P'raps and Prob'ly. But the most famous of them all was a Mite named Dunno. He was called Dunno because he did *not* know everything. In fact, he hardly knew *anything*.

Dunno wore a bright blue hat, bright yellow trousers, a bright orange shirt, and a bright green tie. He was very fond of bright colors. He would dress himself up in his bright clothes and go wandering about the streets making up all sorts of tales and telling them to everybody he met. He loved to tease the girl-Mites. As soon as a girl-Mite caught sight of his orange shirt coming down the street, she would turn around and run home.

Dunno had a friend named Gunky who lived in Daisy Lane. He and Dunno would sit and talk for hours on end. They quarreled twenty times a day, but they always made up.

One day something happened to Dunno that made him the talk of the town. He had gone for a walk in the fields all by himself. Suddenly a May bug came flying past and struck him on the back of the head. Dunno turned a somersault in the air and fell flat on the ground. The May bug kept on flying and was soon out of sight. Dunno jumped up and looked around to see what had struck him, but there was nothing to be seen.

"What could have hit me?" he thought. "Something must have fallen on me."

He looked up in the air, but there was nothing there either—nothing but the sun shining in the sky.

"It must have been the sun," he decided. "A piece must have broken off and fallen on my head."

He turned around and set out for home, and on the way he met a friend named Glass-Eye.

Glass-Eye was a famous astronomer. He knew how to make magnifying lenses from bits of broken bottle. Everything looked bigger when seen through these lenses. By putting several of them together he had made a telescope with which he studied the moon and the stars.

"Glass-Eye," said Dunno, "a very strange thing has happened. A piece of the sun dropped off and hit me on the head."

"How absurd!" laughed Glass-Eye. "If a piece of the sun had hit you, it would have smashed you to smithereens. The sun is enormous. It's even bigger than our earth."

"It couldn't be," said Dunno. "The sun is no bigger than a saucer."

"It just seems to be because it's so very far away. The sun is a great ball of fire. I've seen it through my telescope. If just a little bit of it broke off it would smash our whole town."

"Think of that!" said Dunno. "I never knew the sun was so big. I'll go and tell everybody about it; they may not have heard. But take another look at the sun through your telescope. Maybe it does have a piece out of it after all."

Dunno set out for home again, and he said to everybody he met:

"Have you heard about the sun? It's bigger than our whole earth. Yes, it is! And a terrible thing has happened: a piece has broken off and is falling on us. It'll strike any minute and smash us all to smithereens. Go and ask Glass-Eye if you don't believe me."

Everybody laughed at him because they knew he was always making up stories. But Dunno kept shouting as he ran home, "Save yourselves, everybody! A piece of the sun is falling!"

"A piece of the what?"

"Of the sun! Hurry up! It'll strike any minute, and that'll be the end of us! You don't know what the sun is! It's bigger than our earth!"

"Nonsense!"

"No nonsense at all! Glass-Eye told me so. He saw it through his telescope!"

Everybody rushed outdoors and looked up at the sun. They looked at it until their eyes began to water. They looked at it until there really did seem to be a piece out of it.

"Save yourselves!" shouted Dunno. "Save yourselves as best you can!"

The Mites ran for their things. Blobs snatched up his paints and brushes; Trills snatched up his fiddle and banjo and French horn. Dr. Pillman rushed about the house searching for his medicine bag which had got mislaid. Roly-Poly snatched up his galoshes and umbrella and was just dashing through the gate when he heard Doono call out:

"Take it easy! What are you afraid of? You know what a dunce Dunno is. This is just one of his ideas."

"Ideas!" cried Dunno. "Go and ask Glass-Eye, I tell you."

So they all ran to Glass-Eye and found out that it was, indeed, only something Dunno had made up. How they did laugh!

"How could we have believed such a silly thing?" they said.

"How, indeed?" said Dunno. "Why, I even believed it myself!"

That's the sort of funny fellow Dunno was!

DUNNO TAKES MUSIC LESSONS

Dunno never could do anything right. He never got beyond reading in syllables, and he could only write printed letters. Some people said his head was empty, but that was not true, because he could not have thought *at all* if it had been empty. To be sure, he did not think *much;* but he put his boots on his feet and not on his head, and it takes some thinking to do even that.

He was not a bad sort, all the same. He wanted to learn, but he did not want to work. He wanted to learn without trying, and of course not even the smartest of the Mites could do that.

The boy-Mites and the girl-Mites dearly loved music, and Trills was a very good musician. He had all kinds of instruments and often played them. People praised him very much for his playing. This made Dunno jealous, and one day he said to him:

"Teach me to play. I want to be a musician, too."

"Very well," said Trills. "What instrument do you want to play?"

"Which is the easiest?"

"The banjo."

"Let me have one, and I'll try it."

Trills gave him a banjo. Dunno strummed on it a bit and then said, "It doesn't make enough noise. Give me something louder."

Trills gave him a fiddle.

Dunno sawed away for a little while and then said, "Haven't you something louder?"

"I have a horn," said Trills.

"Let me try that."

Trills gave him a big brass horn. Dunno blew as hard as he could, and it let out a blare.

"That's a good instrument," said Dunno. "It makes a lot of noise."

"Very well, learn to play the horn if you want to."

"Why should I learn?" said Dunno. "I know how without learning."

"No, you don't," said Trills.

"Yes, I do! Listen!" And he blew the horn with all his might.

Bo-o-o-om! Ba-a-m!

"You're just blowing. You're not playing," said Trills.

"Not playing?" said Dunno sharply. "I'm playing very well. I'm making a lot of noise."

"You don't want to make noise; you want to make *music*."

"This is music."

"No, it isn't," said Trills. "I can see you have no ear for music."

"You haven't got an ear yourself," said Dunno angrily. "You're jealous, that's all. You're afraid somebody else will get some of the praise you like so much."

"That's not true," said Trills. "Take the horn and play as much as you like, if you think you don't have to learn. We'll see whether people will praise you!"

"That's just what I'll do," said Dunno.

And he took the horn and began to blow. Since he did not know how, the horn blared and coughed and wheezed. When Trills could stand it no longer, he put on his velvet jacket and the pink bow he wore instead of a necktie and went to see a friend.

That evening when everybody was at home, Dunno took out the horn and began to blow it again. Boom-boom-boom-boom!

"What's that noise?" they cried.

"It's not a noise," said Dunno. "It's me playing."

"Stop it this very minute," said Doono. "It gives me a headache."

"That's just because you aren't used to it. Once you get used to it, it won't give you a headache."

"But I don't want to get used to it."

But Dunno went on blowing. Boom-boom-girrr-girrr-boom-boom!

"Stop it!" cried all the Mites. "Get out of here with that horrid horn of yours!"

"Where shall I go?"

"Go out into the fields and play there."

"No one will hear me there."

"Must you have someone hear you?"

"Of course I must."

"Then go oudoors and play to the neighbors."

Dunno went out and began to blow his horn in front of the house next door. The neighbors came out and asked him not to make so much noise. He went to another house, but he was sent away from there, too. When the same thing happened at a third house, he blew for all he was worth just for spite. This made all the people angry. They came rushing out of their houses and drove him away. It was all he could do to escape them with his horn.

And he has not played it since.

"Nobody appreciates my music," he said. "They don't understand it yet. When they do understand it, they'll want to hear it, but it will be too late. I won't play for them."

HOW DUNNO BECAME AN ARTIST

Blobs was a very good artist. He always wore a long shirt called a smock. He looked very splendid in his smock, standing in front of his easel, his palette in hand and his long hair thrown back. Anyone could see he was an artist.

When the Mites refused to listen to Dunno's music, he decided to become an artist. One day he came to Blobs and said, "Listen, Blobs, I've decided to be an artist. Give me some paints and a brush."

Blobs, who was very generous, gave Dunno all his old paints and brushes. Just at that moment, Dunno's friend Gunky came to see him.

"Sit down, Gunky," said Dunno, "and I'll paint your picture."

Gunky was only too glad to have his picture painted. He sat down and Dunno set to work. He wanted to make Gunky handsomer than he really was, so he gave him a red nose, green ears, blue lips, and orange eyes. Gunky was anxious to see his portrait. He was so anxious that he kept fidgeting in his chair.

"If you don't stop fidgeting, the picture won't look like you at all," said Dunno.

"Does it look like me now?" asked Gunky.

110

"Very much," said Dunno as he painted in a purple mustache.

"May I see it?" asked Gunky when the portrait was finished.

Dunno showed it to him.

"Do I look like *that?*" cried the amazed Gunky.

"Of course you do."

"What did you give me a mustache for? I haven't got a mustache."

"Well, you will have one some day."

"And why did you paint my nose red?"

"To make it prettier."

"And my hair blue? Is my hair really blue?"

"Yes, it is," said Dunno, "but if you don't like it, I can make it green."

"It's a very bad portrait," said Gunky. "Let me tear it up."

"I won't let you tear up a work of art," said Dunno.

Gunky tried to take the portrait away from him, and they had a fight. They made such a lot of noise that Doono and Dr. Pillman and some other Mites came running.

"What are you fighting about?" they asked.

"Look at this," said Gunky. "Whose portrait do you think it is? Does it look like me?"

"Not in the least," answered the Mites. "It looks more like a scarecrow."

"That's just because it has no name on it," said Dunno. "If I put a name on it you'd see right away who it was."

He picked up a pencil and wrote in big printed letters: GUNKY. Then he hung the picture on the wall.

"Let it hang here where everybody can see it," he said.

"I will not," said Gunky. "As soon as you go to bed I'll take it down and tear it up."

"I won't go to bed. I'll stay up all night and watch it," said Dunno.

Gunky was so angry that he slammed the door and went home.

Dunno did stay up all night. When everybody else was asleep, he painted pictures of all his friends. He painted Roly-Poly so fat that he couldn't get him all in the picture. He painted Swifty with long skinny legs and a dog's tail. He painted Shot astride his dog Dot. He gave Dr. Pillman a thermometer instead of a nose. He painted donkey ears on Doono. In a word he made them all look very foolish. In the morning he wrote names on all the pictures and hung them up. It was a real picture gallery.

The first to wake up was Dr. Pillman. As soon as he saw the paintings, he began to laugh. He liked them so much that he put on his glasses to get a better look at them. He examined each picture in turn, laughing very hard.

"Good for Dunno!" he said. "I never had such a good laugh in my life!"

At last he came to his own picture.

"Who is this?" he asked in a stern voice. "Me? It couldn't be me. No likeness at all. Take it down."

"Why?" asked Dunno. "Let it hang there with the others."

"You must be mad, Dunno!" said Dr. Pillman angrily. "Or, perhaps, there's something wrong with your eyes. What makes you think I have a thermometer instead of a nose? I'll have to give you a big dose of castor oil tonight when you go to bed."

Dunno disliked castor oil very much.

"Please don't," he muttered. "I agree that the picture doesn't look like you." And he took it down and tore it up.

The next one to wake up was Shot. He, too, liked the pictures. He almost died laughing. But the moment his eyes fell on his own, he stopped laughing.

"Very bad," he said. "It doesn't look like me. If you don't take it down, I'll never let you go hunting with me again."

And so Dunno had to take Shot's picture down, too.

The same thing happened with the others. Each of the Mites liked everyone's portrait but his own.

The last of the Mites to wake up was Blobs who always slept later than anyone else. When he saw his picture on the wall, he was furious and said it was no portrait at all—just a mess of paint that had nothing to do with art. He tore it down and took his paints and brushes away from Dunno.

Gunky's portrait was the only one that was left hanging on the wall. Dunno took it down and went to see his friend.

"You can have your picture if you want it, Gunky!" he said. "And then you and I will be friends again."

Gunky took the portrait and tore it into little pieces.

"Very well, let's be friends," he said, "but promise never to paint me again."

"I'll never paint *any*body again," said Dunno. "What's the use? You try so hard and get nothing but blame. I don't want to be an artist any more."

HOW DUNNO BECAME A POET

When nothing came of Dunno's efforts to become an artist, he decided to become a poet. He knew a poet who lived in Dandelion Street. The real name of this poet was Turnips, but since all poets like to have beautiful names, he chose another for himself. He called himself Poesy.

One day Dunno went to see Poesy and said to him, "Teach me how to write. I want to be a poet."

"Have you any talent?" asked Poesy.

"Of course I have. I'm very talented," said Dunno.

"We shall see about that," said Poesy. "Do you know how a rhyme is made?"

"A rhyme? What's that?"

"A rhyme is made by finding words that end in the same sound—like, 'tickle, pickle,' or 'berry, cherry.' Is that clear?"

"It is."

"Then give me a rhyme for 'waiter.' "

"Mister," said Dunno.

"No," said Poesy. " 'Mister' doesn't rhyme with 'waiter.' "

"Why not?" said Dunno. "They both end in the same sound."

"Not just the last sound. Next to the last has to rhyme, too—like, 'mother, brother,' or 'tender, fender.' "

"Oh, I see!" cried Dunno. " 'Mother, brother,' 'tender, fender.' That's fun!"

"Then think of a rhyme for 'scissors,' " said Poesy.

"Zizzers," said Dunno.

"What are zizzers?" asked Poesy. "There's no such word as zizzers."

"Isn't there?"

"Of course there isn't."

"Then 'fizzers.' "

"What are fizzers?" asked Poesy, more surprised than ever.

"Fizzers? Why, things that fizz."

"You just made that up," said Poesy. "There is no such word. You've got to choose real words, and not just make up any old word."

"And what if I can't choose a real word?"

"That means you have no poetic talent."

"Very well, you think of a rhyme for scissors," said Dunno.

"Just a minute," said Poesy.

He stood in the middle of the room, crossed his arms on his chest, cocked his head on one side, and began to think. Then he threw back his head and stared at the ceiling and thought. Then he put his chin in his hand and stared at the floor and thought. When he had done all this he began to walk up and down, muttering to himself.

"Scissors, mizzers, bizzers, nizzers, tizzers . . ." He went on muttering for a long time, and at last he said: "Oh, brother! There just isn't any rhyme to that word!"

"You see!" gloated Dunno. "You yourself gave me a word that has no rhyme, and then you say I have no talent."

"Maybe you have, but for goodness' sake leave me alone," said Poesy. "My head's going around. Write anything you like as long as it rhymes and makes sense, and that will be a poem."

"Is it really so easy?" said Dunno.

"Yes, all you need is talent."

Dunno went home, and as soon as he got there he sat down and began to write poetry. All day long he walked up and down, staring now at the floor, now at the ceiling, holding his chin in his hand and muttering to himself. At last the poems were ready.

"Listen, everybody!" he said. "I've written some poems."

"How nice! What are your poems about?" said his friends.

"About all of you," said Dunno. "The first one's about Doono:

> Doono went out for a walk one day
> And jumped over a lamb that stood in his way.

"What?" cried Doono. "When did I ever jump over a lamb?"

"That's just for the sake of the rhyme," explained Dunno.

"And for the sake of the rhyme you dare to make up all sorts of lies about me?" asked the infuriated Doono.

114

"Yes, I do," said Dunno. "I could not make up real things, could I?"

"You just try doing it again!" warned Doono. "Have you made up lies about the others, too?"

"Here's one about Swifty.

> Hungry Swifty, I am told,
> Ate an iron that was cold.

"Hear that?" cried Swifty. "Hear what he says about me? I never ate a cold iron in my life!"

"Don't shout. I said it was cold just for the sake of the rhyme."

"But I never ate a hot one, either," cried Swifty.

"Well, I didn't say you ate a hot one, so there's nothing for you to get excited about," said Dunno. "Now listen to my poem about P'raps:

> Under his pillow P'raps found
> A cake that weighed a half a pound.

P'raps ran over to his bed and looked under the pillow. "There's no cake under my pillow," he said.

"You don't understand poetry," said Dunno. "Of course, there's no cake there. I just said there was for the sake of the rhyme. I've written a poem about Dr. Pillman too."

"We've got to put a stop to this, friends," cried Dr. Pillman. "Are we to stand calmly by and let him go on telling lies about us!"

"No, we aren't!" everybody agreed. "We won't have any more of it! They aren't poems at all. He's just making fun of us."

But Doono, Swifty, and P'raps wanted to hear the other poems.

"Let him read them," they said. "If he read about us, why shouldn't he read about you?"

"We won't have it! We won't listen!" they cried.

"Very well, if you don't want to listen, I'll go and read them to the neighbors," said Dunno.

"What!" they cried. "Disgrace us in front of the neighbors! If you do, you had better not come home!"

"Oh, all right, I won't read them," said Dunno. "Don't be angry with me."

And he resolved never to write another poem.

HOW DUNNO TOOK A RIDE
IN A SODA-WATER CAR

Bendum and his helper Twistum were very good tinkers. They looked exactly alike, except that Bendum was the least bit taller and Twistum was the least bit shorter. Both of them wore leather jackets, and in their pockets they always carried files, wrenches, screwdrivers, and other tools. If the pockets hadn't been made of leather they would have been torn off long ago. Their caps were also made of leather and they had goggles on them. Bendum and Twistum pulled down the goggles when they were working, to keep the dust and dirt out of their eyes.

All day long Bendum and Twistum sat in their shop repairing frying pans, saucepans, teakettles, oil stoves, and grinders; and when they had nothing to repair they would make tricycles and scooters for the boy-Mites.

One day, without saying a word to anybody, Bendum and Twistum shut themselves up in their shop and began to make something. For a whole month they hammered and sawed and filed and soldered without showing anybody what they were working on, and when the month was up it turned out they had made an automobile.

The automobile ran on a mixture of soda water and syrup. In the middle of the car was a seat for the driver, and in front of this seat was the soda-water tank. The soda water ran out of the tank into a pipe leading to a brass cylinder with a piston in it. Under the pressure of the soda water the piston went up and down, up and down, and made the wheels go around. Above the driver's seat was another tank. In it was syrup, which ran through a pipe and greased the engine. Soda-water cars of this sort were very popular among the Mites. But the car that Bendum and Twistum made had one very important improvement: there was a little rubber tube hanging out of the soda-water tank so that the driver could take a sip whenever he wanted it without stopping the car.

Swifty learned to drive the car, and if anyone asked him for a ride, he never refused.

Treacly-Sweeter asked more often than anyone else because he knew he could drink as much soda-water as he liked in the car. Dunno also enjoyed a ride. But Dunno wanted to learn to drive himself, and so one day he said to Swifty, "Let me steer."

"You don't know how," said Swifty. "This is an automobile, and you've got to know how to handle it."

"What's there to know?" Dunno said. "I've seen what to do—just pull levers and turn the wheel. It's very simple."

"It looks simple, but it's really very hard. You'll kill yourself and smash the car."

"All right, Swifty," said Dunno sulking. "The next time you ask me for something I won't give it to you either."

One day when Swifty was out, Dunno saw the car standing in the yard. He climbed into it and began pulling levers and pressing pedals. At first nothing happened, but all of a sudden the car gave a sputter and began to move. Some Mites who were looking out of the window saw this and ran out of the house.

"What are you doing?" they cried. "You'll run into something!"

"No, I won't," said Dunno. But at that very moment he ran into the dog kennel and smashed it to bits. Fortunately, Dot was not inside, or he would have been smashed, too.

"Just look what you've done!" cried Doono. "Stop the car this very minute!"

Dunno was frightened. He wanted to stop the car, but he didn't know how. He pulled this lever and that, but instead of stopping, the car went faster than ever. There was a summerhouse standing in the yard. Bang! Crash! The summerhouse lay in ruins. Boards came falling about Dunno's ears. One of them struck him on the back, another in the head. He kept turning the steering wheel back and forth.

"Open the gates or I'll smash everything!" he called out as the car raced around the yard.

The Mites opened the gates and Dunno drove the car into the street. There was such a commotion that all the townsfolk came running out of their houses.

"Out of the way!" shouted Dunno as the car tore along.

Doono, Bendum, P'raps, Dr. Pillman, and some other Mites ran after it but they couldn't catch up. Dunno went tearing about the town, unable to stop the car. At last it headed for the river and tumbled headlong down the steep bank. Dunno fell out and lay unconscious on the river bank. The car sank to the bottom of the river.

Doono, Bendum, P'raps, and Dr. Pillman carried Dunno home. They thought he was dead, but as soon as they laid him on the bed he opened his eyes.

"Am I still alive?" he groaned as he looked about him.

"You are," said Dr. Pillman, "but please lie still. I must look you over."

He undressed Dunno and examined him.

"Strange as it may seem, not a bone is broken," he said when he had finished. "But you have a few splinters in you."

"A board hit me on the back," explained Dunno.

"I'll have to take the splinters out," said Dr. Pillman, shaking his head.

"Will it hurt?" asked the frightened Dunno.

"Not at all. Here, I'll take the biggest one out first."

"Ouch!" cried Dunno.

"Why, did it hurt?" asked Dr. Pillman in surprise.

"Of course it did!"

"Well, you'll have to grin and bear it. It doesn't *really* hurt."

"It does so! Ouch! Ouch! Ouch!"

"Anyone would think I was cutting your throat, the way you shout! What are you shouting for?"

"It hurts! You said it wouldn't, but it does!"

"Don't make so much noise. There's only one splinter left."

"Leave it there. I don't mind having one splinter in me."

"I can't. It'll get infected."

"Ouch! Oooo!"

"That's all. I'll just paint it with iodine and everything is finished."

"Will the iodine hurt?"

"Oh, no. Iodine doesn't hurt. Lie still."

"O-o-u-u-ch!"

"Come now! If you're so fond of riding in cars, you've got to take the consequences."

"Oh, oh! It stings!"

"It won't last long. Now I must take your temperature."

"Oh, don't! Please don't!"

"Why not?"

"It'll hurt."

"It doesn't hurt to have your temperature taken."

"You always say it doesn't hurt, but it always does."

"Silly! Haven't I ever taken your temperature before?"

"No, you haven't."

"Well, now you'll see it really doesn't hurt," said the doctor, and he went to get the thermometer.

As soon as he was gone Dunno jumped out of bed, leaped through the window, and ran off to Gunky's. When Dr. Pillman came back with the thermometer, Dunno was gone.

"A fine patient!" muttered the doctor. "Here I am doing my best to make him well, and, instead of thanking me, he jumps out of the window and runs away! He ought to be ashamed of himself!"

PART II

A FEAST OF FOLK TALES

for all ages

Irina Zheleznova, who has so painstakingly translated most of the folktales (*skazki* in Russian) you are about to read, has written a message to English-speaking children:

> I am sure you all know that Russia is a huge country. It is the largest country in the world. Its neighbors are Alaska in the east and Scandinavia in the west. In the south it stretches far, far to the Caucasus and Pamir Mountain ranges, and in the north it reaches out into the Arctic Ocean. . . .
>
> When the rays of dawn light up the sky in the far-eastern part of the country, the sun is already beginning to set in the west of Russia; and while icy winds blow in northern Yakutia, roses bloom in Tashkent. . . .
>
> Many different nationalities live in this vast land—one hundred and sixty-seven! Each of them has its own customs and traditions, and nearly every one has its own language. The Chukchi language, for instance, bears as little resemblance to Russian as Arabic does to English.
>
> And each of these peoples of the Soviet Union has its own folktales.
>
> The Chukchi and Nenets tales, as well as those of other peoples in Russia's far north, take us into the snowy tundra, a barren realm of fierce frosts and howling blizzards where the dog and the reindeer are man's best friends. [Today reindeer are also used for mobile children's libraries in these regions.] In the tales of Central Asia, caravans of camels plod over the scorching sands. Other unfamiliar scenes and images rise before us when we read the Russian tales, mainly from the European part of the country; in these, fearless young heroes gallop on horseback over hills and dales that are green in summer and carpeted with snow in winter, while their lovely princesses sit patiently waiting for them in their log towers.

Irina Zheleznova then adds: "Do you know why I have translated all these folktales? It was because I enjoyed reading them so much."

You will not find any of your old friends in these *skazki*. Jack the Giant Killer will not be there, nor Little Red Riding Hood, nor Cinderella, nor Puss-in-Boots; but you will make friends with new heroes as well as with new good fairies, you will get to know other witches and monsters, and you will enjoy new magic.

Some of the Russian and Belorussian folktales offered here resemble versions found in other languages. They were included because of their elements of originality, unique Slavic flavor, and special color.

Everyone, young and old, is invited to this feast of folktales.

LITTLE COCK, FEATHER FROCK

A Russian Folktale

ADAPTED BY ALEKSEI TOLSTOY

Once upon a time a Cat, a Blackbird, and a Little Cock lived in a little house in the forest. Every day the Cat and the Blackbird went deep into the forest to chop wood, but Little Cock stayed home. Before leaving they would warn Little Cock:

"We are going far away, and you must stay and keep house. But don't make any noise, and if the Fox comes, don't look out of the window."

When the Fox found out that the Cat and the Blackbird had left, he hurried to the little house, sat down under the window, and began to sing:

Little Cock,
Feather Frock,
~~With your comb so red,~~
And your glossy head,
Will you look out, please,
I will give you some peas.

Little Cock looked out of the window, and the Fox seized him and carried him off to his hole. Little Cock cried:

The Fox is taking me
Beyond the rivers deep,
Across the mountains steep.
Blackbird and Cat,
Come and save me!

The Cat and the Blackbird heard Little Cock, ran after the Fox, and took Little Cock from him.

When the Cat and the Blackbird went to the forest to chop wood again, they warned Little Cock:

"Little Cock, don't look out of the window. We shall go very far today, and may not hear you when you cry."

When they left, the Fox hurried to the little house and began to sing:

Little Cock,
Feather Frock
With your comb so red,
And your glossy head,
Will you look out, please,
I will give you some peas.

Little Cock sat still, so the Fox sang again:

Boys and girls ran by today,
And scattered wheat upon the way.
The hens are pecking it in flocks,
But won't give any to little cocks.

Little Cock looked out of the window and said:

Cluck, cluck, cluck, please tell me, Fox,
Why won't they give any to little cocks?

Then the Fox seized Little Cock and carried him off to his hole. Little Cock cried:

The Fox is taking me
Beyond the rivers deep,
Across the mountains steep.
Blackbird and Cat,
Come and save me!

The Cat and the Blackbird heard Little Cock and started after the Fox. The Cat ran and the Blackbird flew. When they caught up with the Fox, the Cat scratched and the Blackbird pecked, and they rescued Little Cock.

The Cat and the Blackbird again made ready to go deep into the forest and chop wood. They again warned Little Cock:

"Don't listen to the Fox and don't look out of the window. We shall go much farther today and shall not hear you when you cry."

So once more the Cat and the Blackbird went deep into the forest to chop wood. Along came the Fox. He sat down under the window and sang:

Little Cock,
Feather Frock,
With your comb so red,
And your glossy head,
Will you look out please,
I will give you some peas.

Little Cock sat still, so the Fox sang again:

Boys and girls ran by today,
And scattered wheat upon the way.
The hens are pecking them in flocks,
But won't give any to little cocks.

Little Cock looked out of the window and said:

Cluck, cluck, cluck, please tell me, Fox,
Why won't they give any to little cocks?

The Fox seized Little Cock and carried

him off to his hole beyond the rivers deep, across the mountains steep.

Little Cock cried and cried with all his might, but the Cat and the Blackbird did not hear him. When they came home, they could not find Little Cock.

The Cat and the Blackbird followed the Fox's tracks. The Cat ran and the Blackbird flew. At last they came to the Fox's hole. The Cat began to play and sing:

> I'll play a pretty tune,
> For Brother Fox I'll croon.
> Does my brother roam,
> Or sleeps he in his home?

The Fox heard the song and said to himself:

"Who is it that plays so well and sings so sweetly? I must see who it is."

The Fox came out of his hole. The Cat and the Blackbird seized the Fox and began to beat him. They beat him and beat him until he ran away as fast as his legs could carry him.

The Cat and the Blackbird took Little Cock, put him in a basket, and carried him home.

And to this day they all live happily in their little house in the forest.

THE COCK AND THE BEAN

A Russian Folktale

There once lived a Cock and a Hen. One day the Cock was digging in the garden and he dug up a bean.

"Cluck-cluck-cluck. Eat the bean, Hen," cried the Cock.

"Cluck-cluck-cluck. Thank you, Cock," the Hen replied. "Eat it yourself!"

The Cock pecked at the bean and took one swallow, and the bean got stuck in his throat.

"Please, Hen," he said, "go and ask the River to give me some water to drink."

So what did the Hen do but run to the River.

"River, River, give me some water to take to the Cock, for a bean has got stuck in his throat."

But the River said: "Go to the Lime Tree and ask for a leaf; then I will give you the water."

So what did the Hen do but run to the Lime Tree.

"Lime Tree, Lime Tree, give me a leaf! I will take the leaf to the River, and the River will give me some water to take to the Cock, for a bean has got stuck in his throat."

But the Lime Tree said: "Go to the Peasant's Daughter and ask for a thread."

So what did the Hen do but run to the Peasant's Daughter.

"Peasant's Daughter, Peasant's Daughter, give me a thread! I will take the thread to the Lime Tree. The Lime Tree will give me a leaf to take to the River. And the River will give me some water to take to the Cock, for a bean has got stuck in his throat."

Said the Peasant's Daughter: "Go to the Combmaker and ask for a comb; then I will give you the thread."

So what did the Hen do but run to the Combmaker.

"Combmaker, Combmaker, give me a comb! I will take the comb to the Peasant's Daughter. The Peasant's Daughter will give me a thread to take to the Lime Tree. The Lime Tree will give me a leaf to take to the River. And the River will give me some water to take to the Cock, for a bean has got stuck in his throat."

Said the Combmaker: "Go to the Baker and get me some buns, then I shall give you the comb."

So what did the Hen do but run to the Baker.

"Baker, Baker, give me some buns! I will take the buns to the Combmaker. The Combmaker will give me a comb to take to the Peasant's Daughter. The Peasant's Daughter will give me a thread to take to the Lime Tree. The Lime Tree will give me a leaf to take to the River. And the River will give me some water to take to the Cock, for a bean has got stuck in his throat."

Said the Baker: "Go to the Woodcutter and get me some firewood first!"

So what did the Hen do but run to the Woodcutter.

"Woodcutter, Woodcutter, give me some firewood to take to the Baker. The Baker will give me some buns to take to the Combmaker. The Combmaker will give me a comb to take to the Peasant's Daughter. The Peasant's Daughter will give me a thread to take to the Lime Tree. The Lime Tree will give me a leaf to take to the River. And the River will give me some water to take to the Cock, for a bean has got stuck in his throat."

The Woodcutter gave the Hen the fire-wood.

The Hen took the firewood to the Baker. The Baker gave her some buns to take to the Combmaker. The Combmaker gave her a comb to take to the Peasant's Daughter. The Peasant's Daughter gave her a thread to take to the Lime Tree. The Lime Tree gave her a leaf to take to the River. And the River gave her some water to take to the Cock.

The Cock drank the water and the bean went down.

"Cock-a-doodle-doo!" crowed the Cock.

THE DOUGHNUT

A Russian Folktale

Once upon a time there lived an old man and his wife. Now, one fine day the old man said to his wife:

"Old woman, scrape out the flour bin and sweep out the corn bin, try and scrape up some flour to make us a doughnut."

So the old woman took a fowl's wing, scraped out the flour bin and swept out the corn bin, and she scraped up two handfuls of flour.

She made the dough with sour cream, shaped the doughnut, fried it in butter, and put it on the window sill to cool.

The Doughnut lay still for a while, but then it up and went rolling. It rolled off the window sill on to the bench, off the bench and down to the floor, over the floor to the door, then hop-skip over the doorstep, down the steps, into the yard, and out of the gate, farther and farther away.

It rolled and rolled along the road till it met a Hare.

"Doughnut, Doughnut, I'll eat you up," said the Hare.

"Oh, don't eat me up, Hare. Let me sing you a song:

I'm a Doughnut round,
I was fried and browned,
From a flour bin scraped,
From a corn bin swept.
I've sour cream inside,
In butter I was fried.
They left me to cool,
But I'm no fool!
Grandpa didn't get me,
Grandma didn't get me,
And you, Hare, won't get me either!"

And away it rolled before the Hare could blink an eye. It rolled and rolled till it met a Wolf.

"Doughnut, Doughnut, I'll eat you up," said the Wolf.

"Oh, don't eat me up, Gray Wolf! Let me sing you a song:

I'm a Doughnut round,
I was fried and browned,
From a flour bin scraped,
From a corn bin swept.
I've sour cream inside,
In butter I was fried.
They left me to cool,
But I'm no fool!
Grandpa didn't get me,
Grandma didn't get me,
The Hare didn't get me,
And you, Gray Wolf, won't get me either!"

And away it rolled before the Wolf could blink an eye. It rolled and rolled till it met a Bear.

"Doughnut, Doughnut, I'll eat you up," said the Bear.

"No, you won't, old Bandy Legs!

I'm a Doughnut round,
I was fried and browned,
From a flour bin scraped,
From a corn bin swept.
I've sour cream inside,
In butter I was fried.
They left me to cool,
But I'm no fool!
Grandpa didn't get me.
Grandma didn't get me,
The Hare didn't get me,
The Wolf didn't get me,
And you, Bear, won't get me either!"

And away it rolled before the Bear could blink an eye. It rolled and rolled till it met a Fox.

"Doughnut, Doughnut, where are you rolling?"

"Down the road, as you see."

"Doughnut, Doughnut, sing me a song!"

And the Doughnut sang:

"I'm a Doughnut round,
I was fried and browned,
From a flour bin scraped,
From a corn bin swept.
I've sour cream inside,
In butter I was fried.
They left me to cool,
But I'm no fool!
Grandpa didn't get me,
Grandma didn't get me,
The Hare didn't get me,
The Wolf didn't get me,
The Bear didn't get me,
And you won't get me either, Foxie!"

And the Fox said:

"Oh, what a fine song! It's such a pity I can't hear well. Do get on my nose, Doughnut dear, and sing a bit louder, that I may hear."

So up jumped the Doughnut on to the Fox's nose and sang the same song a bit louder.

But the Fox said: "Doughnut, dear, sit on my tongue and sing your song, it won't take you long!" The Doughnut hopped on to the Fox's tongue, and—snap!—the Fox gobbled him up.

LITTLE GIRL AND THE SWAN-GEESE

A Russian Folktale

Once there was a peasant and his wife and they had a little girl and a little boy.

"Daughter," said the mother to her Little Girl, "we are going out to work, so look after your Little Brother. If you are a good girl and do not go out of doors, we shall buy you a new kerchief."

Father and Mother went away. But Little Girl forgot what she had been told. She seated Little Brother on the grass by the window and ran away to play with her friends.

Suddenly a flock of Swan-Geese swooped down, caught up Little Brother, and carried him off on their wings.

Little Girl came home, but—alas!—Little Brother was gone. She gasped, ran here and there, but not a sign of him was to be found.

She called him and sobbed, crying that she would catch it from Father and Mother, but Little Brother did not answer.

So out she ran into the open field but could see nothing save some Swan-Geese flying far beyond the dark woods. Suddenly she was sure it was they who had carried her brother off. Folks said the Swan-Geese were wicked birds who stole little children.

So off ran Little Girl after the birds. She ran and ran till she came to an Oven.

"Oven, Oven, tell me where the Swan-Geese have flown?"

"Eat one of my rye loaves, and I will tell you," said the Oven.

"What, me eat a rye loaf? At home we do not eat even wheaten loaves!"

So the Oven did not tell her. Little Girl ran on a bit farther and saw an Apple Tree.

"Apple Tree, Apple Tree, tell me where the Swan-Geese have flown?"

"Eat one of my wild apples, and I will tell you," said the Apple Tree.

"At home we do not eat even apples from the garden!"

So the Apple Tree did not tell her. Little Girl ran on till she came to Milk River and Fruit-Jelly Shores.

"Milk River and Fruit-Jelly Shores, tell me where the Swan-Geese have flown?"

"Have some of my jelly with milk and I will tell you."

"At home we do not eat even jelly with cream."

So Milk River did not tell her.

All day long she ran about the fields and woods. When evening came there was nothing left for her to do but go home. All at once, what should she see but a hut on hen's feet with one tiny window, turning round and round.

Inside the hut sat Baba-Yaga, the witch, spinning flax. And on the bench sat Little Brother playing with silver apples.

Little Girl went in.

"Good evening, Granny!"

"Good evening, Little Girl. What brings you here?"

"My frock is wet through with dew, so I have come in to dry."

"Sit down then and spin some flax."

Baba-Yaga gave her the spindle and went out. Little Girl was sitting there spinning, when all of a sudden a Mouse ran out from under the stove and said to her:

"Little Girl, Little Girl, give me some porridge and I will tell you something."

Little Girl gave him some porridge, and Mouse said:

"Baba-Yaga has gone to make a fire in the bathhouse. She will steam you and wash you, roast you in the oven, and eat you up."

Little Girl began crying and trembling with fear, but the Mouse went on:

"Hurry, take Little Brother and run away, and I will spin the flax for you."

So Little Girl took Little Brother in her arms and ran off.

Baba-Yaga came up to the window every once in a while and said:

"Are you spinning, Little Girl?"

And Mouse would answer: "Yes, I am, Granny."

Baba-Yaga made a fire in the bathhouse and came for Little Girl. But the hut was empty. Baba-Yaga cried: "Fly away, Swan-Geese, fly and catch them! Little Girl has carried off Little Brother!"

Little Girl ran until she came to Milk River, and what should she see there but the Swan-Geese coming after her and her brother.

"Milk River, Milk River, hide me, do!" cried Little Girl.

"Eat some of my plain fruit-jelly."

Little Girl ate some and said thank you.

So Milk River hid her and Little Brother in the shadow of its Fruit-Jelly Shores. And the Swan-Geese flew past without seeing them.

Little Girl ran on again. But the Swan-Geese turned back and flew straight toward her. At any moment they would see her. What was she to do? She ran up to the Apple Tree.

"Apple Tree, Apple Tree, hide me, do!"

"Eat my wild apples."

Little Girl ate one quickly and said thank you. The Apple Tree hid her among its leaves and branches. The Swan-Geese flew past without seeing her.

Little Girl picked up her brother and ran on again. When she had almost reached home the Swan-Geese caught sight of her. They honked and flapped their wings, and in another minute would have torn Little Brother out of her arms.

Little Girl came running to the Oven.

"Oven, Oven, hide me, do!"

"Eat one of my rye loaves."

Little Girl popped a piece of a loaf into her mouth and crawled into the Oven with her brother.

The Swan-Geese flew round and round screaming and honking, but after a while they gave up the chase and flew back to Baba-Yaga.

Little Girl said thank you to the Oven and ran home with Little Brother.

And before long Father and Mother came home.

TINY HAVROSHECHKA

A Russian Folktale

There are good people in the world and some who are not so good. There are also people who are shameless in their wickedness. Tiny Havroshechka had the bad luck to fall in with such as these.

She was an orphan and these people took her in and brought her up only to make her work till she couldn't stand up. She wove and spun and did all the housework and had to answer for everything.

Now, the mistress of the house had three daughters. The eldest was called One-Eye, the second Two-Eyes, and the youngest Three-Eyes.

The three sisters did nothing all day but sit by the gate and watch what went on in the street, while Tiny Havroshechka sewed, spun, and wove for them and never heard a kind word in return.

Sometimes Tiny Havroshechka would go out into the field, put her arms around the neck of her brindled cow, and pour out all her sorrows to her.

"Brindled, my dear," she would say, "they beat me and scold me, they don't give me enough to eat, and yet they forbid me to cry. I am to have five poods * of flax spun, woven, bleached, and rolled by tomorrow."

And the cow would say in reply:

"My pretty one, you have only to climb into one of my ears and come out through the other, and your work will be done for you."

And just as Brindled said, so it was. Tiny

Havroshechka would climb into one of the cow's ears and come out through the other. And lo and behold! there lay the cloth, all spun, woven, bleached, and rolled.

Tiny Havroshechka would then take the rolls of cloth to her mistress, who would look at them and grunt and put them away in a chest, then give Tiny Havroshechka even more work to do.

And Tiny Havroshechka would go to Brindled, put her arms round her and stroke her, climb into one of her ears and come out through the other, pick up the ready cloth and take it to her mistress.

One day the old woman called her daughter, One-Eye, and said to her:

"My good child, my pretty child, go and see who helps the orphan with her work. Find out who spins the thread, weaves the cloth, and rolls it."

One-Eye went with Tiny Havroshechka into the fields and she went with her into the woods, but she forgot her mother's command and she basked in the sun and lay down on the grass.

And Havroshechka whispered:

"Sleep, little eye, sleep!"

One-Eye shut her eye and she fell asleep. While she slept Brindled wove, bleached, and rolled the cloth.

The mistress learnt nothing, so she sent for her second daughter, Two-Eyes.

"My good child, my pretty child, go and see who helps the orphan with her work."

Two-Eyes went with Tiny Havroshechka, but she forgot her mother's command and she, too, basked in the sun and lay down on the grass.

---

* A *pood* is a Russian weight equal to about 36 pounds.

131

And Tiny Havroshechka murmured: "Sleep, little eye! Sleep, the other little eye!"

Two-Eyes shut her eyes and she dozed off. While she slept Brindled wove, bleached, and rolled the cloth.

The old woman was very angry, and on the third day she told her third daughter, Three-Eyes, to go with Tiny Havroshechka, to whom she gave more work to do than ever.

Three-Eyes played and skipped about in the sun until she was so tired that she lay down on the grass.

And Tiny Havroshechka sang out: "Sleep, little eye! Sleep, the other little eye!"

But she forgot all about the third little eye.

Two of Three-Eyes' three eyes fell asleep, but the third eye looked on and saw everything. It saw Tiny Havroshechka climb into one of the cow's ears and come out through the other and pick up the ready cloth.

Three-Eyes came home and told her mother what she had seen. The old woman was overjoyed, and on the very next day she went to her husband and said: "Go and kill the Brindled Cow."

The old man was astonished and tried to reason with her.

"Have you lost your wits, old woman?" he said. "The cow is a good one and still young."

"Kill it and say no more," the wife insisted.

The old man began to sharpen his knife. Tiny Havroshechka knew what her father was about to do. She ran to the field and threw her arms round Brindled.

"Brindled, my dear," she said, "they are going to kill you!"

"And the cow replied: "Do not grieve, my pretty one, and do what I tell you. Take my bones, tie them up in a handkerchief, bury them in the garden, and water them every day. Do not eat of my flesh and never forget me."

The old man killed the cow, and Tiny Havroshechka did as Brindled had told her to. She went hungry, but she would not touch the meat, and she buried the bones in the garden and watered them every day.

After a while an apple tree grew out of them, and a wonderful tree it was! Its apples were round and juicy, its swaying boughs were of silver, and its rustling leaves were of gold. Whoever drove by would stop to look at the tree, and whoever came near marveled.

A long time passed by and a little time. One day One-Eye, Two-Eyes, and Three-Eyes were out walking in the garden. And who should chance to be riding by at the time but a young man, handsome and strong and rich and curly-haired. When he saw the juicy apples, he stopped and said to the girls teasingly:

"Fair maidens! Her will I marry amongst you three who brings me an apple off yonder tree."

And off rushed the sisters to the apple tree, each trying to get ahead of the others.

But the apples which had been hanging very low and seemed within easy reach, now swung up high in the air way above the sisters' heads.

The sisters tried to knock them down, but the leaves came down in a shower and blinded them. They tried to pluck the apples off, but the boughs caught in their braids and unplaited them. Struggle and stretch as they would, they could not reach the apples and only scratched their hands.

Then Tiny Havroshechka walked up to the tree, and at once the boughs bent down and the apples came into her hands. She gave an apple to the handsome young stranger. He thanked her and said:

"Fair Maiden! I shall marry thee who brought me an apple from yonder tree."

From that day on Tiny Havroshechka knew no sorrow, for she and her husband lived happily ever after.

THE CUCKOO

A Nenets* Folktale

Once upon a time there lived a poor woman who had four children.

The children would not listen to their mother. From morning till evening they ran about and played in the snow.

When they came in out of the cold, they brought whole drifts of snow into the *choom* ** on the soles of their deerskin

boots, and it was the mother who had to clean up after them. And whenever they got their clothing wet, she had to dry it. They would not listen to their mother and would not help her with the work.

One summer day she was out catching fish on the river. It was a difficult task for her, but none of the four children would help.

So hard was the mother's life and the work she did that she fell ill.

She lay in the choom and called to her

---

* *Nenets* are people of an ethnic group in the extreme northwestern area of the Soviet Union.

** A *choom* is a tent made of animal skins.

133

children, begging them to bring her some water.

"My throat feels very dry, children," she said. "Please, please bring me a drink of water."

She pleaded with them again and again, but the children would not go.

Said the eldest son: "I have no boots."

Said the second son: "I have no hat."

Said the third son: "I have no coat."

And the fourth made no reply at all.

"The river's close," the mother said. "You don't need your coat to fetch the water. My mouth feels terribly dry. I'm very thirsty!"

The children laughed and ran out of the choom. They played outside a long time and never gave a thought to their mother.

At last the eldest became hungry, and he glanced into the choom. He looked and saw his mother standing in the middle of the tent. She was putting on her *malitsa*, her deerskin coat.

As he looked, the malitsa was suddenly covered with feathers.

The mother took up the plank she used for scraping animal hides, and the plank at once turned into a bird's tail.

She touched her metal thimble, and it became a beak.

Her arms were changed to wings.

The mother was transformed into a bird, and she flew out of the choom.

Then the eldest son cried: "Look, brothers, look, that bird's our mother, and she's flying away!"

At this the children ran after the mother and cried: "Mother, we've brought you water!"

And the mother replied: "Cuck-oo, cuck-oo! Too late, too late! The free lake waters spread before me. I'm off to the lake!"

The children ran after their mother, calling to her and holding out a dipper of water.

The youngest son cried: "Mother, Mother! Come home! Here's some water! Drink, Mother!"

But the mother called back from the distance: "Cuck-oo, cuck-oo, cuck-oo! Too late, Son, I won't come back."

The children kept running after their mother for many days and many nights. They ran over stones, they ran over swamps, and they ran over hills. Their feet were so sore and bruised that they bled. Wherever they passed, they left a track of red.

But the Cuckoo, their mother, did not return.

And ever since red moss has been creeping over the tundra.* And as for the Cuckoo, to this day she never builds nests, nor does she bring up her children herself.

* The *tundra* is any of the vast, treeless plains of the arctic regions of the Soviet Union.

AYOGA

A Nanaian* Folktale

Once there lived a little girl named Ayoga. Everyone loved her and said there was no one so pretty as she among the people of the region.

This quite turned Ayoga's head, and she would often stop whatever it was she was doing to admire herself. She would look and never get her fill of looking. She would smile at her image in the polished surface of a copper pan or admire her reflection in the river.

Ayoga now had no time for anything, for she was constantly admiring herself.

---

* *Nanaian* is the language spoken by an ethnic group living in the extreme northeastern part of Russian Siberia, near Manchuria.

One day her mother said:

"Please fetch some water, Daughter."

But Ayoga replied:

"I might fall into the river."

"Hold on to a bush, and you won't fall," her mother said.

"I might scratch my hands," Ayoga said.

"Put on your mittens."

"They might tear."

And all the while she kept staring at herself in the copper pan and thinking how pretty she was.

"If they tear, you can sew them up again with a needle and thread," the mother said.

"The needle might break."

"Take a thick needle."

"I might prick my finger."

"Use a thimble."

"The thimble might crack."

Just then the neighbors' little girl came up, and she said to Ayoga's mother:

"Let me fetch the water!"

And she went to the river and brought the water.

Ayoga's mother mixed some dough, she made flat cakes and she baked them over the fire.

When Ayoga saw the flat cakes, she cried:

"Give me a flat cake, Mother!"

"It's hot, you'll burn your fingers," the mother replied.

"I will put on my mittens."

"The mittens are wet."

"I will dry them in the sun."

"They will get warped."

"I will stretch them out again."

"You'll tire your hands," the mother said. "Why should you work, Daughter, and mar your beauty? I'd better give the flat cake to the little girl who is not afraid of spoiling her hands."

And the mother took the flat cake and gave it to the neighbors' little girl.

Ayoga was very angry. She went to the river, sat down on the bank, and looked at her reflection in the water. And the neighbors' little girl stood beside her, munching her flat cake.

Ayoga's mouth began to water, and she kept glancing back at the little girl. She craned her neck so hard that she stretched it out, and it became very, very, long.

Said the other little girl to Ayoga:

"Here, you can have the flat cake, I don't mind!"

At this Ayoga flew into a terrible rage and grew quite white with fury. She began to hiss. She spread out her fingers and waved her hands. Suddenly her hands changed into wings.

"I don't need your old flat cake, go away, go-go-go!" she cried.

And losing her foothold on the bank, Ayoga fell into the water with a splash and turned into a wild goose. She swam about and she cried:

"Oh, how pretty I am, I ayo-ga-ga-ga. . . . Oh, how pretty I am!"

She swam and she swam about by herself till she quite forgot how to speak. She forgot all the words she ever knew. She only remembered her own name, for she greatly feared lest she, the beautiful one, be taken for someone else.

To this day, whenever she sees anyone, she cries:

"Ayo-ga-ga-ga! . . . Ayo-ga-ga-ga!"

THE GIRL AND THE MOON MAN

A Chukchi* Folktale

There once lived among the Chukchi a man who had only one child, a daughter. The girl was her father's best helper. She went every summer far away from the camping grounds to watch over her father's herd of deer. Every winter she would take the herd ever farther. Only once in a while would she return to the camp for food.

One winter night, as they were riding to the camp, the deer that was harnessed to the sledge lifted his head and glanced up at the sky.

"Look! Look!" he cried.

The girl looked up and saw the Moon Man coming down the sky on a sledge drawn by two reindeer.

"Where is he going and why?" the girl asked.

"He wants to carry you away," her deer replied.

The girl was much alarmed.

"What am I to do? He might really carry me off with him!" she cried.

Without a word the deer began raking away the snow with his hoof until he had scooped out a hole.

"Come, get in this hole, quick!" he said.

The girl got into the hole, and her deer began kicking snow over her. Very soon the girl vanished, and there was only a mound of snow to show where she was.

The Moon Man came down from the sky, stopped his reindeer, and got out of his sledge. He walked all around, looking about him and searching for the girl. But he could not find her. He even went up to the mound, but he never guessed who was under it.

"How very strange!" said the Moon Man. "Where could the girl have got to? I think I'll go away now and come down again later. I'll surely find her then and carry her away with me."

With this he got into his sledge, and his deer bore him off into the sky.

As soon as he had gone, the girl's deer scraped the snow away, and the girl came out of the hole.

"Let us go to the camp quickly!" she said, "or else the Moon Man will see me and come down again. I shall not be able to hide from him a second time."

She then got into her sledge, and her deer whisked her away as quick as lightning. They soon reached the camp, and the girl ran into her father's igloo. But her father was not there. Who would help her now?

Said her deer:

"You must hide, for the Moon Man will be after you."

"Where shall I hide?" the girl asked.

"I will turn you into something else—a block of stone, perhaps," said the deer.

"No, that won't do, he will find me."

"A hammer."

---

* *Chukchi* is the language spoken by an ethnic group in the far northeastern end of Russian Siberia.

"That won't do, either."

"A pole."

"No."

"A hair of the hide hanging over the door."

"No, no!"

"What then? I know, I'll turn you into a lamp."

"All right."

"Well, then, crouch down."

The girl crouched down. The deer struck the ground with his hoof, and the girl was turned into a lamp that burned so brightly that it lit up the whole igloo.

Meanwhile the Moon Man had been searching for the girl among the deer, and he now came rushing into the camping site.

He tied his own deer to a post, entered the igloo, and began looking for the girl. He looked everywhere, but he could not find her. He searched in between the poles that supported the top of the igloo, he searched inside every utensil, he examined every hair on the skins, every twig under the beds, every bit of earth on the floor. But the girl was nowhere to be found.

As for the lamp, he did not notice it, for though it shone brightly, the Moon Man was just as bright.

"Strange," said the Moon Man. "Where can she be? I shall have to go back to the sky."

He left the igloo, climbed into his sledge,

and was about to ride away when the girl ran up to the skin flap over the door and, leaning out, let out a peal of merry laughter.

"Here I am! Here I am!" she called to the Moon Man.

The Moon Man got out of the sledge and rushed into the igloo. But the girl had again turned into a lamp.

The Moon Man began to search for her. He looked over every twig and every leaf, every hair on the skins and every bit of earth, but he did not find the girl. It looked as though he would have to go back without her.

But no sooner had he left the igloo and climbed into his sledge than the girl once more leaned out from behind the flap.

"Here I am! Here I am!" she called with a laugh.

The Moon Man rushed into the igloo again and began to look for her. He searched for a long time, he rummaged through and turned over everything, but he did not find her.

The Moon Man was so weary from the search that he became thin and he became weak, and could barely move his legs or lift his arms.

Now the girl was no longer afraid of him. She took on her proper shape, rushed from the igloo, threw the Moon Man on his back, and tied his hands and feet with a rope.

"O-oh!" groaned the Moon Man. "You will kill me, I know! Kill me, then! I deserve it, it is all my own fault, for I wanted to carry you off from the Earth. But before I die, cover me with skins and let me get warm. I am so cold!"

The girl was very much surprised.

"You—chilled?" she said. "Why, you always live up in the sky, you have no home, no igloo, you belong in the open, and that is where you must stay. What need have you of my skins!"

Then the Moon Man began to plead with the girl, and he spoke to her in this wise:

"Since I am homeless and doomed to be so forever, let me go free to roam the sky. Your people will watch me up in the sky. The sight of me will give them pleasure. Let me go free, and I will be a beacon for your people guiding them across the plains. Let me go free, and I will turn night into day. Let me go free, and I will measure the year for your people. First I will be the Moon of the Old Bull, then the Moon of the Birth of the Calves, then the Moon of the Leaves, then the Moon of Warmth, then the Moon of the Shedding of Antlers, then the Moon of Love among the Wild Deer, then the Moon of the First Winter, and then the Moon of the Shortening Days."

"And if I let you go free and you become strong again, will you not then come down from the sky and carry me off with you?"

"Oh, no, never! I shall try to forget the very way to you. You are far too clever. I shall never come down from the sky again. Only let me go free, and I will light up the sky and the earth!"

And the girl let the Moon Man go free. He rose up into the sky and flooded the earth with moonlight.

THE RICH MAN AND THE POOR MAN

A Caucasian* Folktale

RETOLD IN VERSE BY SAMUEL MARSHAK

A poor man went to his rich friend,
And said, with gracious smile:
"I've come to ask if you would lend
Your ass to me awhile."

"My ass, alas, is out today,"
The rich man made reply.
"At nine o'clock it went away,
I don't know where or why."

"Too bad, too bad," the poor man said,
"I'll bid you, then, good day,"
But at that moment, in the shed,
An ass began to bray.

"You lied to me!" the poor man cried.
" 'My ass is out' forsooth!
But even if its master lied,
The ass has told the truth."

"I lied?!"—the rich man's face grew red—
"I cannot let that pass!
It's me you should believe, instead
Of trusting a mere ass!"

The poor man turned without a word
And climbed the pathway steep.
On coming to a grove he heard
The bleating of a sheep.

The thirsty sheep had left the flock
In search of water cool.
It now was standing by a rock,
And drinking at a pool.

The poor man caught it, tied its feet,
And put it on his back.
He then continued in the heat
To climb the rugged track.

The rich man came that afternoon:
"You stole my sheep, they say.
I want it back and want it soon,
I want it straightaway."

"No sheep of yours is in my shed,
Go search another place,"
The poor man to the rich one said,
And turned away his face.

The rich man was about to go,
When from behind a wall,
He heard a bleat he seemed to know—
A most familiar call.

"My sheep is here!" he roared in rage.
"I hear it calling me.
It's a disgrace for one your age
To lie so shamelessly!"

"You trust that foolish sheep in there?"
The poor man calmly said.
"Far better would it be, I swear,
To trust your friend instead."

---

* *Caucasia* is a region of the Soviet Union between the Black Sea and the Caspian.

THE FROG PRINCESS

A Russian Folktale

Long, long ago there was a Czar who had three sons. One day, when his sons were grown to manhood, the Czar called them to him and said:

"My dear sons, before I grow old I should like to see you married and to rejoice in the sight of my grandchildren."

And the sons replied:

"If that is your wish, Father, then give us your blessing. Whom would you like us to marry?"

And the Czar replied: "You must each of you take an arrow and go out into the open field. Shoot the arrows, and wherever they fall, there will you find your brides."

The sons bowed to their father, and each of them taking an arrow went out into the open field. There they drew their bows and let fly their arrows.

The eldest son's arrow fell in a nobleman's courtyard and was picked up by the Nobleman's Daughter. The middle son's arrow fell in a rich merchant's yard and was picked up the Merchant's Daughter. And as for the youngest son, Prince Ivan, his arrow

shot up and flew away he knew not where. He went in search of it and he walked on and on till he reached a marsh, and what did he see sitting there but a Frog with the arrow in its mouth.

Said Prince Ivan to the Frog:

"Frog, Frog, give me back my arrow."

But the Frog replied:

"I will if you marry me!"

"What do you mean, how can I marry a frog!"

"You must marry me, for I am your destined bride."

Prince Ivan felt sad and crestfallen. But

there was nothing to be done, and he picked up the Frog and carried it home. And the Czar celebrated three weddings. His eldest son he married to the Nobleman's Daughter; his middle son, to the Merchant's Daughter; and poor Prince Ivan—to the Frog.

Some time passed, and the Czar called his sons to his side.

"I want to see which of your wives is the better needlewoman," said he. "Let them each make me a shirt by tomorrow morning."

The sons bowed to their father and left.

Prince Ivan came home, sat down and hung his head. And the Frog hopped over the floor and up to him and asked:

"Why do you hang your head, Prince Ivan? What is it that troubles you?"

"Father bids you make him a shirt by tomorrow morning."

Said the Frog:

"Do not grieve, Prince Ivan, but go to bed, for morning is wiser than evening."

Prince Ivan went to bed, and the Frog hopped out on to the porch, cast off its frog skin, and turned into Vasilisa the Wise and Clever, a maiden fair beyond compare.

She clapped her hands and cried:

"Come hither, my women and maids, make haste and set to work! Make me a shirt by tomorrow morning, like those my own father used to wear."

In the morning Prince Ivan awoke, and there was the Frog hopping on the floor again, but the shirt was all ready and lying on the table wrapped in a pretty towel. Prince Ivan was overjoyed. He took the shirt and brought it to his father who was busy receiving the gifts from his two elder sons.

The eldest son offered the shirt his wife had made, and the Czar took it and said:

"This shirt will only do for a poor peasant to wear."

The middle son offered the shirt the Merchant's Daughter, his wife, had made, and the Czar took it and said:

"This shirt will only do to go to the baths in."

Then Prince Ivan laid out his shirt, all beautifully embroidered in gold and silver, and the Czar took one look at it and said:

"Now that is a shirt fit for a Czar to wear on holidays!"

The two elder brothers went home, and they spoke among themselves and said: "It seems we were wrong to laugh at Prince Ivan's wife. She is no Frog, but a Witch."

Now the Czar called his sons again.

"Let your wives bake me some bread by tomorrow morning," said he. "I want to know which of them is the best cook."

Prince Ivan hung his head and went home.

And the Frog asked him:

"Why are you so sad, Prince Ivan?"

Said Prince Ivan:

"You are to bake some bread for my father by tomorrow morning."

"Do not grieve, Prince Ivan, but go to bed. Morning is wiser than evening."

And her two sisters-in-law, who had laughed at the Frog at first, now sent an old woman who worked in the kitchen to see how she baked her bread.

But the Frog was sly and guessed why the old woman had come. The Frog made some dough, broke off the top of the stove and threw the dough down the hole. The old woman ran to the two sisters-in-law and told them what she saw, and they did as the Frog had done.

And the Frog hopped out on to the porch, turned into Vasilisa the Wise and Clever, and clapped her hands.

"Come, my women and maids, make haste and set to work! By tomorrow morning bake me some soft white bread, the kind I used to eat at my own father's house."

In the morning, Prince Ivan woke up, and there was the bread all ready and lying on the table and prettily trimmed with all kinds of things—flowers on the sides and a town with walls and gates on the top.

Prince Ivan was overjoyed. He wrapped the bread in a towel and took it to his father, who was just receiving the loaves his elder sons had brought. Their wives had dropped the dough into the stove as the old woman had told them to do, and the loaves had come out lumpy and charred.

The Czar took the bread from his eldest son, looked at it, and sent it to the servant's hall. He took the bread from his middle son and did the same with it. But when Prince Ivan handed him his bread, the Czar said:

"Now this is bread fit for a Czar to eat on holidays!"

And the Czar bade his three sons come and feast with him on the morrow together with their wives.

Once again Prince Ivan came home sad and sorrowful and hung his head very low. And the Frog hopped over the floor and up to him and said:

"Croak, croak, why are you so sad, Prince Ivan? Is it that your father has grieved you by an unkind word?"

"Oh, Frog, Frog!" cried Prince Ivan. "How can I help being sad? The Czar has ordered me to bring you to his feast, and how can I show you to him!"

Said the Frog in reply:

"Do not grieve, Prince Ivan, but go to the feast alone, and I will follow later. When you hear a great tramping and thundering, do not be afraid, but if they ask you what it is, say 'That is my Frog riding in her carriage.'"

So Prince Ivan went to the feast alone, and his elder brothers came with their wives, who were dressed in their finest clothes and had their brows blackened and roses painted on their cheeks. They stood there, and they mocked Prince Ivan.

"Why have you come without your wife?" they teased. "You could have brought her in a handkerchief. Wherever did you find such a beauty? You must have searched all the swamps for her."

Now the Czar with his sons and his daughters-in-law and all the guests sat down to feast at the oaken tables covered with embroidered clothes. Suddenly there came a great tramping and thundering, and the whole palace shook and trembled. The guests were frightened and jumped up from their seats.

But Prince Ivan said: "Do not fear, honest folk. That is only my Frog riding in her carriage."

And there dashed up to the porch of the Czar's palace a gilded carriage drawn by six white horses, and out of it stepped Vasilisa the Wise and Clever. Her gown of sky-blue silk was studded with stars, and on her head she wore the bright crescent moon, and so beautiful was she that it cannot be pictured and cannot be told, but she was a true wonder and a joy to behold! She took Prince Ivan by the hand and led him to the oaken tables covered with embroidered cloths.

The guests began to eat, to drink, and to make merry. Vasilisa the Wise and Clever drank from her glass and poured the last few drops into her left sleeve. She ate some swan meat and threw the bones into her right sleeve.

And the wives of the elder sons saw what she did and they did likewise. Then the time came to dance. Vasilisa the Wise and Clever took Prince Ivan by the hand and began to dance. She danced and she whirled and she circled round and round, and everyone watched and marveled. She waved her left sleeve, and a lake appeared. She waved her right sleeve, and white swans began to swim upon the lake. The Czar and his guests were filled with wonder.

Then the wives of the two elder sons began to dance. They waved their left sleeves, and only splashed mead over the guests. They waved their right sleeves, and bones flew about on all sides, and one bone hit the Czar in the eye. The Czar was very angry and drove out both his daughters-in-law.

In the meantime, Prince Ivan ran home, and finding the frog skin, threw it into the stove and burnt it.

Now Vasilisa the Wise and Clever came home, and she at once saw that her frog skin was gone. She sat down on a bench, very sad and sorrowful, and she said to Prince Ivan:

"Ah, Prince Ivan, what have you done! Had you but waited just three more days, I would have been yours for ever. But now I must leave you. Farewell. Seek me beyond the Thrice-nine Lands in the Thrice-ten Kingdom where lives Koshchei the Deathless." And Vasilisa the Wise and Clever turned into a gray cuckoo bird and flew out of the window.

Prince Ivan cried and wept for a long time, and then he bowed in all four directions and went off he knew not where to seek his wife, Vasilisa the Wise and Clever. Whether he walked a short distance or long one is not known. But after a while he met a little old man, who was as old as old can be.

"Good morrow, good youth!" said he, "what do you seek and whither are you bound?"

Prince Ivan told him of his trouble, and the little old man who was as old as old can be said:

"Ah, Prince Ivan, why did you burn the frog skin? It was not yours to wear nor yours to burn. Vasilisa the Wise and Clever was born wiser and more clever than her father, and this so angered him that he turned her into a frog for three long years. Ah well, it can't be helped now. Here is a spool of thread for you. Follow it without fear wherever it rolls."

Prince Ivan thanked the little old man who was as old as old can be, then followed the ball of thread wherever it rolled. He soon met a bear in an open field. Prince Ivan took aim and was about to kill it.

But the bear spoke up in a human voice and said:

"Do not kill me, Prince Ivan. Who knows but you may have need of me some day!"

Prince Ivan took pity on the bear, spared him and went on. He looked, and—lo!—there was a drake flying overhead. Prince Ivan took aim.

But the drake said to him in a human voice:

"Do not kill me, Prince Ivan. Who knows but you may have need of me some day!"

And Prince Ivan did not kill the drake and went on. Just then a hare appeared. Prince Ivan took aim quickly and was about to shoot it.

But the hare said in a human voice:

"Do not kill me, Prince Ivan. Who knows but you may have need of me some day!"

And Prince Ivan spared the hare's life and went farther. He came to the blue sea and he saw a fish lying on the sandy shore, gasping for breath.

"Take pity on me, Prince Ivan," said the fish, "throw me back into the blue sea!"

Prince Ivan threw the fish into the sea and walked on along the shore. Whether a long time passed or a short time no one knows, but by and by the spool of thread rolled into a forest, and there in the forest stood a little hut on chicken's feet, spinning round and round.

"Little hut, little hut, stand as once you stood, with your face to me and your back to the wood," said Prince Ivan.

The hut turned its face to him and its back to the forest, and Prince Ivan entered. And there, on the edge of the stove ledge, lay Baba-Yaga the Witch with the Switch—in a pose she liked best, with her crooked nose to the ceiling pressed.

"What brings you here, good youth?" asked Baba-Yaga. "Is there aught you come to seek? Come, good youth, I pray you, speak!"

Said Prince Ivan:

"First give me food and drink, Baba-Yaga, and steam me in the bath, and then ask your questions."

So Baba-Yaga gave him food and drink, steamed him in the bath, and put him to bed, and then Prince Ivan told her that he was seeking his wife, Vasilisa the Wise and Clever.

"I know where she is," said Baba-Yaga. "Koshchei the Deathless has her in his power. It will be hard getting her back, for it is not easy to get the better of Koshchei. His death is at the point of a needle, the needle is in an egg, the egg is in a duck, the duck is in a hare, the hare in a stone chest, and the chest at the top of a tall oak tree which Koshchei the Deathless guards as the apple of his own eye."

Prince Ivan spent the night in Baba-Yaga's hut, and in the morning she told him where the tall oak tree was to be found. Whether he was long on the way or not no one knows, but by and by he came to the tall oak tree. It stood there and its leaves rustled as it swayed, and the stone chest was at the top of it and very hard to reach.

All of a sudden, lo and behold! the bear came running and it pulled out the oak tree roots and all. Down fell the chest, and it broke open. Out of the chest bounded a hare, and away it tore as fast as it could. But another hare appeared and gave it chase. It caught up with the first hare and tore it to bits. Out of the dead hare flew a duck, and it soared up to the very sky. But in a trice the drake was upon it and it struck the duck so hard that it dropped the egg, and down the egg fell into the blue sea.

At this Prince Ivan began weeping bitter tears, for how could he find the egg in the sea! But all at once the fish came swimming to the shore with the egg in its mouth. Prince Ivan cracked the egg, took out the needle, and began trying to break off the point. The more he bent it the more Koshchei the Deathless writhed and twisted. But all in vain. For Prince Ivan broke off the point of the needle, and Koshchei fell down dead.

Prince Ivan then hurried to Koshchei's palace of white stone. Vasilisa the Wise and Clever ran out to him and kissed him on his honey-sweet mouth. And Prince Ivan and Vasilisa the Wise and Clever returned to their home and lived together long and happily till they were quite, quite old.

THE MAGIC FIDDLE

A Belorussian Folktale

Once upon a time there lived a boy who from his earliest years played on a pipe. He would cut himself a reed, while tending bullocks, make a pipe out of it, and begin to play, and the bullocks would stop nibbling the grass, prick up their ears, and listen. Hearing him, the birds in the forest would be silent, and even the frogs in the swamps would stop croaking.

The boy would go off to tend the horses at night, and it would be gay and merry in the meadows, with the lads and lasses singing and joking, as young people should. The night would be beautiful and warm, and the ground fairly steaming.

And when the boy would start playing on his pipe, all the lads and lasses would grow quiet. To each it seemed that a kind of balm was soothing his troubled heart, and that some unknown force was lifting him up to the bright stars in the deep blue sky.

---

* *Belorussia* is the western part of the Soviet Union bordering on Poland, Lithuania, Latvia, and the Ukraine.

The night herdsmen would sit there without stirring, forgetful of their aching, weary limbs and empty stomachs. They would sit there and listen. And each felt he could listen forever to the enchanting melody. When the music would stop, no one would so much as move from his place lest he frighten away the magical voice that like a nightingale poured out songs through the groves and forests.

Then the pipe would play again, a sorrowful tune this time, and sadness would descend on all. . . . Peasant men and women on their way home late at night from their master's fields would stop and listen and they never seemed to have their fill. Their lives would rise before them—the poverty and the suffering, the cruel master and judge and stewards. Their hearts would grow so heavy that they longed to give voice to their sadness in loud lamentations, as they would have done for a dear departed soul or for a son sent off to the wars.

But the sad tune would soon change to a

gay one. Then the peasants would throw down their scythes, rakes, and pitchforks, and with arms akimbo they would begin to dance.

So great was the piper's magic power that his music could do with the heart whatever he wished.

When the piper grew to manhood, he made himself a fiddle and with it roamed the land. Wherever he went he would play his fiddle. Wherever he went he would be treated as the most welcome of guests and would have good things heaped on him.

For many a year did the fiddler wander over the land—a joy to good folk, but a plague to cruel lords. A thorn in their side was he to the masters, for wherever he played the serfs no longer obeyed their lords.

So the lords decided to do away with the fiddler, and first one then another man did they order to shoot or to drown him. But no one was willing to kill the fiddler for the peasants loved him, and the stewards thought him a sorcerer and were afraid of him.

Then the lords called up the demons from the nether world, and together they plotted against him. For, of course, everyone knows that lords and demons are tarred with the same brush.

One day when the fiddler was walking in the forest, the demons sent twelve hungry wolves against him. The wolves stood in the fiddler's path. They gnashed their teeth, and their eyes gleamed like coals. And the fiddler had no weapon in his hand save the bag with his fiddle in it.

"My end has come," he thought.

So he took his fiddle from the bag, for he wished to hear music just once more before his death. He leaned against a tree and drew his bow across the strings.

The fiddle spoke out like a living thing, and its sweet music resounded in the forest. The bushes and the trees became suddenly stilled, not a single leaf stirred. The wolves, jaws gaping, their hunger forgotten, stood frozen to the spot, listening.

And when the music stopped, the wolves moved off as in a trance to the depths of the forest.

The fiddler walked on. The sun was setting beyond the forest, its golden rays flecking the tops of the trees. When he came to the bank of a river, he sat down to rest, took out his fiddle and began to play. So well did he play that earth and sky gave ear to him, seeming ready to listen forever. Then he struck up a gay tune, and all around began to dance—the stars whirled like snow in a blizzard, the clouds floated across the sky keeping time, and fish leaped up and thrashed about until the river seethed like boiling water.

Even the king of the water sprites joined the dancing, and such capers did he cut that the river overflowed its banks.

The demons were frightened and bounded out of their backwaters. But though they gnashed their teeth in fury, there was nothing they could do to the fiddler.

And the fiddler, seeing that the king of the water sprites was flooding the people's fields and gardens, stopped playing, put the fiddle into his bag, and went on his way.

He walked and he walked, and all of a sudden two young lords came running up to him.

"We have a ball tonight," they said. "Come and play for us, fiddler, we shall pay you well."

The fiddler thought it over, and what was he to do! The night was dark, and he had nowhere to sleep and no money either.

"Very well," said he, "I'll play for you."

The young lords brought the fiddler to a

palace where there were so many young lords and ladies that there was no counting them.

Now, on the table stood a large bowl, and one by one the lords and ladies were continually running to it. Each in turn thrust a finger into the bowl and then passed it across his eyes.

The fiddler, too, went up to the bowl, dipped in his finger and passed it across his eyes. No sooner had he done so than he saw that this was no palace at all, but the nether world itself; and these were no lords and ladies, but devils and witches.

"Oh, so that's the kind of ball it is!" said the fiddler to himself. "Just you wait, I'll play you a fine tune!"

So he tuned up his fiddle and his bow struck its living strings. And all around him was shattered to dust, and the devils and witches were scattered far and wide and were never seen again.

PILIPKA AND BABA-YAGA

A Belorussian* Fairy Tale

Once there lived a man and his wife. They had no children, and the wife was always sorrowing and grieving that she had no one to rock in the cradle and to kiss and fondle.

One day the husband went to the forest, chopped out a log from an alder tree, and brought it home to his wife.

"Here," he said, "rock this."

The wife put the log in the cradle, and she began rocking it and singing as she rocked:

"Little son, rock-a-bye, you are white of body and dark of eye."

She rocked the log one day, and she rocked it the next, and on the third day she looked, and there was a little baby boy lying in the cradle!

The husband and wife were overjoyed.

They called their little son Pilipka [Chip], and began caring for him tenderly.

When Pilipka grew up, he said to his father:

"Make me a golden boat, Father, and a silver paddle. I want to go fishing."

And the father made him a golden boat and a silver paddle and sent him to the lake to catch fish.

Pilipka set to fishing in earnest, and he fished whole days and nights on end. Indeed, so well were the fish biting that he would not even go home, and his mother would bring his dinner to him.

She would come to the lake and call:

"Pilipka, my son, the day is half done, and here is a pie for you to try!"

And Pilipka would make for the shore, throw the fish he had caught out onto it, and, having eaten his mother's pie, paddle to the middle of the lake again.

---

* *Belorussia* is the western part of the Soviet Union bordering on Poland, Lithuania, Latvia, and the Ukraine.

Now Baba-Yaga the Witch with the Switch, hearing how his mother called to Pilipka, decided to steal him from her.

She took a sack and a poker, came to the lake, and began calling:

"Pilipka, my son, the day is half done, and here is a pie for you to try!"

Pilipka thought that it was his mother calling and paddled to the shore. Baba-Yaga hooked his boat with her poker, dragged it up on the bank, and, seizing Pilipka, thrust him into the sack.

"Aha!" she cried, "you won't be catching fish any more!"

And throwing the sack over her shoulder, she carried it off with her into the forest thicket. But the way to her house being long, she soon grew tired, sat down to rest and fell asleep. And Pilipka crawled out of the sack, filled it full of heavy stones, and went back to the lake again.

When Baba-Yaga woke up, she caught up the sack and carried it home with many moans and groans.

She brought it home, and she said to her daughter:

"Roast this fisherman for my dinner!"

She shook the sack out on the floor, and—lo!—nothing but stones dropped out of it.

Baba-Yaga flew into a rage.

"I'll show you how to fool me!" she cried at the top of her voice. Running to the lake shore again, she began calling to Pilipka:

"Pilipka, my son, the day is half done, and here is a pie for you to try!"

Pilipka heard her and called back:

"I know you well! You are not my mother, but Baba-Yaga. My mother's voice is ever so much thinner."

And though Baga-Yaga kept calling him, Pilipka did not heed her.

"Never you mind," said Baba-Yaga to herself, "I'll make me a thin little voice."

And she ran to the blacksmith.

"Blacksmith, blacksmith, sharpen my tongue and make it thinner," said she.

"Very well," said the blacksmith. "Just put it on my anvil."

So Baba-Yaga stuck out her long tongue and laid it on the anvil, and the blacksmith took his hammer and pounded away at it until it became quite thin.

After that Baba-Yaga ran to the lake, and she called to Pilipka in a thin little voice:

"Pilipka, my son, the day is half done, and here is a pie for you to try!"

Pilipka heard her and thought it was his mother calling. He paddled in to shore, and

Baba-Yaga snatched him up and thrust him into her sack.

"You won't fool me any more!" Baba-Yaga cried, overjoyed, and without stopping to rest she took him straight home. She shook him out of the sack and said to her daughter:

"Here he is, the cheat! Light the stove and roast him for dinner."

And with these words she went out.

And her daughter lit the stove and, bringing a spade, said to Pilipka:

"Lie down on the spade, I'll put you into the stove."

And Pilipka lay down on the spade with his legs sticking up in the air.

"Not that way!" Baba-Yaga's daughter cried. "I shan't be able to put you into the stove if you hold your legs up."

Pilipka dropped his legs, letting them hang down over the spade.

"Not that way!" Baba-Yaga's daughter cried again.

"Then how?" Pilipka asked. "Show me!"

"How stupid you are!" exclaimed Baba-Yaga's daughter. "This is the way it's done. Look!"

And she stretched herself out on the spade. Pilipka snatched up the spade and shoved it into the burning stove. After that he closed the stove and put Baba-Yaga's poker against it so that her daughter could not jump out.

He ran out of the hut, and lo! there was Baba-Yaga walking toward it. Pilipka leaped up into a tall and leafy sycamore tree and hid himself in the branches.

Baba-Yaga came into the hut, she sniffed and she smelled the smell of roasting meat. She took the roast out of the stove, ate up the meat, and, throwing the bones out into the yard, began rolling over them, saying:

"On these bones I did fall-fall, o'er these bones I will roll-roll, for I have eaten of Pilipka's flesh."

And Pilipka called to her from his hiding place:

"On these bones you may fall-fall, o'er these bones you may roll-roll, but you have not eaten of my flesh."

Baba-Yaga heard him and she grew black with rage. She ran to the sycamore tree and began gnawing at it with her teeth. She gnawed and she gnawed, and she broke her teeth; but the tree stood there as tough and as strong as ever.

Baba-Yaga ran to the blacksmith.

"Blacksmith, blacksmith," cried she, "forge me a steel ax!"

The blacksmith forged her an ax.

Baba-Yaga rushed with it to the sycamore tree and began chopping it down.

Said Pilipka:

"Strike no tree, but strike a rock!"

Said Baba-Yaga:

"Strike no rock, but strike the tree!"

Said Pilipka again:

"Strike no tree, but strike a rock!"

Here the ax suddenly struck a rock and became all chipped and blunted.

Baba-Yaga gave a howl of rage, snatched up the ax and returned to the blacksmith to have it sharpened.

Pilipka looked, and he saw that the sycamore tree was beginning to lean over to one side. Baba-Yaga had chopped it nearly through, and he had to hurry to save himself before it was too late.

Just then a flock of geese flew over.

"Geese, geese, do not screech, drop me down a feather each," he called to them. "To my mother and father I will fly with you, and there I will pay for your service true!"

The geese dropped him a feather each, and of these feathers Pilipka fashioned himself half a wing.

Then a second flock of geese came flying. And Pilipka called to them and said:

"Geese, geese, do not screech, drop me down a feather each. To my mother and father I will fly with you, and there I will pay you for your service true!"

And the second flock dropped him a feather each.

After that came a third and a fourth flock, and all the geese dropped Pilipka a feather each.

Pilipka fashioned himself a pair of wings and flew after the geese.

Just then Baba-Yaga came running from the blacksmith shop, and she began chopping down the sycamore tree again. She chopped so hard that the chips flew. She chopped and she chopped, and the sycamore tree fell on her with one great cr-r-r-ash! and killed her.

And Pilipka came flying home with the geese. When his mother and father saw him they were overjoyed. They seated him at the table and treated him with all sorts of good things to eat.

And to the geese they gave oats and ale, and that is the end of this long-short tale.

HOW VASIL VANQUISHED THE DRAGON

A Belorussian* Folktale

Whether it was so or not, whether it is true or false, let us hear what the tale has to tell.

And so here it is.

To a certain land there once came a most fearful and terrible Dragon. He dug himself out a deep hole by a mountain in the midst of a forest, and lay down to rest.

Whether he rested long or not no one now recalls, but the moment he rose he shouted loudly for all to hear:

"Come, folk, men and wives, old and young. You must each of you bring me a tribute each day. One of you can bring me a cow, another a lamb, and a third a pig! He who obeys, will live. But he who does not, will die, for him I will devour!"

The people were frightened, and they began paying the Dragon the tributes he asked for. This went on for a long time, till at last there came a day when there was nothing left to bring, for the people were now as poor as can be. But the Dragon was of the kind that could not let a day pass without gorging himself. So he began flying from village to village, seizing people and carrying them off to his lair.

---

* *Belorussia* is the western part of the Soviet Union bordering on Poland, Lithuania, Latvia, and Ukraine.

The people went about wailing like lost souls, vainly trying to find a way to be delivered from the cruel Dragon.

Now at that very time a man named Vasil came to those parts, and he saw that the people went about sad and crestfallen, wringing their hands and weeping loudly.

"What is the trouble?" he asked. "Why is everyone weeping?"

The people told him of their trouble, and Vasil tried to comfort them.

"Calm yourselves," said he. "I will try to save you from the Dragon."

And taking a heavy cudgel, he went to the forest where the Dragon lived.

The Dragon saw him and, rolling his great green eyes, asked: "Why have you come here with that cudgel?"

"To give you a beating!" Vasil replied.

"My, how brave you are!" said the Dragon. "You had better run away while you still can, for I need only blow once and you will be blown clear away from here, a full three *versts!*" *

Vasil smiled.

"Don't you boast, you old scarecrow," said he. "I've seen worse monsters than you. We'll see which of us can blow the harder. Go on, blow!"

And the Dragon blew so hard that the leaves rained down from the trees, and Vasil was thrown to his knees.

"Ha, that's nothing!" said he, springing to his feet. "Why, it's enough to make a cat laugh! Now let *me* try. Only first you must tie something over your eyes if you don't want them to jump out of their sockets."

The Dragon tied a kerchief over his eyes, and Vasil came up and struck him such a blow on the head with his cudgel that sparks flew from the Dragon's eyes.

"Can it be that you are stronger than I?"

the Dragon asked. "Let's try again and see which of us is fastest at crushing a rock."

And the Dragon seized a rock weighing all of a hundred *poods* * and squeezed it with his claws so hard that the dust rose up in clouds.

"There's nothing to that!" laughed Vasil. "Let's see you squeeze it so that the water will run from it."

The Dragon was frightened. He was beginning to think that Vasil was the stronger of the two and, glancing at Vasil's cudgel, said:

"Ask me what you will and you shall have it."

"I don't need anything," Vasil replied. "I have plenty of everything in my house, more than you have."

"Can that be true?" asked the Dragon in disbelief.

"If you don't believe me, come and see for yourself!"

So they got into a cart and drove off.

By now the Dragon was becoming very hungry. He saw a herd of bullocks on the edge of a forest, and he said to Vasil:

"Go and catch a bullock and we'll have a bite to eat."

And Vasil went to the forest and began stripping bast from some linden trees. The Dragon waited and waited, and at last went to look for him.

"What is taking you so long?" he asked him.

"Can't you see I am stripping bast from linden trees," Vasil replied.

"What do you need bast for?"

"To make some rope so as to catch us five bullocks for dinner."

"What do we need five bullocks for? One

---

* A *verst* is a distance of about ⅔ mile.

* A *pood* is a Russian measure of weight of about 36 pounds.

is enough." And the Dragon caught a bullock by the nape of the neck and dragged it to the cart.

"Now go and bring us some wood to roast the bullock," said he to Vasil.

And Vasil sat down under an oak tree in the forest, filled his pipe, and began to smoke.

The Dragon waited for him a long time and, at last losing patience, went to look for him.

"What is taking you so long?" he asked Vasil.

"I want to bring a dozen oaks or so, so I'm trying to pick the thickest among them."

"What do we want with a dozen oaks? One is enough," said the Dragon. Giving one wrench, he pulled out the thickest of the oaks.

He roasted the bullock and invited Vasil to join him.

"Go ahead and eat," said Vasil. "I'll have something at home. What's one bullock for me—just a bite!"

The Dragon ate the bullock and licked his lips.

They rode on and soon came to Vasil's house. The children saw their father coming from a distance, and they cried out joyously:

"Father's coming! Father's coming!"

But the Dragon did not catch the words and asked:

"What are the children shouting?"

"They are pleased that I am bringing you home for their dinner. They're very hungry."

By now the Dragon was badly frightened, so he jumped from the cart and took to his heels. But he missed the road and landed in a bog. The bog was very deep, so deep indeed that the bottom could not be reached, and the Dragon was drowned. And that was the end of him.

HOW THE BROTHERS FOUND THEIR FATHER'S TREASURE

A Moldavian* Folktale

Once upon a time there lived a man who had three sons. He was a hard-working man. He never idled, but labored from early morn to late at night. He seemed never to be tired and always did everyting well and on time.

As for his sons—tall, handsome, and strong lads all three—they did not like work.

The father labored in the fields, in the garden, and in the house while his sons sat around chatting idly in the shade of a tree, or went fishing in the Dniester River.

"Why do you never work and help your father?" their neighbors would ask.

"Why should we work?" the sons would

Moldavia is one of the fifteen Soviet Socialist Republics; it is in the southwestern part of European Russia.

reply. "Father takes good care of us, and does all the work very well by himself."

And so it went from year to year.

The sons grew to manhood. Their father aged, became weak, and could no longer work as before. The garden around the house was neglected and the fields were overgrown with weeds. The sons saw this, but they disliked work so much that they did nothing about it.

"Why do you sit there, my sons, idling the hours away?" their father would ask them. "I worked when I was young, and now your time has come."

"Oh, it'll never be too late to work," the sons replied.

The old man, deeply troubled that his sons were such idlers, fell ill with grief and took to his bed.

By now the family was in the direst straits. Nettles and thistles stood so high in the garden that the house was barely visible.

One day the old man called his sons to his bedside.

"My sons," he said to them, "my end has come. How are you going to live without me? You don't like work and don't know how to work."

The sons' hearts were filled with anguish, and they burst into tears.

"Speak to us, Father, give us your dying counsel," begged the eldest son.

"Very well!" the father replied. "I'll tell you a secret. You know that your mother and I toiled hard and unsparingly. Over many long years, bit by bit, we saved for you a treasure—a pot of gold. I buried it near the house, but I no longer remember just where. Find that treasure and you will live without poverty and never know need."

With that he bade his sons good-bye and breathed his last.

The sons buried their old father and mourned his death. Then one day the eldest son said:

"Well, brothers, we are poor indeed, for we haven't even money to buy bread. You remember what our father said before he died. Let us look for the pot of gold."

They took their spades and began digging small holes near the house. They dug and they dug, but they could not find the pot of gold.

Said the middle brother:

"If we dig in this way, my brothers, we shall never find our father's treasure. Let us dig up all the ground around the house!"

The brothers agreed. Again they took up their spades, and they dug up all the ground round the house, but they still found no pot of gold.

"Let us dig once more, but deeper," said the youngest brother. "Perhaps our father buried the pot of gold deep down."

Once again the brothers agreed, for they were very eager to find their father's treasure.

They set to work, and the eldest brother, who had been digging a long time, suddenly felt his spade strike something big and hard. His heart beat with excitement, and he called to his brothers:

"Come quickly! I have found father's treasure!"

The middle brother and the youngest brother came running to help their elder brother.

They worked very, very hard, but what they dug up from the ground was not a pot of gold but a large rock.

The brothers were disappointed.

"What shall we do with the rock?" they said. "It's no use leaving it here. Let us carry it away and throw it in a gully."

No sooner said than done. They got rid of the rock and began digging again. They worked all day long, never stopping to eat or to rest, and they dug up all the garden. The soil under their spades became soft and crumbly, but no pot of gold did they find.

"Well," said the eldest brother, "now that we have dug up the soil, it's no use leaving it barren. Let us plant vines here!"

"That's a good idea!" the two younger brothers agreed. "At least our labors will not have been wasted."

So they planted some grapevines and began tending them carefully.

A short time passed by, and they had a fine, large vineyard with ripened, sweet, juicy clusters of grapes.

The brothers gathered in a rich harvest. They put aside the grapes they needed for themselves and sold the rest.

Said the eldest brother:

"It was not in vain, after all, that we dug up our land, for we found the treasure of which father spoke before he died."

156

HOW A MUZHIK DINED WITH THE HAUGHTY LORD

A Ukrainian Folktale

Once upon a time there lived a lord who was both rich and haughty. There were few people with whom he would have anything to do. And as for the *muzhiks*,* he refused altogether to consider them human beings, saying that an evil smell, the smell of earth, came from them; and he ordered his servants to chase them away if any of them ventured near.

One day the muzhiks got together and began talking about the lord.

"I saw the lord quite close; I met him in the field," said one.

"And I looked over the fence yesterday and saw the lord having coffee on the balcony," said another.

Just then a third muzhik, the poorest of the poor, came up and laughed on hearing them.

"Pooh, that's nothing," said he. "Anyone could peek at the lord over the fence. If I so wish, I will dine with him!"

* A *muzhik* is what a simple peasant was called in czarist Russia.

"What do you mean! Dine with him, indeed!" laughed the first two muzhiks. "Why, the moment he sees you he'll have you thrown out. He won't let you near the house!"

And the two muzhiks began jeering at the third and calling him names.

"You're a liar and a braggart!" they cried.

"I am not!"

"Well, if you dine with the lord, you'll get three sacks of wheat and two bullocks from us; but if you don't, you'll do everything we tell you to do."

"Very well," the muzhik replied.

He came into the lord's courtyard, and when the lord's servants saw him they

rushed out of the house and started to chase him out.

"Wait!" the muzhik said. "I have good tidings for the lord."

"What are they?"

"That I will tell to no one but the lord himself."

So the lord's servants went to the lord and told him what the muzhik had said.

The lord felt curious, for the muzhik had come not to ask for anything, but to bring news. Perhaps it was something that might prove useful. . . .

"Show him in!" said the lord to his servants.

The servants let the muzhik into the house, and the lord came out to speak to him.

"What are the tidings you bring?" he asked.

The muzhik glanced at the servants.

"I should like to talk with you in private, my lord," said he.

By now the lord's curiosity was thoroughly aroused, and he ordered the servants to leave them.

Said the muzhik in an undertone as soon as they were alone: "Tell me, gracious lord, what might be the cost of a piece of gold as big as a horse's head?"

"What do you want to know for?" asked the lord.

"I have my reason."

The lord's eyes gleamed, and his hands began to itch.

"It's not for nothing that the muzhik asks me such a question," said he to himself. "He must have found some treasure."

And he tried to worm out an answer from the muzhik.

"Tell me, my good man, why do you want to know about it?" he asked again.

Said the muzhik with a sigh: "Well, if you don't wish to tell me, you needn't. And now I must be going, for my dinner is waiting for me."

The lord forgot to be haughty. He was fairly trembling with greed.

"I'll outwit this muzhik," thought he to himself, "and get that gold away from him." And to the muzhik he said: "Look here, my good man, why should you hurry home? You can have dinner with me if you are hungry. Come, servants, make haste and set the table, and don't forget the vodka!"

The servants at once set the table and served the vodka and cold dishes, and the lord began to regale the muzhik and offer him this and that.

"Drink, my good man, drink, and eat your fill! Don't stand on ceremony!" said he.

And the muzhik did not refuse and ate and drank heartily, while the lord kept heaping his plate and refilling his glass.

Said the lord when the muzhik had eaten till he could eat no more: "And now go quickly and bring me your piece of gold the size of a horse's head! I shall know much better than you how to dispose of it. And as a reward I'll give you a ruble."

"No, my lord, I won't bring you the gold," the muzhik said.

"Why ever not?"

"Because I haven't got it."

"What?! Then why did you want to know the cost of it?"

"Just out of curiosity!"

The lord fell into a great rage. He went purple in the face and he stamped his feet.

"Get out of here, fool!" he cried.

Said the muzhik in reply:

"I am not the fool you think me, O most gracious lord! I had my bit of fun at your expense, and I have won into the bargain my wager of three sacks of wheat and two round-horned bullocks. It takes brains to do that!"

And with that he went away.

THE STORY OF ZARNIYAR WHO HAD ALL HER WITS ABOUT HER

An Azerbaijan* Fairy Tale

What shall I tell you about? I know. I'll tell you about a merchant named Mamed who lived in the city of Misar, journeyed to strange lands, and traded in goods of all kinds.

One day he bethought him to set off to a far-off land. He bought a large number of all kinds of goods, hired servants, and bidding farewell to his family set off on his way with his caravan.

He went to one place and then to another, and at last he came to a city he had never heard of before.

Here he decided to rest after his long travels, and he put up with his servants at a caravansary.

As he sat eating and drinking, a stranger came up to him.

"Ho there, merchant!" said the man. "You must have come from distant parts if you do not know the customs of this city."

"And what are the customs of this city?" Mamed asked.

"I'll tell you what they are. Every merchant who comes here must present a worthy gift to the Shah. In return, the Shah invites the merchant to his palace and plays a game of *nardi* with him."

What was Mamed to do? He had to go to the Shah whether he wanted to or not. So, choosing the costliest fabrics he had in his possession, he laid them out on a golden tray and set off for the palace.

The Shah received the gifts and began asking the merchant what city he came from, what goods he was trading in, and where he had been. Mamed answered him truthfully, and the Shah heard him out and said:

"Come to my palace tonight, and you and I will play nardi."

In the evening Mamed came to the palace, and there was the Shah waiting for him with the nardi board set up before him.

"Listen to my rules, merchant," said the Shah. "I have a learned cat. It can balance seven lighted lamps on its tail all night long, from evening to morning. Now if it proves able to balance the lamps all the time we are playing, all your riches and all your wares will be mine, and I will order you to be bound and thrown in a dungeon. But if the cat so much as moves from its place, my whole treasury will be yours and you can do with me whatever you wish."

What was the merchant to do? To run away was not possible, to protest was out of the question. There was no way out but to accept the Shah's conditions. So he sat there and cursed himself for having come to that city.

"It's easy enough to lose one's life here, to say nothing of one's possessions!" thought he.

The Shah now called his learned cat, and the cat came and twirled its tail and sat down in front of him.

"Bring the lamps!" the Shah commanded.

---

* *Azerbaijan* is one of the Soviet Socialist Republics; it is in the southeastern part of European Russia.

At once seven lamps were brought in by the servants and placed on the cat's tail.

The Shah picked up the pieces, and the game began.

The merchant kept glancing at the cat as he moved the figures over the board. And the cat sat there as if turned to stone—not moving, not even stirring.

So a day passed and a night, and then another two days and two nights, and Mamed continued to play nardi with the Shah while the cat sat there as before.

At last Mamed could bear it no longer.

"I cannot play any more!" he cried. "You win, Shah!"

That was all the Shah was waiting for.

He called his servants and said to them: "Bring to me all the merchant's wares and all his gold. And as for the merchant himself, bind him and throw him in a dungeon!"

So the Shah's servants seized Mamed and did all the Shah had ordered them to do.

Mamed, confined to the dungeon, cursed himself for not having had the sense to pass the city by and under his breath berated the Shah and his learned cat.

But now we will leave Mamed where he is and tell you about his wife Zarniyar.

Zarniyar stayed quietly at home waiting for her husband, but he did not come and there was no sight or sign of him.

"Perhaps something has happened to him?" thought she.

For a long time she lived with these anxious thoughts until one day Mamed's servant, his face streaked with dirt and his clothes in tatters, came running to her.

"Mistress, mistress!" cried he. "The Shah of a far-off land has imprisoned the master and has seized all his goods and all his gold. I alone ran away, barely escaping with my life. What are we going to do?"

Zarniyar asked the servant to tell her everything that had taken place. After that she gave orders for a large number of mice to be caught and a large chest to be filled with them. Then, taking a quantity of silver and gold, she dressed herself up in man's clothing, hid her long hair under a high fur cap, and set off at the head of a caravan to rescue her husband.

She journeyed without halting and without delays of any kind and at last arrived at the city where her husband was languishing in the dungeon.

To some of her servants she gave orders that they should wait at the caravansary for her, to others that they should accompany her to the palace of the Shah.

Then, taking a large tray of chased gold,

she laid out on it many valuable gifts and set off for the palace, her servants carrying the chest full of mice behind her.

When they neared the palace, Zarniyar said to her servants: "While I am playing nardi with the Shah, you must let the mice into the chamber, one by one."

The servants remained at the door with the chest, and Zarniyar entered the Shah's chamber.

Said she to the Shah: "Long years to you, O Ruler of rulers! As is the custom of your country, I have brought you a valuable gift."

Taking her for a man, the Shah received Zarniyar with great honors, put the choicest delicacies before her and invited her to join him in a game of nardi.

"What will your conditions be, O Ruler of rulers?" asked Zarniyar.

Said the Shah: "We shall play until my learned cat moves from its place."

"And what if your learned cat does move from its place?" Zarniyar asked.

"Then I shall admit that I have lost the game, and you shall do with me what you wish."

"Very well," said Zarniyar. "Let it be as you say."

The Shah called his learned cat, and the cat padded in and sat down very solemnly on the rug in front of him. Then the Shah's servants appeared bringing seven lamps, which they placed on the cat's tail.

The Shah then began playing nardi with Zarniyar. He kept smiling as he played, waiting for this young merchant to admit himself the loser.

Zarniyar's servants now opened the chest and let a mouse into the Shah's chamber.

When the cat saw the mouse its eyes be-

gan to glitter and it made as if to move from its place. But the Shah looked at it so sternly that it quietened at once and seemed frozen to the spot.

In a little while Zarniyar's servants let several more mice into the chamber. The mice began running up and down the floor and scuttling about near the walls. Now this was too much for the learned cat. It gave one miaow, and, jumping up suddenly— whereupon all the seven lamps dropped to the floor—began chasing the mice all over the room.

Shout as the Shah might, his learned cat would not listen to him.

Then only did Zarniyar call her servants, who rushed into the room, tightly bound the Shah hand and foot and began beating him with leather thongs, until he called for mercy.

"I will let out all my captives," cried he, "and will give them back all I took away, only spare me!"

Zarniyar's servants continued whipping the Shah, and the Shah screamed at the top of his voice. But although his people heard him they would not come to his aid, for all had long grown weary of his cruelty and greed.

Zarniyar then ordered the release of her husband and all who were with him, and had the Shah thrown into the dungeon.

After that Zarniyar and Mamed returned to their native city of Misar and continued to live there in peace and happiness, eating and drinking of the best in the land. And so must you do, too.

Three apples have fallen from the sky. One is for me, the second for the teller of this tale, and the third for him who listened to it.

A MOUNTAIN OF GEMS

A Turkmenian* Folktale

In a certain village there once lived an old widow who had one son, Mirali by name. They were very poor. The old woman combed wool and took in washing and in this way managed to earn enough to feed herself and her son.

When Mirali grew up, his mother said to him:

"I haven't the strength to work any more, my son. You must find yourself work of some kind to do, and so earn your keep."

"Very well," said Mirali, and off he went in search of a living. He went here, and he went there, but nowhere could he find anything to do.

After a time he came to the house of a certain *bai*.**

"Do you need a workman, bai?" Mirali asked.

"I do," the bai replied.

And he hired Mirali on the spot.

A day passed, and the bai did not ask his new workman to do anything at all. Another day passed, and the bai gave him no orders of any kind. A third day passed, and the bai seemed not so much as to notice him.

So Mirali went to him and asked:

"Shall I be getting any work to do, master?"

"Yes, yes," the bai replied, "tomorrow you will come with me."

The following day the bai ordered Mirali to slaughter a bull and to skin it, and this being done, to bring four large sacks and prepare two camels for a journey.

The bull's hide and the sacks were put on one of the camels, the bai climbed onto the other, and they started off on their way.

When they got to the foot of a distant mountain, the bai stopped the camels and ordered Mirali to take down the sacks and the bull's hide. Mirali did so, and the bai then told him to turn the bull's hide inside out and lie down on it. Mirali could not understand what this was for, but he dared not disobey and did as his master told him.

The bai rolled up the hide into a bundle with Mirali inside it, strapped it tight, and hid himself behind a rock.

By and by two large birds of prey flew up, seized in their beaks the hide, which had the fresh smell of meat about it, and carried it off with them to the summit of an inaccessible mountain.

Here the birds began to peck and claw at the hide and to pull it in different directions. The hide tore, Mirali rolled out, and the birds, seeing him, were frightened and flew away bearing the hide away with them.

Mirali got to his feet and began looking about him.

The bai saw him from below and shouted:

"What are you standing there for? Throw down to me the colored stones that are lying at your feet!"

Mirali looked and saw that indeed a great number of precious stones were strewn

---

* *Turkmenia* is a republic of the USSR, in Central Asia, north of Iran.

** *Bai* is the name given to a rich, sometimes titled, man in old Turkmenia.

162

about everywhere. There were diamonds and rubies and sapphires and emeralds and lumps of turquoise. The gems were large and beautiful, and they sparkled in the sun.

Mirali began gathering the gems and throwing them down to the bai, who picked them up as fast as they fell and filled his two large sacks with them.

Mirali kept on working until a thought struck him that turned his blood cold.

"How shall I get down from here, master?" he called to the bai.

"Throw me more of the stones," the bai called back, "and I shall tell you how to get down from the mountain afterward."

Mirali believed him and went on throwing down the gems. When the sacks were filled to the top, the bai hoisted them on to the camels' backs.

"Ho there, my son!" called he with a laugh to Mirali. "Now you understand the kind of work I give my workmen to do. See how many of them are up there on the mountain!"

And saying this, the bai rode away.

Mirali was left on the mountain all alone. He began looking for a way to climb down, but there were abysses and precipices on all sides and men's bones lay about everywhere. They were the bones of those who, like Mirali, had been the bai's workmen.

Mirali was terrified.

Suddenly there came a rush of wings overhead, and before he could turn around a huge eagle had pounced upon him. He was about to tear Mirali to pieces, but Mirali did not lose his presence of mind. Grasping the eagle's legs with both hands, he held them in a tight grip. The eagle let out a cry, rose up into the air, and began flying round and round, trying to shake off Mirali. At last, exhausted, it dropped to the ground at the foot of the Mountain of Gems, and when Mirali released his hold it flew away.

In this manner Mirali was saved from a terrible death.

He went to the market and began looking for work again. Suddenly he saw the bai, his former master, coming toward him.

"Do you need a workman, bai?" Mirali asked him.

Now it did not enter the bai's head that any workman of his could have remained alive—it had never happened before—and, mistaking Mirali for another, he hired him and took him home with him.

Soon after, the bai ordered Mirali to slaughter a bull and skin it. This being done, he told him to get ready two camels and bring four sacks.

They made their way to the foot of the same mountain, and, just as before, the bai told Mirali to lie down on the bull's hide and wrap himself in it.

"Show me how it is done, for it is not quite clear to me," said Mirali.

"What is there to understand? Here is the way it's done," the bai replied. And he stretched himself out on the hide which had been turned inside out.

Mirali at once rolled the hide up into a bundle, with the bai inside it, strapped it tight and stepped away.

"Wait, my son," the bai cried. "What have you done to me!"

But at that moment two birds of prey flew up, seized the bull's hide, and flew off with it to the mountain top. Once there, they began to tear at it with their beaks and claws; but seeing the bai, they were frightened and flew away. The bai scrambled to his feet.

"Come, bai, do not waste time—throw down the gems to me, just as I did to you," Mirali called from below.

Only then did the bai recognize him, and he began trembling with fear and rage.

"How did you get down from the mountain?" he called to Mirali. "Answer me quickly!"

"Throw down more of the gems, and when I have enough, I'll tell you how to get down from the mountain," Mirali replied.

The bai then began throwing down the gems, and Mirali picked them up as fast as they fell. When the sacks were full, Mirali hoisted them on to the camels' backs.

"Come, bai, look around you," he called to him. "The bones of the men whom you drove to their death are strewn about everywhere. Why do you not ask them how to get down from the mountain? As for me, I am going home."

And turning the camels around, Mirali set off for his mother's house.

The bai rushed about on the mountain top, shouting threats and pleas. But it was all in vain, for who was there to hear him?!

THE FERN GIRL

A Yakut* Folktale

They say that one morning a little old woman, the mistress of five cows, rose and went out to the field.

In the big and wide field she saw a horsetail—a fern with five shoots. She pulled it out without breaking the root or any of the shoots, brought it to her *yurta,*** and put it on her pillow. Then she went out again and sat down to milk her cows.

There she sat, when all of a sudden she heard a tinkling of bells in the yurta. The old woman dropped her milk pail, spilling the milk in her haste. She ran into the yurta and looked around, but everything was as it had been—there lay the horsetail fern on the pillow, just a fern like any other. The old woman went out once more. She sat down to milk her cows, when suddenly she again heard a tinkling of bells. She ran into the yurta, spilling the milk in her haste, and

whom did she see sitting on her bed but a girl of rare beauty. The girl's eyes sparkled like precious stones and her brows were like two black sables. The fern had turned into a girl!

The old woman was overjoyed.

"Stay with me and be a daughter to me," said she to the girl.

And so the two started living in the yurta together.

One day a young hunter named Kharzhit-Bergen went to the taiga to hunt. He saw a gray squirrel and he shot an arrow. He kept on shooting arrows from early morning till sunset, but never once did he hit the squirrel.

The squirrel bounded up a spruce tree, leaped from the spruce tree to a birch tree and then on to a larch tree, and settled in a pine tree by the little old woman's yurta.

Kharzhit-Bergen ran up to the pine tree and shot another arrow. The squirrel darted away again, and the arrow fell into the

---

* *Yakutia* is a Soviet Socialist Republic in northeastern Asiatic Russia.

** A *yurta* is a tent.

164

smoke hole of the little old woman's yurta.

"I want my arrow, old woman, give it back to me!" Kharzhit-Bergen shouted, but the little old woman did not come out and made no reply.

Kharzhit-Bergen was very angry. He flushed with rage and he ran into the yurta.

There before him sat the beautiful girl. Such was her loveliness that it took his breath away and made his head swim. Without a word he ran out, jumped on his horse, and galloped home.

"O my parents," said he, "the little old woman, the mistress of five cows, has a most beautiful girl in her yurta. Send matchmakers to her, for I want her for my wife."

Kharzhit-Bergen's father at once sent nine men mounted on nine horses for the girl.

The matchmakers came to the little old woman's yurta, they saw the girl, and such was her beauty that it took their breath away. Then, coming to their senses, they all left the yurta—all but one, the oldest and most respected among them.

"Little old woman," said he, "will you not give this young girl to Kharzhit-Bergen to be his wife?"

"That I will," the little old woman replied.

Then they asked the girl if she was willing, and the girl said that she was.

"You will have to pay a big ransom for the bride," said the little old woman. "You must give me as many cows and horses as my field will hold."

The cows and horses were soon driven to the little old woman's field, and so many were they that one lost count of them.

Then they dressed the girl in fine new clothes, they dressed her quickly and well. They brought a dappled horse, they bridled him with a silver bridle, they saddled him with a silver saddle, and they hung a silver whip at his side. Kharzhit-Bergen took his bride by the hand, led her out, put her on the dappled horse, and rode homeward with her.

They were riding along when suddenly Kharzhit-Bergen saw a fox on the road.

Said Kharzhit-Bergen, for he could not help himself:

"I am going to ride after the fox, but will soon be back. And you must follow this road till you reach the place where it branches off in two directions. On the eastern side a sable skin will hang, and on the western side will hang the hide of a bear with a white throat. Do not turn down the western road. Follow the road where you see the sable skin."

And with these words, he galloped away.

The girl rode on alone, and in due time she reached the fork in the road. But no sooner was she there than she forgot Kharzhit-Bergen's instructions. She turned down the road where the bearskin was hanging and soon came to a large iron yurta.

Out of the yurta, dressed in clothes of iron, there stepped the eighth devil's daughter. She was altogether hideous.

The devil's daughter seized the girl, dragged her off her horse, pulled off all of her fine clothes, and dressing herself in them, threw the girl over the yurta. After that she mounted the dappled horse and rode eastward.

Kharzhit-Bergen caught up with her when she was nearing his father's yurta. But he saw nothing and guessed nothing, for the devil's daughter had covered her face with a heavy veil.

All Kharzhit-Bergen's kin gathered to welcome the bride. Nine handsome young men and eight girls came out to the tethering post to meet her.

The girls spoke amongst themselves, and they said:

"The bride has only to open her mouth and speak one word, and the prettiest beads will drop out and roll over the ground." And they brought thread so as to string the beads.

The young men spoke amongst themselves, and they said:

"The bride has only to take one step and wherever she passes black sables will follow in her footsteps." And they got ready their bows and arrows so as to shoot the sables.

But when the bride started to speak, frogs dropped from her mouth, and when she took one step, mangy stoats ran after her. All who had come to meet the bride stood aghast and grew sad at heart.

But they spread a carpet of green grass from the tethering post to the bridegroom's yurta and, taking the bride by the hand, led her there.

The bride went into the yurta and, using the crowns of three young larch trees, made up a fire in the hearth.

After that there was a wedding feast, and everyone ate and drank and played games and made merry. No one guessed that this was not the real bride at all, for the devil's daughter would not remove her veil. Everyone thought that she was shy.

Soon after this the little old woman came to her field to milk her cows. She looked, and she saw that a new horsetail with five shoots had grown up in the selfsame spot, and it was even more slender and straight than the first one.

The little old woman dug up the horsetail together with the root, took it to her yurta, and put it on her pillow. Then she went back to the field and began milking the cows. Suddenly she heard the tinkling of bells in the yurta. She went inside, and

whom did she see there but the very same girl, looking more beautiful than ever.

"How is it that you are here, why have you come back?" the little old woman asked.

"O my mother," the girl replied, "when Kharzhit-Bergen and I were on our way to his yurta, he told me that he was going to ride after a fox and that I was to follow the road where a sable skin was hanging and in no wise to turn down the road where a bear's hide had been hung. But I forgot his warning, took the wrong road, and soon came to an iron yurta. The eighth devil's daughter met me, she pulled off my clothes, and dressing herself in them threw me over her iron yurta. After that she mounted my dappled horse and rode away. Some gray dogs seized me in their jaws and dragged me to the wide field near your yurta, and I came to life again in the guise of a horsetail fern. Ah, Mother, will I ever see Kharzhit-Bergen again?"

The little old woman heard her story and tried to comfort her.

"Do not be troubled, you will see him," said she. "And in the meantime, stay with me as before and be my daughter."

And so the fern girl began living in the little old woman's yurta again.

The dappled horse learned that the fern girl had come to life, and he spoke to Kharzhit-Bergen's father in a human voice and said:

"Know that Kharzhit-Bergen left his bride alone as he was bringing her home, and she had to ride on by herself. When she reached the fork in the road she turned down the path where the bear's hide was hanging and came to an iron yurta. The eighth devil's daughter rushed out, pulled off her fine clothes and dressed herself in them, and then she threw her over the iron yurta.

Now the devil's daughter lives in your yurta, and you have her for your daughter-in-law. And as for my true mistress, she has come to life again. You must bring her back to your yurta and give her to your son in marriage, else things will go hard with you. The devil's daughter will pull down your hearth and your yurta, she will make your life a misery and will put you all to death."

Hearing this, the old man ran into the yurta.

"Where did you bring your wife from, my son?" asked he of Kharzhit-Bergen. "Who is she?"

"She is the daughter of the little old woman, mistress of five cows," Kharzhit-Bergen replied.

Said the father: "The dappled horse has been complaining to me." And Kharzhit-Bergen's father told his son what the dappled horse related to him.

The devil's daughter heard Kharzhit-Bergen's father, and she turned back with fear and rage.

Kharzhit-Bergen heard his father, and he grew red with anger.

He seized the devil's daughter, dragged her out of the yurta, and drove her away.

After that Kharzhit-Bergen set off on horseback for the little old woman's yurta. He leaped from his horse by the tethering post, and the little old woman saw him and hurried out of her yurta. She was very happy, just as if someone thought lost had been found again or as if someone who had died had come back to life. From the tethering post to the yurta she spread a carpet of green grass and she slaughtered her best and fattest cow and her best and fleshiest horse and began preparing the wedding feast.

As for the fern girl, she looked at Kharzhit-Bergen and she burst out crying.

"Why have you come for me?" she asked him. "You let the daughter of the eighth devil give my body to the gray dogs. How can you come here now? There are more maids in the world than there are perches, there are more women in the world than there are pikes. Go and ask for a wife among them. I will not marry you!"

"I never gave you to the daughter of the eighth devil," said Kharzhit-Bergen. "I never gave you to the gray dogs. When I rode off to the taiga after the fox I showed you the road you had to take. I did not tell you to go and meet your death."

The little old woman brushed the tears from the fern girl's right eye, she brushed the tears from her left eye, and she seated herself between the fern girl and Kharzhit-Bergen.

Said the little old woman:

"How is it that you who died and then came back to life, you who were lost and then found, how is it that you do not rejoice? You must love each other as before, you must live in friendship and peace. Heed my words, both of you, and do as I say."

The girl obeyed, and she said softly: "Very well, I will do as you say, I will forgive and forget."

At this Kharzhit-Bergen jumped to his feet and began dancing and capering about and embracing and kissing the fern girl.

Then they saddled the dappled horse with a silver saddle and they bridled him with a silver bridle; they covered him with a silver horsecloth and they hung a silver whip at his side. And the fern girl they dressed in the best of finery, and she and Kharzhit-Bergen set off on their way.

They rode on and on. Winter they knew by the snow that fell, summer they knew by the rain that poured, autumn they knew by

the fog that hung over the fields. On and on they rode.

All Kharzhit-Bergen's kin, all his nine brothers came out to meet the bride. From the tethering post to the yurta they spread a carpet of green grass.

"When the bride comes," said they to themselves, "she will take a step and then another, and wherever she walks sables will leap from her footprints."

And with this in mind, they began making bows and arrows and they worked so hard that the skin peeled from the palms of their hands.

And Kharzhit-Bergen's eight sisters began spinning thread, and they too worked so hard that the skin came off their fingers. They waited for the bride and they said to themselves:

"When she comes, she will speak up in silvery tones, and precious red beads will drop from her mouth."

Then Kharzhit-Bergen arrived with his bride, and two of his sisters tied their horses to the tethering post. They caught the bride

in their arms and they let her down to the ground. The bride spoke up in silvery tones, and red beads dropped from her mouth, and the girls began gathering the beads and threading them on a string. The bride walked to the yurta, and black sables ran from her footprints, and the young men took their bows and arrows and began aiming at the sables.

The bride came into the yurta and, using the crowns of three young larch trees, made a fire in the hearth.

A gay wedding feast was held. Guests gathered from all the villages. There were singers among them and dancers, storytellers and wrestlers, and tumblers too.

For three days the feast went on and then it was over, and the guests went home on foot and on horseback.

And Kharzhit-Bergen and his wife set up house together. They lived in friendship and in peace, they lived happily and they lived long, and it is said that their grandchildren are living still.

THE GOLDEN CUP

A Buryat* Folktale

It is said that long, long ago, in olden times, there lived a mighty Khan named Sanad.

One day he decided to remove himself and all his people to new lands where the camping sites were better and the pastures richer. But the way to those lands was long and hard.

Before leaving, Sanad Khan ordered all the old people to be left behind.

"The old people will be a burden to us on the way," he said. "Not one old man or old woman must we have with us. He who does not carry out my command will be severely punished."

It was a cruel order, and the people's hearts were heavy. But there was nothing they could do, they had to act as the Khan willed. For they all feared the Khan and dared not disobey him.

One only of Sanad Khan's subjects, a young man named Tsyren, vowed that he would not abandon his old father.

The son and father agreed that Tsyren would hide the old man in a large leather sack and, in secret from Sanad Khan and everyone else, carry him to the new lands. And as for what might happen later, well they would take their chances.

Sanad Khan left the old camping site and together with his people and herds set out for the far-off lands in the north. And with them, in a large leather sack slung across his horse's back, went Tsyren's old father. Un-

known to the others, Tsyren gave his father food and drink. And whenever they made camp, he would wait until it was quite dark, untie the sack, and let the old man out that he might rest and stretch his aching limbs.

So they rode for a long time till they reached the shores of a great sea. Sanad Khan ordered his people to halt and camp for the night.

One of the Khan's attendants went down to the water's edge and noticed at the bottom of the sea something that sparkled and gleamed. He took a closer look and saw that it was a large golden cup of very unusual shape. Returning at once to the Khan, he told him that a precious golden cup was lying at the bottom of the sea close to the shore.

Sanad Khan, without thinking twice, ordered the cup to be delivered to him at once. But since no one dared or was willing to dive into the sea, the Khan gave orders that they draw lots.

The lot fell upon one of the Khan's own men. The man dived in, but he never came up again.

They cast lots again, and the man upon whom the lot fell leapt into the sea from the top of a steep cliff, but he too was never seen again.

In this way many of Sanad Khan's people lost their lives.

But the merciless Khan did not for a moment think of giving up his venture. On his orders, his subjects, one after another, dived unprotesting into the sea and perished.

---

* The *Buryats* are a nomad people in the southeastern part of European Russia.

At last it was Tsyren's turn to dive in after the cup. Before doing so, Tsyren went to the place where he had hidden his father to bid him good-bye.

"Farewell, Father," said Tsyren. "We are going to die, both of us, you and I."

"What has happened? Why must you die?" the old man asked.

Tsyren then explained that the lot had fallen upon him to dive to the bottom of the sea after the cup.

"But not one of those who dived in came up again," said he. "And so I am to perish in the sea by the Khan's orders, and you will be found here and killed by his servants."

The old man heard him to the end and said:

"If this goes on, you will all be drowned in the sea without ever getting the golden cup. The cup is not at the bottom of the sea at all. Do you see that mountain, not far from the sea? The golden cup is standing at the top of it. What you take to be the cup is only its reflection. How is it that none of you thought of that?"

"What shall I do?" Tsyren asked.

"Climb the mountain, find the cup, and deliver it to the Khan. It should not be difficult to find it. The cup sparkles so that it can be seen from afar. However, it may be that the cup stands on a cliff too steep for you to climb. In that case, this is what you must do: wait until some roes appear on the cliff and find a way of startling them. The roes will rush away and push the cup in their haste. Waste no time then, but snatch it up quickly or else it will fall into a deep, dark ravine and be lost to you for ever."

Tsyren thanked his father and at once made for the mountain.

It was not easy to climb to the top of it. Tsyren clutched at shrubs, trees, and sharp rocks, and he scratched his face and hands till the blood appeared, and he tore his clothing. At last, when he had all but

reached the top, Tsyren saw the golden cup. It was very beautiful. It stood on a high and inaccessible cliff, and it sparkled and shone.

Tsyren saw that he would never be able to climb the cliff. So, heeding his father's words, he waited for the roes to appear.

He had not long to wait. Several roes soon made their appearance on the cliff. They stood there calmly gazing down. Tsyren gave a loud shout. The roes were startled and began rushing to and fro on the cliff. They soon overturned the golden cup, and it came rolling down, and Tsyren caught it nimbly as it fell.

Pleased and happy, he made his way down the mountain with the cup in his hands, went to Sanad Khan, and placed it before him.

"How did you get this cup from the bottom of the sea?" the Khan asked him.

"It was not there that I found it," Tsyren replied, "but on the top of yonder mountain. What we saw in the sea was only the cup's reflection."

"Who told you that?" asked the Khan.

"I thought of it myself," Tsyren replied.

The Khan said no more and let him go.

The following day, Sanad Khan and his people moved on.

They journeyed a long time, and at last they reached a great desert. Here the sun had baked the earth and had burnt up all the grass. There was no river anywhere about, nor even a stream. The men and the cattle began to suffer from a terrible thirst. Sanad Khan sent men in all directions in search of water, but try as they would, no water could they find, for all around was dry, scorched land. The people were in despair. They did not know what to do or where to go.

Tsyren secretly made his way to where he had left his father.

"What are we to do, Father, tell me?" he asked. "We are all dying of thirst, and so are the cattle."

"Let a three-year-old cow go free," said the old man, "watch it closely. Whereever it stops and starts sniffing at the ground, there begin to dig."

Tsyren let loose a three-year-old cow, and the cow hung its head low and began wandering from place to place. At last it stopped and began sniffing at the hot earth, drawing in the air noisily.

"Dig here," said Tsyren.

The people began digging, and they soon reached a large underground spring. Cool, clear water gushed out and flowed over the ground. Everyone drank his fill and was cheered and heartened.

Sanad Khan called Tsyren to his side and asked him.

"How is it that you were able to find an underground spring in this desert?"

"I knew certain signs that told me where it was," Tsyren replied.

The people drank some more, rested, and moved on again. They journeyed for many days, and then they halted and pitched camp. Unexpectedly it began to rain heavily in the night, and the rain put out the campfire. Hard as they tried, the people could not light the fire again. They were chilled to the bone and wet, and they did not know what to do.

Then someone noticed what seemed to be the light of a campfire on the top of a distant mountain.

Sanad Khan at once gave orders that the fire be brought down from the mountain.

The people rushed to fulfill the Khan's orders. First one, then another, then a third climbed the mountain. Each found the fire, which flamed beneath the thick branches of a large spruce tree, and also a hunter who was warming himself by it. Each took away with him a burning log. But not one succeeded in carrying his log as far as the camp, for the heavy rain put out the flame.

Sanad Khan was very angry, and he gave orders for all who went to get the fire but returned without it to be punished.

When Tsyren's turn came to fetch the fire, he crept to where he had hidden his father and asked him:

"What is to be done, Father? How is the fire to be carried from the mountain to the camp?"

"Do not take the burning logs," said the old man, "they'll smoulder on the way and be put out by the rain. Take a large pot with you and fill it full of burning coals. Only in this way will you be able to bring the fire to the camp."

Tsyren did as his father told him, and he brought down from the mountain a potful of live coals. The people made fires, dried and warmed themselves and cooked their food.

When Sanad Khan learned who it was that had brought them the fire, he ordered Tsyren to come to him.

Tsyren came, and the Khan began shouting at him angrily:

"How is it that you who knew how to bring the fire kept silent about it?" he raged. "Why did you not speak up at once?"

"Because I did not know how to do it myself," Tsyren told him.

"Yet you were able to do it. How was it so?" the Khan insisted.

And so persistently did he ply him with questions that Tsyren finally confessed that he had only been able to carry out the Khan's commands because of his father's good advice.

"Where is your father?" the Khan asked.

Said Tsyren: "I carried him all the way in a large leather sack."

Then Sanad Khan commanded the old man to be brought before him, and he said to him: "You need hide no longer, you may ride freely with the rest. Old people are no burden to the young, for age has wisdom."

SILVER HOOF

*A Folktale from The Urals**
ADAPTED BY PAVEL BAZHOV

There was an old man named Kokovanya in our village. He had none of his own family left, so he thought he'd take some orphan into his hut to be a child to him.

He asked the neighbors if they knew of anyone, and they told him: "Grigory Potapov's children were left orphans not long ago. The bailiff sent the older girls to the manor sewing room, but there's a little girl of six nobody wants. That would be the child for you."

But Kokovanya said: "I'd be clumsy with a lass. A lad would be better. I'd teach him my trade and he'd help me when he got bigger. But what can I do with a lass? What can I teach her?"

But then he thought about it all again. "I knew Grigory and his good wife too," he said. "They were hard workers and merry folk. If the lass takes after them it won't be dull in my hut. I'll adopt her. But maybe she won't come?"

"Well, her life's none too sweet," the neighbors said. "The bailiff gave Grigory's cottage to some poor devil and told him to look after the orphan till she grew up. But he's got a dozen of his own. They haven't

---

* The *Urals* or Ural Mountains form the traditional boundary between Europe and Asia; they separate the Russian plains from the Siberian lowlands.

enough for their own mouths. And the wife nags at the orphan child and begrudges her every crust. The girl is little, but she's big enough to understand. She feels it. Wouldn't you say she'd want to get away from there? And then you'll talk to her a bit, and she'll take to you."

"Yes, that's true," said Kokovanya. "I'll talk to her kindly."

When the next holiday came round he went to the place where the orphan lived. He found the hut crowded with folk, young and old. A little girl sat by the stove petting a brown cat. The child was small and the cat was small too, so thin and bedraggled it was a wonder anyone would let it in. The child was stroking the cat, and it purred so you could hear it all over the hut.

Kokovanya looked at the girl and asked: "Is that Grigory's lass?"

"The same," said the goodwife. "And as if it's not enough feeding her, she's got to

drag in that mangy beast too. We can't get rid of it. And it scratches the children. And then on top of all I've got to feed it!"

"They must tease it, your children," said Kokovanya. "When she has it, it purrs." Then he turned to the child. "Well, Podaryonka,* how'd you like to come and live with me?"

The child stared.

"How did you know I'm called Daryonka?" she asked.

"It just came," he said. "I didn't think, I didn't know, I just happened on it."

"But who are you?" the child asked.

"I'm a sort of hunter," said Kokovanya. "Summertime I wash sand and look for gold; and winters I go to the woods and look for a certain goat, but I never catch sight of him."

"Will you shoot him if you do?"

"No," said Kokovanya, "I shoot ordinary

---

* The word *podaryonka* means "little gift."

goats, but that one I won't. I want to see where he stamps his right forefoot."

"What for?"

"Come and live with me, and I'll tell you all about it," said Kokovanya.

The little girl wanted very much to hear about the goat, and she could see Kokovanya was a merry, kind old man. So she said: "I'll come. But take my Pussy too. Look how good she is."

"That's as sure as I stand here," said Kokovanya. "Only a fool would leave behind a cat that sings like that. She'll be as good as a balalaika * in the hut."

The goodwife heard their talk, and she was as glad as could be to get the orphan off her hands. She started putting Daryonka's things together in a hurry. She was afraid Kokovanya might change his mind.

The cat, too, seemed to understand what was happening. She kept rubbing against their legs and purring: "R-r-right! You'r-r-re r-r-right!"

So Kokovanya took the orphan home. He was tall and bearded, and she was a bit of a thing with a button nose. Down the street they went with the bedraggled cat trotting along behind.

That was how they came to live together —Grandad Kokovanya, the orphan Daryonka, and Pussy. The days passed. They didn't get rich, but they had enough and there was plenty for everyone to do.

In the morning Kokovanya went to work, Daryonka tidied the hut and made soup and porridge, while Pussy hunted mice. In the evening they were all at home, very comfortable and merry.

The old man was a wonderful teller of tales. Daryonka loved to listen, and Pussy

---

* A *balalaika* is a Russian instrument somewhat like a guitar but with a triangular shape.

would lie purring: "R-r-right! You'r-r-re r-r-right!"

But after every story Daryonka would remind the old man: "Now, tell me about the goat, Grandad. What is he like?"

At first Kokovanya tried to put her off, but then he told her:

"That's a very special goat. On his right forefoot he's got a silver hoof. And when he stamps with that silver hoof he leaves a gem there. If he stamps once there's one gem, if he stamps twice there are two, and if he begins to paw the ground there'll be a whole pile."

He told her this and then he was sorry, because after that Daryonka could talk of nothing but the goat.

"Grandad, is he a big goat?"

Kokovanya told her he was no taller than the table, with thin legs and a pretty head. But Daryonka kept on: "And has he got horns, Grandad?"

"Yes, he has, and fine ones too. Ordinary goats have two horns, but this one's got antlers, with five tines."

"And does he eat people, Grandad?"

"No, he doesn't eat people, he eats grass and leaves, and he may nibble a bit of hay from the stacks in winter."

"And what color is he?"

"In summer he's brown like Pussy here, and in winter he's silver-gray."

Autumn came and Kokovanya got ready to go to the woods. He wanted to find out where the goats were feeding. But then Daryonka started begging and pleading.

"Take me with you, Grandad! I might get a look at the goat, even if he's a long way off!"

"A long way off you wouldn't know him," said Kokovanya. "All goats have horns in autumn. And you wouldn't see how many tines this one has. In the winter, now—that's different. Ordinary goats haven't got horns then, but Silver Hoof has them all the time. So then you can know him even when he's far away."

With that he managed to quiet her. Daryonka stayed at home, while Kokovanya went to the woods. On the fifth day he came back.

"A lot of goats are feeding near Poldnevsk this year," he said. "That's where I'll go when winter comes."

"But how'll you sleep in the woods in winter?" asked Daryonka.

"I've got a hut there, by the glade where we go mowing," he said. "It's a sound one with a window and a stove. I'm all right there."

Then Daryonka started up again: "Will Silver Hoof feed there too?"

"Who knows? He may."

Then the child kept on with her begging and pleading: "Take me with you, Grandad! I'll stay in the hut. Maybe Silver Hoof will come up close and then I'll see him."

At first the old man wouldn't hear of it. "What! Take a little girl into the woods in winter! You'd have to go on skis and you don't know how. You'd sink in the snow. What would I do with you? You'd freeze too!"

But Daryonka kept begging: "Take me, take me, Grandad! I can ski a little bit!"

Kokovanya talked this way and that, but at last he thought to himself: "What if I do take her after all? If she tries it once she won't ask again."

"All right," he said, "I'll take you. Only see you don't start crying when we get to the woods or asking to go home."

When real winter came, Kokovanya loaded a hand sled with two sacks of rusks, some hunting supplies, and other things he'd need. Daryonka made herself a little bundle too. She took some scraps of cloth to make a dress for her doll, a spool of thread and a needle, and then she put in a rope too. I may be able to catch Silver Hoof with it, she thought.

She was sorry to leave the cat, but there was nothing else to be done with it. She stroke it and talked to it and explained all about everything.

"Grandad and I are going to the woods, Pussy, and you must stay here and catch all the mice. When we see Silver Hoof we'll come back home again, and I'll tell you all about it."

Pussy looked up with clever eyes and purred: "R-r-right! You'r-r-re r-r-right!"

So Kokovanya and Daryonka set off. And all the neighbors stared in amazement. "The old man must be in his dotage. Taking a little maid like that to the woods in winter!"

Just as Kokovanya and Daryonka were leaving the last houses behind, they heard all the dogs making a big fuss and commotion, barking and howling as though some wild beast was about. They looked around, and there was Pussy running down the middle of the street, spitting and hissing at the dogs. Pussy was a fine big cat now, and able to look after herself. There wasn't a dog anywhere that would dare a fight with her.

Daryonka wanted to catch Pussy and take her back home, but just try to catch her! She ran into the woods and up a tree in a flash. Get her out of there if you can! Daryonka called and called, but Pussy wasn't to be coaxed down. So what could they do? They had to go on. And when they looked around, there was Pussy running along near them, off to one side. That was how they came at last to the hut.

So all three of them lived there. And Daryonka liked it. "It's nice here," she said. Kokovanya agreed, "Yes, it's more cheerful." And Pussy curled up in a ball by the stove and purred loudly: "R-r-right! You'r-r-re r-r-right!"

There were a lot of goats that winter. Ordinary goats. Kokovanya brought one or two home every day. The hides piled up and the meat was salted—far too much to be taken back on the hand sled. Kokovanya saw he would have to go home for a horse, but how could he leave Daryonka alone in the woods with only the cat? But Daryonka had got used to the woods and she spoke of it herself.

"Grandad, why don't you go to the village for a horse? We ought to take the salt meat home."

Kokovanya was surprised.

"What a wise head on those little shoulders! As sensible as a grown woman. Thought of it all by yourself! But won't you be frightened, all alone?"

"Why'd I be frightened?" she answered. "You say yourself the hut's a good strong one, the wolves can't get in, and besides, they don't come here. And I've got Pussy with me. I won't be frightened. But come back soon all the same!"

Kokovanya left. And Daryonka stayed behind alone with Pussy. She was quite used to being alone in the daytime when Kokovanya was tracking goats. But when it began to get dark she felt a bit scared. So she looked at Pussy and saw she was comfortable and contented. That made Daryonka feel better. She sat down by the window and looked out toward the glade and—there!—something like a little ball bounced out of the woods. It came closer and she saw it was a goat. He had thin legs and a slender head, and five tines on his horns. Daryonka ran out at once, but she found nothing there. She waited and waited, and at last went back to the hut. "I must have dreamed it," she said, "it was just my fancy."

Pussy purred: "R-r-right! You'r-r-re r-r-right!"

Daryonka went to bed, taking the cat with her, and slept soundly till morning.

Another day passed. No Kokovanya. Daryonka felt bored and lonely but she did not cry. Instead she stroked the cat.

"Don't fret, Pussy," she said. "Grandad'll come tomorrow, you'll see."

Pussy only sang her usual song: "R-r-right! You'r-r-re r-r-right!"

Again Daryonka sat by the window looking at the stars. She was thinking of going to bed when she suddenly heard a pitter-pitter-pat behind the wall of the hut. She jumped up, frightened, and there was the pitter-pitter-pat by the other wall, then back by the first one again, then by the door, and at last up on the roof. It was not loud, it sounded like very quick, light footsteps.

Suddenly Daryonka thought to herself: "What if that's the goat that came yesterday?" She wanted so badly to see it that even fright couldn't hold her back. She opened the door and peeped out, and there was the goat, quite close, standing as quiet as could be. He raised his front foot to stamp and a silver hoof gleamed on it, and the horns had five tines. Daryonka did not know what to do, so she called it as she would an ordinary nanny goat or billy goat.

How that goat laughed! Then he turned and ran across the glade. Daryonka went back into the hut and told Pussy all about it.

"I've seen Silver Hoof! I saw his horns and I saw his hoof. Only I didn't see him stamp and leave precious stones. He'll show me that next time."

The third day passed and still no Kokovanya. Daryonka's face was quite clouded. She even cried a bit. She wanted to talk to Pussy, but Pussy was gone. Then Daryonka got really frightened and ran out to look for the cat.

It was a light night with a full moon. Daryonka looked around and there was the cat, quite close, sitting in the glade with the goat in front of her. Pussy was nodding her head and so was the goat, as if they were having a talk. Then they began running about in the snow.

The goat ran here and there, then he stopped and stamped.

They ran about the glade for a long time, and disappeared in the distance. Then they came right up to the hut again. The goat jumped up on the roof and began stamping with his silver hoof. And precious stones flashed out like sparks—red, green, light blue, dark blue—every kind and color.

It was then that Kokovanya returned. But he did not know his hut. It was covered with precious stones, sparkling and winking in all colors. And there stood the goat on top, stamping and stamping with his silver hoof, and the stones kept rolling and rolling down.

Suddenly Pussy jumped up there too and stood beside the goat purring loudly—and then there was nothing, no Pussy and no Silver Hoof.

Kokovanya scooped up half a hatful of gems, but Daryonka begged him: "Don't touch any more of them, Grandad! I want to look at the gems just as they are in the morning."

Kokovanya did as she asked. But before morning heavy snow fell and covered everything.

They cleared the snow away afterward, but they couldn't find anything. Well, they didn't do so badly after all, with what Kokovanya had collected in his hat.

So it all ended well, though it was a shame about Pussy. She was never seen again, and Silver Hoof didn't come back either. He'd come once, that was enough.

But after that people often found stones in the glade where the goat had run about. Most of them were green ones, chrysolites, folk call them. Have you ever seen them?

THE MIGHTIEST OF THEM ALL

A Kazakh* Folktale

ADAPTED BY VICTOR VAZHDAEV

Once upon a time there lived a man named Makbul. He had a daughter. When his daughter became a young woman, Makbul said to her: "My daughter, I should like to know whom you will choose to marry."

"Father," she answered, "if you will allow me to choose for myself, then I confess that I should like to marry the strongest thing in the whole world. Man does not seem to have much strength, and I am still but a young maid and need a protector!"

"Daughter," said old Makbul, "You are indeed asking for a lot! Everyone knows, that which is strongest in this world is the Sun. But I love you so much, my dear, that I am ready to grant your every wish."

Saying this, Makbul took his daughter by the hand and they set off to speak to the Sun.

They walked for a long time. At last they reached that faraway place where the plains end. They did not stop there, however, but went on and on.

After a time they saw that everything had become so bright that by comparison the brightest day, in the most cloudless weather, on the most treeless plain, seemed like the darkest hour, in the darkest night, in the deepest abyss on earth.

The blinding light that now surrounded them turned everything into the yellowest of yellows—sky, earth, road, even the grass and the flowers. All was bathed in this light that was the yellowest of yellows.

But old Makbul and his daughter did not halt, they did not turn back, but went tirelessly farther and farther. When they came to the end of this land of light, they saw that again everything had changed.

And how it had changed! Now the heat was so intense that by comparison the hottest hour of the hottest day of the hottest summer in the hottest place on earth seemed like the coldest day in the coldest year in the coldest place in the world. That is how hot it was! And this heat turned everything a red-red, just like fire. The fire-red road stretched into the fire-red distance over the fire-red earth under the fire-red sky!

But old Makbul and his daughter went tirelessly on, moving ever forward.

At last they reached the Sun. The Sun was round, merry, and blinding.

Makbul placed his daughter in front of himself and said:

"Sun, do you see that she is as graceful as a young Arab mare, that her braids are like the branches of the weeping willow, her face the color of white corn, her brows like birds' wings, her lashes like arrows, and that all of her is like a ravishing desert mirage? Do you agree, Sun, that there is none more fair in the whole world?"

"I agree," said the Sun, "that there is none more fair."

---

* The *Kazakh* Soviet Socialist Republic is in the central part of Asiatic Russia.

"Sun!" Makbul then said, "you are the largest, the hottest, the brightest, the strongest! . . . My daughter is so young and so delicate that she would like to marry the strongest thing in the world. That is why we have come to you."

"Wait a minute, Makbul!" said the Sun, interrupting the old man. "I am willing to take your daughter as my wife. But you are mistaken, I am not the strongest thing in the world."

"But it is you who banishes the night!" exclaimed Makbul. "It is you who warms the earth! You nourish with your rays the forest, the grasses, and all that grows! If you did not exist there would be eternal night, eternal hunger, and eternal death! Who can it be that is mightier than you!?"

"Look," said the Sun pointing downward.

Makbul lowered his eyes to the ground.

Hot sunrays beamed over the earth. Suddenly, however, from somewhere, like flocks of sheep, numberless clouds moved over the whole sky. The sunrays now could no longer pierce the clouds to reach the earth, and they were lost in the mass of the threatening clouds.

"The Cloud is stronger than I," said the Sun. "He does not let my rays through to shine upon the earth. He is like a veil hiding me from the world, from its people, and against him I am powerless. Do you still want to give me the hand of your daughter in marriage?" the Sun asked sadly and with such a somber face that the weather became at once gloomy.

Makbul was at a loss to know what to say, and was silent for a while.

"No, Sun, I shall not marry you!" said Makbul's daughter. "Let us go, Father. I thought there was nothing stronger than the Sun in the whole wide world, but that is not so!"

And they went to speak to the Cloud.

"Cloud, do you see my daughter?" asked Makbul.

And as before the Sun, the girl appeared before the Cloud in all her beauty.

"I see her," answered the Cloud.

"Do you see, Cloud, that she is as graceful as a young Arab mare, that her braids are like the branches of the weeping willow, her face the color of white corn, her brows like birds' wings, her lashes like arrows, and that all of her is like a ravishing desert mirage? Do you agree, Cloud, that there is none more fair in the whole world?"

"I agree," said the Cloud, "that there is none more fair on earth."

"Cloud," Makbul then said, "we thought that the strongest in the world was the Sun, but you have proved your greater strength. Tell me, do you agree to take my daughter to be your wife?"

"I agree," said the Cloud, "but you are mistaken if you think that I am the strongest. There is a thing mightier than I."

Saying this, the Cloud shuddered. He began to move waving his misty sleeves; his long coat billowed out like a sail; his cheeks were about to burst; and gliding off to the side he barely managed to cry out: "Woe is me, woe! The restless Wind chases me all over the earth, to wherever it fancies! Never, never does he give me peace!"

And the huge, heavy, mighty looking Cloud broke into sobs, pouring over the earth torrents of rain-tears.

"Let's go to the Wind," said the girl. "Who wants so tearful a bridegroom as the Cloud? The Wind is no doubt the strongest!"

And they set off to call on the Wind.

Br-r-r! It was frightening to approach the house where the Wind lived. There was such a din and such whistling all about! Believe us, nothing else could be heard there. And to make yourself heard you had to shout with all your might.

"Stop droning and moaning!" shouted Makbul. "We want to talk to you."

At first the Wind looked out the window. How gloomy, angry, and unkempt he looked, as if he had slept and slept and was not at all slept out.

"Speak up!" he grunted, "and be quick about it! I have no time to stand around having talks with you."

Makbul was glad, and so was his daughter. At last, they thought, they had found the strongest! The Wind will not become gloomy like the Sun, he will not sob like the Cloud. This is indeed a bridegroom!

Makbul now placed his daughter in front of himself and spoke to the Wind as he had spoken to the Sun and the Cloud.

The Wind listened to what the old man had to say, knit his shaggy brows, breathed into his shaggy beard, and what hurricanes, what blizzards, what cyclones did he bring down upon the earth! The door to the Wind's house was flung open, the shutters flapped noisily against the walls, and so impatient was the Wind that he himself flew out the window.

"You wicked old man!" he roared at Makbul. "Why did you come to laugh at me? Don't you know that for a thousand years now I have thrown myself against the Mountain that stands in my way? Each time I think that now I shall succeed in rolling him off my path! But there he always stands, Giant Mountain. He does not stir, and when I strike against him I scatter in all directions, like water flowing over a boulder!"

And stamping his foot, the Wind shook his shaggy head, howled, whistled, and threw himself once more against the Mountain.

"Let us go to Giant Mountain!" said Makbul's daughter. "Of what good is the Wind as a bridegroom? Giant Mountain is no doubt the strongest of all!"

"Hello, Giant Mountain!" said Makbul respectfully.

"Hello, Giant Mountain!" said the girl even more respectfully.

"Hello!!" the Mountain answered in a thunderous voice.

Makbul and his daughter were at a loss to know how to begin.

"Speak up, old man," said the unreachable Mountain as kindly as he could. "Speak up, do not be afraid. I am so big, so strong, that I cannot talk more softly."

Then Makbul explained everything to the Mountain.

"All this is true," he said, after hearing out Makbul. "The Cloud is stronger than the Sun, the Wind is stronger than the Cloud, and I am stronger than the Wind. All this is true! I am willing to take your daughter to be my wife. But you should know that below, in the foothills, lives some kind of creature. He does with me as he pleases, and I am powerless before him. Even at this very moment I feel that something has been stuck into my side which burns and pricks. . . ."

And, barely did Giant Mountain utter these words, when, without any warning, there was such a thud, as if something had been shot out of a huge cannon. The Mountain rocked, and one of its unreachable peaks split into huge rocks, which rolled down its side! And nothing was left of the peak—as if it never existed! From the Emerald Lake hidden by this peak, foaming and splashing, the Emerald River burst forth and cascaded down in a waterfall, gathered and flowed swiftly in a foamy, transparent current toward the Parched Desert.

As if enchanted, Makbul and his daughter stood rooted to the ground staring at the hidden river. They looked and marveled at this wonder, and saw, as in a fairy tale, the Parched Desert turn into a Flowering Valley!

And Giant Mountain, when the rain of rocks ceased and the noise of the river became more steady and calm, himself astonished at what had just happened, said:

"I look and I am amazed! There never was in the world anything so beautiful as my Emerald Lake! And now there appears even a more beautiful sight, an Emerald River! The Parched Desert has become a Flowering Valley. How much beauty has been added!"

Even the old Mountain had never heard, had not known that such a thing could be done!

"Yes, friend Makbul," said he turning to the old man, "your daughter is incomparable, and I am willing to take her as my wife, but I am not worthy. Go below, to the foothills. Look there for a being that compared to me is small, but he is really the most mighty. He does with me as he pleases. Go to him."

And old Makbul left with his daughter, descended to the foot of the Mountain in search of the mysterious, most mighty being.

They walked and walked, and looked and looked, and then they saw . . . a man.

His shoulders were broad, his hands were strong, his face was handsome. His eyes shone with contentment and youth. There he stood, merely a man, no different from other men. The same as they were. He smiled at them.

"Hello," said Makbul.

"Hello," said his daughter.

"Hello!" the man answered.

"Tell us, please, do you happen to know where there lives that unknown being that is stronger than any in this world?" asked Makbul.

"Please explain more clearly whom you mean," said the man. "I don't understand what you want to know." And Makbul told him everything.

"*I* am the strongest," said the man.

"You!?" Makbul said with surprise.

"You!?" asked the girl, and she blushed.

"And who are you??" Makbul and the daughter said in one voice.

"I am a Master Builder!" the man answered. "I dig into mountains to get from them the treasure that they hold—iron, ore, gold, and precious stones. I have dug a tunnel through the thickness of Giant Mountain and have laid steel rails over the length of this tunnel. Trains now run over these rails to bring out the treasure. I have built bridges over precipices, and men and machines ride over these bridges as over the ground."

"And did you do all this yourself?" exclaimed Makbul.

"Oh, Great One!" said Makbul's daughter, "if you have done all this yourself, you are indeed the greatest wizard on earth and the strongest being!"

"No," answered the man. "I did not do all this alone, but with other men. We are many, we are countless!"

"What a marvel!" said Makbul. "A whole army of Great Ones! And are they all as strong as you?"

"Much stronger! Among us there are such mighty men that I cannot hope to vie with them. But our strength is not so much in our hands as in our brain, our will, and our knowledge. We have solved mysteries of nature. We have solved the mystery of friendship among people. But we are not

'Great Ones.' We are just simple folk—like you, honorable elder, and you, beautiful maiden.

"We want man to live happily on earth. At the will of man, canals water dry lands, strong stone houses are built against the worst hurricanes. Electricity gives man light and warmth. Airplanes, trains, and ships overtake the wind. And there are ever new wonders to be discovered by man."

"Truly you must be the mightiest of them all, mightier than the Sun, the Cloud, the Wind, or the Mountain! Will you take my daughter to be your wife?"

"I will!" the man answered.
And they were wed.

[*This is a tale from the Kazakhistan Soviet Republic, a desert region developed in recent years into an agriculturally productive area—"a desert turned into a garden." In this version the old tale has been given a modern ending. It is understandable that in such a land, where the unsuspected riches of the soil came to fruition with the aid of up-to-the-minute technological achievements of men, that Man should be regarded as "the mightiest of them all"—the mightiest of all the mighty forces of nature—and that his inventions should be considered miracles.*]

PART III

STORIES, VERSE, AND FABLES

for boys and girls from eight to eleven

FAVORSKY

TWO STORIES BY MAXIM GORKY

Maxim Gorky (1868–1936) wrote grim novels, plays, and short stories for adults. But he was one of the first major Russian writers to advocate a separate, lighthearted literature for children. In 1933 he conducted a countrywide poll in the Soviet Republic, asking its young what kind of stories they liked to read. The many thousands of answers were analyzed and the results were presented in an important report to a large gathering of children's authors. A new kind of literary trend was thus begun. Its emphasis was on the gay story, the folktale, and biographies of outstanding people.

Here are two humorous stories by Maxim Gorky: "A Fish Story," and "Simple Ivanushka."

A FISH STORY

One day a boy named Yevseika sat at the edge of the sea fishing. Fishing can be very boring, especially when the fish are stubborn and won't bite. It was a hot day and Yevseika began to doze from the heat and the boredom and—splash!—he fell into the water.

The water was deep but that didn't scare him! He swam quietly for a while, then dove down and immediately found himself at the bottom of the sea. He sat down on a rock that was covered with soft red seaweed and looked around him; it was very pleasant down there, at the bottom of the sea!

A starfish moved about slowly, some long-whiskered lobsters glided noiselessly over the rocks, a crab was swimming sideways, and everywhere, thick as cherries on trees, sea anemones clung to the rocks. And wherever he gazed Yevseika saw all kinds of strange-looking things—water lilies swaying although there was no breeze, tiny shrimp darting about like flies, a large turtle dragging itself along the sea floor while two green baby fish hovered over its shell like butterflies, and a hermit crab carrying its own shell as he moved over and down some white rocks. Looking at the hermit crab Yevseika remembered a couple of lines from a poem about a poor old peasant:

> His cart was his only home—
> He never wandered therefrom.

Suddenly Yevseika heard a piercing sound over his head, like a clarinet note: "Who are you?"

He looked up and saw a huge fish with silver-gray scales, bulging eyes, and a grinning mouth. It looked as if it had already been fried.

"Was it you who just spoke to me?" Yevseika asked the fish.

"I!"

Yevseika was surprised and said with some annoyance, "How could it be you? Fish don't talk!"

And to himself he thought: "That's strange! I can't understand German at all, but fish language I understand without any trouble. I must be getting pretty smart!" Feeling quite satisfied with himself, Yevseika looked around him again.

A small, frisky fish was circling over him laughing and saying, "Look at that! What a freak arrived here today—it has two tails! And no shell—phooey! And only two fins!"

Some of the little fish, more daring, swam right up to Yevseika's nose and teased.

"Aren't *you* pretty!"

Yevseika's feelings were beginning to be hurt.

"What creatures!" he thought. "Don't they understand that they are looking at a man?!"

And he tried to grab the little fish but they darted away, pushing each other with their noses and with their sides. Singing in chorus, they now turned to teasing the crabs:

Crabs live under rocks—females and males—
Feeding on nothing but fishes' tails;
Fishes' tails are tasteless and dry—
Never do they taste a juicy fly! Why?!

The largest of the crabs, moving its whiskers fiercely, muttered as it tried to catch the mischievous little fish in its claws, "When I catch you I'll cut out your tongues!"

"What a grouch he is!" thought Yevseika.

Then the huge fish with the clarinet voice spoke to him again.

"What makes you think all fish cannot speak?"

"My father told me," Yevseika said.

"And what is a—father?"

"Well, someone like me, only bigger, and with a mustache. When he is not cross he's very nice."

"Does he eat fish?"

Yevseika was afraid to tell the truth. Looking up through the water, wishing he were at home or in some other familiar place, he saw a greenish sky and a sun that looked yellow like a brass tray. This made him feel even a little more scared, and he answered the huge fish, "No, my father does not eat fish. They have too many bones."

"What ignorance!" the huge fish cried. "Not all of us are boney. For instance, in my family . . ."

"I better change the subject," Yevseika thought and he politely asked the huge fish, "Have you ever been up there—above the water?"

"What for?" the fish sneered, "there's nothing to breathe with up there."

"But there are lots of tasty flies there," Yevseika said.

"FLIES!?" and the huge fish looked at Yevseika with unfriendly suspicion. "May I ask why you came down here?" he added, wondering whether Yevseika was a fisherman.

"I'm a goner!" Yevseika said to himself. "Now he will surely eat me up." And pretending to be without a worry in the world, he answered, "Oh, just to take a walk and cool off."

"Hmm," the huge fish didn't seem to believe him. "Are you sure you weren't drowned?" he asked.

"I should say not!" Yevseika said, pretending to be deeply offended. "Not at all! If I wanted to I could get up and . . ."

He tried to stand up but couldn't. He felt as if a very heavy quilt held him down. He couldn't even turn or move.

"I think I'm going to cry," Yevseika said to himself, but he remembered just in time that tears cannot be seen under water and decided that in that case it wasn't worth crying. Perhaps there was some other way to get out of his predicament.

By now Yevseika was surrounded by countless sea creatures. A porkfish, looking like a poorly drawn piglet, was sliding down his leg. "I'd like to have a closer acquaintance with you," he hissed.

A bubble fish hovered near his ear, pouting and puffing. "What a sight!—neither lobster, fish, nor shellfish—what a sight!" he mumbled.

"You just wait," Yevseika said to the bubble fish, "some day I'm going to be an aviator!"

A lobster crawled up to Yevseika's knees and said politely, "Allow me to ask—what time is it?"

A jellyfish swam by looking exactly like a wet handkerchief. A shrimp tickled Yevseika behind the ear. Baby lobsters got tangled in his hair and pulled at it hard as they tried to free themselves. "Ouch! Ouch!" Yevseika screamed, but not too loudly—trying hard to look carefree and pleasant, the way his father sometimes looked when he knew he deserved the scolding he was getting from his wife, Yevseika's mother.

There were even more fish around him now, swimming about with their eyes bulging—eyes that were dull and meaningless, like arithmetic. And they were muttering, "How can he live without whiskers, or shells, and with two tails? He resembles none of *us*. Well, it's true he might be a distant relative of the octopus."

"Is that so?" Yevseika nearly said out loud. And he whispered to himself, "I bet they don't even know that I got two 'A's' in Russian last year!"

And he tried to look as if he had heard not a word of what the fish had just said about him. He even tried to whistle an I-don't-care whistle, but that was impossible because water filled his mouth at once, like a stopper.

The huge talkative fish kept pestering him, "Do you like it down here?"

"No . . . I mean yes. I like it. But I like it at home, too!" And as soon as Yevseika said this he was sorry and worried. "Perhaps this will make the huge fish angry and he will start eating me," he thought. And to change the subject again, Yevseika said very loudly. "Let's play a game. Let's have some fun. Do you want to?"

The huge talkative fish liked this idea. He grinned, opening his round mouth and showing his pink gills. He also wagged his tail and cried in a shrill, shrill voice, "It's fun to play games—it's fun, it's fun!"

"Let's swim up," Yevseika said as if he had just thought of the idea.

"What for?" the huge fish wanted to know.

"Oh, come on! We can't swim down, can we?—we're already at the bottom. And up there, above the water, there are some flies."

"Flies! Do *you* love flies?"

Yevseika loved only his mother, his father, and ice cream, but he answered: "Yes . . ."

"Very well, let's swim up," the huge fish said, turning so that his head pointed upward. Yevseika immediately climbed on the huge fish's back.

And, holding on to his gills, he shouted: "I'm ready!"

"Let go, you little monster—you are pulling too hard at my gills," the huge fish yelled.

"That's nothing—don't worry!" Yevseika reassured him.

"What do you mean—don't worry? A real fish like me can't live without breathing!"

"For Pete's sake—you argue too much! If you want to play then let's play. . . ." Yevseika said, not caring any more that he sounded angry. "I knew that I could swim up from the bottom of

the sea," he said to no one in particular, very pleased with himself
and smiling up at the sun. The sun seemed to be winking at him
for some strange reason. And he thought to himself, "If I could
hold on until we come up a bit more than I could manage to get to
the top myself."

The huge fish stopped talking and swam upward gracefully like
a dancer, singing at the top of his piercing voice.

> The hungry trout
> Swam about
> Looking for his dinner.

> He caught a fly
> And soon did fry—
> The fisherman was the winner . . .

Small fish followed them chanting in chorus:

> Poor, poor trout!

Yevseika and the huge fish swam ever higher and faster. Suddenly Yevseika felt the air on his face.

"Oh!"

He looked around him. It was very bright. The sun's beams played over the water; green waves splashed against the shore humming their soft, unchanging tune. He saw his fishing rod being carried farther and farther out to sea by the outgoing waves.

Yevseika noticed that he was again sitting on the same rock from which he had fallen into the water. He felt his clothes—they were dry! Strange. . . . He rubbed his eyes and yawned.

SIMPLE IVANUSHKA

Once upon a time there lived a young man whom everyone called Simple Ivanushka. He was handsome and healthy, but somehow, no matter what he did or how he did it, the result was not what it should have been. In truth, everything he did was silly.

One day a farmer hired Ivanushka as a helper. The farmer and his wife decided to go to town the next day, and the farmer's wife said to Ivanushka: "You will remain here with the children, look after them, and feed them."

"Feed them what?" asked Ivanushka.

"Take some water, add some flour and some potatoes—be sure to cut them up—and make some soup."

And the farmer said to Ivanushka: "Watch the door. See to it that the children do not run off into the woods."

Then the farmer and his wife left.

Ivanushka soon woke the children, lifted them down from the shelves that served as their beds, and set them down on the floor. Then he sat down behind them, saying to himself: "I am now looking *after* them, just as my master told me to do."

The children sat for a while on the floor playing quietly. They soon felt hungry and asked Ivanushka for food. He got to work at once preparing their meal. He dragged into the hut a large bucket of water, poured a whole sack of flour into it and a bushel of potatoes, and mixed them all well with a large spade.

"And whom do I have to cut up?" he asked out loud.

The children heard him ask this question and were scared. "Maybe he is going to cut us up!" they thought, and they stole out of the hut on tiptoe.

When Ivanushka saw them disappear into the woods, he scratched his head—as every Russian peasant does when he is puzzled.

"How can I look after them now? I have to watch the door, too, so that it does not run away!" He then looked down at the bucket full of water, flour, and potatoes. "Cook yourself, soup," he said, "while I go to look after the children."

He took the wooden door off its hinges, lifted it onto his shoulder, and carried it with him into the woods.

Soon he met a Bear. The Bear was surprised at what he saw, and bellowed: "Look here young man—why are you bringing wood into the woods?"

And Ivanushka told him what had just happened.

The Bear sat back on his haunches and laughed and laughed. "What a fool you are, Ivanushka! I think I am going to eat you up!"

"You better eat up my master's children," Ivanushka said, "so that next time they will obey their father and mother and not run away into the woods."

At this, the Bear laughed even harder—he rolled on the ground in helpless laughter. "I have never seen such a stupid fellow! Come with me, Simple Ivan, I want to show you to my wife."

And he led Ivanushka to his den. As Ivanushka followed him, the door he was carrying over his shoulder kept catching on the branches of the pine trees.

"Why don't you get rid of that door!" the Bear said.

"No, I can't! I promised my master I'd watch it—so watch it I must!"

They soon arrived at the Bear's den, and the Bear said to his wife: "Look at what I brought you—this is Simple Ivanushka. He is a riot, a one-man circus!"

"Auntie, have you seen the children?" Ivanushka immediately asked the Mother Bear.

"Mine are at home—they are asleep."

"Show them to me," Ivanushka said, "maybe they are the ones I am looking for."

The Mother Bear showed him her three little cubs.

"No, these are not the ones. I had only two," he explained.

The Mother Bear realized also how simple Ivanushka was.

"But yours are human children!" she said to Ivanushka.

"Well, yes," he answered, "but they are all small creatures, it's kind of hard to tell which are whose."

"Isn't he odd!" the Mother Bear said. Turning to her husband, she suggested, "Mikhail Potapich, let us not eat him up; let him live with us and be our servant."

"Very well," her husband agreed. "Although he *is* a human, he is a harmless fellow."

The Mother Bear then handed Ivanushka a basket made out of linden bark. "Go and gather some wild strawberries," she said. "When my cubbies wake up I'll have a treat for them."

"All right—this I can do," said Ivanushka. "But you watch the door for me."

Simple Ivan went to the strawberry patch, filled the bark basket —and his tummy—with ripe strawberries, and then started back to the Bear's den, singing at the top of his voice.

> Oh, have you ever heard
> A singing ladybird?
>
> The chant of the ant?
>
> The words of the lizard—
> That four-legged wizard?

When he reached the Bear's den he shouted, "Here are your strawberries!"

The three cubs came running, and they growled, pushed one another, and turned somersaults as they devoured their favorite treat.

Ivanushka looked at the happy cubs. "It is too bad that I cannot be a bear," he said, "so that I, too, can have children!"

The Bear and his wife, hearing this, roared with laughter, "Oh my, it is impossible to live with one like him—we'd die laughing!"

"You know what?" Ivanushka said to the Bears. "You watch that door and I'll go look for the children. If they get lost my master will be furious."

The Mother Bear then said to her husband, "Misha, you go and help him find the children."

"Yes, I better help him," the Bear agreed. And he added, shaking his head, "He *is* a strange one!"

Ivanushka and the Bear went off together chatting like friends. They followed this path and that in search of the farmer's children.

"You know, Ivanushka," the Bear said in a friendly way, "you're quite stupid sometimes."

"And you?—are you clever?" Ivanushka asked the Bear.

"Who me?"

"Yes, you!"

"I don't know."

"I don't know either," Ivanushka said. "Are you *mean?*"

"No, why should I be mean?" the Bear replied.

"I think mean people are stupid. I am not mean either. That means that neither one of us is really stupid," Ivanushka concluded.

"My, how well you reason!" the Bear said with surprise.

Suddenly they saw two children fast asleep under a bush.

"Are these yours?" the Bear asked.

"I don't know. Let's find out. Mine are hungry."

"Are you hungry?" he asked them.

"We're starved!" they answered.

"Yes," Simple Ivanushka said, "that means they are mine. I'll take them back to the village and you, Uncle Bear, please go and fetch the door. I have to hurry and cook that soup."

"Very well," the Bear said. "I'll bring the door."

Ivanushka walked behind the children, looking *after* them as he had been told to do by his master. As he walked, he sang gaily:

> The beetle as is his habit,
> Catches each day a rabbit.
>
> The fox hidden behind some trees,
> Gazes, gapes, at what he sees.

Soon they came to the farmer's hut. The farmer and his wife had returned from town. They had found in the middle of the room the bucket with the flour and the potatoes, the door gone, and no children. They had sat down on a bench, and cried and cried.

"What are you crying about?" Simple Ivanushka asked them.

When they saw that their children were safe they cheered up and hugged them. Then they asked Ivanushka, pointing to the mess in the bucket: "What is this?"

"Soup!"

"Is this the way to make soup?"

"How do I know how to make soup?"

"And where is the door?"

"Someone will bring it right away." And looking out of the window, Ivanushka said, "There it comes."

The farmer and his wife also looked out of the window and saw the Bear walking in the middle of the road dragging the door, as frightened villagers scattered in all directions—some climbing onto roofs, others climbing up trees. The dogs were also scared, and they scurried behind fences and gates barking and snarling at the Bear. Only a red-feathered rooster bravely remained where he was. He stood in the middle of the road flapping his wings and crowing loudly and shrilly at the Bear:

> Cock-a-doodle-doo!
> I'll lock you in the zoo!

THE JUMP

LEO TOLSTOY

A ship was on its homeward journey. The weather was pleasant. All the passengers were on deck. A monkey was scampering over the ship amusing the passengers, everyone was laughing.

Suddenly the monkey ran over to a twelve-year-old boy, the son of the ship's captain, and snatched his cap from his head. The monkey put the cap on her head and quickly climbed up the mast. Again everyone laughed, and the boy didn't know whether to laugh or to get angry.

The monkey perched herself on the first crossbeam of the mast, took off the cap, and began to tear it with her teeth. She seemed to be teasing the boy. He shouted threats at her, but she continued to tear his cap, doing it even harder.

The crowd below began to laugh louder. The boy got more angry and went after the monkey on the mast. He quickly climbed the rope to the first crossbeam, but the monkey climbed higher even more rapidly. They boy kept after her. Within a moment they were both at the top of the mast. There the monkey, holding on by one foot to a rope, stretched herself full length and hung the cap on the end of the last crossbeam. Then she climbed to the very tip of the mast and sat there mocking the boy.

From the mast to the end of the highest crossbeam on which the cap now hung was a distance of about six feet. To reach the cap the boy had to let go of the rope and the mast.

But, forgetting all danger, he stepped onto the crossbeam.

Everyone on deck was watching with interest what the boy and the monkey were up to. But when they saw that the boy had let go of the rope and stepped onto the crossbeam, they froze with terror.

If he slipped he would kill himself falling to the deck. Everyone looked on in silence waiting to see what would happen next.

Suddenly someone below cried in panic. The boy heard the cry, looked down, and began to teeter. Just then the captain of the ship, the boy's father, came out of his cabin onto the deck. He was carrying a rifle to shoot seagulls. When he saw his son on the uppermost crossbeam, he at once aimed the rifle at him and shouted: "Jump into the water! Or I'll shoot!" The boy wavered. "Jump! One, two . . ." As soon as his father cried "three," the boy jumped.

He fell like a rock into the water. Instantly several seamen jumped from the ship into the sea. Within forty seconds the boy came to the surface. The seamen grabbed him and pulled him up to the deck. In a few moments water began to come from his mouth and nose and he began to breathe.

When the captain saw this he suddenly uttered a cry and ran into his cabin before anyone could see that he was weeping.

POOR PEOPLE

LEO TOLSTOY

In a small fisherman's cabin, near the edge of the sea, Zhanna, a fisherman's wife, sat by the fire mending an old sail. It was dark and cold outside. The wind was howling. There was a storm over the sea. But in the cabin it was warm and cozy. The earthen floor had been swept clean and a comforting fire was spluttering and hissing softly in the fireplace. Five young children were asleep on a wide bed in the corner.

Zhanna's husband had put out to sea early that morning and

had not yet returned. She kept listening to the drone of the waves and the fury of the wind. She was worried.

The old wooden clock struck ten—then eleven, and still he did not return. Zhanna thought of her fisherman husband—how he didn't spare himself and would stay out fishing in cold weather and in storms. She, too, worked from morning till night. But they never had enough to eat. The childern didn't have shoes and went about barefoot both in winter and in summer. Zhanna was grateful though that they were strong and healthy. Then she thought of her husband again and she said to herself, "Where is he now? May the Lord watch over him!"

It was too early to go to bed. She put down her sewing, wrapped herself in a heavy shawl, lit a lantern, and went outside to see if the sea was calming down, whether the beacon was still burning in the lighthouse, and if she could see her husband's boat coming in. But she saw nothing in the black darkness.

Zhanna remembered that she had intended to visit her neighbor, the widow, who was very poor and ill and had two small children to care for. Life had been very hard for this woman. "I'll go and stay with her for a while," Zhanna thought.

She approached her neighbor's hut and knocked. There was no answer. Zhanna pushed the door open and entered. It was damp, cold, and dark inside. She raised the lantern to see where the sick woman was. She saw her lying on a small bed that stood right across from the door. The woman was lying very quietly, her head was tilted way back. She did not move at all. Her face was as white as the pillow, and her arm hung limply from the side of the bed.

And on the same bed, near the dead mother, two little children were sleeping. They were curly haired and chubby. They had been covered carefully with the mother's threadbare shawl and with her dress. Evidently the dying woman had tried to care for her young ones to the very last moment of her ebbing life. The children were breathing easily and sleeping peacefully.

Zhanna wrapped the children in her shawl and took them home

with her. She put the sleeping orphans near her own children and drew the curtain across the bed.

She was pale and shaken. "What will her husband say? After all, they had five children of their own and a lot of care they were. Why did she bring the others!" Zhanna sat there, at the bed, for a long time, worrying.

It finally stopped raining and it was getting light outside, but the wind continued to howl. Suddenly the door to the cabin was opened, a stream of cold sea air blew into the room and a tall dark-skinned man entered.

"It's me, Zhanna," her husband said.

"Oh, it's you! Thank God!" Zhanna said but she didn't dare look him in the face.

"The weather was awful," he continued. "I hardly caught anything and the nets got torn. I was lucky to get back alive. And what did you do while I was away?"

"I? . . ." she began, and grew paler. "I sat here sewing. It was scarey. I worried about you."

They were silent for a while.

"Our neighbor, the widow, died! Death was not easy for her. How her heart must have ached for her two little ones. . . ."

Zhanna said no more. Her husband frowned. Then his face grew thoughtful and he looked troubled. After a while he said:

"We'll have to take them in. We'll manage to survive—somehow. Hurry and get them."

But Zhanna did not move.

"Why don't you go? Don't you want to take them in? What's wrong with you, Zhanna?"

"Here they are. I've already brought them," Zhanna said, parting the bed curtain.

THE BURGLAR

KONSTANTIN PAUSTOVSKY

We were becoming desperate. We didn't know how to catch that thieving tomcat. He burglarized us every night, and he hid himself during the day so cleverly that none of us could find him. This tomcat had no conscience. He was a vagabond, a bandit. We called him the Burglar.

He would steal anything: fish, meat, cream, and bread. One time he even got after a jar of worms that was carefully put away in the shed—thinking, no doubt, that it contained some tasty tidbit for him. He overturned and broke it. He didn't eat the worms, but the chickens came running and swallowed every one of them. Our plans for fishing were ruined for the day.

After that, we spent nearly a month trying to locate the red-furred thief. Some of the village boys tried to help. One day they came to us with the news that they had seen the cat at dawn, scampering through the orchards, carrying in his mouth several perch fish. We rushed down to the cellar and, sure enough, ten fat perch were missing.

This was not a petty theft—this was robbery, and in broad daylight!

We vowed to catch that tom this time and bring him to justice for his banditry.

We caught him that very evening. He had snatched a large piece of sausage from the table and climbed into a tree with it.

We began to shake the tree. The cat dropped the sausage, and it fell on Ruvim's head. The crook looked down at us with wild eyes and hissed threateningly. But nothing could save him. With a dreadful howl he jumped from the tree, landed on the ground, and, taking off like a kicked football, hid way under the house.

It was a small house in the corner of a neglected garden. It was cluttered outside and inside with fishing rods, hunting equipment, and sacks of fruit. We used it only for spending the night. The days, from dawn till dark, we spent on the shores of the countless lakes, fishing. We cooked our catch outdoors on a fire that we built right at the edge of the water. To get to the lakes, we had to tramp down paths through tall, fragrant grass and tall-stemmed wild flowers. The flowers brushed against us as we passed, leaving us covered with yellow flower dust. We would return in the evening tired from a day in the hot sun, carrying the remainder of our catch, to hear new stories about the robber.

But this evening we caught him. He had squeezed himself into a narrow hole under the house. We threw an old fishing net over the hole and waited. But the cat did not come out. He sat there, howling from time to time.

An hour passed, two, three. . . . It was time to go to bed, but the cat kept howling and whining under the house, and it got on our nerves.

We decided to summon Lenka, the son of the village shoemaker. Lenka was famous for his fearlessness and quickness. We assigned to him the task of dragging the cat out from under the house.

Lenka tied a fish to a long piece of rope and threw it into the hole where the cat was hiding. The cat grabbed the fish in his teeth. Lenka pulled at the rope. The cat held on to the fish. Lenka kept pulling the rope with the cat and the fish at the end of it. Soon the thief appeared, and Lenka grabbed him and held on to him by the scruff of his neck.

For the first time we had a good look at the animal. He looked like a genuine tomcat—the homeless and uncared-for variety.

Ruvim asked thoughtfully. "What do we do with him now?"

"Let's give him a good beating," I said.

"It won't do any good," Lenka said tersely. "He's had this kind of character from childhood. Try instead to feed him properly, and every day.

The cat glared at us, waiting for his fate to be decided.

We followed Lenka's advice, dragged the cat into the larder, and gave him a sumptuous supper—fried pork, jellied perch, and cheese pancakes with sour cream.

He ate for a whole hour. Then he came out of the larder and sat down on the house steps. Soon he began to wash himself while watching us with his suspicious and impudent eyes.

After a thorough cleansing, he sneezed several times and began to rub the sides of his head against the wooden step—again and again. This was supposed to express his satisfaction. We thought he would rub his fur right off his head. But he finally stopped, turned on his back, caught his tail between his teeth, chewed on it for a while, spit, stretched out, and fell asleep peacefully, snoring lightly.

From that day the red tomcat lived with us and stopped stealing.

One morning he even performed a noble and unexpected act. A few of our hens got up on the table in the garden and began to peck at some left-over food on the plates. The tomcat came up stealthily and with a frightening battle cry jumped on the table. With a wail of despair the hens took flight with a long-legged rooster at the head of the retreating squad. The cat pursued the rooster on three legs, striking at him with the fourth. Feathers and dust flew in all directions.

From that day the hens were careful not to steal. Whenever they saw the cat, they scurried under the house. And the cat walked about like a master and a watchman. He would rub his head against our legs, asking for gratitude, as he left locks of his red fur on our trousers.

We changed his name from "Burglar" to "Cop," although my friend Ruvim maintained that this was not a nice thing to do. We were sure, however, that the police would not mind.

THE THREE FAT MEN

YURI OLESHA

Outside Russia, Yuri Olesha (1899–1960) is known mainly for his novels, short stories, and plays for adults.

His fantasy for children, *The Three Fat Men,* has won for him widespread and lasting popularity among the Soviet young. The book has run to thirty editions, has been made into a film, and has become a stage classic, performed in most of the 47 children's theaters in the Soviet Union.

This legend has many moods, fantastic characters and situations, but the core of its story is as true as history.

We have space, unfortunately, only for Part I of the book, but a good deal happens on every page.

It would be unkind to give away the plot. Perhaps some enterprising publisher will make the whole of *The Three Fat Men* available to young English-speaking readers. Here are the first three episodes.

TIBUL

Doctor Gaspar Arnery Has a Busy Day

The time of magicians has passed. And there probably never were any to begin with. They must have been made up to amuse very little children. But there did exist very clever jugglers who could fool the crowd watching them, and that is why people believed they were wizards and magicians.

Once upon a time, there was a doctor whose name was Gaspar Arnery. A simple-minded person, or an idler at a country fair, or a dull student might have taken him for a magician; for the doctor could do wonderful and unusual things that seemed just like magic.

Doctor Gaspary Arnery was a scientist. He had studied a hundred different sciences, and there was not another person in all the land as wise and learned as he. Everyone knew how wise he was—the miller,

207

the soldiers, all the ladies, and even the Palace ministers. This is the
song the school boys sang about him:

Doctor Gaspar Arnery—
What a clever man is he!
He can trap the slyest fox,
He can crack the hardest rocks,
He can fly from here to Mars,
He can reach the farthest stars!

One lovely day in June, Doctor Gaspar Arnery decided to set off on a
long walk to gather some grasses and beetles for his collection. He was
not young any more and was therefore afraid of the wind and the rain.
Whenever he left the house he would tie a warm scraf around his neck,
put on a pair of glasses to keep the dust out of his eyes, and take along
his walking stick to lean on and keep him from stumbling. When he
started out he always took a lot of trouble to have everything just so.

It was a beautiful day. The sun did nothing but shine, the grass was so
green it made your mouth water just to look at it, the air was full of
dandelion fuzz, birds chirped, and there was a sweet breeze.

"Ah, how lovely," said the doctor. "But I'd better take my cape, just
in case. Summer days are so changeable. It might begin to rain."

When he had made sure that everything was in order at home, he
wiped his spectacles clean, picked up his green leather bag and set off.

The best places for gathering grasses and beetles were out in the
country beyond the town, near the Palace of the Three Fat Men. This
was where the doctor usually went. The Palace of the Three Fat Men
stood in the middle of a huge park. The park was surrounded by deep
moats. There were black iron bridges across them. And the bridges
were guarded by Palace Guards in black oilskin hats with yellow feathers. All around the park, as far as the eye could see, were meadows full
of flowers, small groves of trees, and ponds. It was a wonderful place for
walks. The most unusual kinds of grasses grew there, the prettiest
beetles buzzed there, and the birds always sang there most sweetly.

"It's too far to walk all the way to the Palace park," the doctor
thought. "I'll only go to the end of town and then I'll take a cab."

There was a big crowd in the square near the town gates.

"Is it Sunday today?" the doctor wondered. "No, I don't think so. It's
Tuesday."

He came a little closer.

The entire square was full of people. There were workers in gray jackets with green cuffs, sailors with weather-beaten faces, rich merchants in colored vests and their wives in great pink shirts; there were vendors with pitchers, trays, cans of ice cream, and braziers with roasted chestnuts; there were skinny street performers dressed in green, yellow and other brightly colored costumes, looking like patchwork quilts; there were very little boys pulling shaggy dogs by the tails.

Everyone was pushing toward the town gates. The gates were as tall as a house and were made out of iron. They were now shut tight.

"Why are the gates shut?" the doctor wondered.

The crowd was noisy, people were shouting and arguing, but it was impossible to understand what it was all about. The doctor went over to a young woman holding a big gray cat.

"Would you kindly tell me what's going on?" he asked. "Why are there so many people here? Why is everyone so angry? And why are the town gates closed?"

"The Guards won't let anyone out."

"Why not?"

"So they won't be able to help those who have left and are now on their way to the Palace of the Three Fat Men."

"I'm sorry, Miss, but I don't understand what you mean."

"My goodness! Don't you know that Prospero the Gunsmith and Tibul the Acrobat have led the people to storm the Palace of the Three Fat Men?"

"Prospero the Gunsmith?"

"Yes. There are Guards on the other side of the gates. No one is allowed to leave the town. And the Palace Guards will kill off everyone who has joined with Prospero."

Just then they heard several faint shots. The crowd roared.

"I seem to have missed a very important event," the doctor thought. "That's because I stayed at home this past month, working day and night, and my door was locked. I simply had no idea of what was going on."

In the distance a cannon boomed several times. The sound bounced like a ball and rolled along on the wind. Doctor Gaspar was not the only one to get frightened and stumble backward. The crowd scattered. Children began to cry. Pigeons flew up flapping their wings loudly, and the dogs began to howl.

The cannon boomed again and again. Then the crowd began to push forward toward the gates, shouting:

"Prospero! Prospero!"

"Down with the Three Fat Men!"

Doctor Gaspar didn't know what to do. He was well known, and now many people recognized him. Some rushed toward him, as if he could shield them. But the doctor himself was close to tears.

"What's going on out there? How can we find out? Maybe the people are winning, but then again maybe they've all been killed?"

A dozen people ran toward the corner of the square where three narrow streets met. An old house with a high tower stood there. The doctor decided to climb up to the tower, too. There was a laundry on the street level of the house and a winding staircase led up to the tower from the dark room inside. Some light came through the tiny windows but it was hardly enough to see by. Everyone climbed slowly and with difficulty, because the stairs were rickety and there was no railing. Imagine how hard it was for Doctor Gaspar to reach the top! When he had climbed only twenty steps, the others heard him shout in the darkness.

"Help! My heart's bursting! And I've lost the heel of my shoe!"

As for his cape, the good doctor had lost it back on the square, after the cannon had boomed for the tenth time.

There was a platform at the top of the tower with a stone railing all around it. Here one could see for at least thirty miles away. But there was no time to admire the landscape, though it was really pretty. Everyone was looking toward the scene of battle.

"I have a pair of binoculars. I always take along a pair of binoculars with eight lenses," Doctor Gaspar said. "Here, have a look," he added and unhooked the strap.

The binoculars were passed around.

Doctor Gaspar saw a great many people in the fields. They were running toward the town. They were fleeing. From afar they looked like colored flags. Palace Guards on horseback were pursuing them.

The doctor thought it all looked like a picture in a magic lantern. The sun was shining brightly, the grass glittered, cannon balls burst like puffs of cotton. The powder flames shot up just as if someone were catching sunbeams in a mirror. The horses pranced, reared up, and spun around. A white smoke veiled the park and the Palace of the Three Fat Men.

The running men were getting closer and closer. Many of them fell on

210

the way. From the top of the tower they looked like colored flags falling on the grass.

A cannon ball whizzed over the square.

Someone dropped the binoculars.

The cannon ball burst, and everyone standing on the platform at the top of the tower rushed back down the stairs.

The locksmith caught his leather apron on a hook. He turned around, saw something terrible, and shouted at the top of his voice:

"Run for your lives! They've captured Prospero the Gunsmith! They'll be inside the gates any minute!"

There was a mad scramble in the square.

The crowd rushed away from the gates and ran down the little streets leading off the square. The noise of the shooting was deafening.

Doctor Gaspar and two other men stopped on the third floor landing. They looked through the narrow window built into the thick wall. There was just room for one of them to have a good look. The other two could only get a peep over his head. Doctor Gaspar was one of the two who could only peep. But even that was more than enough to see the horrible things that were going on.

The great iron gates flew open. About three hundred people rushed through them. These were workers in gray cloth jackets with green cuffs. Many of them fell to the ground bleeding.

The Guards galloped right over them, swinging their swords and shooting. The yellow feathers in their shiny hats fluttered in the wind. The horses opened their foaming red mouths and rolled their eyes.

"Look! Look! There's Prospero!" the doctor cried.

They were dragging him along at the end of a rope. He stumbled, fell, and rose again. His red hair was matted with blood, and there was a big noose tied around his neck.

"Prospero has been captured!" the doctor cried again.

Just then a cannon ball hit the laundry. The tower leaned, swayed, steadied for a moment, and then came crashing to the ground.

The doctor tumbled downstairs, losing his other heel, his walking stick, his bag, and his spectacles on the way.

Ten Scaffolds

It was a lucky fall. Doctor Gaspar did not crack his head, nor break his bones. But no matter how luckily one may fall from a toppling tower, it's far from pleasant, especially if you are not young—or, rather, are old, as Doctor Gaspar Arnery was. The good doctor fainted from fright.

When he came to, it was evening. He looked about.

"Oh, dear! My spectacles are broken. When I look around without them, I see things just as badly as someone with good eyes when he puts on spectacles. It's most distressing."

Then he began to grumble about his lost heels.

"I'm short enough as it is, and now I'll be at least an inch shorter. Perhaps even two inches shorter, since I lost both heels. No, I guess I'll be only one inch shorter after all."

He was lying on top of a pile of broken bricks. The tower had crumbled, all but a narrow piece of wall that stuck up out of the ground like a bone. He could hear the sound of music coming from afar. It was a lively waltz, carried on the wind. The doctor raised his head. Broken black beams hung above him. Stars were shining in the blue-green evening sky.

"I wonder where the music's coming from?"

The doctor was beginning to feel chilly without his cape. There was not a sound to be heard in the square. He groaned as he picked himself up from among the fallen stones. Then he stumbled on someone's boot. The locksmith was lying across a beam, gazing up at the sky. The doctor shook him. But the locksmith did not move. He was dead.

He left the square. There were people lying in the road. The doctor bent over each one and saw the stars reflected in their eyes. He touched their foreheads. They were dead.

"What a misfortune!" he whispered. "That means the people have been beaten. What will become of us?"

Half an hour later he reached a crowded, brightly lit street. He was very tired. He was hungry and thirsty, too. Here the town looked as it always did.

The doctor stood at a crossing, resting from his long walk. "How strange," he thought. "There are colored lights shining in the windows, carriages roll by, glass doors open and shut. There are Chinese lanterns swinging over the dark waters. It's just as if it were yesterday here. Don't they know what happened this morning? Didn't they hear the shooting and the cries of the wounded? Don't they know that the people's leader, Prospero the Gunsmith, has been captured? But perhaps nothing really happened, perhaps it was all a bad dream?"

"He was dragged through the town with a rope around his neck. Poor man!" he heard someone say.

"They've put him in an iron cage. And the cage is in the Palace of the Three Fat Men," said a fat coachman in a light blue top hat with a ribbon on it.

Just then a fine lady and a little girl came up to buy some roses from a street flower vendor.

"Whom have they put in a cage?" the fine lady asked.

"Prospero the Gunsmith. The Guards captured him."

"Thank goodness!" she said.

Her daughter began to cry.

"Why are you crying, silly?" the fine lady said. "Are you sorry for the gunsmith? You shouldn't be. He's a very bad man. Now, just look at these lovely roses."

There, in bowls that were full of water and leaves, the large roses floated like swans.

"Take these three. And stop crying. They're all rebels. If you don't put them in iron cages, they'll take away our houses and fine clothes and our roses."

A boy ran by. First he pulled at the lady's embroidered cape, then he tugged at the girl's pigtail.

"Hey, Countess!" he shouted. "Prospero the Gunsmith is locked up in a cage, but Tibul the Acrobat is free!"

"You dreadful boy!"

The lady stamped her foot and dropped her bag. The flower girls laughed. A fat coachman lost no time in asking the fine lady if she would care to get in his carriage and drive away.

The fine lady and her daughter drove off.

"Hey, you!" one of the flower girls shouted to the boy. "Come back here and tell us what you know."

Two drivers climbed down from their boxes. Shuffling forward in their long coats with five small capes attached to the collars, they came up to the flower girls.

"That's some whip! It sure is a beauty!" the boy thought as he looked at the coachman's long whip. He would have loved to have one like it, but he knew he never would.

"What did you say?" the coachman asked in a deep voice. "Did you say Tibul the Acrobat is free?"

"So I heard. I was down at the docks. . . ."

"Didn't the Guards kill him?" the other coachman asked in an equally deep voice.

"No, they didn't. Pretty Miss, will you give me a rose?"

"Wait, silly! Tell us what happened."

"Well, it was like this. At first they thought Tibul had been killed. So they looked for him among the dead, but couldn't find him."

"Perhaps they tossed him in the river?" one of the coachmen said.

At that point a beggar joined them.

"Who was tossed into the river?" he asked. "Tibul the Acrobat isn't a kitten to be tossed into the river! He's alive! He escaped!"

"Tibul is alive!" the flower girls cried joyfully.

214

The boy stole a rose from one of the bowls and dashed off. Several drops from the wet flower landed on the doctor. He wiped them off his face. They were as bitter as tears. Then he came closer to hear what else the beggar had to say.

But something happened then that stopped the conversation. A strange procession was coming down the street. At the head of it were two men on horseback carrying lighted torches, which flowed in the wind like fiery beards. Rolling slowly behind them was a black carriage with a coat of arms painted on the door.

Behind the carriage came the carpenters. There were a hundred carpenters in all.

Their sleeves were rolled up, they were ready for work. They wore aprons and carried their saws, planes, and tool boxes. Guards rode along both sides of the procession. They had to keep reining in their horses, for the animals wanted to gallop off.

"What's going on? What's all this about?" people in the street asked each other anxiously.

Sitting in the black carriage with the coat of arms on the door was an official of the Council of the Three Fat Men. The flower girls were frightened. They pressed their hands to their cheeks as they looked at his head. It could be seen through the carriage window. The street was brightly lit. The black-wigged head bobbed up ond down. It looked as if a big bird was inside the carriage.

"Move along! Get moving!" the Guards shouted.

"Where are the carpenters going?" a little flower girl asked the Captain of the Guards.

"The carpenters are going to build scaffolds! Now do you understand? The carpenters are going to build ten scaffolds!" he shouted right in her face and so fiercely that her hair blew in all directions.

"Oh!"

The flower girl dropped her bowl. The water with the floating roses poured out on the pavement.

"They're going to build scaffolds!" the doctor repeated in terror.

"Yes, scaffolds!" the Guard shouted, turning back and baring his teeth. "Scaffolds for all the rebels! They'll all have their heads chopped off! All who dare rise up against the Three Fat Men!"

The doctor felt dizzy. He thought he might faint.

"It's been too much for one day," he thought. "Besides, I'm awfully hungry and tired. I'd better hurry back home."

Yes, it was about time the doctor got some rest. He was so overcome by all that had happened, by all he had seen and heard, that he didn't even think that his fall together with the tower earlier in the day was very unusual. He was not even bothered by the loss of his hat, cape, walking stick, and the heels of his shoes. Worst of all, though, was that he had lost his spectacles. So he hired a cab and headed for home.

Star Square

As the doctor drove along the broad paved streets, a chain of street lights rushed past the carriage. The lights were like glass balls. The carriage rolled along embankments, past high stone walls on which bronze lions holding shields in their paws stuck out their long tongues. Below, the water flowed sluggishly, black and shiny as tar. The town was reflected upside down in the water; it was trying to float away, but it couldn't get loose and melted in soft golden ripples instead. He rode over bridges that were curved like arches. From below or from the opposite bank they looked like cats arching their iron backs before springing. There were sentries at the approach to every bridge. They sat around on their drums, smoking their pipes, playing cards and yawning as they stared at the stars. Doctor Gaspar looked about and listened as he drove on.

From the streets, from the houses, from the open tavern windows and from behind the park fences he could hear snatches of a song.

> *They've caught the horrid Prospero*
> *And caged him like an ape,*
> *With an iron collar round his neck—*
> *To see he won't escape!*

A drunken fop was singing it, too. The fop's aunt had just died. She had a lot of money and not a single other relative. The fop had just inherited all his aunt's money. That is why he was angry at the people for rising up against the rule of the Three Fat Men.

There was a big act on at the animal show. Three fat and hairy monkeys on a wooden stage were supposed to be the Three Fat Men. A terrier was playing the mandolin. A clown dressed in a bright red suit with a golden sun on his back and a golden star on his stomach was reciting a poem to the music.

These Three Fat Men—
  so fat are they,
They drink and gobble
  night and day.
The only pastime that
  they know
Is to watch their bellies
  grow.
Beware, fat pigs, the time
  will come
When you will pay for
  what you've done.

"The time will come!" bearded parrots screeched from all sides.

There was a terrible din. The animals in the cages began to bark, growl, chatter, and whistle.

The monkeys dashed to and fro on the stage. It was hard to tell their arms from their legs. Finally, they jumped down, scrambling over the heads and shoulders of the screeching audience. The fattest men there were making the most noise. Their faces red with anger, they threw their hats and canes at the clown. A fat lady shook her umbrella at him and caught another fat lady's hat with it.

"Oh! Ah!" the other fat lady screamed, and she waved her arms because her wig had come off together with her hat.

One of the monkeys clapped its hand on the lady's bald head as it rushed by. She fainted dead away.

"Ha-ha-ha!"

"Ha-ha-ha!" the rest of the crowd laughed. These people were much thinner and were more shabbily dressed.

"Bravo! Bravo!"

"Get 'em!"

"Down with the Three Fat Men!"

"Long live Prospero! Long live Tibul! Long live the people!"

Just then someone shouted still louder:

"Fire! The town's on fire!"

Everyone made a dash for the doors, pushing and shoving and turning over the benches. The animal keepers were trying to catch the monkeys.

The driver of the doctor's carriage turned around, pointing with his whip:

"The Guards are setting fire to the artisans' quarters," he said. "They want to find Tibul the Acrobat."

The pink glow of fire was spreading over the town and lighting up the dark houses.

When the doctor's carriage reached the main square, which was called Star Square, it could go no farther, for there were many other carriages, men on horseback, and people crowding them from all sides.

"What's going on here?" the doctor asked.

But no one answered, because they were all busy craning their necks, trying to see what was going on in the square. The doctor's driver stood up on his box and also looked in that direction.

This is how Star Square got its name: It was surrounded by tall houses and covered with a glass top, somewhat like a huge circus. In the middle of the glass top, so high that it took your breath away, was the largest lamp in the world. It was a tremendous round glass ball hung on heavy cables with an iron band around it that made it look like the planet Saturn. The light it cast was so beautiful and so unlike anything else in the world that people had named the wonderful lamp "Star." And that is how the square came to be known as Star Square.

No other light was needed in the square, nor in the houses, nor in any of the nearby streets. The Star lit every nook and cranny in every house, and the people who lived there never used lamps or candles.

The driver was looking over the carriages and over the tops of the coachmen's hats.

"What can you see? What's going on there?" the doctor asked anxiously, peering over his driver's back. But Doctor Gaspar was short and couldn't see a thing, especially since he was nearsighted and had lost his spectacles.

The driver told him all he saw. And this is what he saw.

There was great excitement in the square. People were running to and fro across the round space. It seemed as if the whole place were spinning like a merry-go-round. People rushed about to get a better view of what was happening above.

The great lamp was as bright as the sun. It blinded them. People threw back their heads and shielded their eyes with their hands.

"There he is! There he is!" they cried.

"There! Over there!"

"Where? Where?"

"Higher up!"

"Tibul! Tibul!"

Hundreds of fingers pointed to the left. They were pointing to a very ordinary-looking house. All the windows on all six floors of the house had been thrown wide open. Heads stuck out of every window. The heads looked very colorful; some had on tasseled nightcaps, some had on pink bonnets with red curls sticking out, some had on kerchiefs. Higher up, in the rooms where poor young poets, artists, and actors lived, there were happy-looking beardless faces lost in clouds of tobacco smoke and lovely young women whose golden hair lay like a cloud on their shoulders. The house, with its open windows and brightly-colored heads poking out, was just like a large cage of goldfinches. The owners of all these heads were trying to see something very important that was happening on the roof. This was just as impossible as trying to see your own ears without a mirror. These people who wanted to see the roof of their own house used the crowd below as a mirror. Those on the ground could see everything; they were shouting and waving their arms. Some were overjoyed, others were terribly angry.

A tiny figure was moving along the roof. It was slowly and carefully climbing down the steep incline. The iron roofing clattered under its feet.

The little figure waved its cape for balance, just as a tightrope-walker in the circus uses a Chinese umbrella.

It was Tibul the Acrobat.

The people shouted:

"Bravo, Tibul! Bravo, Tibul!"

"Hang on! Remember how you walked a rope at the fair!"

"He won't fall down! He's the best acrobat in the land!"

"This isn't the first time we've seen him walk up and down a rope."

"Bravo, Tibul!"

"Run! Save yourself! Free Prospero!"

Others were angry. They shook their fists and bellowed:

"You won't escape, you stupid clown!"

"Faker!"

"Rebel! They'll shoot you like a hare!"

"Watch out! We'll pull you off that roof and drag you to the scaffold! Ten scaffolds will be ready tomorrow!"

Tibul continued his dangerous journey.

"Where did he come from?" the people wondered. "How did he get to the square? How did he get to the roof?"

"He escaped from the Guards," others said. "He escaped and disappeared. Then he was seen in different parts of the town, he climbed from roof to roof. He's as quick as a cat. And his skill comes in handy. That's why he's so famous."

Guards appeared in the square. People were now running to the side streets to get a better view. Tibul stepped over the railing and stood at the very edge of the roof. He stretched out his arm. His green cape was wound around it and fluttered like a flag.

People were used to seeing him with this cape and dressed in yellow and black harlequin tights at the fairs and marketplaces. Now, high up under the glass top, his small, thin body looked like a wasp crawling up the wall of a house. Every time the cape flapped in the wind, it seemed as if the wasp were opening its shiny green wings.

"I hope you fall and break your neck! They'll shoot you, wait and see!" shouted the drunken fop who had inherited a fortune from his aunt.

The Guards took up their positions. Their officer ran up and down scowling. He had a large gun. His spurs were as long as runners.

Suddenly it became very quiet. The doctor clapped his hand to his heart, for it was beginning to jump like an egg in boiling water.

Tibul stopped for a second at the edge of the roof. He had to get to the other side of the square; from there he could escape to the workers' quarter.

The officer stood in the center of the square in a bed of blue and yellow flowers. Beside him was a pool and a fountain spouting from a round stone bowl.

"Wait!" the officer said to the soldiers. "I'll shoot him down myself. I'm the best shot in the regiment. I'll show you how it's done. Watch!"

Nine steel cables stretched from the nine houses surrounding the square to the center of the glass top. They supported the Star. It was just as if nine long black rays had spread over the square from the Star's wonderful flame.

Who knows what Tibul was thinking then? He was probably saying to himself: "I'll cross over the square on this wire as I walked a rope at the fair. I won't fall. This cable is attached to the lamp. The other one goes from the lamp to the house on the other side. If I cross both cables, I'll reach the other side—and safety."

The officer raised his gun and took aim. Tibul walked along the edge of the roof to where the cable began, stepped on to it, and began moving along it toward the lamp.

The crowd gasped.

He would move very slowly, then suddenly, he would take several quick steps, nearly running, but placing his feet carefully and balancing with his outstretched arms. It looked as if he would fall at any minute.

His shadow now appeared on the wall. The closer he got to the lamp, the bigger and paler his shadow became, the lower it slid down the wall.

It was a long drop to the ground.

When he was halfway to the lamp, the officer's voice boomed out.

"I'm going to shoot! He'll fall right into the pool. One! Two! Three!"

There was a loud bang.

Tibul continued along the cable, but for some strange reason it was the officer who toppled into the pool.

He had been shot.

One of the Guards held a smoking pistol. He had just killed the officer.

"Long live the people!" the other Guards shouted.

"Long live the Three Fat Men!" their enemies shouted and began shooting at Tibul from all sides.

He was now only two steps from the lamp. Tibul raised his cape to keep the blinding light from his eyes. Bullets whizzed past him. The crowd below shouted with joy.

Bang! Bang!

"Missed him!"

"Hooray! They missed!"

Tibul climbed on to the iron ring of the lamp.

"Just wait!" his enemies threatened. "He wants to cross to the other side. We'll get him when he goes down the other cable."

Suddenly something quite unexpected happened. Tibul's figure, which seemed black against the bright light, crouched on the iron ring and turned a lever. Something clicked, clanged—and the lamp went out! This took everyone by surprise. The square became as still and as dark as the inside of a trunk.

The next moment something clanged very high up. A light patch appeared in the dark top. Everyone saw a little bit of sky with two twinkling stars. Then a small black figure climbed through the patch, and there was the sound of running feet across the glass top.

Tibul the Acrobat had escaped.

The horses had been frightened by all the shooting and the sudden darkness. The doctor's carriage nearly turned over. The driver reined in the horses and took another road.

Thus, after a most unusual day and a most unusual evening, Doctor Gaspar Arnery finally returned home.

The night was ending. Doctor Gaspar made ready for bed.

Among the hundred different sciences he had studied was History. The doctor had a large leather-bound book. In it he wrote down his thoughts about important events.

"One must always keep things in good order," said the doctor raising his finger. And so, even though he was very tired, he pulled a chair over to the table, opened his leather-bound book and began to write.

"The workers, the miners, the sailors, all the poor working people of the town, rose up against the rule of the Three Fat Men. The Guards won the battle. Prospero the Gunsmith has been captured, but Tibul the Acrobat escaped. A Guard shot his officer on Star Square. That means all the soldiers will soon refuse to fight against the people and protect the Three Fat Men. But I am worried about Tibul."

The doctor heard a scraping noise behind his back. He turned around and faced the fireplace. A tall man in a green cape had just climbed down the chimney and stepped into the room. It was Tibul the Acrobat.

AFTER SCHOOL

V. ZHELEZNIKOV

This story was published in *Murzilka,* a children's magazine which has existed for the past hundred years. It is published for children from six to ten years of age and has a circulation of 1,000,000 copies. A number of the best children's writers contribute to it regularly. For many years the celebrated young children's poets, Samuel Marshak and Agnya Barto, were its editors. It is a contemporary story.

When school was dismissed, I went to the classroom for first graders. I would not have gone there but our neighbor had asked me to look after her little son when school was over. After all, it was the first of September and the first day of school.

I ran into the classroom and found it empty. Everyone had already left. I was about to turn around and go on my way when I noticed someone sitting in the last row. Very little of her could be seen above her desk.

It was a little girl—and not at all the little boy for whom I had come. As is the custom for girl first graders on the first day of school, she wore a white apron and white bows in her hair—big ones.

It was strange for her to be sitting there alone. All the other children had gone home and were probably already eating soup or jello while they were telling their parents and other members of the family circle about the wonders of school. But this one sat there waiting for heaven knew what.

"Little girl," I said, "why don't you go home?"

No answer.

"Have you lost something?"

She continued her silence and sat there like a stone statue.

I didn't know what to do. I tried to think of a way to make this "stone statue" move. I went to the blackboard and began to draw.

I drew a first-grade girl who had come home from school and was having her dinner. Then I drew a mommie, a daddy, and two grand-mas. The girl was eating with relish, both cheeks bulging with some delicious food, while the others were looking at her, straight into her mouth. It turned out to be an amusing picture.

"You and I," I said, "are hungry. Isn't it time for us, too, to go home?"

"No," she replied. "I'll not go home!"

"I suppose you're going to sleep here all night?"

"I don't know."

Her voice was sad and low, more like a mosquito buzz than a human voice.

I looked again at my picture and my stomach began to rumble. I was getting very hungry.

"Well, too bad, she is a strange one," I said to myself. I left the room and was on my way to the exit when my conscience began to nag, and I turned back.

"Listen," I said to her, "If you don't tell me why you are sitting there, I'll call the school doctor. And he—one, two, three,—he'll call 'Emergency,' there will be an ambulance, the siren, and off to the hospital you'll go." I decided to scare her a little. I am scared of the school

doctor myself. He forever says: "Breathe, don't breathe . . . ," and he sticks the thermometer under your arm. It is as cold as an icicle.

"All right," she blurted out, "so I'll go to the hospital!"

"Can't you tell me," I almost shouted, "what's happened?"

"My brother is waiting for me. He's in the yard . . ."

I looked out—and, sure enough, a little boy was sitting there on a bench. The yard was deserted.

"So what?"

"So this—I promised to teach him today all the letters of the alphabet."

"Boy, you sure can make promises," I said. "In one day—the whole alphabet?! Perhaps you're planning to finish the whole school in one year. You're quite a liar."

"I didn't lie. I just . . . didn't know."

I could see that she was about to cry. She lowered her eyes and shook her head in a certain way which meant the tears were on their way.

"It takes weeks to learn to write all the letters. It's not so simple."

"Mother and Father went far away, and my brother Seryozha misses them terribly. And so I told him, 'I'll start going to school, I'll learn all the letters, and we'll write Mommie and Daddy a letter. He has already told all the boys on our street about it. But all we wrote all day in class today is sticks!" She barely managed to hold back the tears.

"Sticks!" I said, "that's fine, that's simply great! Letters are made out of sticks." And I went over to the board and wrote the letter "A"—I printed it. "This is the letter 'A'. It is made out of three sticks."

Well, I never intended to become a teacher, but I had to distract her somehow so that she would not start crying.

"And now," I said, "let's go to your brother. I'll explain everything to him."

We left the room, went to the school yard, and walked over to her brother. We walked like little kids, holding hands. She had thrust her tiny hand into mine. It was a soft little hand, with fingers like tiny pillows, and warm.

I thought to myself: if any of the boys saw me they'd laugh at me for walking hand in hand with a first-grade girl. But how could I push her hand away?—after all, she was a human being.

And this important Seryozha sat there, swinging his legs. He pretended not to see us.

"Listen, fellow," I said to him. "I want to explain something to you. . . . You know, it takes almost a whole year to learn the whole alphabet. It's not so easy. . . ."

"That means she didn't learn it!" he said and looked at his sister with scorn. "Then she didn't have to promise."

"We wrote only sticks all day," the little girl said desperately, "but letters are made out of sticks."

He didn't even listen to her. He rose from the bench, put his hands in his pockets, lowered his head, and shoved off like a duck. He had paid no attention to me. I got tired of the whole affair. I always seemed to get mixed up in other people's business.

"I did learn the letter 'A'!" his sister cried after him. But he didn't even turn around.

I caught up with him.

"Listen," I said. "You can't blame her. Learning is complicated. When you start school you'll find out. Do you think that the astronauts Gagarin and Titov mastered the whole alphabet in one day? They, too, sweated it out. And you complain . . ."

"All day I've been memorizing the letter I was going to write my Mommie," he said.

His face looked so gloomy that I thought it was wrong of his mother to have left him behind. If parents go off to distant places, let them take their children along. Children don't get scared of long trips or fierce frosts.

"Don't worry," I said to him. "I'll come over after supper, and I'll write everything down just as you dictate it."

"Good!" the little girl said. "We live in that house behind the iron fence. Won't that be good, Seryozha?"

"All right," Seryozha nodded, "I'll wait for you."

I saw them enter their courtyard. Their little figures soon began to disappear behind the iron fence and some bushes.

Then I heard a loud voice, the teasing voice of a boy: "Well, Seryozha, did your sister learn the whole alphabet today?"

Seryozha stopped, and his sister ran into the house.

"Do you know how long it takes to learn the whole alphabet? It takes a whole year!" Seryozha shouted.

"Oh, is that so? Then your letter will have to wait a whole year—and your parents, too," the other boy said in a nasty way.

"No, I have a friend. He finished the first grade long ago, and he will come this evening and write my letter!"

"You're lying," the other boy said. "You're a big liar! Can you tell me his name?"

Silence.

In another second I expected to hear the triumphant cry of the tease, but I didn't let this happen. I climbed up to the stone ledge below the iron fence and stuck my head through the bars.

"Do you want to know his name? It's Yurik," I said.

The tease's mouth fell open with surprise. Seryozha said nothing. He was not the kind to kick someone who was down.

I jumped off the ledge and started for home.

I don't know why, but I was in a pretty good mood. I even felt like singing.

A MERRY FAMILY

NIKOLAI NOSOV

It is no news that Soviet schoolchildren are diligently trained to value the importance and fascinations of science. The ways in which young boys and girls are encouraged in this are less well known, and they are manifold. Quite effective is the manner in which scientific themes are used in young children's stories. For instance, going about some home project with scientific precision is made interesting and dramatic in fiction.

Here is the climax to an entertaining story which tells how a pair of schoolboys, inseparable friends, go about building a homemade incubator to hatch a family of chicks. Nearly all of their classmates are drawn into the enterprise. There is a trial-and-error plot and good characterization of the boys and even of the chicks!

The boys have taken turns sitting up all night, for twenty-one nights, to keep the correct temperature in the incubator. Then comes . . .

The Hardest Day of All

Working together was fun and the time passed quickly. At last the twenty-first day arrived. It was a Friday. We had everything ready for the brood. We found a large pot in the shed and lined it with felt to make a warming pan for the newborn chicks. Now it stood ready on top of a pan of hot water, waiting for the first chick to hatch.

Mishka and I had wanted to stay up the night before, but Vadik Zaitsev had got his mother to allow him to do night duty, and he wouldn't hear of us being there too.

"I don't need you hanging around when I'm on duty," he said. "You can go to bed."

"But what if the chicks begin hatching during the night?" we said.

"So what? As soon as a chick comes out I'll drop it into the pot and let it dry off."

"Don't you dare drop it!" I said, horrified. "You must be very gentle with chicks."

"Don't worry, I'll be gentle. Now you go off to bed like good little boys. Don't forget you're on duty tomorrow. So you'd better have a good night's rest."

"All right," agreed Mishka. "Only be sure to wake us if the chicks begin hatching."

Vadik promised.

We went to bed, but I couldn't sleep for a long time and lay there worrying about the chickens. Next morning I woke up very early and ran to Mishka's right away. He was up already too, and was sitting beside the incubator examining the eggs.

"I don't see any sign yet."

"Too early, probably," said Vadik.

Vadik soon went home because the night was over and our watch was on. When he had gone, Mishka decided to examine all the eggs once more. We began turning them over and looking for some tiny little hole which the chick inside would make with its beak. But there wasn't so much as a crack in any of the shells. We closed the incubator and sat for a long time without speaking.

"Suppose we break open one and see if there's a chick inside or not?" I suggested.

"No, you mustn't. Not yet," said Mishka. "The chick is still breathing through its skin and not through its lungs. As soon as it begins breathing with its lungs it will crack open the shell by itself. If we crack it too soon the chick will die."

"But they must be already alive inside," I said. "Maybe you can hear them move if you listen carefully?"

Mishka took an egg out of the incubator and put it to his ear. I bent over him and put my ear to it too.

"Be quiet!" growled Mishka. "How can I hear anything with you snoring into my ear!"

I held my breath. It was very quiet, so quiet you could hear the watch ticking on the table. Suddenly the bell rang. Mishka jumped and nearly dropped the egg. It was Vitya. He wanted to know whether the chicks had begun to hatch yet.

"No," said Mishka. "It's too early."

"All right. I'll drop in again before school," said Vitya.

He went away and Mishka took the egg out again and put it to his ear. He sat like that for a long time with his eyes closed, listening intently.

"I can't hear a sound," he said at last.

I took the egg and listened too. But I could not hear anything either.

"Perhaps the embryo is dead?" I said. "We ought to try the others."

We took the eggs out one by one and listened to each separately, but not one of them gave any sign of life.

"They couldn't all be dead, could they?" said Mishka miserably. "One of them at least must be alive."

The bell rang again. This time is was Senya Bobrov.

"What are you doing up so early?" I asked him.

"I came to find out how the chicks are coming along."

"They aren't coming along at all," Mishka answered. "It isn't time yet."

Seryozha arrived next.

"Well, any chicks yet?"

"You are too impatient," said Mishka. "Don't expect the chicks to start hatching from early morning!"

Seryozha and Senya sat for a while and then left. Mishka and I began listening to the eggs again.

"No, it's no use," he said wretchedly, "I don't hear a thing."

"Perhaps they're keeping still just to fool us?" I suggested.

Then Yura Filippov and Stasik Levshin came, and after them, Vanya Lozhkin. They kept coming one after the other, and by the time we were due to leave for school it began to look like a general assembly. We called my little sister Maya and told her what to do if the chicks began hatching while we weren't there, and left with the others for school.

I don't know how we lived through that day. It was the hardest day in our lives. It seemed to us that someone was deliberately stretching out the time and making every lesson ten times longer than usual. We were all terribly afraid that the chickens would begin to hatch while we were in school and that Maya would not manage by herself. The last class was the worst. We thought it would never end. It was so long that we began to wonder whether we hadn't missed the bell. Then we thought that perhaps the bell was out of order. Or that Aunt Dunya, the custodian, had forgotten to ring the last bell and had gone home and we'd have to sit in school until tomorrow morning. The whole class was fidgety and nervous. Everybody sent little notes to Zhenya Skvortsov, the only one of us who possessed a wrist watch, asking what time it was. But as luck would have it Zhenya had left his watch at home that day. It was so noisy in class that Alexander Yefremovich had to stop several times to ask for silence. But the noise continued. Finally Mishka raised his hand to say that it was time to dismiss us, but just at that moment the bell rang and everyone sprang up and rushed to the door. Alexander

Yefremovich made us all sit down again and said no one must leave his desk until the teacher left the room. Then he turned to Mishka.

"Did you want to ask me something?"

"No, I just wanted to say that it was time to dismiss us."

"But you raised your hand before the bell rang?"

"I thought the bell was out of order."

Alexander Yefremovich shook his head, picked up the class book, and went out of the room. The boys dashed into the hall and down the stairs. There was a jam at the exit, but Mishka and I managed to push our way through. We rushed headlong down the street with the others tearing after us.

Five minutes later we were home. Maya was sitting at her post by the incubator sewing a new dress for her doll.

"Has anything happened?" we asked.

"Nothing."

"How long is it since you looked into the incubator?"

"Quite a long time ago. When I turned over the eggs."

Mishka went to the incubator. All the boys crowded around, craning their necks and standing on tiptoe. Vanya Lozhkin climbed on to a chair to see better, but he fell off and nearly knocked Lyosha Kurochkin down. But Mishka couldn't bring himself to raise the lid. He was afraid to look.

"Come on, lift it! What are you waiting for?" someone said.

At last Mishka lifted the lid. The eggs lay at the bottom as before, looking like big white pebbles.

Mishka stood for a while without saying anything, then he turned them over carefully one by one and examined them from all sides.

"Not a single crack!" he announced dejectedly.

The boys stood around in silence.

"Maybe they won't hatch at all," said Senya Bobrov. "What do you think?"

Mishka shrugged his shoulders: "How can I tell? I'm not a sitting hen!"

We tried not to worry and settled down to wait patiently. But that was easier said than done. We couldn't stop worrying however hard we tried, and every ten minutes we peeped inside the incubator. The other boys were anxious too and kept coming in for the latest news bulletins. Everyone asked the same question: "Well, what's happening?"

After a while Mishka stopped answering and only shrugged his shoulders, but he had to shrug them so often that by the end of the day his shoulders were hunched right up to his ears.

As the evening wore on the boys stopped coming. Vitya, our group leader, was the last to drop in. He sat with us for a long time.

"Perhaps you miscalculated?" he said.

We began counting again but there was no mistake. This was the twenty-first day and it was coming to an end but there were no chicks.

"Never mind," Vitya tried to console us. "We'll wait till morning. They may hatch during the night."

I persuaded my mother to let me stay over at Mishka's place, and we decided to sit up all night and watch. We sat for a long time by the incubator in silence. We had nothing to talk about any more. We couldn't even daydream because we had lost our hopes. Soon the street cars stopped running and it grew very quiet. The street light outside the window went out. I lay down on the sofa. Mishka dozed sitting up, but he nearly fell off the chair. So he came over and lay beside me on the sofa, and we fell asleep.

When we woke up it was daylight, and everything was as before. The eggs still lay in the incubator, not so much as a crack in any of them, and not a sound inside.

All the boys were terribly disappointed.

"What could have happened?" they asked. "We followed all the instructions carefully, didn't we?"

"I don't know," said Mishka, shrugging his shoulders.

Only I knew what had happened. Of course the embryos had died that time when I overslept. The temperature had gone down and they had perished from the cold—died before their lives had properly begun! I felt very guilty before the boys. All their trouble would be for nothing, and all because of me! But I couldn't tell them all this just then. I decided to confess later on, when the whole incident would be forgotten and they wouldn't feel so bad about losing the chicks.

Mishka and I were dejected that day in school. All the boys looked at us with such sympathy, as if we were in mourning for somebody; and when Senya Bobrov took it into his head to call us the "chickabiddies," just out of spite, the others jumped on him and said he ought to be ashamed of himself. Mishka and I felt uncomfortable.

"I'd rather they were sore at us!" said Mishka.

"Why should they be?"

"Well, look at all the work they've put in. They have every right to be sore."

After school some of the boys dropped in, but soon they stopped coming. All except Kostya Devyatkin, who came once or twice. He was the only one who hadn't given up hope yet.

"See," Mishka said to me. "Now all the boys are angry with us. But should they be? Anyone can make a mistake."

"But you said yourself they have a right to be sore."

"Well, maybe they have," replied Mishka irritably. "You, too. It's all my fault."

"Why is it your fault? Nobody is blaming you for anything," I said.

"Yes, it is. But you won't be too angry with me, will you?"

"Why should I be?"

"Oh, because I'm such a good-for-nothing. It's all my bad luck. Nothing I do ever comes to any good."

"That's not true. It's me who spoils everything," I said. "It's all my fault."

"No, it isn't. It's my fault. I killed the chicks."

"You killed them?"

"I'll tell you, only promise you won't be angry?" said Mishka. "Once I fell asleep early in the morning, and when I woke up and looked at the thermometer it had gone up to 104 degrees. I opened the lid quickly to let the eggs cool off, but I suppose it was too late."

"When was that?"

"Five days ago."

Mishka looked terribly guilty and miserable.

"Well, you needn't worry," I said to him. "The eggs were spoiled long before that."

"Before what?"

"Before you overslept."

"Who spoiled them?"

"I did."

"You? How?"

"I also overslept, and the temperature went down, and so the eggs were spoiled."

"When did that happen?"

"On the tenth day."

"Why didn't you say anything before?"

"I was afraid to. I thought perhaps the chicks hadn't died after all. But now I know they did, and it was I who killed them."

"And you let the boys do all that work for nothing," said Mishka, looking fiercely at me, "just because you were afraid!"

"Well, I thought maybe it would be all right. The boys would have decided to go on with it anyway, otherwise we would never know whether the chicks had died or not."

"Oh, is that so!" Mishka said indignantly. "Anyhow you ought to have owned up right away so we could all decide together what to do instead of you deciding for everybody else."

"Look," I said, "Why are you yelling at me? Why didn't you own up yourself? You also overslept, didn't you?"

"I guess I did," said Mishka, contrite. "I'm a dope. You can punch me in the nose if you like."

"Never mind, I won't do anything of the kind. But don't you go telling the boys what I've told you," I said.

"I'll tell them tomorrow. Not about you, but about myself. Let everyone know what a jerk I am."

"All right, then I'll confess too," I said.

"No, you'd better not."

"Why not?"

"Well, you know them. They always laugh at us because we do everything together. We go to school together, do our lessons together, and even get low marks together. Now they'll say we overslept our watch together too."

"Let them say what they like," I said. "Besides, I couldn't shut up and let them laugh just at you, could I?"

When We Lost Hope

That sad day drew to a close and evening came again. The situation in the kitchen remained unchanged: the incubator was warm, the lamp still burned, but our hopes were dead. Mishka sat silently staring at the egg in his hand. We couldn't make up our minds whether to crack it open or wait awhile. All of a sudden, he sat up with a start and stared at me with wide-open eyes. I thought he had seen a ghost behind me and I turned around quickly. But there was nothing there. I turned back to Mishka.

"Look!" he said hoarsely, stretching out his hand with the egg in it.

At first I couldn't see anything at all, but then I saw what looked like a small crack.

"Did you knock it against something?"

Mishka shook his head.

"Then—then—the chick did it?"

Mishka nodded.

"Are you sure?"

Mishka shrugged his shoulders.

I carefully lifted the bit of broken shell with my nail, making a small hole in the egg. The same moment a tiny yellow beak thrust itself through the hole and then disappeared.

We were so excited we couldn't speak and just hugged each other with joy.

"Hurrah! It's happened!" shouted Mishka, and burst out laughing. "Now what do we do? Whom do we tell first?"

"Wait a minute!" I said. "What's the rush? Where are you off to?"

"We've got to tell the boys!" He rushed to the door.

"Wait!" I said. "Put the egg back first."

Mishka zoomed back and put the egg into the incubator. At that moment Kostya arrived.

"We've got one chick!" shouted Mishka.

"You're fibbing!"

"Word of honor!"

"Where is it?"

Mishka lifted the incubator lid and Kostya looked inside.

"Where's the chick? All I see is eggs."

Mishka had forgotten exactly where he had put the egg with the crack in it, and now he couldn't find it. Finally he found it and showed it triumphantly to Kostya.

Kostya shouted with delight. "Look, there's a real chicken's beak sticking out of it!" he cried.

"Of course it's real. Did you think it was some circus trick?"

"Wait here. You hang on to that egg and I'll go and call the others," said Kostya.

"Okay, go and get them. They didn't believe there would be any chicks at all. No one came in all evening."

Kostya ran out and we heard him go clattering down the stairs, three steps at a time.

"Golly!" cried Mishka. "I haven't told Mother yet!" He ran to call his mother, and I snatched up the egg and ran off to show it to my mother.

Mother looked at it and told me to run and put it back in the incubator at once, otherwise it might cool down and the chicken would catch cold.

I rushed back to Mishka's place and there he was in the kitchen all excited and his mother and father were standing laughing at him. As soon as he saw me Mishka pounced on me.

"Did you see where I put that egg? I've turned the whole incubator upside down and I can't find it anywhere!"

"What egg?"

"You know—the one with the chick in it!"

"Here it is," I said.

When Mishka saw the egg in my hands he nearly had a fit.

"You silly ass! What do you mean by picking up the egg and running off with it!"

"Calm down," said Mishka's mother. "All that fuss about an egg!"

"But, Mother, it isn't an ordinary egg. Look at it!"

Mishka's mother took the egg and looked at the tiny little beak showing through the hole. His dad looked at it too.

"Hm," he said smiling. "Remarkable!"

"There's nothing remarkable about it," said Mishka with an important air. "It's just a natural phenomenon."

"You're a natural phenomenon yourself," laughed Mishka's dad. "There's nothing remarkable about the chicken of course. What's remarkable is that it hatched out in *your* incubator. I must admit I didn't think anything would come of it."

"Why didn't you say so then?"

"Why should I? I'd rather you spent your time breeding chickens than running wild in the street."

At that point Maya came into the kitchen. She put her eye to the hole, and just then the chick stuck out its beak.

Maya screamed. "He wanted to peck me!" she cried. "You naughty little chick, you! Not out of your shell and fighting already."

"You mustn't shout at a newborn chick like that!" said Mishka. "You'll frighten it." He took the egg and laid it back in the incubator.

At that moment there was a noise outside on the stairs and the sound of running feet. Soon the kitchen was full of boys. The egg had to be taken out again and shown around.

"Boys," cried Mishka. "Let's have the egg. We've got to put it back in the incubator or the chicken will catch cold." But no one paid any attention to him. We had to take it away by force.

"Aren't there any cracks in the other eggs yet?" Vitya asked.

We inspected the other eggs but there was no sign of any more cracks.

"No, Number 5 is the only one," said Mishka.

"Perhaps they'll hatch later on," said the boys.

"It doesn't matter," said Mishka. "Even if only one chick hatches, I'll be satisfied."

"Shouldn't we break open the shell and let the chick out?" said Senya Bobrov. "He must be uncomfortable, sitting in there."

"Oh no," said Mishka. "You mustn't touch the shell. The chick's skin is still too tender and you can hurt it."

When the boys had gone, Mishka examined the eggs once more and found another crack.

"Look," he shouted. "Number 11 is beginning to hatch out too!"

I looked, and sure enough there was a crack in the egg that had Number 11 written on it.

We sat down by the incubator, nearly bursting with happiness.

"You and me are certainly the lucky ones," said Mishka. "I bet very few people are as lucky as we are."

Night came. Everyone had gone to bed long ago, but Mishka and I didn't feel the least bit sleepy.

The time went very fast. At about two o'clock in the morning two more eggs cracked, Numbers 8 and 10. And the next time we looked into the incubator there was a real surprise waiting for us. There among the eggs sat a tiny newborn chick. It was trying to stand on its legs, but it kept toppling over.

I nearly choked with excitement.

I picked up the chick. It was still wet and instead of feathers it had silky yellow down sticking untidily all over its tender pink back.

Mishka opened the warming pot, and I put the chick inside. We added hot water to the pan underneath so the chick would be cozy.

"It's very warm in there, he'll soon dry out and look nice and fluffy," said Mishka.

He took the two halves of the shell out of the incubator. "It's a wonder how such a huge chick could fit into such a little shell!" he said. And the chick really did look huge compared with the shell. But after all, he had been curled up inside it with his legs tucked up under him and his head twisted around. And now he had straightened out and was standing on his spindly little legs with his neck stretched out.

Mishka was still looking at the broken shell when suddenly he cried out: "Look, this is the wrong chick!"

"What do you mean, the wrong chick?"

"It's not the first one! The first one that cracked the shell was Number 5, this is Number 11!"

Sure enough the shell had the figure "11" written on it.

We looked into the incubator. Number 5 was still in the shell, lying where we had put it.

"What's the matter with it?" I said. "It was the first to crack the shell and now it won't come out!"

"It's probably too weak to break the shell itself," said Mishka. "Let it lie a little while, perhaps it'll get stronger."

The Mistake

We were so busy that we didn't notice morning had come until we saw the sun shining in the window. Sunbeams played on the kitchen floor, making the room look bright and gay.

"I suppose the boys will be coming soon," said Mishka. "They won't be able to hold out."

The words were hardly out of his mouth when two of them arrived—Zhenya and Kostya.

"Want to see a miracle?" cried Mishka and he picked the newborn chicken out of the warming pan. "There! A miracle of nature."

The boys examined the chick gravely.

"And three more eggs have cracked!" Mishka exclaimed. "Look!"

The chick evidently didn't like the cold. When we held him in our hands it began to fidget, but as soon as we put him back into the pan he quieted down.

"Have you fed him?" asked Kostya.

"Oh no," said Mishka. "It's too soon to feed him. You only feed them the day after they're hatched."

"I bet you haven't slept all night," Zhenya said when he arrived to get the latest news.

"No. . . . We've been too busy."

"Then you'd better go and take a nap, and I'll take over for awhile," suggested Kostya.

Mishka and I lay down on the couch and went to sleep at once. To tell the truth I had felt sleepy for a long time. The boys woke us up about ten o'clock.

"Come and look at miracle Number 2!" cried Kostya.

"Miracle number what?" I muttered, still half asleep. I looked around and saw that the kitchen was full of boys.

"Here it is!" they cried and pointed to the saucepan.

Mishka and I jumped up and ran to look into it. There were two chicks there now. One of them was fluffy and round and as yellow as egg powder. A real beauty!

"Isn't he splendid!" I said. "Why is the first one so mangy looking?"

The boys laughed. "That one is the first one!"

"Which one?"

"The fluffy one."

"No, it isn't. It's that skinny one."

"The skinny one has just hatched out. The first one has dried out, and that's why he's fluffy."

"Isn't that great!" I said. "Then the second one will be fluffy, too?— when he dries?"

"Of course."

"What number is that?" Mishka asked.

The boys looked puzzled.

"I thought you knew all the eggs are numbered," said Mishka.

"No, we didn't look for any number," said Kostya.

"We can see by the shell," I said. "The shell must still be inside."

Mishka looked into the incubator and let out a yell. "Look! There are two more brand-new chicks in there!"

Everybody made a dash for the incubator. Mishka carefully took out the two new chicks and showed them to us. "There they are, the little eagles!" he said proudly, and put them into the warming pan with the other two.

Now we had four chicks. They sat huddled together for warmth.

Mishka then took the broken shells out of the incubator and looked for the numbers. "Numbers 4, 8, and 10," he said. "But which is which?"

Of course you couldn't tell now what shell they had hatched from. The boys laughed.

"Number 5 is still lying there in the incubator," I said.

"What's the matter with it? Maybe it's dead?" said Mishka.

We got out Number 5 and widened the hole a little. The chick was lying quietly inside. It moved its head.

"Hurrah, it's alive!" we shouted and laid it back inside the incubator.

Mishka checked over the remaining eggs and found another crack, in Number 3. The boys clapped their hands.

Things were really humming at last!

It was Sunday. Since there was no school that day, the boys spent the whole day in our kitchen. Mishka and I sat beside the incubator—the place of honor. To the right, near the stove, stood the warming pan with the newborn chicks inside; on the stove was the pot of hot water; and on the window sill were the boxes with the oats, which were already a bright green. The boys laughed, told jokes and all kinds of interesting stories.

"Have you figured out why they didn't hatch when they were supposed to?" one of the boys asked. "You expected them on Friday."

"I can't imagine what happened," replied Mishka. "The manual says that they are supposed to hatch on the twenty-first day, and this is the twenty-third. Maybe the people who wrote the book made a mistake."

"If anyone made a mistake, it's probably you," said Lyosha Kurochkin. "When did you put the eggs in the incubator?"

"On the third. It was on a Saturday. I remember perfectly, because the next day was Sunday."

"There's something wrong," said Zhenya Skvortsov. "You put the eggs in on Saturday, and the twenty-first day comes out to be on Friday."

"He's right," said Vitya Smirnov. "If you started on Saturday, the twenty-first day ought to be on Saturday. There are seven days in a week and twenty-one days make exactly three weeks."

"Three times seven is twenty-one!" laughed Senya Bobrov. "At least that's what the multiplication table says."

"I don't know about the multiplication table but that's how we figured it," said Mishka huffily.

"How did you count?"

"I'll tell you," said Mishka, counting on his fingers. "The 3rd was the first day, the 4th was the second, the 5th, the third . . ."

He counted all the way up to Friday and got twenty-one days.

Senya looked puzzled. "That's funny. According to the multiplication table the twenty-first day comes on Saturday, and when you count on your fingers it comes out on Friday."

"Show us again how you counted," said Zhenya.

"Look," said Mishka, bending his fingers again, "Saturday, the 3rd, was the first day; Sunday, the 4th, was the second day . . ."

"Just a minute! You're wrong! If you began on the 3rd, you shouldn't count that day."

"Why?"

"Because the whole day wasn't over. The first 24 hours didn't pass until the 4th. That means you ought to count from the 4th."

Suddenly Mishka and I both saw it in a flash. Mishka tried counting the new way and it came out right.

"Of course," he said, "the twenty-first day was yesterday."

"Then everything came out as it should have," I said. "We put the eggs in the incubator on Saturday evening, and the first crack appeared on Saturday evening. Exactly twenty-one days later."

"You see how much trouble you can avoid by knowing how to count correctly," said Vanya Lozhkin.

Everyone laughed.

"Yes," said Mishka, "if we hadn't made that mistake we could have saved ourselves a lot of worry and bother."

The Birthday Party

By the end of that day there were already ten chickens sitting in our warming pan. The last to appear was Number 5. He didn't want to come out of his shell, not for anything, and we had to break off the top to help him out. If we hadn't done that, he would still have been sitting there. He was smaller than the other birds and weaker, probably because he had been in the shell so long.

Toward evening only two eggs were left in the incubator. They looked very sad lying there all by themselves and there was still no sign of a crack in them. We kept the lamp on in the incubator but they didn't hatch out that night either. All the newborn chicks spent the night very comfortably in the warming pan, and in the morning we let them down on the floor—ten yellow balls of fluff cheeping for all they were worth. Some stood quite firmly on their little legs, others were still wobbly. Some even tried to run, but they weren't very good at it. Sometimes they pecked with their little beaks at small spots on the floor and even at the shiny heads of nails on the floorboards.

"Look at that. They're hungry!" cried Mishka.

We quickly boiled an egg, chopped it up fine and spread it on the floor, but the chicks didn't know what to do with it. We tried to feed them out of our hands.

"Eat, you silly things," we said. But the chicks didn't even look at the food. Just then Mishka's mother came into the kitchen.

"They won't eat any egg, Mom," Mishka said.

"You must teach them."

"How? We told them to eat, but they won't listen to us."

"That's not the way to teach chicks. You have to tap on the floor with your finger."

Mishka sat down beside the chicks and tapped on the floor next to the egg crumbs. The chicks watched the finger pecking at the food and they began imitating it. In a few minutes they had eaten up all the egg. Then we put out a saucer of water, and they drank it up. You didn't have to teach them that. Then they got into a huddle, and we put them back in the pan to warm up.

When Marya Petrovna, our teacher, came into the classroom that day, we all ran to meet her with the news that our chicks had hatched. She was very pleased.

"So this is your chicks' birthday," she said. "I congratulate you."

We all laughed, and Vitya Smirnov said, "We must have a birthday party for them. Let's have it today."

Everyone approved of the idea. "Yes, let's. Let's! Marya Petrovna, will you come to our chicks' birthday party?"

"Thank you, I'll come with pleasure," Marya Petrovna said. "I'll bring them a present too."

"We must all bring them presents!" the boys cried.

When we came home from school Mishka and I waited impatiently for the guests to arrive. We were dying to see what sort of presents the chicks would get.

Senya Bobrov came first with a bouquet of flowers.

"What's that for?" said Mishka.

"For the chickens. That's my present."

"Whoever heard of flowers for chicks. They can't eat flowers, can they?"

"They don't have to eat them. They'll look at them and smell them."

"What an idea! As if they haven't seen flowers before."

"Of course they haven't. Get me a jar to put them in. You'll see how nice they'll look." We got a jar and put the flowers in water.

The next to arrive were Seryozha and Vadik. They both brought bunches of snowdrops.

"What is everybody bringing flowers for?" said Mishka scowling.

"Don't you like our presents?" said Vadik offended. "It isn't nice to look gift horses in the mouth."

We put their flowers in water too.

Then Vanya Lozhkin came and brought a pound of oatmeal. Mishka looked doubtful. "I'm afraid they won't eat it."

"You can try," said Vanya.

"No, we'd better wait and ask Marya Petrovna."

Just then Marya Petrovna came. She carried something wrapped in newspaper. It turned out to be a bottle filled with what looked like milk.

"Milk!" shouted Mishka. "We never thought of giving them milk!"

"This is buttermilk," said Marya Petrovna. "It is just what they need for the first few days. You'll see how they like it."

We let the chicks out of the pot and poured the buttermilk into a saucer and gave it to them. They drank it up with gusto.

"That's what I call a real present for chicks," said Mishka delighted. "You have to know what to bring to a chicken's birthday party."

The guests kept coming one after another. Vitya and Zhenya brought millet. Then Lyosha Kurochkin came running in with a baby's rattle.

"I didn't know what to bring, and I saw these rattles in a store on the way here, so I bought them one."

"A brilliant idea," said Mishka sarcastically. "The perfect birthday gift for a chicken."

"How was I to know what to buy? Besides, they might like the rattle for all you know."

He ran over to the chickens and shook the rattle over their heads. They stopped pecking at the buttermilk and lifted their heads to listen.

"See that?" cried Lyosha overjoyed. "They like it!"

Everyone laughed. "All right," Mishka said, "now let them eat in peace."

I asked Marya Petrovna whether we could feed them oatmeal. She said they ate any sort of meal provided it was cooked.

"How do you cook it?" Mishka wanted to know.

"Just the way you cook cereal," said Marya Petrovna.

Mishka and I wanted to cook the cereal at once, but just then another guest arrived—Kostya Devyatkin.

"Have you brought a present?" the boys asked.

"Of course I have," said Kostya, pulling two pies out of his pocket.

"What a funny present," laughed the boys.

"You always have pies at birthday parties, don't you?" said Kostya.

"What's inside them?" Mishka asked suspiciously.

"Rice."

"Rice?" cried Mishka.

He snatched the pies out of Kostya's hand and began scooping the rice out of them.

"Hey! What are you doing!" said Kostya. "Don't you believe me?"

But Mishka didn't answer. He scooped all the rice into a saucer and put it in front of the chicks. They began pecking at it right away.

When Maya saw that everyone had brought gifts for the chicks, she went to her room and brought a piece of red ribbon, cut it into little strips, and tied a red bow around each chick's neck. We put the jars of flowers down on the floor near the chicks, and—what with the flowers, the ribbons, and the saucers of buttermilk, rice, and fresh water—it really did begin to look like a birthday party.

After the chicks had enough to eat and drink, we took off their ribbons and put them back into the warming pan. Marya Petrovna advised us to fence off a part of the kitchen for them and keep a pot of hot water to warm themselves against.

We showed her our incubator and the two eggs still lying inside.

"I'm afraid those won't hatch any more," said Marya Petrovna. "But it doesn't matter. You have done very well as it is."

"I was afraid nothing would come of it, because I overslept once and the temperature went down," I said.

"They can cool down quite a bit without being harmed," said Marya Petrovna. "After all, the hen doesn't sit on her eggs all the time. Once a day she goes off to get something to eat, leaving the eggs uncovered. Incubator eggs are also cooled off once a day so as to create the natural conditions for the embryo to develop. It is much worse to overheat them."

"I overheated them once," said Mishka. "The temperature went up to 104 degrees."

"Most likely you noticed it before any serious harm was done," said Marya Petrovna. "But it you had let the temperature remain high for a long time, the eggs would surely have been spoiled."

That evening we broke open the two remaining eggs. In both of them we found undeveloped embryos. Life had stopped and the chicks had died before they were born. Perhaps it was the result of overheating.

We switched off the lamp; it had burned for exactly twenty-three days. The mercury in the thermometer gradually went down. The incubator cooled off. But in the saucepan near the stove was our happy family—ten fluffy chicks.

To the Country

Our little family of chicks lived very happily. They felt quite all right as long as they were close together. But if any one of them strayed away from the others he would start cheeping nervously and running about looking for his brothers, and he wouldn't calm down until he had found them.

Maya had wanted to take her chick away from the very beginning, but we wouldn't let her. Then one day she said she wouldn't wait any more and she picked one of the chicks up and took it to her room.

Half an hour later she came back in tears.

"I can't stand it! I can't stand to hear him cry. I thought he'd get used to it after a little while, but he keeps crying so pitifully I can't stand it!"

As soon as she put the chick on the floor, he made straight for the other chicks huddled together in the corner.

We fenced off part of the kitchen for them, spread a piece of oilcloth on the floor and put an iron pot of hot water on it. We covered the pot with a pillow to keep the water from cooling off too quickly. The chicks nestled under the pillow around the warm pot and felt as comfy as if they were nestling under the mother hen's wings. The pot with hot water took the place of the brood hen.

Sometimes we took them out into the yard, but it was dangerous for them there: too many stray dogs and cats prowling about. So they spent most of the time indoors, and we were very much afraid that they were not getting enough fresh air. One chick worried us particularly. He was smaller than the others and less lively. He was a thoughtful sort of chick. He often sat quietly by himself instead of running about with the others, and he ate very little. That was Number 5, the one that had cracked his shell first but hatched out last.

"We really ought to pack them up and take them to the country," said Mishka. "I'm afraid they might get sick here."

But we could not bear the thought of parting with them, and so we kept putting it off from day to day.

One morning Mishka and I came to feed the chicks as usual. By now they had learned to know us and they came running from near the warm pot to meet us. We had brought them a plate of millet gruel, and they rushed to it. Pushing one another out of the way and jumping over one another's heads, each one tried to get ahead of the others. One of them even got on the plate with his feet.

"Where's Number 5?" said Mishka.

Number 5 usually hung behind the others. Since he was the weakest he got pushed aside, and we usually had to feed him separately. Sometimes he didn't eat anything, but he always came running with the others because he didn't want to be left alone. But this time there was no sign of him. We counted the chicks and found that one was missing.

"Maybe he's hiding behind the pot?" I said. I looked behind the pot, and there he was lying on the floor. I thought he was just taking a rest. I stretched out my hand and picked him up. His little body was quite cold, and his head hung down lifelessly on his skinny little neck. He was dead.

We stared at him for a long time, feeling so sad we could not speak.

"It's our fault," Mishka said at last. "We ought to have taken him to the country. He would have become strong there in the fresh air."

We buried Number 5 in the back yard under a lime tree, and the very next day we packed the others in a basket and set out for the country. All the boys came to see us off.

Maya wept bitterly when she kissed her own chick good-bye. She wanted terribly to keep him; but she was afraid he would be lonesome for his little brothers, so she agreed to let us take him to the country.

We covered the basket with a shawl and went off to the station. The chicks were warm and comfortable in the basket, and they sat quietly all the way, cheeping softly to one another. The passengers looked at us curiously when they heard the chicks cheeping and guessed what we had in the basket.

"Well, my young poultry farmers, you've come for more eggs, I suppose?" laughed Aunt Natasha when she saw us.

"No," said Mishka. "We've brought you some chicks instead."

Aunt Natasha peeped into the basket.

"Heavens alive!" she cried. "Where on earth did you get all those chicks?"

"We hatched them in our own incubator."

"You're joking! You must have bought them in some bird shop."

"No, Aunt Natasha. Remember those eggs you gave us a month ago? Well, we've brought them back to you, but now they're chicks."

"Well I never!" cried Aunt Natasha. "You'll want to be poultry farmers or something like that when you grow up, I suppose."

"We don't know yet," said Mishka.

"But aren't you sorry to part with the chicks?"

"Yes," replied Mishka. "But you see, it isn't good for them to live in town. Here the air is pure and fresh, and they have more room to run about. The hens will lay eggs for you, and the cocks will crow. One of the chicks died, and we buried him under the lime tree."

"You poor dears," said Aunt Natasha, putting her arms around Mishka and me. "But never mind. It can't be helped. All the others are fine and strong."

We let the chicks out of the basket and watched them running about in the sunshine.

We spent all day in the country. We went for a walk in the woods and took a dip in the river. The last time we had been there it was early spring and the fields had still been bare. At that time the tractors had been busy in the fields turning up the soil. Now the fields were covered with green shoots which spread in a huge green carpet as far as you could see.

It was nice in the woods. All sorts of beetles and other insects crawled about in the grass, butterflies fluttered about everywhere, and birds sang on every tree. It was so beautiful that we didn't want to go home. We decided we would come here in the summer, build a tent at the river, and live there like Robinson Crusoe.

But finally it was time to go. We went back to Aunt Natasha's to say good-bye. She gave us each a piece of cake to eat on the train and made us promise that we'd come and spend the summer holidays with her. Before leaving, we went into the back yard for a last look at our chicks. They seemed quite at home already and were running about among the trees and bushes cheeping merrily. But they still kept close together and went on cheeping so that if any of them strayed away in the grass he could easily find the others.

"Good-bye family!" said Mishka. Then he delivered a farewell speech: "Have a nice time in the fresh air and sunshine; get big and strong and grow up to be fine healthy birds. Always keep together and stand up for one another. Remember you are all brothers, children of the same mother . . . er . . . I mean the same incubator, where you all lay side by side when you were still plain ordinary eggs and couldn't run about or talk . . . er . . . cheep, I mean. . . . And don't forget us, because we made the incubator; and that means if it wasn't for us, you wouldn't be here, and you wouldn't know how wonderful it is to be alive!

"That's all."

RAGS, BORYA, AND THE ROCKET

M. BARANOVA AND Y. VELTISTOV

Excitement, suspense, and interesting scientific details characterize this story about space dogs and a couple of earthbound would-be scientists, the boys Borya and Gena.

Rags, Borya's pet dog, runs away after he is frightened, shaken, and singed in an experiment the boys conduct with a homemade rocket. Eventually Rags is picked up by two dog trainers of the Institute for Space Research. The now unfriendly and untrusting Rags is renamed "Snapper" by his trainers; his painful experience with the boys' experiment has temporarily soured his personality. In the meantime, Borya and Gena, helped by Lyuba, their neighbor and occasional playmate—a girl full of daydreams and bright ideas—continue their search for Rags.

When Rags, now called Snapper, completes his first of five space flights after a long and trying training period, and does this bravely and in good spirits, he is renamed "Courageous." Rags-Snapper-Courageous becomes a space celebrity! But all these changes of his name thwart Borya and his chums in locating the long-lost pet.

Here is an important part of the story, resolving the plot.

Five . . . Four . . . Three . . . Two . . .
One . . . Blast-off!

Like a sentry the rocket stood in the middle of a field that was rust-red with last year's dry grass. The rocket's sharp point was aimed at the very center of the blue dome of the sky. High in the rocket, its black eye—the open hatch—looked out on the vast field, at the people bustling below, at the cabin of the elevator sliding up and down along its slender body, at the low, lumbering automobiles.

Only one person was neither working nor hurrying. With his legs planted wide apart, he was looking up at the black eye of the hatch.

It was Dr. Dronov, the head space physician. He was not busy just then because he was neither an engineer nor a mechanic. The engineers and mechanics were most preoccupied running around the rocket, jumping onto the elevator, inspecting this and that—examining their prize creation from all sides. The doctor, however, was waiting his turn. He had not come only to observe idly the activity around the rocket.

"Cyclops!" * Dr. Dronov mused, gazing admiringly at the silver shaft. "You beautiful one-eyed giant! You have had countless parents and nurses. Scientists thought about you for numberless days and nights. Engineers created you in blueprints and tables, and in their imaginations. Your great steel body still holds the warmth of the workers' hands. And your stout heart, your engines, in which soon will rage a thousand-degree fire, was conjured up in the furnaces of the metallurgists. And your blood—your light, fiery blood, was poured into you by the chemists. But how far would you fly, great giant, if you had no brain? Be grateful to the physicists for your clever instruments. And, of course, you will be wise to remember the mathematicians on your space trip—they planned your every move. Yes, you have had so many parents that you cannot even remember them all.

"When the Italians named you 'rocket,' which means an ordinary pipe in their language, they never dreamed you would become so mighty. The ground will tremble and shake, mighty rocket, when you push off from the earth, rushing up into space to look at the stars with your one eye."

"It's time," someone's voice interrupted Dr. Dronov's thoughts. Vasily, a young physician and Dr. Dronov's assistant, and Valya, a medical student and lab technician, joined him. They were holding the dogs in their arms. Both wore their white laboratory smocks: they had just taken blood samples from the dogs, weighed them, recorded their pulse on tape, and measured their temperatures. Snapper and Duffer, already strapped to their trays, were calm. They only wagged their tails, recognizing Dr. Dronov.

"We're ready," said Dr. Dronov.

They walked to the rocket.

The elevator crept upward. The dogs looked down at the grass, so rapidly moving away from them, but the people accompanying them looked up.

The elevator stopped at the open hatch. The doctors fastened the dogs' trays into the rocket capsule. They connected the wires sticking

---

* *Cyclops,* in Greek mythology, is one of a race of giants who had only one eye, in the middle of the forehead.

out from under the clothing of the "pilots" to the apparatus. They checked everything, again looking over the cabin.

They satisfied themselves that everything in this capsule—resembling a hat—was in order. Inside, it was a little world in itself. The glass-wool insulation protected the pilots from heat, for during flight the rocket shell would get as hot as a tea kettle on the stove. For breathing there was a balloon of oxygen mixed with air. There were control instruments that would record on tape the information given by the transducers about the dogs' condition and transmit it by radio. There was the faithful companion of the flyer, the accelerograph, whose leaping graph tells of the invisible forces of gravity. And the movie camera, hanging over the heads of the travelers, would take pictures of them from the first minute to the last. At the same time it would take pictures of the clock, so the doctors would know exactly when everything took place, and would be able to compare the film strip with the reports of the instruments.

Only the parachute was not visible. It was somewhere under the floor, packed in a solid capsule. When necessary, it would open.

"What do you think?" Dr. Dronov asked.

"Excellent, as far as I can see," Vasily said. "Well, then, stewardess, say good-bye," he said turning to Valya.

"So long, Snapper. Bye-bye, Duffer!" Valya said. "Take it easy. Everything will be all right!"

"Till we meet again!" the men said.

The hatch was covered, and there remained for observation only a porthole a little smaller than a saucer. Valya, Dr. Dronov, and Vasily looked into it in turn. Then they went down on the elevator and only the blue sky remained visible through the porthole.

The dogs lay next to each other, spread out on their trays. Snapper looked about calmly. Duffer seemed quite indifferent; she yawned. They lay for quite a long time, not suspecting that the event for which they had trained so long had begun. The instruments were already making their reports, air was coming out of the balloon, and the movie camera was quietly whirring away.

The field around the rocket soon became deserted. The people all went down the steps into a shelter, over which sparkled the glass of stereoscopes. The mechanics were the last to leave.

The hour of preparation was coming to a close. The engineers were at their posts, at the instrument panels. Their faces were calm. They waited for the commander to press the button that would give the signal for the blast-off.

All eyes were on the commander. Nobody spoke. There was total silence. One could only hear the clock ticking off each second with its big second hand.

Vasily could not understand why the commander did not look excited. With his shaved head and stocky figure in a soft lounge jacket, he reminded him of his mathematics teacher at school. This teacher had always been composed, even during examinations, when the whole class seethed with excitement. One could understand that. But this imperturbable commander, how could he be sure that nothing would go wrong with the rocket?

"Get ready!" the commander ordered, and began to count down, "Five . . . Four . . . Three . . . Two . . . One . . . Blast-off!"

On the television screen the spectators saw a bright flash light up the rocket from below and a cloud of smoke surround its body. In the next moment the sound of the explosion hit the door of the shelter.

Slowly, as if making up its mind, the rocket rose above the cloud of smoke, let out a stream of flame, and, pushing a column of bright rose-colored gases toward the ground, rushed skyward. It gathered speed with every second. With a flash of golden lightning it diminished into a small shining speck.

At this moment Vasily remembered his instruments and hurried to them, but his way was barred by a wall of people's backs. The servants of the mighty rocket, workers, mechanics, and engineers, were standing around the screen in a solid ring, glued to the sight of the jumping green line. None of them could read what the jumping line was saying but they were watching attentively all the same, because it was telling the story of the passengers.

Stepping on toes and excusing himself, Vasily made his way to the apparatus. Valya hurried him on. She was almost in tears. What was the use of having learned to understand the language of the instruments and having taken examinations at the Institute, if now she couldn't get to see a thing? The instruments would write everything on a tape, of course, and she would read and reread the tape later, but nonetheless she was a blunderhead. With Dr. Dronov it was different; he had guessed how it would be and had taken his seat beforehand at the screen.

At last Valya and Vasily reached the screen.

In the rocket, a sudden peal of thunder burst in on the passengers. The dogs turned their heads this way and that, trying to understand where the strange frightening noise was coming from. They did not know that it was the burst of the melody of their flight—that they were flying!

In its headlong rush the rocket carried the capsule higher and higher. Leaving behind the paths of birds, the highest mountain peaks, and the ceiling of jet planes, it went through the clouds and into the upper layers of the stratosphere, where meteors flashed like falling stars and where the iridescent northern lights were as familiar a sight as neon signs in the streets of the cities of the earth. Even in these fascinating regions, the rocket did not stop but continued its journey to a height where instead of air there were only invisible particles of gas, and where our passengers would have perished instantaneously had it not been for the protection afforded by the pressurized cabin. It was a pity Snapper and Duffer could not look out of the porthole.

At first the vibration shook them, and then the invisible forces pinned their heads down and sat on them. Their chests were compressed, their hearts pounded, and their bodies felt as though they were filled with lead. But they did not panic; they lay quietly. Suddenly the engines stopped.

Imagine yourself unexpectedly flying up to the ceiling. You were on the floor a moment ago and suddenly you are floating in the air. That's what happened to our space passengers; it took their breath away. It was as if a mighty hand held them up gently. They could not feel their heads or their paws or their tails. They became lighter than feathers. Were it not for the belts, they would have soared like birds. It was astonishing! You only felt like that in dreams.

This amazing situation cheered Snapper and his eyes began to sparkle merrily. He could now look through the porthole and saw an inky-black sky and a blinding sun. It was beautiful and terrible.

Then Snapper looked around the cabin and noticed that a ray of sunlight peeping through the porthole was projected onto the opposite wall, forming a spot of light. The spot remained still for a while and then jumped off the wall and fell on Snapper's left eye. He squinted, sneezed, and shook his head, and when he opened his eyes, the spot of light was on the ceiling. But there, too, it did not sit quietly but began to jump from place to place.

Snapper's eyes became narrow little slits, his tail began to wag happily, and from his throat came short sounds resembling laughter. He gave himself up to the game wholeheartedly, but he did not understand the meaning of the game the spot of light was playing. If a man had been there, he would have known that the reflection was not jumping from wall to ceiling by chance. In a state of weightlessness an astronaut does not know "up" from "down"; he is suspended and does not feel the motion of flight. But the sun's ray tells him, "Your rocket, with the engine turned off, at first was flying up, then came to a standstill, turned nose down and is now falling to earth. Now it will go into the solid layers of the atmosphere. Beware! Beware!"

The ray of sun was right. The rocket described an enormous arc, turning various sides to the sun and then, still revolving round its axis, began descending.

254

On earth the doctors also knew that the most dangerous struggle would now take place. In its descent a rocket goes through intricate turns, falling through the air like a barrel rolling downhill. It must be a harrowing experience to be inside a falling rocket.

If only the parachutes would open promptly!

True enough, as if by a secret signal, invisible forces attacked Snapper and Duffer, pummelling them without mercy. Their chests heaved, their backs ached, their insides were squeezed. Everything grew dark before their eyes from the blows they were receiving on their heads. The blows they were given on their backs made the blood rush to their heads and a red film appear before their eyes. It was as if the evil forces of gravity were taking their revenge for the few moments of pleasure the dogs had during the period of weightlessness. Snapper and Duffer endured everything, even when the unemotional instruments could not stand the sharp jolts and stopped writing.

The doctors ran out of the shelter. They were followed by all the others. Everyone looked into the clear calm sky until their eyes hurt, searching for the falling rocket and not finding it.

The blood throbbed in their temples. Where was the rocket?! A thin wisp of smoke appeared in the blue sky. It was the scarcely visible trace of the red-hot head of the rocket. It appeared and then disappeared again, leaving the sky as empty as the plain below.

Then a white kerchief flashed in the heights with the suddenness of a shot. It did not disappear, but gradually spread out into a white sail that slowly floated down to earth. The outlines of the round cupola of the parachute and its precious weight, the triangular tip of the rocket, grew clearer.

The sun shone and silence reigned. Only somewhere in the heavens a lark was signing.

Silently the people ran across the field, as if by some prearranged signal. In front ran the doctors, their white smocks billowing out like wings.

They rushed to the parachute.

Cars hooted, overtaking the runners. Some of the people jumped on their running boards, others waved the cars off, trusting their own legs better.

The engineers gathered in the parachute. Dr. Dronov and Vasily together tried to look into the porthole and see if the passengers were alive.

"Are they alive?" Valya asked in alarm, stamping her foot impatiently. "Answer, for heaven's sake!"

The doctors did not answer. They quickly opened the hatch, pulled out the trays with the dogs on them, and untied the straps.

"Hurrah! They're alive, alive!" Valya cried and shook the shoulders of somebody or other, probably an engineer. "Hurrah, comrades!"

The engineer she was shaking was squatting on his heels and running his hand over the rocket, evidently blind to everything else. He had not heard Valya and was blinking confusedly.

"What a character!" Valya said in an offended tone. "They're alive, everything's all right!"

"Yes, of course, that's fine!" It finally penetrated; the engineer stood up. "Congratulations." He shook hands with Valya and then with the doctors. "Congratulations, congratulations! It's a great day! Excuse me, I have to go."

He again sat down by the rocket and from his face it was evident that he was distressed. Dr. Dronov understood the man: the descent had not been altogether successful; as the specialists say, it had been hard.

But one way or another, these rocket engineers had done a good job. Snapper and Duffer had returned safe and sound in the rocket that was now lying on the ground. The sides of this darkened, heated shaft deserved to be patted in the way a test pilot pats an unmanageable plane after he has landed it in spite of everything.

Duffer lay on the ground panting heavily, her long pink tongue hanging out; what had happened had obviously overwhelmed her. But Snapper jumped up and shook himself energetically, as after a bath. The warm sun, the smell of the earth and the grass, and the happy familiar voices made him immensely joyful. With a squeal he rushed around Vasily, leaping and bounding about like a merry sunbeam. It was as if a spring that was impossible to stop was unwinding inside him.

Valya watched this wild dance of joy and laughed. Vasily joined in with his deep bass voice. Dr. Dronov's eyes sparkled. The distressed engineer came up and also smiled. Then more and more people came. The merriment was catching.

"Come on, little fellow! Give us a Russian dance!" someone yelled, and everyone saw that it was the calmest person of them all, the commander of the launching.

Soon Valya rang a little bell, and the dance broke off. Snapper obediently ran to his dish. Duffer got up and followed him. The dogs ate hungrily. They finished their supper with pieces of sausage, for which Snapper willingly stood on his hind legs, begging like a circus dog. "Look," he seemed to be saying, "the ordeals of the flight have not spoiled my appetite."

"Oh, what a little rascal you are, Snapper!" Vasily said, shaking his head in mock reproach.

"What? What did you call him?" asked the commander of the launching. "Snapper? Why Snapper? A brave, jolly fellow like that, and you call him Snapper?"

Vasily did not know what to say. Dr. Dronov came to the rescue.

"You see," he explained, "Snapper was his former name. But now he's called something else. . . . *Courageous*—that's it. Sounds good, doesn't it? *Courageous*."

One day in July, Vasily again led two of his charges out of the gate on leashes, and behind him Valya carried a cage with a gray rabbit that was chewing indifferently.

The special plane flew off. Its passengers were awaited at the launching site by a slender silver rocket.

Courageous flew three more times, and each flight was more successful than the last. Deceleration was smoother than before. As the doctors said, "the system for retrieving the passengers proved to be reliable."

Courageous behaved like an experienced cosmonaut. When the engines roared, he remembered the invisible pressure and laid his longish muzzle down on his paws in advance, assuming a comfortable position. During weightlessness he played with the sun's reflection as before, gazed at the bright sun in the porthole, and discovered later that the invisible "boxers" had softened their blows. Each time he landed he performed his wild dance of joy, ate candies, had his picture taken, and stuck his tongue out at the photographer.

Two other little white dogs joined the crew. They were Snowflake and Pearl; and there was a quiet rabbit called Marfushka. The new dogs were inexperienced astronauts. When one of them was nervous or capricious, Courageous would put him in his place by growling and lightly pulling at an ear. The crew minded him.

"These dogs have my respect!" Vasily said to Valya. "Marfushka, now, is an indifferent creature; she does nothing but chew all day long.

You take this sky-scout by the ears and she doesn't object. But the courage of those little dogs amazes me. Have you noticed, Valya, that our Snapper is now not only a fine cosmonaut but a real commander? He has great talent as a leader."

"Please," Valya interrupted. "Don't spoil my best worker by praising him too much. See, he heard you and is beginning to liven up Pearl, who is still shivering—the poor thing."

But Vasily, on the contrary, raised his voice calling to the photographer:

"Oh, Kulik, Kulik, you missed the real hero!" Vasily was referring to Courageous.

Vasily did not know that that very morning Kulik's new film was being shown in Moscow movie theaters and that Courageous was looking at the surprised audience. A foreign visitor had already telephoned the Institute:

"Do you have a dog named Courageous? I should like very much to photograph him for my newspaper."

"By all means, come over," the Professor answered into the telephone, and he smiled ironically, "now that Courageous has become a film star he'll have no more time for training."

Is It Rags or Not?

Gena ran into the Smelov apartment with the air of a conqueror.

"Turn it on, turn it on quick!" he cried breathlessly.

In confusion Borya turned on the light.

"Not that, silly, the TV. Turn it on, Rags is there."

"Rags? How? Why?" Borya wanted to ask, but there was no time to say anything. He rushed to the set and began to turn the knob.

"We are in one of the rooms of the Institute of Space Research," said the voice of the announcer. There was no picture. Bands of light ran over the screen. Suddenly they vanished. Several people in white smocks appeared. On some sort of shaking apparatus sat a dog dressed like a parachutist. It had a long, thin muzzle like Rags.

"Is that him?" whispered Gena.

Borya shook his head doubtfully. That dog with the long, well-groomed fur was too quiet and too sure of himself.

"Courageous is training," said the announcer.

Then Borya said firmly, "No, it's not him. . . ."

Later they laughed over a merry little dog who jumped and showed off, moving his great fluffy ears in a funny way.

Suddenly the long-thin-faced dog appeared again. He was now sitting in a rocket chamber and turning his head, watching a spot of reflected sunlight which had jumped in through the porthole. His face expressed such limitless trust and curiosity that he could only be Rags.

"It's him!" Borya jumped off his chair. "It's him! Let's go to the Institute right away!"

"To the Institute?" asked Gena. "They'll kick us out."

"Then what shall we do? Sit here and do nothing?"

"We have to think up something. Let's call Lyuba!"

They sent a fat little boy who was playing in the sandbox beneath the window to fetch Lyuba. That lover of adventure appeared without delay.

"I knew it, I knew it," she rattled, coming into the room. "I was going along and said to myself: 'Something is bound to happen.' And it did!"

"Sit down," Borya said rather sternly, indicating a chair.

Lyuba meekly sat down.

"Listen, we'll begin today. You'll have to . . . Three tousled heads bent over a map of the district.

An hour later Lyuba was seen hurrying through the courtyards. She ran into an entrance and a minute later rushed out, whispered something to a girl with a pail in her hand, and ran off.

She met an old lady with a shopping bag. Lyuba talked to her, even carried her shopping bag to the entrance. The old lady, being rather deaf, for a long time could not understand what the girl wanted. But Lyuba persisted until she understood, and then dived into the house.

At one building, a boy bigger than Lyuba did not want to let her into the courtyard. But the girl said something to him, after which he stopped waving his arms, squatted down on his heels and began to draw a sort of plan in the sand. They looked around the court together and went into various entrances, where the boy pointed out certain doors and where Lyuba dropped envelopes into the letterboxes. Until late in the evening she was seen flitting about through the courtyards.

That day many boys and girls of the neighborhood received the following notice:

"If it is important to you who will be the first to fly to the moon, if you are a friend of science and of cosmonauts, come with your dog tomorrow at eleven o'clock to Rose Boulevard. There you will be met by the staff of LYGEB."

Rose Boulevard was so called because an enormous rose bush grew in the main flowerbed. Until eleven o'clock on that sunny day in August the boulevard looked as usual. Babies were dozing peacefully in their carriages. Nurses and grandmothers were scolding mischievous children for throwing balls into the flowerbeds. Pensioners were dozing, their faces covered with newspapers. Domino players were slamming their pieces down on the table, oblivious to everything.

The scene was suddenly transformed, as if by an earthquake tremor. The pensioners roused themselves and started up from their benches, the nurses stopped scolding the children, and the hands of the domino players froze in mid-air, in the act of smacking their dominoes down. If the benches had been able to move, they would have turned around to face the unusual procession that marched down the boulevard, filling it with shouting and barking. About twenty sun-tanned children proudly led on leashes mongrels, huskies, boxers, Alsatians, and cuddlesome thin-legged poodles. A girl in a red dress and two boys leading the procession were the only ones without dogs.

"It looks as if they've opened a dog show," said an old lady.

"So it seems."

"But where are the judges?"

"Most likely it's those three in front."

The onlookers were not far from right. It was of course the undertaking of LYGEB—*L*yuba, *G*ena and *B*orya. It was they who had sent the mysterious invitations. It took all of Lyuba's initiative to find out in one day all the names and addresses of the dog owners. And here they all were.

The plan of LYGEB was simple. From Rose Boulevard they would go to the Institute of Space Research and say: "We have brought you some dogs. If they are needed for the exploration of outer space, we will give them to you. And please show us Rags."

Borya had described in detail the great aim of the LYGEB plan. But he made no mention of Rags.

"Are you willing to give them your dogs?" he asked.

"Of course we are!" the owners of the dogs had answered, gazing sadly at their pets, who were wagging their tails.

"That's fine," Borya had said. "Now we have to pick out the best specimens. After all, they'll have to fly into outer space!"

Gena had lined them up, Lyuba had written down the names of the dogs and had given each a plus or a minus, according to the opinion of Borya, who looked over the future celebrities critically. It turned out that half of them had cosmic names. One after another they came up: Venus, Mars, Pluto; there were two Rockets and even one Sputnik. On the whole Borya was pleased with the inspection. But seeing a long-haired Scotch terrier, he wrinkled his nose. He remembered the song the boys had sung at the dog show, "The dog has a beard and a mustache, too, ha, ha, hee, hee. . . ."

"A scarecrow. We don't need that kind," Borya had said crossly to the owner, a girl in a yellow dress.

"You haven't any right to talk like that!" the girl had said in a tearful voice. "My dog isn't groomed but he's very brave. Look at this!" She took a paper from a little handbag.

Everybody gathered round Borya, who unfolded the paper and read:

The District Militia Station expresses its gratitude to Olga Zatsepova for the capture of a thief by her terrier.

Station Chief Solovyov

The certificate had a seal on it.

"What's his name?" Lyuba had asked, sitting on her heels and stroking the shaggy hero gently.

"His name is 'The Hair of Veronica.' That's the name of a constellation. Vronnie, for short."

"We'll take your Vronnie," Borya had agreed. "Let's go!"

The procession triumphantly wound its way along the street, followed by the curious glances of passers-by. On the way from Rose Boulevard to the Institute, the friends of science and cosmonauts had to undergo a number of trials. They heroically withstood the onslaught of curious boys and the raids of stray dogs, who tried to start fights with their proud relatives. At one moment two dogs appeared from around a corner and took on an Alsatian. When the big dog grew angry and jumped on them, the fur flew. It was all the children could do to save the silly things from his sharp fangs.

But everything turned out well. The procession arrived at its destination without losing a single member.

The neat two-story house, shaded by trees, met them with silence. The dogs promptly lay down on the grass, worn out by the heat.

An old watchman appeared from the gatehouse. He looked over the hushed company and asked sternly, "Whom did you want to see?"

"The Chief," Gena answered for everybody.

The watchman snorted: "Imagine that! And I'm supposed to interrupt the scientists for such nonsense."

"We're not here for nonsense. We're friends of science," Borya tried to explain.

"We know all about your science—climbing over fences!" the guard said.

"I can see that you don't read the papers," Gena said with dignity. "And you are supposed to be a watchman at the Institute of Space Research!"

"He's trying to teach me!" the old man flew into a rage. "Why, the Professor himself shakes my hand. I said I won't let you in, and that's that."

"But we won't go away!" the children shouted.

A man with a preoccupied look came out, attracted by the noise. After hearing both sides, he told the angry watchman that this was a serious business and that one should thank the children and not drive them away.

"You know best," the old man answered, frowning.

"Well, let's see your dogs," the doctor said to the children and began to select little mongrels.

"This one, and this one, and this one here," he pointed them out. "And the terrier, of course. You're not sorry to part with him, are you?"

"No, of course not!" Vronnie's mistress sighed.

The donated dogs were led away.

"How about us?" The owners of the Alsatians were disappointed.

"Your dogs are fine for other purposes. They can serve excellently on the frontiers, for instance. Unfortunately, they aren't suitable for us. I'll make up a list of the owners of the selected dogs. You can come and visit them. Thanks a lot, children!"

Borya, suddenly afraid that the doctor would go away before he could find out about Rags, touched his sleeve.

"Please, couldn't you show me my dog?"

"Your dog? Is he here, at the Institute?"

"I had a dog, Rags. He's now called Courageous. I recognized him on television."

"But Courageous, my friend, was called Snapper and not Rags. And then, he was a stray dog."

"All the same, it's him," Borya insisted. "I can prove it. I'll just look at him and say, 'Here, Rags!' And he'll come right over. You'll see!"

The doctor was a kind person and he understood Borya's feelings.

"Well, maybe so," he said after a moment, "maybe it is he. But there's nothing I can do about it at the moment. Courageous is not in town."

"Is he in the country?"

"On vacation. Good-bye." And he turned to go.

"Wait a minute, wait a minute!" Lyuba rushed forward.

The doctor stopped. "What can I do for you, young lady?"

"I wanted to tell you that he's been looking for Rags a whole year. Are you quite sure that Courageous used to be called Snapper?"

"Yes. We all know that."

There was nothing else to say. Borya, his head lowered dismally, was drawing a half-circle in the sand with his toe.

"Come," Gena touched him lightly on the shoulder. "We'll come back some other time."

Borya Gives an Interview

There came at last a morning when the star-gazer awakened to the surprising and joyful news. "Has it really happened?" he asked, as if doubting that the day he had dreamed of had dawned and was shining peacefully.

Young or old, a person hardened by life or a boy with radiant eyes, the star-gazer's heart beat joyfully on that morning, in May, 1960, when he heard about the ship.

It was not a sailing vessel, nor a battle cruiser, nor an airliner that filled our dreamer with happiness, but a newborn spaceship. It was flying around the globe. And the dreamer decided, "A spaceship has been built, and this means it will soon have a human passenger. It can't be otherwise!"

And again news traveled around the globe as fast as the spaceship. It sounded Russian whether given in English, German, or French. Everyone who announced it knew that overhead flew not a little ball but a whole room, airy, warm, and comfortable. And around it was outer space which was almost empty, and where the pressure of gases was a hundred billion times weaker than inside the giant Sputnik. One shuddered to think of it. What if the walls of the chamber did not withstand the stress and the capsule exploded?

But the craft made one revolution around the earth after another, and in the cabin it was as warm and airy as before, just like home.

Since there was such a durable room there would soon be somebody to occupy it!

The dreamer could barely wait till twilight to see this new and brightest star. He would not need field glasses or a telescope; he would see it with his naked eye!

But there will be no skipper on this ship. It will be a ship without a captain—an empty ship with only cargo and not a human being on it. But was the captain needed? Why should we risk his life? For there is dangerous radiation in space. Meteors fly there a hundred times faster than bullets. It is dangerous to collide with them even if they are minute particles because they can pierce the walls of the capsule. A man would be helpless against them. While he evaluated the danger, a second or two would be lost, during which the spacecraft would fly many miles. So was it not better to trust the ship's electronic brain?

Yes, it was better to trust the computers. They will lead the rocket, evade the dangers, and, when necessary, change the spaceship's course.

But eventually there would have to be a commander of the spaceship. He would be the one to investigate the lunar craters and unravel the secrets of Mars. He would be the one to stop the rocket in its course in order to wait for the arrival of an unknown planet. He would be the one to control the computers! The computers were only mechanical navigators; the commander would be a man!

The star-gazers meditated along these lines while they waited to see the spaceship in the skies, and thought of voyages to distant stars.

Among them was the future spaceship commander—the first one. Like the others, he gazed at the sky and wanted very much to be in the spaceship. But that was yet impossible. For not a single spacecraft had landed, so far, and the doctors were still not convinced of the possibility of a reëntry from space safe for man. Everyone was aware of the problems of making space flight completely safe for human beings and watched the developments of space science.

Not much time passed before the radio began to announce interesting reports:

In the Soviet Union research in the upper layers of the atmosphere and in outer space continues with the help of geophysical rockets.

In accordance with the research program, another in the series of single-stage ballistic rockets was launched in June, 1960.

The launching was successful. The rocket reached an altitude of 682,240 feet.

The animals on board were landed in good condition.

The dog Courageous completed his fifth flight into space.

The last two of these matter-of-fact announcements attracted a number of impatient reporters to the Institute. As always, they were in a great hurry. But the objects of their interest caused some delay; somewhere in the Institute building, doctors were checking them over.

Other reporters crowded around the entrance and made fun of their colleagues arriving late. A puffing, tousled fellow rushed up, a tape recorder dangling from his shoulder. "Have they left already?" he asked breathlessly.

"They refused to leave without seeing you!" somebody said. "Hurry and pull out your microphone. The broadcast is about to begin! Comrades," the clown said in the voice of a radio announcer, "we are in the courtyard of the Institute for Space Research. Allow me to introduce you to the world-famous cosmonaut, and request him to say a few words about his health. Can you hear that crunching sound? Our astronaut happens to be Rabbit Starlet. She's eating her breakfast of cabbage with noisy zest. We can assume, therefore, that she's in excellent health!"

The radio reporter with the tape recorder listened to this speech, laughed with the rest, and said: "Go on, joke about the sound of cabbage. But, how about it?—can you journalists reproduce in your notebooks the sound of a storm? I traveled to the Pacific Ocean with this tape recorder and microphone to catch the howling of the ocean winds. How would your mute paper convey the force of the elements?"

The contest of wits was interrupted by the appearance of a girl dressed neatly in a white robe. She was immediately surrounded by the reporters. It was Valya. She smiled, pleased with the attention, with the morning's freshness, and with the awareness of having recently become a doctor.

"Where are the heroes?" the reporters asked.

"They are still being checked over, but they'll soon be brought out. What can I tell you in the meanwhile? Perhaps I can tell you about the flight?"

"No, tell us about yourself. How does it feel to be a space doctor?"

Valya blushed. How had they found out that she would now be training test dogs?

"There isn't much to tell," Valya said. "I finished secondary school, came here to work as a laboratory assistant, and continued with my studies at the Institute. I am now a doctor. That is all."

"Here they are!" someone cried out.

In the open doorway stood Vasily with two little white dogs. Immediately a commotion started around the little space travelers. The photographers arranged the three astronauts—Starlet was also brought out—in all possible combinations.

A cameraman used up a whole roll of movie film, interrupting the newspaper photographers. The reporters badgered the doctors with the most irrelevant questions. Vasily could not satisfy their curiosity, for he did not know the facts, about Courageous' food preferences. They wanted to know if he liked steak better than chocolate, or vice versa. He couldn't remember a time when Courageous had refused any kind of food.

Only the man with the tape recorder looked on all this commotion with any degree of calm. When the photographers subsided, he approached the little astronauts.

"Be a good fellow and give a big bark," he said, holding the microphone near Courageous. His tone was so sincere that none of his colleagues even smiled.

Squinting in the sun, his tongue lolling from the heat, Courageous looked seriously at the man, not understanding what he wanted.

But Malek suddenly leaped forward and, jumping high, licked the radio reporter on the nose with all his canine spontaneity.

"Well!" the reporter exclaimed. "Will *you* bark for me?"

Malek barked joyfully.

After recording these important sounds for the public, the man with the tape recorder crossed the courtyard, settled himself in the grass, and began to speak into his microphone.

"We are in the courtyard of the Institute that sent the dogs Courageous and Malek and the rabbit Starlet on their journey into space. The noise you hear is from the reporters interviewing them—if I may be allowed the expression—the returned cosmonauts. . . ."

The reporters did not hear the rest of what the man said into the microphone, for their attention was suddenly diverted.

The Institute's watchman was the only person who had noticed two small figures slipping through the bars of the iron fence. He was about to grab them when they dashed through the bars, ran forward, and their excited young faces interrupted all conversation.

"Rags! Rags!" the tow-headed boy shouted as he ran toward the dogs.

Courageous dashed to meet him with great bounds, dragging his long leash in the grass. Ecstatically, he jumped up to the boy's chest, giving him a lick on the face.

Borya squatted down on his heels, lifted Rags into his lap, raised his face, and looked into his loving eyes. He began to talk to him in a strange, choking voice that expressed both his grief and despair of the past months and his happiness at this reunion.

"Rags, Rags," Borya cried, seeing but not believing—not yet—that his pet was near him. "It's me, remember? Do you recognize me? I thought I'd never, never see you again. Boy, how you've grown! And you're so strong! Do you like it here, Rags? Did you miss me?"

Rags looked into the face of his former master and his tail said that he had long ago forgotten his grievance, that he had missed him and was glad to see him. Not only glad but happy!

Rags turned to look at Vasily, who was coming toward them squinting his eyes behind his thick glasses, and wagged his tail faster. Yes, he was happy to see and hear Borya. Besides that, he remembered how well off he was here with this kind man, so he was doubly happy.

"Is this your dog?" Vasily asked in surprise. "Glad to meet you."

Borya sprang to his feet, beaming.

"Yes, it's my Rags! I've been looking everywhere for him. And then . . ." He didn't finish, becoming aware of all the curious eyes staring at him.

"What a meeting!" said one of the reporters, grinning. "You say, sonny, that Courageous was called Rags? Strange."

Questions were showered upon Borya: "How did you lose him?" "What did he like to do?" "Did he like steak when you had him?" "How long did you look for him?" They asked so many questions that Borya

had to tell everything he knew about Rags, right from the beginning.

The other trespasser was ignored. Only one journalist paid any attention to him: "I knew it, I knew you'd be here!"

"Daddy!" Gena cried, overjoyed. "We've found Rags!"

"I saw it all," Anatoly Karatov said.

When Borya finished his tale, Karatov went up to him. "I'm glad for you, Borya. I was very sorry when you lost your dog."

"It was our fault—Gena's and mine," Borya confessed. "But then," and his eyes narrowed slyly, "if Rags hadn't disappeared, he would never have become Courageous! Now the whole world knows him!"

Borya paused, full of amazement at his discovery, and turned to Vasily.

"Doctor, may we come here sometimes to visit him? Gena and I, and a girl Lyuba? We won't get in the way."

"Of course," Vasily agreed. "Be sure to come and visit us."

"Borya, Borya!" Gena punched his friend, "you lucky stiff! You found Rags, and he's a famous astronaut!" Then Gena looked at his father sadly, as if to say that happiness was unequally distributed in this world. Journalist Karatov did not like dogs.

Borya was saying good-bye to Rags.

"I'll come," he said in his ear. "Don't worry! I'll come to see you again."

THE OLD GENIE HOTTABYCH

LAZAR LAGIN

I recently had the opportunity to conduct a minor literary poll—in several classes in Moscow schools—of the currently most popular children's books. *The Old Genie Hottabych* was, without a doubt, a great favorite.

The story is a combination for children of *A Thousand and One Nights* and *Aladdin's Lamp,* but with a distinctly scientific-age touch. The Genie performs miracles aplenty, of course. But the miracles of mathematics and science he sees all around him *in Moscow* after his liberation from a bottle (in which he had been held prisoner for the last two thousand years) astound him no less, and perhaps even more, than *his* magic astounds his modern host.

He is an ambitious Genie and wants to learn. The schoolboy who had set him free and his school chum become the Genie's tutors. Their old pupil is as full of pranks as he is of scientific curiosity.

Here are the first few adventures of the old Genie and the boy Volka.

A Most Unusual Morning

At 7:32 that morning a playful sunray slipped through a tear in the curtain and settled on the nose of Volka Kostylkov, a sixth-grade student. Volka sneezed and woke up.

Just then he heard his mother say in the next room, "Don't wake him yet, Alyosha. Let the child sleep a bit longer; he has an examination today."

Volka winced. When, oh when, would his mother stop calling him a child!

"Nonsense!" he could hear his father answer. "The boy's nearly twelve. He might as well get up and help us pack. Before you know it, this "child" of yours will be using a razor."

How could he have forgotten about the packing! Volka threw off the blankets and dressed hurriedly. How could he have forgotten such a day!

This was the day the Kostylkov family was moving to an apartment in a new six-story building. Most of their belongings had been packed the night before. Mother and Grandma had packed the dishes in a little tin tub in which once, very long ago, they had bathed Volka. His father had rolled up his sleeves and, with a mouthful of tacks and just like a shoemaker, had spent the evening hammering down the crates of books.

Then they had all argued as to the best place to put the things so as to have them handy when the truck arrived in the morning. Then they had their tea on a bare table—as at a picnic. Then they decided their heads would be clearer after a good night's sleep, and they all went to bed.

In a word, there was just no explaining how he could have forgotten that this was the morning they were moving to the new apartment for which they had waited so long.

The movers came before breakfast was quite over. The first thing they did was to open wide both halves of the door and ask in loud voices, "Well, can we begin?"

"Yes, please do," both Mother and Grandma answered and began to bustle about.

Volka marched downstairs, solemnly carrying the sofa pillows to the waiting truck.

"Are you moving?" a boy from next door asked.

"Yes," Volka answered casually, as though he was used to moving from an old apartment to a new one every week and there was nothing very special about it.

The janitor Stepanych walked over, slowly rolled a cigarette and began an unhurried conversation as one grown-up talking to another. Volka felt dizzy with pride and happiness. He gathered his courage and invited Stepanych to visit them at their new home. The janitor said, "With pleasure." A serious, important, man-to-man conversation was beginning, when all at once Volka's mother's voice came through the open window. "Volka! Volka! Where can that dreadful child be?"

Volka raced up to the now strangely large, empty apartment, in which pieces of old newspapers and old medicine bottles were lying forlornly about the floor.

"There you are at last!" his mother said. "Take your precious aquarium and get right into the truck. I want you to sit on the sofa and hold the aquarium on your lap. Be sure the water doesn't spill on the sofa."

It's really strange, the way parents worry when they're moving to a new apartment.

Well, the truck finally choked as if exhausted and stopped at the attractive entrance of the new building. The movers quickly carried everything upstairs and were soon gone.

Volka's father opened a few crates and said, "We'll do the rest in the evening." Then he left for the factory.

Mother and Grandma began unpacking the pots and pans, while Volka decided to run down to the river. His father had warned him not to go swimming without him because the river was very deep, but Volka soon found an excuse. "I have to go in for a dip to clear my head. How can I take an exam with a sluggish brain!"

It's wonderful, the way Volka was always able to think of an excuse when he was about to do something he was not allowed.

How convenient it is to have a river near your house! Volka told his mother he'd go sit on the embankment and study his geography. And he really and truly intended to spend about ten minutes leafing through the textbook. However, he got undressed and jumped into the water the minute he reached the river. It was still early and there was not a soul about. This had its good and bad points. It was nice, because no one could stop him from swimming as much as he liked. It was bad, because there was no one to admire what a good swimmer and especially what an extraordinary diver he was.

Volka swam and dived until he became blue. Finally, he had had enough. He was ready to climb out when he changed his mind and decided to dive into the clear water just once more.

As he was about to come up for air, his hand hit a long hard object. He grabbed it and surfaced near the shore, holding a strange-looking slippery, moss-covered clay vessel. It resembled an ancient Greek vase called an amphora. The neck was sealed tightly with a green substance and what looked like a seal was imprinted on top.

Volka weighed the vessel in his hand. It was very heavy. He caught his breath. A treasure! An ancient treasure of great scientific value! How wonderful!

He dressed quickly and dashed home to open it in the privacy of his room.

As he ran along, he could visualize the notice which would certainly appear in all the papers the next morning. He even thought of a head-line: "A Pioneer Aids Science."

Yesterday, a pioneer * named Vladimir Kostylkov came to his district militia station and handed the officer on duty a treasure consisting of antique gold objects that he found on the bottom of

---

* *The Pioneers* is a nationwide organization of Soviet children aged nine to fifteen.

the river, in a very deep place. The treasure had been handed over to the Historical Museum. According to reliable sources, Vladimir Kostylkov is an excellent diver.

Volka slipped past the kitchen, where his mother was cooking dinner. He dashed into his room, nearly breaking his leg as he stumbled over a chandelier lying on the floor. It was Grandma's famous chandelier. Very long ago, before the Revolution, his grandfather had converted it from a hanging oil lamp. Grandma would not part with it for anything in the world, because it was now a treasured memory of Grandfather. Since it was not elegant enough to be hung in the dining room, they decided to hang it in Volka's room. That is why a huge iron hook had been screwed into the ceiling.

Volka rubbed his sore knee, locked the door, took his penknife from his pocket, and, trembling with excitement, scraped the seal off the bottle.

The room was immediately filled with choking black smoke while a noiseless explosion of great force threw him up to the ceiling, where he remained suspended from the hook by the seat of his pants.

The Old Genie

While Volka was swaying back and forth on the hook, trying to understand what had happened, the smoke began to clear. Suddenly, he realized there was someone else in the room. It was a skinny, sunburnt old man with a beard down to his waist and dressed in an elegant turban, a white coat of fine wool richly embroidered in silver and gold, gleaming white silk puffed trousers, and petal-pink morocco slippers with upturned toes.

"Hachoo!" the old man sneezed loudly and prostrated himself. "I greet you, O Wonderful and Wise Youth!"

Volka shut his eyes tight and then opened them again. No, he was not seeing things. The strange old man was really there. Kneeling and rubbing his hands, he stared at the furnishings of Volka's room with lively shrewd eyes, as if they were all a goodness-knows-what sort of a miracle.

"Where did you come from?" Volka inquired cautiously, swaying back and forth under the ceiling like a pendulum. "Are you . . . from an amateur troupe?"

"Oh no, my young lord," the old man replied grandly, though he

remained in the same uncomfortable position and continued to sneeze. "I am not from the strange country of Anamateur Troupe you mentioned. I come from this most horrible vessel."

With these words he scrambled to his feet and began jumping on the vessel, from which a wisp of smoke was still curling upward, until there was nothing left but a small pile of clay pieces. Then, with a sound like tinkling crystalware, he yanked a hair from his beard and tore it in two. The bits of clay flared up with a weird green flame until soon there was not a trace of them left on the floor.

Still, Volka was skeptical. You must agree, it's not easy to accept the fact that a live person can crawl out of a vessel no bigger than a bottle.

"Well, I don't know . . ." Volka stammered. "The vessel was so small, and you're so big compared to it."

"You don't believe me, O despicable one?!" the old man shouted angrily, but immediately calmed down; once again he fell to his knees, hitting the floor with his forehead so hard that the water shook in the aquarium and the sleepy fish began to dart about. "Forgive me, my young savior, but I am not used to having my words doubted. Know thou most blessed of all young men, that I am none other than the mighty Genie Hassan Abdurrakhman ibn Hottab, that is, the son of Hottab, famed in all four corners of the world."

All this was so interesting it made Volka forget he was hanging under the ceiling on a chandelier hook.

"A 'gin-e'? Isn't that some kind of a drink?"

"I am not a drink, O inquisitive youth!" the old man flared up again, then took himself in hand once more and calmed down. "I am not a beverage, but a mighty, unconquerable spirit. There is no magic in the world which I cannot do, and my name, as I have already had the pleasure of conveying to your great and extremely respected attention, is Hassan Abdurrakhman ibn Hottab, or, as you would say in Russian, Hassan Abdurrakhman Hottabych. If you mention it to the first Ifrit or Genie you meet, you'll see him tremble, and his mouth will go dry from fear," the old man continued boastfully.

"My story—hachoo!—is strange, indeed. And if it were written down, it would serve as a good lesson for all those who seek learning. I, most unfortunate Genie that I am, disobeyed Sulayman, son of David (on the twain be peace!)—I and my brother, Omar Asaf Hottabych. Then Sulayman sent his Vizier Asaf, son of Barakhiya, to seize us, and he brought us back against our will. Sulayman, David's son (on the twain be peace!), ordered two bottles brought to him: a copper one and a clay one. He put me in the clay vessel and my brother Omar Hottabych in the copper one. He sealed both vessels and imprinted the greatest of all names, that of Allah, on them and then ordered his Genies to carry us off and throw my brother into the sea and me into the river, from which you, O my blessed savior—hachoo, hachoo!—have fished me. May your days be prolonged. O . . . begging your pardon, I would be indescribably happy to know your name, most handsome of all youths."

"My name's Volka," our hero replied as he swayed gently to and fro under the ceiling.

"And what is your fortunate father's name, may he be blessed for eternity? Tell me the most gentle of all his names, as he is certainly deserving of great love and gratitude for presenting the world with such an outstanding offspring."

"His name's Aleksei. And his most gentle . . . most gentle name is Alyosha."

"Then know thou, most deserving of all youths, Volka ibn Alyosha, that I will henceforth fulfill all your wishes, since you have saved me from the most horrible imprisonment. Hachoo!"

"Why do you keep on sneezing?" Volka asked, as though everything else was quite clear.

"The many thousand years I spent in dampness, deprived of the beneficial rays of the sun, in a cold vessel lying on the bottom of a river, have given me, your undeserving servant, a most tiresome running nose. Hachoo! Hachoo! But all this is of no importance at all and unworthy of your attention. Order me as you wish, O young master!" Hassan Abdur-rakhman ibn Hottab concluded fervently with his head raised, but still kneeling.

"First of all, won't you please rise," Volka said.

"Your every word is my command," the old man replied obediently and rose. "I await your further orders."

"And now," Volka mumbled uncertainly, "if it's not too much trouble . . . would you be kind enough . . . of course, if it's not too much trouble. . . . What I mean is, I'd really like to be back on the floor again."

That very moment he found himself standing beside old man Hottabych, as we shall call our new acquaintance for short. The first thing

Volka did was to grab the seat of his pants. There was no hole at all.

Miracles were beginning to happen.

The Geography Examination

"Order me as you wish!" Hottabych continued, gazing at Volka devotedly. "Is there anything that grieves you, O Volka ibn Alyosha? Tell me and I will help you."

"My goodness!" Volka cried, glancing at the clock ticking away loudly on the table. "I'm late! I'm late for my exam!"

"What are you late for, O most treasured Volka ibn Alyosha?" Hottabych asked in a business-like way. "What does that strange word 'ex-am' mean?"

"It's the same as a test. I'm late for my test at school."

"Then know thou, O Volka, that you do not value my powers at all," the old man said in a hurt voice. "No, no, and no again! You will not be late for your exam. Just tell me what your choice is: to hold up the exam, or to find yourself immediately at your school gates?"

"To find myself at the school," Volka replied.

"Nothing could be simpler! You will now find yourself where your young and honorable spirit draws you so urgently. You will stun your teachers and your schoolmates with your great knowledge."

With the same pleasant tinkling sound the old man once again pulled a hair from his beard, then a second one.

"I'm afraid I won't stun them," Volka sighed, quickly changing into his school uniform. "To tell you the truth, I have little chance of getting an 'A' in geography."

"In geography?" the old man cried and raised his thin hairy arms triumphantly. "So you're to take an exam in geography?! Then know thou, O most wonderful of all wonderful ones, that you are exceptionally lucky, for I know more about geography than any other Genie—I, your devoted Hassan Abdurrakhman ibn Hottab. We shall go to school together, may its foundation and roof be blessed! I'll prompt you invisibly and tell you all the answers. You will become the most famous pupil of your school and of all the schools of your most beautiful city. And if anyone of your teachers does not accord you the greatest praise, he will have to deal with me! Oh, they will be very, very sorry!" Hottabych raged. "I'll turn them into mules that carry water, into homeless curs covered with scabs, into the most horrible and obnoxious toads—

276

that's what I'll do to them! However," he said, calming down as quickly as he had become enraged, "things will not go that far, for everyone, O Volka ibn Alyosha, will be astounded by your answers."

"Thank you, Hassan Hottabych," Volka sighed miserably. "Thank you, but I don't want you to prompt me. We Pioneers are against prompting as a matter of principle. We're conducting an organized fight against prompting."

Now, how could an old Genie who had spent so many years in prison know such a scholarly term as "a matter of principle"? However, the sigh his young savior heaved to accompany his sad and honorable words convinced Hottabych that Volka ibn Alyosha needed his help more than ever before.

"Your refusal grieves me," Hottabych said. "After all, no one will notice me prompting you."

"Ha!" Volka said bitterly. "You don't know what keen ears our teacher Varvara Stepanovna has."

"You not only upset me, you now offend me, O Volka ibn Alyosha! If Hassan Abdurrakhman ibn Hottab says that no one will notice, it means no one will notice!"

"Not a single soul?" Volka asked again, just to make sure.

"Not a single soul. The words which I will have the pleasure of telling you will go straight from my deferential lips to your greatly respected ears."

"I really don't know what to do, Hassan Hottabych," Volka said sighing. "I really hate to upset you by refusing. All right, have your own way! Geography isn't mathematics or grammar. I'd never agree to even the tiniest prompt in those subjects, but since geography isn't really the most important subject. . . . Come on, let's hurry!" He looked at the old man's unusual clothing with a critical eye. "Hm-m-m . . . D'you think you could change into something else, Hassan Hottabych?"

"Don't my garments please your gaze, O most noble of Volkas?" Hottabych asked unhappily.

"Sure they do, they certainly do," Volka answered diplomatically. "But you're dressed . . . if you know what I mean . . . our styles are a little different. . . . Your clothes will attract too much attention."

"But how do respectable, honorable gentlemen of advanced age dress nowadays?"

Volka tried to explain what a jacket, trousers, and a hat were, but though he tried very hard he wasn't very successful. He was about to despair, when he suddenly glanced at his grandfather's portrait on the wall. He led Hottabych over to the time-darkened photograph, and the old man gazed long at it with curiosity, surprised to see clothing so unlike his own.

A moment later, Volka, holding Hottabych's arm, emerged from the house. The old man was magnificent in a new linen suit, an embroidered Ukrainian shirt, and a straw hat. The only things he had refused to change, complaining of three-thousand-year-old corns, were his slippers. He remained in his pink slippers with the upturned toes, which, in times gone by, would have probably driven the most stylish young man at the Court of Caliph Harun al Rashid out of his mind with envy.

When Volka and the transformed Hottabych approached the entrance of Moscow Secondary School No. 245,* the old man looked at himself in the glass door and was quite pleased with what he saw.

The elderly doorman, who was sedately reading his paper, put it aside with pleasure at the sight of Volka and his companion. It was hot and the doorman felt like talking to someone.

Mounting several steps at a time, Volka dashed upstairs. The corridors were quiet and empty, a true and sad sign that the examination had begun and that he was late.

"And where are you going?" the doorman asked Hottabych good-naturedly as he was about to follow his young friend.

"He's come to see the principal," Volka shouted from the top of the stairs.

"You won't be able to see him now. He's at an examination. Won't you please come by again later on in the day?"

Hottabych frowned angrily.

"If I be permitted to, O respected old man, I would prefer to wait for him here." Then he shouted to Volka, "Hurry to your classroom, O Volka ibn Alyosha! I'm certain that you'll astound your teachers and your comrades with your great knowledge!"

"Are you his grandfather or something?" the doorman inquired, trying to start up a conversation. Hottabych said nothing. He felt it beneath his dignity to converse with a doorkeeper.

"Would you care for a cup of tea?" the doorman continued. "The heat's something terrible today."

---

* A Soviet *Secondary School* is a ten-year school for children from the ages of seven to seventeen.

278

He poured a full cup of tea and, turning to hand it to the untalkative stranger, found to his utter surprise that the old man had disappeared into thin air. Shaken by this unnatural occurrence, the doorman gulped down the tea intended for Hottabych, poured himself a second cup, and then a third, and did not stop until there wasn't a drop left. Then he sank into his chair with exhaustion and began to fan himself with his newspaper.

All the while, a no less unusual scene was taking place on the second floor, right above the doorman, in classroom 6B. The teachers, headed by the principal Pavel Vasilyevich, sat at a table covered with a heavy cloth used for special occasions. Behind them was the blackboard hung with various maps. Facing them were rows of solemn pupils. It was so quiet in the room that one could hear a lonely fly buzzing monotonously near the ceiling. If the pupils of 6B were always this quiet, theirs would undoubtedly be the most disciplined class in all of Moscow.

It must be noted, however, that the quiet in the classroom was not only due to the hush accompanying any examination, but also to the fact that Volka Kostylkov had been called to the board—and he was not in the room.

"Vladimir * Kostylkov!" the principal repeated and looked at the quiet children in surprise.

It became still more quiet.

Then, suddenly, they heard the loud clatter of running feet in the hall outside, and at the very moment the principal called "Vladimir Kostylkov" for the third and last time, the door burst open and Volka, very much out of breath, gasped:

"Here!"

"Please come up to the board," the principal said dryly. "We'll speak about your being late afterward."

"I . . . I feel ill," Volka mumbled, saying the first thing that came to his head as he walked uncertainly toward his examiners.

While he was wondering which of the slips of paper laid out on the table he should choose, old man Hottabych slipped through the wall in the corridor and disappeared through the opposite one into an adjoining classroom. He had an absorbed look on his face.

Volka finally took the first slip his hand touched. Tempting his fate,

---

* *Vladimir* is the formal version for the name Volka.

he turned it over very slowly, but was pleasantly surprised to see that he was to speak on India. He knew quite a lot about India, since he had always been interested in that country.

"Well, let's hear what you have to say," the principal said.

Volka even remembered the beginning of the chapter on India word for word as it was in his book. He opened his mouth to say that the Hindustan Peninsula resembled a triangle, and that this triangle bordered on the Indian Ocean and its various parts—the Arabian Sea in the West and the Bay of Bengal in the East—that two large countries, India and Pakistan, were located on the peninsula, that both were inhabited by kindly and peace-loving peoples with rich and ancient cultures, etc., etc., etc. But just then Hottabych, standing in the adjoining classroom, leaned against the wall and began prompting diligently, cupping his hand to his mouth like a horn.

"India, O my most respected teacher . . . !"

And suddenly Volka, contrary to his own desires, began to pour forth the most atrocious nonsense.

"India, O my most respected teacher, is located close to the edge of the Earth's disc and is separated from this edge by desolate and unexplored deserts, as neither animals nor birds live to the east of it. India is a very wealthy country, and its wealth lies in its gold. This is not dug from the ground as in other countries, but is produced, day and night, by a tireless species of gold-bearing ants, which are nearly the size of a dog. They dig their tunnels in the ground, and three times a day they bring up gold sand and nuggets and pile them in huge heaps. But woe be to those Indians who try to steal this gold without due skill! The ants pursue them and, overtaking them, kill them on the spot. From the north and west, India borders on a country of bald people. The men and women and even the children are all bald in this country. And these strange people live on raw fish and pine cones. Still closer to them is a country where you can neither see anything nor pass, as it is filled up to the top with feathers. The earth and the air are filled with feathers, and that is why you can't see anything there."

"Wait a minute, Kostylkov," the geography teacher said with a smile. "No one has asked you to tell us of the views of the ancients on Asia's geography. We'd like you to tell us the modern, proved facts about India."

Oh, how happy Volka would have been to display his knowledge of the subject! But what could he do if he was no longer in control of his speech and actions! In agreeing to have Hottabych prompt him, he became a toy in the old man's well-meaning but ignorant hands. He wanted to tell his teachers that what he had told them obviously had nothing to do with modern geography. But Hottabych, on the other side of the wall, shrugged in dismay and shook his head; and Volka, standing in front of the class, was compelled to do the same.

"That which I have had the honor of telling you, O greatly respected Varvara Stepanovna, is based on the most reliable sources, and there exist no other, more scientific facts on India than those I have just, with your permission, revealed to you."

"Please keep to the subject. This is an examination, not a masquerade. If you don't know the answers, it would be much more honorable to admit it right away. What was it you said about the earth's disc, by the way? Don't you know that the earth is round?"

Did Volka Kostylkov, an active member of the Moscow Planetarium's Astronomy Club, know that the earth was round? Why, any first grader knew that. But Hottabych, standing behind the wall, burst out laughing, and no matter how our poor boy tried to press his lips together, a scornful smirk escaped him.

"I presume you are making fun of your most devoted pupil! If the earth were round, the water would run off it, and then everyone would die of thirst, and all the plants would dry up. The Earth, O most noble and honored of all teachers and pedagogues, has always had and does now have the shape of a flat disc, surrounded on all sides by a mighty river named 'Ocean.' The Earth rests on six elephants, and they in turn are standing on a tremendous turtle. That is how the world is made, O teacher!"

The board of teachers gazed at Volka with rising surprise. He broke out in a cold sweat from horror and the realization of his own complete helplessness. The other children could not quite understand what had happened to their friend, but some began to giggle. It was really funny to hear about a country of bald people, about a country filled with feathers, about gold-bearing ants as big as dogs, and about the flat earth resting on six elephants and a turtle. As for Zhenya Bogorad, Volka's best friend and one of the class Pioneer leaders, he became really worried. He knew that Volka, as chairman of the Astronomy Club, at least knew that the earth was round—if he knew nothing else. Could it be that he had suddenly decided upon some mischief, and during an examination, of all times! Volka was probably ill, but what ailed him? What kind of a strange, strange disease did he have? And then, it was very bad for their Pioneer group. So far, they had been first in all the exams, but now Volka's stupid answers would spoil everything, though he was usually a disciplined Pioneer! Goga Pilukin, a most unpleasant boy at the next desk (nicknamed "Pill" by his classmates), hastened to rub it in.

Turning to Zhenya, he said, "That takes care of your group, Zhenya dear," he whispered with a malicious giggle. "You're sinking fast!"

Zhenya shook his fist at Pill.

"Varvara Stepanovna!" Goga whined. "Bogorad just shook his fist at me."

"Sit still and don't tattle," Varvara Stepanovna said and turned back to Volka, who stood before her more dead than alive.

"Were you serious about the elephants and the turtle?"

"More serious than ever before, O most respected of all teachers," Volka repeated after the old man and felt himself burning up with shame.

"And haven't you anything else to add? Do you really think you were answering the question?"

"No, I've nothing to add," Hottabych said behind the wall, shaking his head.

And Volka, helpless to withstand the force that was pushing him toward failure, also shook his head and said, "No, I've nothing to add. Perhaps, however, the fact that in the wealthy land of India the horizons are framed by gold and pearls."

"It's incredible!" his teacher exclaimed.

It was difficult to believe that Kostylkov, usually a well-behaved boy, had suddenly decided to play a silly joke on his teachers, and at such an important time! He was running the risk of a second examination in the autumn.

"I don't think the boy is quite well," Varvara Stepanovna whispered to the principal.

Glancing hurriedly and sympathetically at Volka, who stood numb with grief before them, the committee held a whispered conference.

Varvara Stepanovna suggested, "What if we ask the child another question, just to calm him? Say, from last year's book. Last year he got an 'A' in geography."

The others agreed, and Varvara Stepanovna once again turned to the unhappy boy.

282

"Now, Kostylkov, don't be nervous. Tell us what a horizon is."

"A horizon?" Volka said with new hope. "That's easy. A horizon is an imagined line which . . ."

But Hottabych came to life behind the wall again, and Volka once again became the victim of prompting.

"The horizon, O most revered one," Volka corrected himself, "I would call the horizon that brink where the crystal cupola of the Heavens touches the edge of the Earth."

"It gets worse as he goes on," Varvara Stepanovna moaned. "How would you have us understand your words about the crystal cupola of the Heavens—literally or figuratively?"

"Literally, O teacher," Hottabych prompted from the next room.

And Volka was obliged to repeat after him, "Literally, O teacher."

"Figuratively!" someone hissed from the back of the room. But Volka repeated, "Naturally, in the literal sense and no other."

"What does that mean?" Varvara Stepanovna asked, still not believing her ears. "Does that mean you consider the sky to be a solid cupola?"

"Yes."

"And does it mean there's a place where the earth ends?"

"Yes, there is, O my most highly respected teacher."

Behind the wall Hottabych nodded approvingly and rubbed his hands together smugly.

A strange silence fell on the class. Even those who were always ready to laugh stopped smiling. Something was definitely wrong with Volka. Varvara Stepanovna rose and felt his forehead anxiously. He did not have a fever.

But Hottabych was really touched by this. He bowed low and touched his forehead and chest in the Eastern manner and then began to whisper. Volka, driven by the same awful force, repeated his movements exactly.

"I thank you, O most gracious daughter of Stepan! I thank you for your trouble. But it is unnecessary, because, praised be Allah, I am quite well."

All this sounded extremely strange and funny. However, the other children were so worried about Volka that not a shade of a smile crossed a single face. Varvara Stepanovna took him by the hand, led him out of the room, and patted his bowed head.

"Never mind, Kostylkov. Don't worry. You're probably overtired.

Come back when you've had a good rest. All right?"

"All right," Volka said. "But upon my word of honor, Varvara Stepanovna, it's not my fault! It isn't really!"

"I'm not blaming you at all," the teacher answered kindly. "I'll tell you what: let's drop in on Pyotr Ivanych."

Pyotr Ivanych, the school doctor, examined Volka for ten whole minutes. He made him close his eyes and hold his arms out before him with his fingers spread apart; then he tapped his knee and drew lines on his chest and back with his stethoscope.

By then Volka came to himself. His cheeks turned pink again and his spirits rose.

"The boy's perfectly well," said Pyotr Ivanych. "And if you want my opinion, he's an unusually healthy child! I think he was probably overworked. He must have studied too much before his exams, because there's nothing wrong with him. And that's all there is to it!"

Just in case, though, he measured some drops into a glass, and the unusually healthy child was forced to drink the medicine.

Suddenly, Volka had an idea. What if he could profit from Hottabych's absence and take his geography examination right there, in the doctor's office?

"By no means!" Pyotr Ivanych said emphatically. "By no means. Let the child have a few days of rest. Geography can wait."

"That's quite true," the teacher sighed with relief, pleased that everything had turned out so well in the end. "And you, my young friend, run along home and have a good rest. When you feel better, come back and take your exam. I'm positive you'll get an 'A!' What do you think, Pyotr Ivanych?"

"Such a Hercules as he? Why, he'll never get less than an 'A+'!"

"Ah . . . and don't you think someone had better see him home?"

"Oh, no, Varvara Stepanovna!" Volka cried. "I'll be all right."

All he needed now was for a chaperone to bump into that crazy old Hottabych!

Volka now appeared to be in the pink of health, and with an easy heart Varvara Stepanovna let him go home.

The doorman rushed toward him as he was on the way out. "Kostylkov! Your grandpa, or whoever he is, the one who came here with you . . ."

At that very moment, old man Hottabych appeared from the wall. He was as happy as a lark and immensely pleased with himself, and he was humming a little tune.

"Help!" the doorman cried soundlessly and tried in vain to pour himself another cup of tea from the empty kettle. When he put the kettle down and turned around, both Volka Kostylkov and his mysterious companion had disappeared. By then they had already turned the nearest corner.

"Pray tell me, young master, did you astound your teacher and your comrades with your great knowledge?" Hottabych inquired proudly, breaking a rather long silence.

"I astounded them all right!" Volka said and looked at the old man wrathfully.

Hottabych beamed. "I expected nothing else! But for a moment there I thought that the most reverend daughter of Stepan was displeased with the breadth and scope of your knowledge."

"Oh, no, no!" Volka cried in fear, recalling Hottabych's terrible threats. "You were imagining things."

"I would have changed her into a chopping block on which butchers chop up mutton," the old man said fiercely (and Volka was really frightened for his teacher's fate), "if I hadn't seen that she had such great respect for you and took you to the door of your classroom and then practically down the stairs. I realized then that she had fully appreciated your answers. Peace be with her!"

"Sure, peace be with her!" Volka added hastily, feeling that a load had fallen from his shoulders.

During the several thousand years of Hottabych's life, he had often had to do with people feeling sad and gloomy, and he knew how to cheer them up. At any rate, he was convinced he knew how to do so. All that was needed was to give a person that which he had always longed for. But what kind of a present should he give Volka? The answer came to him quite by chance when Volka asked a passer-by:

"Would you please tell me what time it is?"

The man looked at his watch and said, "Five to two."

"Thank you," Volka said and continued on in silence.

Hottabych was the first to speak.

"Tell me, O Volka, how was the man able to tell the time of day so accurately?"

"Didn't you see him look at his watch?"

The old man raised his eyebrows in surprise.

"His watch?!"

"Sure, his watch," Volka explained. "He had a watch on his wrist. The round chrome-plated thing."

"Why don't you have such a watch, O most noble of all Genie-saviors?"

"I'm too young to have such a watch," Volka answered humbly.

"May I be permitted, O honorable passer-by, to inquire as to the time of day?" Hottabych said, stopping the first person he saw and staring at his watch.

"Two minutes to two," the man answered, somewhat surprised at the flowery language.

After thanking him in the most elaborate oriental manner, Hottabych said with a sly grin, "May I be permitted, O loveliest of all Volkas, to inquire as to the time of day?"

And there was a watch shining on Volka's left wrist, exactly like the one the man they had stopped had, but instead of being chrome-plated, it was of the purest gold.

"May it be worthy of your hand and your kind heart," Hottabych said in a touched voice, basking in Volka's happiness and surprise.

Then Volka did something that any other boy or girl would have done in his place, having found himself the proud possessor of his first watch. He raised his arm to his ear to hear it tick.

"It's not wound. I'll have to wind it." To his great disappointment, he found he could not move the winding button. Then he got out his penknife to open the watch case. However, try as he would, he could not find a trace of a slit in which to insert the knife.

"It's made of solid gold," the old man boasted and winked. "I'm not one of those people who give presents made of hollow gold."

"Does that mean there's nothing inside of it?" Volka asked with disappointment.

"Why, should there be anything inside?" the old Genie inquired anxiously. Volka unbuckled the strap in silence and returned the watch to Hottabych.

"All right, then, I'll give you a watch that doesn't have to have anything inside."

Once again a gold watch appeared on Volka's wrist, but now it was very small and flat. There was no glass on it and instead of hands there was a small vertical gold rod in the middle. The face was studded with the most exquisite emeralds set where the numbers should be.

"Never before did anyone, even the wealthiest of all sultans, have a hand sun watch!" the old man boasted again. "There were sun dials in city squares, in market places, in gardens and in yards. And they were all made of stone. But I just invented this one. It's not bad, is it?"

It certainly was exciting to be the only owner of a sun watch in the whole world.

Volka grinned broadly, while the old man beamed.

"How do you tell the time on it?" Volka asked.

"Here's how," Hottabych said, taking hold of Volka's hand gently. "Hold your arm straight out like this and the shadow cast by the little gold rod will fall on the right number."

"But the sun has to be shining," Volka said, looking with displeasure at a small cloud that just obscured it.

"The cloud will pass in a minute," Hottabych promised. True enough, in a minute the sun began to shine once again. "See, it points somewhere between 2 and 3 P.M. That means it's about 2:30." As he was speaking, another cloud covered the sun.

"Don't pay any attention to it," Hottabych said. "I'll clear the sky for you whenever you want to find out what time it is."

"What about the autumn?" Volka asked.

"What about it?"

"What about the autumn and the winter, when the sky is covered with clouds for months on end?"

"I've already told you, O Volka, the sun will shine whenever you want it to. You have but to order me and everything will be as you wish."

"But what if you're not around?"

"I'll always be near by. All you have to do is call me."

"But what about the evenings and nights?" Volka asked stubbornly. "What about the night, when there's no sun in the sky?"

"At night people must surrender themselves to sleep, and not to look at their watches," Hottabych snapped. He had to control himself not to teach the insolent youth a good lesson. "All right then, tell me whether you like that man's watch. If you do, you shall have it."

"What do you mean? It belongs to him. Don't tell me you are going to . . ."

"Don't worry, O Volka ibn Alyosha. I won't touch a hair on his head. He'll offer you the watch himself, for you are certainly worthy of receiving the most treasured gifts."

"You'll force him to and then he'll . . ."

"And he'll be overjoyed that I did not wipe him off the face of the earth, or change him into a foul rat, or a cockroach hiding in a crack of a hovel, or the last beggar . . ."

"That's real blackmail," Volka said angrily. "Tricks like that send a man to jail, my friend. And you'll well deserve it."

"Send me to jail?!" the old man flared up. "Me?! Hassan Abdurrakhman ibn Hottab? And does he know, that most despicable of all passers-by, who I am? Ask the first Genie, or Ifrit, or Shaitan you see, and they'll tell you, as they tremble from fear, that Hassan Abdurrakhman ibn Hottab is the chief of all Genie bodyguards. My army consists of seventy-two tribes, with 72,000 warriors in each tribe; every warrior rules over one thousand Marids and every Marid rules over a thousand Aides and every Aide rules over a thousand Shaitans and every Shaitan rules over a thousand Genies. I rule over them all, and none can disobey me! If only this thrice-miserable of all most miserable passers-by tries to . . ."

Meanwhile, the man in question was strolling down the street, glancing at the shop windows, and in no way aware of the terrible danger hanging over him because of an ordinary watch glittering on his wrist.

"Why, I'll . . ." Hottabych raged on in his boastfulness, "why, if you only so desire, I'll turn him into a . . ."

Each second counted.

Volka shouted, "Don't!"

"Don't what?"

"Don't touch that man! I don't need a watch! I don't need anything!"

"Nothing at all?" the old man asked doubtfully, quickly calming down. The only sun watch in the world disappeared as quickly as it had appeared.

"Nothing at all," said Volka. He heaved such a sigh that Hottabych realized he must apply himself to cheering up his young savior and lifting his gloomy mood.

Hottabych's Second Service

Volka was in the dumps. Hottabych sensed that something was wrong. He never dreamed he had done the boy such a bad turn during the examination, but it was all too clear that Volka was upset. And the one to blame, apparently, was none other than himself, Hassan Abdurrakhman ibn Hottab.

"Would you, O moon-like, feel inclined to listen to stories of most unusual and strange adventures?" he asked slyly. "For instance, do you know the story of the Baghdad barber's three black roosters and his lame son? Or the one about the copper camel with a silver hump? Or about the water carrier Ahmet and his magic pail?"

Volka kept on frowning. This did not stop the old man, and he began hurriedly:

"Be it known to you, O most wonderful of all secondary-school pupils, that once upon a time in Baghdad there lived a skilled barber named Selim who had three roosters and a lame son named Tub. It so happened that Caliph Harun al Rashid once passed his shop. But, O most attentive of all youths, I suggest we sit down on this bench in order that your young legs don't tire during this long and most enlightening story."

Volka agreed. They sat down in the shade of an old linden tree.

For three long hours Hottabych went on and on with the truly interesting story. He finally ended it with these crafty words: "But more marvelous still is the story of the copper camel with a silver hump," and immediately proceeded with it. When he came to the part: "Then the stranger took a piece of coal from the brazier and drew the outline of a camel on the wall. The camel waved its tail, nodded its head, walked off the wall and onto the cobblestones . . ."—he stopped to enjoy the impression his story of a drawing coming to life had made on his young listener.

But Hottabych was in for some disappointment, because Volka had seen enough cartoons in his life. However, the old man's words gave him an idea.

"You know what? Let's go to the movies. You can finish the story later."

"Your every word is my command, O Volka ibn Alyosha," the old man replied obediently. "But do me a favor and tell me what you mean by 'the movies'? Is it a bathhouse? Or, perhaps, that's what you call the

marketplace, where one can stroll and chat with friends and acquaintances?"

"Well! Any child can tell you what a movie is. It's a . . ." At this,
Volka waved his hands around vaguely and added, "Well, anyway,
you'll see when we get there."

Over the Saturn Theater box office was a sign that read: "Children
under sixteen not admitted to evening performances."

"What's the matter, O most handsome of all handsome youths?"
Hottabych inquired anxiously, noticing that Volka had become gloomy
again.

"Nothing much. It's just that we're late for the last daytime performance! You have to be sixteen to get in now. I really don't know what to
do, because I don't feel like going home."

"You won't go home!" Hottabych cried. "In a twinkling of an eye
they'll let us through, surrounded by the respect your truly endless
capabilities command! I'll just have a peek at those bits of paper everyone's handing that stern-looking woman at the entrance."

"The old braggart!" Volka thought irritably. Suddenly, he felt two
tickets in his right fist.

"Come!" Hottabych called, beaming again. "Come, they'll let you
through now!"

"Are you sure?"

"Just as positive as that a great future awaits you!"

He nudged Volka toward a mirror hanging nearby. A boy with a
bushy blond beard on his healthy freckled face looked back from the
mirror at a shocked and gaping Volka.

BE PREPARED, YOUR HIGHNESS

LEO KASSIL

During the forty years that Leo Kassil has been writing books for young Soviet readers, he has invented for his stories a number of fascinating countries. To these imaginary lands he has here added another—Jungahora.

Deliyar Srambuk, an African prince, heir apparent to the throne of Junga-hora, arrives to spend a few weeks at a Pioneer camp on the Black Sea. The Pioneers are a nationwide organization of children from nine to fifteen years of age. Deliyar is not the first royal personage to visit the Pioneers; several princes and princesses had been known to be guests of Soviet children's camps. But this prince's visit results in extraordinary happenings and adventures.

The story is absorbing not only because of the unusual plot and characters, but also because it expresses in an unusual and moving way the idea that "no matter where a person is born, in a shack or in a palace, he is born a legal heir to the blessings on earth attained by all mankind." It is in these words that an important character of the book, a Jungahora poet, Tangaor, speaks of his love of all good people, be they workers, farmers, or *princes*.

Perhaps some day a full version of this fine story will be published in English so that English-speaking children can enjoy all of it.

The Prince of Jungahora

"That's all I need—a prince!" said the camp director into the telephone receiver.

Everyone in the room looked up. Some thought they didn't hear him right, others believed he was jesting, for the director had the reputation throughout the Black Sea camp area of being a terrific wit. Right then, however, he didn't look as if he was intent on being amusing. It seemed that the long-distance call from Moscow, interrupting the meeting that was then being held in his office, had indeed brought some very strange news.

At the other end of the telephone connection, in Moscow, they didn't quite understand the director's answer, for he kept repeating it, as he looked at his assistants with a wry smile:

291

"I'm saying, that's all we need here—that's all that's lacking—a prince!"

Evidently, at least that morning, they were not in the mood for smart retorts in the capital. The receiver grumbled something sternly and the director drew himself up and said in a more businesslike tone:

"Yes, it is clear. I understand," and, his nerves suddenly tense, he motioned to the bookkeeper, Comrade Makarichev, to close the window facing the sea. The tide seemed to him suddenly to be unusually noisy. The bookkeeper closed the window tightly. The room immediately became quiet but stifling. And the waves stole right up to the director's cabin, and, seeming full of curiosity, reached up the wall on tiptoe, as if trying to peek in.

The director, Mikhail Borisovich Kravchukov, moved the receiver away from his ear, looked for an instant at the mouthpiece as if he expected something more to leap out of it, then lowered it with a bang onto the old-fashioned apparatus resembling a small deer with two antlers. Then he turned to his staff. He didn't feel happy, but he tried not to show it. He puffed out his cheeks, shrugged his shoulders, partly in amusement and partly in resignation, and said:

"Well, congratulations! How does it go in Gogol's play, *The Inspector General?*—'I am obliged to announce a most disagreeable bit of news'—a prince is on his way to our camp."

"In what sense?" asked the bookkeeper.

"In the most ordinary sense, or, rather, to be exact, in the most extraordinary sense: a prince, a bona fide 'His Royal Highness'—may he get lost! He is the younger brother of the King of Jungahora, long may he live and reign! and so on, and so forth, and etcetera! We are expecting the heir apparent to the throne of Jungahora. It's a fact! So, what do you think, should we phone the Artek Camp and try to benefit from their experience with royalty? They've had some sort of princes and princesses from Laos or from Cambodia. I believe it was mentioned in the papers. There is no denying it, my friends: I must say, all my life I've dreamed of having in my Pioneer camp such an august personage," the director waxed sarcastic.

"Why August?" the bookkeeper objected. "This is only July. Or is he to be included in the August quota of campers?"

"My dear Comrade Makarichev," sighed Kravchukov, "is it possible that all you've ever read in your life is calendars and plans?"

"What do you mean?" the bookkeeper was offended. "You're giving everyone the wrong impression about me—from time to time I glance at a newspaper."

The director did not pursue the subject of his bookkeeper's reading habits any further.

An Absolute Secret *

Stop here! Wait a minute! I know, I know quite well, my dear boys and girls, that ordinarily you never read prefaces to books. But in this case, I beg you, read it without fail. To make sure that you will, I am placing it here, inside the story. Furthermore, I didn't want the grown-ups to read it. They would most certainly start boring you with their persistent arguments, trying to convince you that this is a fairy tale and that nothing of the sort ever actually happened in the Soviet world. And they will point out that such a country as Jungahora doesn't even exist. They will poke your nose into an atlas and keep repeating, as they do so, that this story is nothing but a fantasy.

I urge you not to argue with them! Pretend that you agree. Let them regard this as a fairy tale—that will be better for all concerned. I, too, will then have some peace. Otherwise all kinds of discussions would develop, and inquiries: where? and what? and who? and whence? And it is possible that some kind of diplomatic complications would result, with so-called international tensions. No, it is far better to let the adults think that this is nothing but a fairy tale. And with you, only with you, will I share the secret that it all really happened, just as I have written it down in this book. For the time being, however, I am obliged to change the name of the country I had in mind, move it just a bit on the map, and give some of the heroes of this true story different names.

All the rest is the honest truth, the real truth, and nothing but the truth. And I also assure you that as soon as it is possible, I'll reveal to you the real name of the country Jungahora and show it to you on the map. And, do you know, I firmly believe that I'll be able to do all this before you, yourselves, become grown-ups and begin to insist that everything amazing and new in this world is a fairy tale!

---

* For those under the age of sixteen only.

But, in the meantime, be discreet. Don't say a thing! Let the adults think that you are reading a fairy tale.

The Important News Is Broadcast

It soon became known in the Pioneer camp Spartacus, located on the shores of the Black Sea, that a real prince was about to arrive to spend the rest of the summer with the other campers.

The director had decided not to ascribe unusual importance to this event and not to inform the boys and girls in advance about the imminent arrival of the uncommon visitor. However, in the course of his telephone conversation with Moscow, when he had asked that the window be closed, he did not notice that the draft had noiselessly opened the door to his office and that at this door someone had been eavesdropping—someone by the name of Taraska, surname Bobunov.

Everyone in Camp Spartacus knew this small round-cheeked Pioneer, and he most certainly knew everyone. There wasn't a slyer, more garrulous, more gossiping youngster in Spartacus, nor, perhaps, in the entire Black Sea camp region. Taraska had several nicknames, all doing justice to his personality.* Noticing him at last at the door, the director shook his head with annoyance, anticipating that his plan to remain casual about the arrival of the royal personage now had not a chance of succeeding.

He called Taraska in, and said: "So, no doubt you've heard all about it. Tell me, Taraska, do you think you could manage not to babble about the matter, for the time being at least, just for a while, so that . . ."

"If it's only for the time being, then I think I could," Taraska said with conviction.

But the for-the-time-being ended for Taraska the minute he stepped out of the director's office. True, he meant to keep his promise. He was even proud to think that he, Pioneer Taras Bubnov, could look as if nothing uncommon had happened, as if he didn't merit special attention, that is, as if he had not been entrusted with so important a secret, perhaps even an official secret. Two boys from the upper camp passed him. They walked by him, poor fellows, without even suspecting what he, Taras, knew!

---

* These nicknames are funny and descriptive in Russian, but unfortunately less so in English. But, here they are anyway: Taraskon, Tartarena, Tarascat.

294

The prince was at that very moment already on his way to Camp Spartacus!

Very soon, however, the secret began to want out—it began to sort of crawl out of Taraska. The secret somehow gave him an itch in the ear, it stuck in his throat, and no matter how hard he scratched his ear and coughed, nothing helped. The secret made his lips feel dry and he had to wet them with his tongue again and again. And his tongue was in the worst state of all—it really felt awful. It fidgeted in his mouth, threatening each moment to blurt out something that would disclose the information he had acquired by painstaking eavesdropping.

In the end Taraska gave in to the temptation, and taking his secret with him, went in the direction of Tent no. 4. Here stayed the most hardened, the most closely knit group of Pioneer boys. They had earned the special privilege of living in tents right on the edge of the sea, instead of occupying the more comfortable summer buildings of the camp situated on the hill and surrounded by flowers and shrubs.

The surf was very rough that morning and the boys had not gone swimming. They were keeping busy with other things. A few of them were tinkering with something or other, others were solving crossword puzzles, and some were playing chess, sitting on benches near the tents.

"Guess what?" Taraska began in a tone that indicated he was hiding something quite extraordinary. "Eh, you guys, guess what!"

No one paid any attention.

"If you promise to listen without noise, racket, or yells, that is, if you can stand to shut up about it for the time being, I'll tell you something that will make you fall off your seats. But, I warn you, it's a secret."

No one even looked in his direction. The boys continued with their occupations. Then someone from inside Tent no. 4 muttered:

"Well, just imagine that!"

"OK, go ahead and think I'm a tattler," Taraska said, addressing the tent.

"Thank you very much for the kind permission, but we'd do it anyway," came from behind the canvas wall of the tent.

"Go ahead, help yourself . . . call me anything you want, call me 'town crier,' anything, see if I care."

"We'll oblige," this also from the tent.

"And Transistor, and Tarantas, just as you wish."

"Will do," came the pitiless answer from Tent no. 4.

"But this time you'll be convinced once and for all that I tell only the honest truth," Taraska declared, still addressing himself to the tent wall but looking around at the boys outside.

"Maybe that's enough of your jabbering," Yaroslav Nesmetnov, the most dignified of the Pioneers of Tent no. 4 said, taking his eyes off the chessboard for a moment right after checkmating his opponent.

"Then why won't you listen to what I have to say?" Taraska complained. "Well, I'll tell you anyway—a prince is coming here. From Jungahora."

At that announcement even those few who had barely looked up at Taraska now turned away.

"What next? Are you sure that we are not expecting the king himself?"

"No, his father, the king, died long ago. I've asked Yuri [the group leader]. The prince's older brother is now king. He is only the heir apparent."

"You don't say . . . and where is he that apparent?" Slava [short for Yaroslav] Nesmetnov said while arranging the chess pieces for a new game.

A boy reading on the doorstep of the adjacent tent looked up at Taraska with mocking perplexity. On the whole, though, Taraska's news did not cause the noise, racket, or jabbering he had warned against. To be sure, even if it had been Taraska who announced that the younger brother of the football champion, Leo Yashin, was coming to the camp, and even if some of the worst skeptics had protested that Yashin had no brother, there would have been some noise.

"Well, what's so remarkable about a prince?" Slava said, cooling off Taraska's excitement. "Let him come and live with us if he wants to. We don't begrudge it to him. Maybe there are no Pioneer camps in his own country."

"What's a prince, a seventh-day wonder or something?" Slava's chess partner agreed with him.

"So, is it his fault that he was born a prince?" Taraska said stubbornly.

"After all, he *could* abdicate if he is against monarchy," the boy with the book said.

At this, Taraska, who for some reason had decided to take the prince under his protection, became indignant.

"How do you know?! Give him time, maybe he will abdicate when it's his turn to . . . to . . . climb . . . no, not climb, what is the word? . . . oh, yes, to ascend to the throne, anyway, to be crowned."

The camper with the book looked up and said to the others: "Say, fellows, where is this so-called Jungahora—in Africa or in Australia?"

"Your guess is as good as mine," Nesmetov said. "If you ever go there, be sure not to get lost on the return trip—that's all I have to say."

The other boy got up, stretched, and announced:

"Just the same, I'll run up to the library. They have a reference book there about different countries—they got it before last summer's festival of nations. The book is called *Nations of the World*."

"That's right," Slava teased, "nations that *exist* in the world, not those invented by Taraskas." Then he added, addressing his partner, "By the way, I don't know about the prince, but I'm grabbing your queen."

It was now time to spread the startling news among the girls. They didn't receive Taraska's news with particular rapture either. They were sitting on the porch of a large summer house. Some were knitting, others were sorting out pebbles or playing games.

"Girls," Taraska said tauntingly and with an air of importance, "I must bring you up to date on current events. But, be careful, don't shriek, please!" And he stuck his fingers into his ears in anticipation of an earsplitting reaction to his news about the imminent arrival of the prince.

To his disappointment no shrieking whatsoever ensued. There was hardly any racket. He even removed his fingers from his ears and looked with astonishment at the young ladies.

"Go ahead, any more lies?" said the oldest of the girls. Everyone called her Tonida, although her name was really Antonida, or Tonya for short.

Tonya Pashukhina had come to Camp Spartacus from a children's home situated not far from the Volga city of Gorky. She had been awarded a summer at this camp for her outstanding group work. It had been her idea to set up what she called the Center for Urgent Friendship at the children's home and in its school. To this center all insults, offenses, and other troubles with which, as everyone knows, the lives of children are always full were immediately reported. The center had gone to work at once so as not to allow anyone to be mistreated, or to straighten matters out at once for the offended one.

Tonya was tall, precise, and a tomboy. She looked serious, spoke in a moderate voice and with emphasis, and pronounced her *o*'s as the people of the Volga region do—fully. Tonida had become a leader among the girls from the day of her arrival. They believed she had the best sense of justice, and they were a little afraid of her. But Tonida didn't like girlish sentimentality. When any one of her playmates tried to show, with a shriek and a hug, admiration of Tonya's feats in the water, Tonya would try to discourage her with a "Don't cling to me and don't be mushy," and she would quickly free herself from the admirer's embrace.

The boys preferred to admire Tonida from a distance. After a first attempt to tease her they had had a taste of the strength of her character, and of her fists.

To everyone's envy, Tonya swam like a dolphin, could "fry pancakes" better than anyone, making the flat stones glide farther than anyone else could over the water's surface, as she cast them into the sea. Once, accepting a dare from the boys, she dove from the Frog Wharf, a high cliff, to the rapturous shrieking of the girls and the approving whistling of the tent occupants. It must be said, however, that after this event Tonida had a not very pleasant interview with the camp director.

"That, my beautiful maiden, doesn't go here," he opened the conversation. "If you don't value your life, think of mine. I am responsible for you. I am not in charge of an alpine camp, and cliff climbers are out of place here. You'll break your neck, kill yourself, then what?"

"What do I care?" Tonida said. She spoke in a low, deep voice. "And who would really be concerned? Who needs me that much?" she added almost defiantly.

When she said this, the director rose from his desk, took Tonida by her shoulders, led her to a large armchair, and sat her down in it. He brought over a chair and sat down opposite her, taking her hands and holding them between his large strong ones.

"That's not good. That's no way to talk. I know your story; I know that you grew up without the love of parents. You are not the only one. Our people have lived through a difficult time. Many fathers and mothers were lost in the war . . ."

"It wasn't the war that took mine," Tonida interrupted.

"I know. I know, my dear, who deprived you of your mother and father.* But their traces have been found, their name has been estab-

---

* The camp director alludes here to the people who perished at the hands of Stalin's secret police.

lished and you carry it, and with honor, from what I've heard. And don't you have girl friends and other friends? 'Who needs you?' you say. Aren't you ashamed to talk that way? It all depends on you whether people need you, or whether you live only for yourself. But I have heard about all that you initiated there in Gorky at your Pioneer club and I have even read about you and remembered it all. I was even glad to see your name on the list of this summer's campers. I thought, that's good that Antonida Pashukhina has chosen us. And you value yourself so little that you take silly risks with your life. Believe me, child, this isn't right. You mustn't . . ."

Tonida now looked at Taraska from under the thick, almost straight brows that gave her an air of inflexibility, and said:

"So what, a prince!" and taking out a rounded comb from her hair, she combed it back from her forehead with the same gesture as a chief would use in removing his helmet. Her large, gray eyes rested disapprovingly on Taraska, who shrank from her look and almost regretted having come over to the girls' part of the camp. "Of what importance is all that to me?" Tonya continued. "You can tell your prince, if and when he comes, that we are not about to become his loyal subjects."

"We've made it!" said Lusya Makhlakova, one of the most spiteful girls in the camp. "any minute now we'll be receiving emperors in our camp."

"And I thought," said another girl, "that there were no more princes in the world. Kings still remain here and there, and they will spend the rest of their lives on their thrones, but what can princes look forward to? It's all so ridiculous."

"But, really, girls, don't you think it will be sort of nice and different to have a prince here?" a small Pioneer said in a timid voice as she was sorting out pebbles in her lap.

"We've already seen enough princes," chimed in another girl.

"By the way, where have you seen that many princes?" Tonida wanted to know.

"Many times . . . for example in 'Cinderella,' and how he went around with a slipper and tried it on everyone . . ."

"Silly, this will not be on the stage, this will be for real."

"What difference does that make?"

Tonida looked sternly at her playmates and said: "I personally think that we must show the prince right from the start that we are not some sort of servile and cringing people, like the ones he is used to in his own country. He's probably used to having everyone scrape and bow before him. Personally, I have no intention of bothering with all those 'Permit me,' 'Allow me,' 'I beg your forgiveness,' 'I regret that . . .' "

Taraska couldn't stand it any more. "I know your kind," he said, "you girls talk big now. Now you talk about high principles, but as soon as he appears you will go into ecstasies: 'Oh, how darling! How cute! May I have your autograph? Permit me to take a picture of you . . .' "

Tonida rose quickly from the porch steps and advanced on Taraska. "Scram, while you can. We have listened to you. Be grateful for that. Disappear, quick, or you'll get something you didn't come for."

In his tent Taraska found the boys bent over the festival book. Slava was reading out loud:

"Jungahora . . . area 194,000 square kilometers . . . population more than five million . . . capital, the city of Hayrajamba, famous for its royal palace, Jaygadang, built in ancient times by slaves. Jungahora spreads over a fertile valley extending almost to the ocean; it is bordered on the northeast by a high mountain range shielding the country from northerly winds. The mountain slopes are covered with thick forests growing high-priced species of trees such as teak and poison ash. In the valley there are vast groves of palm trees. Agriculture is the country's main economic resource. Rice and rubber are the main products. Jungahora is a constitutional monarchy. The king is the head of the state. The most important problems are resolved by the king, in consultation with the parliament and with tribal chiefs. There are no political parties, labor unions, or other social organizations. They are forbidden. Diamond mining is highly developed and diamonds are the country's chief export. Foreign capital plays a significant role in the country's economy."

Just then someone appeared carrying an atlas from the library. Almost knocking their heads together, the boys started to look for the distant torrid land of Jungahora, whose heir apparent was at that very moment mounting the steps to the office of the director of Camp Spartacus.

The story continues with the initiation of the prince into camp life, his gradual understanding of the ways of the Pioneers, his growing friendship with the boys in Tent no. 4, his quarrels with the willful Tonida who eventually becomes his best friend, and with the meeting of the prince and the campers with the poet from Jungahora, Tangaor, who is taking a cure at the Black Sea.

The camp soon hears that a palace revolution has taken place in Jungahora. The prince's brother has been deposed. His power-greedy uncle has become regent and the heir apparent is to return to Jungahora immediately to be crowned the new king. The prince has enjoyed life so much at the camp that he refuses to return to his country. Tonida tries to help him escape from the clutches of his uncle's emissaries. He and Tonida nearly drown in the effort to escape. When, however, the prince learns that Tangaor has left for Jungahora to lead the people against the regent, he agrees to return to his homeland and try to be a good king, helping the poet lead the common people against their enemies. Back home he misses his Pioneer friends, especially Tonya. He writes to them at the camp that he now lives in three hundred rooms and has dozens of elephants, but that he would gladly exchange all this splendor for one real friend.

THE LITTLE HUMPBACKED HORSE

A Tale in Verse

BY PYOTR ERSHOV

The well-known Soviet children's poet, Kornei Chukovsky, who is also an authority on Russian folk literature, has this to say about *The Little Humpbacked Horse:*

A wonderful thing happened in Russia to a certain young man. He had come to the capital to study; surprising himself, and without much effort, he created a book of genius, a lasting addition to Russian literature which has survived more than a hundred years and, without doubt, will survive another century.

The nineteen-year-old round-cheeked, beardless youth who had just left the provincial school bench—how amazed he would have been had someone predicted then, in 1834, the great destiny of his endeavor!

The name of the youth was Pyotr Ershov; his great book was The Little Humpbacked Horse [Konek-gorbunok].

This gay and satirical fairy tale in verse, based on an old folktale, was suppressed by the censors for thirty years (1835–1865) because it was not complimentary to the character of the czar in the story. Later, from time to time, the poem was printed for simple folk and was peddled at fairs and market-places like cloth, religious images, or pastry. After another thirty years this work finally became part of Russian literature. Although originally meant for adults, it became a children's book "by adoption." "Having appropriated this book as their own," adds Chukovsky, "children bequeathed it to their grand-children, their great-grandchildren, and their great-great-grandchildren, and it has become impossible to imagine a generation of Russian children who could get along without it." The tale has since been published in at least fifty editions, thirty of them before 1900.

The English version reproduced here gives the whole story. It was regret-tably necessary, however, to summarize several passages in prose in order to save space. Perhaps this loss is also a gain; it gives the reader a chance to catch his breath. The poem is very dynamic; its tempo, fitting the many lively adven-tures of the hero and his benefactor, Humpback, moves along at a breath-taking pace.

The "preludes" for each of the three parts—for example, "Now the telling of the tale begins"—and the "false" beginning of Part III are typical devices in Russian folk literature, designed to attract and hold the attention of the audience. It is also a distinct feature of the Russian *skazka* to end with a

302

complaint that the storyteller had been at the feast celebrating the happy ending but had not partaken of the refreshments. This gambit was intended to remind the audience to reward the narrator with coins or food for his telling of the tale. These formulas, of course, originated when stories were told orally, often by minstrels.

Not only do thousands of Russian children of today read and love *The Little Humpbacked Horse*, but the tale is also presented in children's theaters throughout the Soviet Union in a full-scale, rollicking performance; and there is always a full house. The play, at least as it is presented at the Central Moscow Children's Theater, has also been transposed, in part, into prose, the verse being retained in the most dramatic and singable episodes.

THE LITTLE HUMPBACKED HORSE

PART ONE

Now the telling of the tale begins.

Past the woods and mountain steep,
Past the rolling waters deep,
You will find a village pleasant,
Where once dwelt an aged peasant.
Of his sons—and he had three—
The first sharp was as could be;
Second was nor dull nor bright,
But the third—a fool all right.
These three brothers garnered wheat,
Brought it to the Royal Seat,
By which token you may know
That they hadn't far to go.
There they sold their golden grain,
Counting carefully their gain,
And, with well-filled money bags,
Home again would turn their nags.

But, upon an evil day,
Dire misfortune came their way—
Someone, between dark and dawn,
Took to trampling down their corn;
Never had such grief before
Come to visit at their door;
Day and night they sat and thought
How the villain could be caught;
Till at last it dawned upon them
That the way to solve the problem,
And to save their crops from harm,
Was each night to guard the farm.

[*As the day drew near its close, the eldest brother with pitchfork and ax in hand started out to stand his watch.*

303

The night was dark and stormy. Fright-
ened, he dived into a haystack and re-
mained there till dawn. When he re-
turned home in the morning, he said
that he had seen no thief. As that day
drew near its close, the second brother
went to stand his watch. A fearful frost
set in. His teeth a-chattering, and nearly
frozen to death, the second brother fled
from his watch. To keep warm he
walked around a neighbor's fence all
night. On the morrow when home he
came, he said that he had seen no one
stealing the grain. Now it was the third
son's turn. . . .]

But he never turned a hair,
Sitting on the oven there
Singing with his foolish might,
"O, you eyes as black as night!"
Then to coax and beg Ivan
Both the elder sons began,
Bade him go and guard the grain;
They grew hoarse, but all in vain.
Father finally said, "Here,
You just listen, Vanya dear.
Go on watch, and if you do,
This is what I'll do for you:
I shall give you beans and peas,
And some pictures, if you please."

At these words Ivan climbed down,
Donned his coat of russet brown,
Pocketed a crust of bread,
And on sentry duty sped.

Night fell and the white moon rose.
On his beat Ivan now goes
Looking sharply all around;

Then he sits upon the ground.
Munching slowly his bread,
Counting stars overhead—
Suddenly, a neigh resounded!
To his feet our sentry bounded;
Peering round with shaded eyes,
In the field a mare he spies.
Now this mare, I'd have you know,
Whiter was than whitest snow,
Silken mane in ringlets streaming
To the ground, all golden gleaming.
"Oh, ho-ho! So this is it!
You're the villain! Wait a bit,
Nasty little plague," said he
And, approaching stealthily,
Seized her tail as in a vise,
Mounted on her in a trice,
Landed on her with a smack—
Back to front and front to back.
But the mare, whose blood was hot,
Started bucking on the spot.
Eyes ablaze with angry glow,
Like an arrow from a bow,
Over the hills and valleys she sped,
Over streams and gullies she fled,
On her haunches reared and pranced,
'Neath the forest branches danced—
By all her wiles and strength, in vain
Did she ply to be free again.
For she found her match at last;
To her tail Ivan stuck fast.

Finally she said to him,
Spent and trembling in each limb:
"Since you sat me, I confess
I am yours now to possess;
Find a place for me to rest,
Care for me as you know best,

But you must let me out to graze.
And at the end of these three days,
Two such handsome steeds I'll bear
As have ne'er been seen, I swear;
Then a third I promise you
Only twelve hands high with two,
Little humps upon his back,
Ears a yard long, and eyes coal black.
If you so wish, why . . . sell the two;
But Ivan, whatever you do,
Part not with the little steed
Though you be in direst need—
Nor for gold, nor silken raiment,
Nor for lucky charm in payment.
Faithful friend to you he'll be,
Where you go on land or sea.
He'll find shade from summer's heat,
Keep you warm in snow and sleet,
Find your food in time of need,
Quench your thirst with cooling mead.
I shall be forever free
And shall roam at liberty."

Now, Ivan thought all this all right,
Found the mare shelter for the night
In an empty shepherd's shack,
Which he shut up with a sack;
Then he homeward made his way
With the early light of day,
Singing merrily, "Heigh-ho,
Vanya would a-wooing go."

[*When Ivan returned home at dawn,
he said not a word about the white
mare. Instead he told his family a cock-
and-bull story about Satan appearing in
the night and flailing the grain with his
tail. Ivan boasted that he had felt no
fear before the devil, had jumped on his
back, beat him, and made him promise
never again to plague good folk and
steal from them. Trusting the devil's
word, Ivan got off his back and went
home.*]

Ivan fell quiet, said no more,
Yawned, and soon began to snore;
While his brothers, though they tried
Not to, laughed until they cried;
Father too could not refrain,
And he laughed and laughed again,
Though it is a sin, they say,
For old men to laugh that way.

Since that night I cannot say
How much time has passed away,
For of this I heard no word—
Nor from man, nor beast, nor bird.
What is this to you or me—
Whether one year passed, or three?
Time can't be recalled, once fled.
Let me tell my tale instead.

[*The white mare with the silken
mane kept her promise to Ivan. She
bore two handsome steeds with golden
hair and a queer little humpbacked
horse. One day Danilo, Ivan's eldest
brother, spied the steeds in the shepherd's shack. He called to his brother
Gavrilo, and together they rushed back
to the shack to gaze at the lovely pair
their fool-of-a-brother had hidden there.
. . .*]

Here two chargers met their gaze—

Snorting, ruby eyes ablaze,
Silken tails in ringlets streaming,
Golden in the shadows gleaming;
And their hoofs, of diamonds made,
Were with monster pearls inlaid.
Yes, it cannot be denied:
Horses fit for czars to ride.
And they nearly burst from spleen
As they stared upon this scene;
The eldest gaped, scratched his head:
"Where did he get them?" he said.
"This just proves the ancient rule:
Fortune favors but the fool.
Say, Gavrilo, let's go down
Sunday to the fair in town,
Sell them to the nobles there;
We will share the takings square,
And with the money, you'll agree,
We can have a merry spree."

Sunday came and found them dressed
For the town in their best;
See them at their icons praying,
Then for Father's blessing staying,
After which—in secret—they
Took the steeds and stole away.

Night her shadows softly spread,
And Ivan set out for bed.
Through the village he went swinging,
Munching his crust, and singing;
Through the meadow he did skip,
With his hand upon his hip;
Into the shack upon his toes,
Like a very lord, he goes.
Everything was in its place—
But the steeds! Of them, no trace!
Only tiny Humpback. How he

Fawned around his feet in glee,
Prancing gaily in delight,
Flapping both ears left and right.
At this sight Ivan wept sore,
As he leaned against the door.
"Oh, my horses black as night,
With your golden manes so bright!
Did not I look after you?
What foul devil stole you? Who?
Plague on him, the dirty dog!
May he perish in a bog!
To the next world, when he goes,
May he trip and break his nose!
Oh, my horses black as night,
With your golden manes so bright!"

Humpback neighed and shook his head:
"Do not fret, Ivan," he said.
"Yes, your loss is great, I know,
But I'll help you in your woe.
Blame the devil for his own deeds—
It was your brothers who stole those
    steeds.
Dry your tears, Ivan. Make haste.
We have not much time to waste.
Mount my back. When I say 'Go,'
Hold to me for all you know;
Though I'm small—that's true, of
    course—
I'm as good as any horse!"

Saying this, he stretched out flat;
On his back Ivan then sat,
Grabbed his ears and held them tight,
Shouting out with all his might;
Little Humpback's sinews quivered,
On his feet he stood and shivered,
Shook his mane and, with a neigh,

Like an arrow sped away.
Only dust clouds marked the course
Of the rider and the horse.
On they flew, as quick as thought;
In a trice, the thieves were caught.

[*Seeing Ivan, his brothers stared and scratched their heads, confused and scared. They confessed their deed, and they pretended to regret it. Then they spoke sorrowfully of their toil, their ailing father, and their poverty. Good-natured Ivan agreed to let them sell the steeds. Together the three brothers set off for the town and the fair. But . . .*]

Soon the sky grew overcast,
Colder, colder blew the blast;
And so they thought to bivouac
In a wood, for to lose the track
Would not do. The steeds were made
Fast within its leafy shade;
There they made themselves at ease,
Ate and drank beneath the trees.
After that, in happy mood,
Each made as merry as he could.

Soon Danilo saw a light
In the darkness of the night;
He nudged Gavrilo on the sly,
Cunningly he winked an eye,
Pointed where the light was burning,
Coughed a muffled cough of warning.
After which he scratched his head,
"Something's burning—yes, a fire!
Just the thing that we require!
Listen now, Vanyushka dear,
Go and fetch some embers here—

For it really slipped my mind,
And I left my flint behind."
To himself says brother Dan:
"May you break your neck, young
    man!"
Thinks Gavrilo, "Do I care?
Lord knows what is burning there.
If the highwaymen beset him,
We for ever can forget him."

[*Ivan mounted Humpback, and together they rode out of sight.*]

Then Gavrilo cried in fright:
"Saints be with us all this night!
Save us, Lord, from evil sin!
Say, what devil's under him?"

Brighter, brighter shone that light,
Swifter, swifter was their flight,
Till they halted where it lay—
There the field was bright as day,
Lit by wondrous brilliant rays—
Cold and smokeless, but ablaze!
Here Ivan, in stark surprise,
Stared and said, "Why, bless my eyes!
Look, there's light in plenty there,
But no smoke or heat! I swear
Now, this *is* a curious light."

Quoth his horse: "Yes, you're quite
    right.
And you very well may stare!
That's the Fire-Bird's feather there!
But, Ivan, for your own sake,
Touch it not, for in its wake
Many sorrows, many woes
Follow everywhere it goes."

[*But Ivan did not heed Humpback's warning. He wrapped the Fire-Bird's feather in a kerchief and hid it in his hat. Then he galloped swiftly back again. To his brothers he said that the fire was merely a burning tree stump.*

Next day the three brothers reached the fairgrounds early. Soon the Mayor arrived at this Hostlers' Fair and, according to custom, officially opened it by giving permission for the buying and selling to start. A great crowd began to gather around the two handsome steeds; seeing the crowd, the Mayor approached. When he saw the beautiful horses, he proclaimed that they were fit only for the Czar. He issued a strict order that they must not be sold without his approval and then . . .]

Straightway to the Czar went he.
"Pardon, Gracious Majesty!"
Cried the Mayor, as he fell prone,
Breathlessly before the throne.
"Be not angry with thy slave;
Suffer me to speak, I crave."
"Speak," vouchsafed the Czar. "Commence,
But be sure your words make sense."
"I shall try, Your Majesty;
I am Lord Mayor here, you see,
Sire, I rode to Hostlers' Fair
With my guard today and there

308

I beheld a crowd, so great
That it blocked up every gate;
When I got inside the Fair,
I saw two such chargers there—
Handsome horses black as night,
Silken manes in ringlets bright,
Golden in the sunlight streaming,
Flowing tails all golden gleaming,
And their hoofs, of diamonds made,
Were with monster pearls inlaid."
Cried the Czar excitedly:
"We shall have to go and see!
And, if they are all you say,
We shall buy those two today.
Come! My coach!" He clapped his
    hands—
Lo!—his coach all ready stands.
He donned his robes and crown with care
And in haste drove to the Fair,
Followed by his Guard of State.

All the people made way,
Kneeled and cheered, "Hurray!"
In reply, the Czar smiled brightly,
Bowed, and from his coach sprang
    lightly. . . .
Charmed by those steeds, the Czar
Gazed at them from near and far—
Praised, and praised them once again,
Softly stroked each golden mane,
Gently patted each steed's spine,
Felt their necks so sleek and fine.
After he had gazed his fill,
He turned round with right good will,
Saying: "My good people, who
Owns these handsome chargers two?
Who's the master?" Here, Ivan,
Arms akimbo like a Pan,*

---
* *Pan* means lord in Polish.

Pushed his brothers both aside,
Puffed his cheeks, and proudly cried:
"Czar, these steeds belong to me.
I'm their owner, here, you see."

[*Whereupon the Czar asked Ivan if
he would sell the chargers. Ivan said he
would rather swap them—for twice-five
caps full of silver. The coins were
counted out and the Czar added five rubles for good measure. Ten of the Czar's
grooms took the horses' bridles and tried
to lead them to the Royal Palace. But
the steeds tripped the grooms and ran,
bridles broken, back to Ivan.*]

Back the Czar drove to Ivan,
And he said, "Look here, my man:
Seems my grooms can't hold those two,
So there's nothing else to do
But for you to come with me.
I shall issue a decree,
To make you Master of my Horse;
Like a lord you'll live, of course,
You'll have raiment of the best,
Gold brocade upon your chest—
On my royal word—you'll see!
Are you willing?" "Well, I'll be . . .
In the Palace I shall live!
And to me the Czar will give
Handsome raiment of the best;
I'll wear gold upon my chest!
Like a lord I'll live in clover,
Rule the Royal Stables over!
Well, I never! Your commission,
I accept, Czar, on condition—
That you never treat me rough
And always let me sleep enough.
Or you'll see no more of me!"

Whistling to his horses, he
Sauntered through the city singing,
Carelessly his mittens swinging,
Followed by his steeds a-prancing
And his humpbacked horse a-dancing
To the rhythm of his song—
And the marvel of the throng.

As for his two brothers, they
Stowed the silver safe away
In their belts; then, in high feather,

Had a drink or two together
And in glee rode home; once there,
Shared the money fair and square;
Married 'mid much joy and laughter,
Lived and prospered ever after.
And the rest of all their days
Spoke of their Ivan with praise.
Let us now forget those two
And, good people, Christians true,
I'll amuse you if I can
With the deeds of our Ivan.

PART TWO

Tales, you know, are quickly spun,
Deeds are sooner said than done.

Once again my tale proceeds
Of Ivan and of his deeds,
Of the little talking gray
Humpbacked horse, so wise and gay.
Goats are grazing on the seas,
Hills are overgrown with trees;
Golden bridle loosely swinging,
See the stallion sunward winging—
Far below him, forests glide;
Thunderclouds on every side
Race across the sky and dash,
Hurling lightning as they crash.
Wait—this is the prelude to
What I shall be telling you.
Have you heard of Buyan Island
Floating on the ocean wild, and
Of the maiden wondrous fair
Sleeping in a casket there?

Forest beasts with gentle tread
Guard her grave, while overhead
Nightingales their music pour.
Stay, my friends, a little more—
Now my prelude's said and done,
And my story again begun.

Well, good friends and Christians true,
Fellow countrymen, look you,
Our Ivan made his merry way
To the Palace that fine day.
There he was Master of the Horse
And did not pine away, of course,
For his brothers and his dad.
(And, indeed, why should our lad?)
He had garments gay in plenty
And possessed five and twenty
Chests, all full of caps and shoes

Out of which to pick and choose.
All he did was eat his fill,
Slake his thirst, and sleep at will.

Now, the Chamberlain began,
As weeks passed, to watch Ivan. . . .
You should know that he had been—
Till Ivan came on the scene—
Master of the Royal Horse;
His was noble blood, of course,
So no wonder that he bore
Malice toward Ivan and swore
That he'd die, but soon or late
He'd drive the upstart from the gate.
But the rogue, his good time biding,
And his double-dealing hiding,
Feigned to be Ivan's best friend
And masked his feelings to this end—
Thinking: "Wait, you peasant lout,
Time will come, I'll turn you out."

So the Chamberlain began,
As weeks passed, to watch Ivan,
And he noticed that he never
Fed or groomed those steeds, or ever
Took them out for exercise;
Yet those steeds—to his surprise—
Always were, whene'er paraded,
Brushed and burnished, manes a-braided,
Tails in flowing ringlets streaming,
Glossy coats like satin gleaming,
Mangers always full of wheat—
Which, it seemed, grew at their feet.
"Now, whatever can this mean?"
Sighed the Chamberlain in spleen.
"Can it be, a goblin sprite
Comes and plays his pranks at night?
Watch him—that's what I shall do.

And it should be easy to
Spin a story in a flash
And to settle that fool's hash.
I shall tell the Court, of course,
That the Master of the Horse
Is a wicked infidel,
And a sorcerer as well;
That Old Nick his soul has taken,
That he has God's Church forsaken."

So, the former Chief of Horse
(Yes, the Chamberlain, of course)
That same evening hid away
In a stall beneath some hay.

Blackest midnight came at last,
Pit-a-pat, his heart beat fast;
Lying there with bated breath,
He peeped out, as still as death,
Waiting for that sprite—when hark!
Loud the door creaked in the dark,
And the horses pawed the ground
As Ivan, without a sound,
Entered—though he looked, of course,
Like the Master of the Horse.
First he barred the door; then he
Doffed his hat most carefully,
And from it he slowly took
Out his kerchief, which he shook
Till the Fire-Bird's feather blazed;
After which, with tender care,
He commenced to groom the pair—
Braided their fine manes so long,
While he sang a merry song;
Meanwhile, crouching there and quiv-
    ering,
Hair all bristling, skin a-shivering,
Stared the Chamberlain in fright

At the joker of the night.
"Oh, so that is it! I see!
Very well! I'll tell the Czar
What a smart young man you are!
Just you wait until tomorrow—
You'll remember me with sorrow!"
But Ivan, quite unaware
Of the evil lurking there,
Gaily sang his little song,
As he braided those manes so long.
After he had groomed each steed,
Filled each tub with cooling mead,
And the bins with choicest corn,
He let out a sleepy yawn,
Wrapped the feather up once more,
And laid himself upon the floor—
By his horses made his bed
With his hat beneath his head.

With the dawn, the Chamberlain
Stretched his limbs to ease the strain;
And, on hearing our Ivan
Snoring loud as Yeruslan,*
He rose, and on his tip-toes crept
Cautiously to where he slept,
He snatched the feather from his hat,
Then he vanished—just like that!

As the Czar woke with a snore,
There he stood right at the door;
Bowing low until his head
Hit the floor, he whined and said:
"To confess, O Majesty,
I have dared to come to thee!
Be not angry with thy slave,

---

* *Yeruslan* was a valiant knight of Russian folklore. He was said to be endowed with fabulous strength.

But suffer me to speak, I crave."
"Speak, without exaggeration
And without prevarication,"
Yawned the Czar. "If you tell fibs,
Know the knout will count your ribs."
Gathering his courage, he
Said: "God bless Your Majesty!
On the Holy Cross, forsooth,
I am telling you the truth.
All the court knows that it's true
That Ivan conceals from you
That which can't be bought or sold—
Not for silver, nor for gold—
It's a Fire-Bird's feather, see,
Which he hides, Your Majesty."
"What! A Fire-Bird's! And he dare,
Cursed varlet, such a rare . . .
Oh, the villain!—wait and see
What a whipping there will be!"
"That's not all," the Chamberlain
Whispered, as he bowed again.
"Were it but the feather, he
Might retain it, Majesty;
But he boasts, as I have heard,
That did you but say the word,
He could bring the Bird of Fire
To your Royal Chamber, Sire."
And the spy, with servile tread,
On all fours approached the bed,
Dropped the treasure, and—once
    more—
Banged his head upon the floor.

Long the Czar enchanted gazed,
Chortled, stroked his beard, amazed;
Bit the feather's end, then he
Placed it under lock and key;
Shouted in impatience and—

As if confirming his command—
Waved his sceptre in the air:
"Hey, you! Fetch me that fool there!"

And the lords-in-waiting ran
Instantly to fetch Ivan.

[*The Czar scolded Ivan for having
concealed the Fire-Bird's feather from
him. He promised to forgive Ivan this
"crime" if he fulfilled his boast and
brought the Fire-Bird itself to the
Palace. Ivan swore he never made this
boast, but the Czar did not believe him.
The Czar threatened to have Ivan put
to death if he did not find the Fire-Bird
and bring it to him. In tears Ivan made
his way to the hayloft where his little
Humpback lay . . .*]

Hearing him, his Humpback ran
Full of glee to meet Ivan;
But, on seeing him in tears,
Almost sobbed and drooped his ears:
"Why, Ivanushka, so sad?
Tell me what's the matter, lad,"
Said he, fawning round his knees.
"Put your mind, Ivan, at ease;
Tell me what has happened, please.
Just confide in me, Ivan;
I shall help you if I can.
And Ivan in bitter tears,
As he kissed his Humpback's ears,
Said: "The Czar—Oh, have you
    heard?—
Bid me bring a Fire-Bird!
Oh, whatever shall I do?"
In reply his horse said, "True,

Your misfortune's great, I know.
But I'll help you in your woe.
You rejected my advice—
Now you have to pay the price:
For remember, when you found
That bird's feather on the ground,
I told you, for your own sake,
Not to touch it—in its wake,
Many sorrows, many woes,
Follow everywhere it goes.
Now, Ivan, you see that I,
When I warned you, told no lie.
But, Ivan—'twixt you and me—
This is easy as can be;
Service lies ahead, my man—
Now go to the Czar, Ivan,
Say to him in language plain:
'Czar, I need the best of grain
And two troughs, then, if you please,
Wine brought in from overseas;
Tell them that they must make haste,
For I have no time to waste—
I'll be off at dawn of day.' "

[*Ivan did as he was bid. The Czar
gave strict commands to fulfill Ivan's
demands. When the dawn began to
peep, Humpback roused Ivan from
sleep. He took the grain and the wine,
and tightly tied the troughs with twine.
He climbed upon his horse's back, and
to the rising sun they sped, in quest of
the Fire-Bird . . .*]

Seven days they rode, I heard;
When the eighth day dawned, they
    stood
In a dark and dense green wood.

"Here," Humpback tossed his head,
"You will see a glade," he said.
"In the middle of this glade,
Stands a hill of silver made.
There it is that every morn,
Fire-Birds flock before the dawn—
Water from the stream to drink.
We will catch them there, I think."

Up the hill Humpback flew—
And he climbed a mile or two;
Then he stopped, tossed his head
(Flapping both his ears) and said:
"Look, it's getting dark, Ivan,
You must watch as best you can.
Mix some wine and grain—enough,
But no more, to fill one trough;
And to hide yourself from sight,
'Neath the other trough sit tight;
Make no sound, and mind you keep
Eyes and ears alert—don't sleep!
You will see at dawn of day
Flocks of Fire-Birds come this way;
They will peck your grain and chatter
In their language—but no matter:
Seize the nearest one, Ivan;
Hold it fast as fast you can;
When you have that Fire-Bird tight,
Shout for me with all your might;
I shall come without delay."
"Won't they burn my fingers, say?"

[*Ivan donned some mittens and sat under the trough, waiting to see what would happen. A flock of Fire-Birds swooped down on the wine-soaked grain. They screamed and hopped as they got drunk. Ivan caught one of the Fire-Birds and quickly called for Humpback. The little horse appeared and urged him to put the Fire-Bird into his sack and hold on tightly to it. But Ivan wanted to catch more Fire-Birds —there were so many and they were such strange and lovely creatures. So Ivan then and there . . .*]

With his sack he beat the air.
In a blinding blaze of light
Started up the flock in fright,
Wheeling in a ring of fire,
Soaring to the clouds and higher.
While Ivan with crazy laughter
Waved his mittens, running after,
Yelling madly—just as though
He had swallowed lye, you know.
When the birds had gone from view,
Our Ivan, without ado,
Made the royal treasure fast,
And set off for home at last.

Finally, they reached the Court,
And the Czar cried: "Have you brought
Me the Fire-Bird?" while he eyed
His attendant by his side,
Who (the Chamberlain, I mean)
Stood and bit his nails in spleen.
"Yes, of course," replied Ivan.
"Then where is it, my young man?"
"Wait a minute and you'll see!
Bid them first, Your Majesty,
Shut the chamber casement tight,
And draw the shades against the light."
All the lords-in-waiting ran,
Closed the casement for Ivan.
Flinging down his sack with pride,

315

"Come on out, my dear," he cried.
Blinded by the flood of light,
They all screened their eyes in fright;
And the Czar, in accents dire,
Shouted: "Gracious! We're on fire!
Water!—call the fire brigade!
See the fire this fool has made!"
Tears a-streaming from his eyes,
Our bird-catcher, laughing, cries:
"No, no. This is not a fire—
It is but your Fire-Bird, Sire.
It's a lovely plaything, see,
That I've brought Your Majesty!"
Said the Czar for all to hear:
"Vanya, friend, I love you, dear.
And in token of my joy,
Be my Royal Groom, my boy!"

Then the former Chief of Horse
(Yes, the Chamberlain, of course)
Muttered to himself in hate:
"No, you ill-bred milksop—wait!
You won't always prosper so—
Have all that fool's luck. Oh no!
I'll get you in trouble, yet!
Yes, I will, my little pet!"

[*Now, one evening some three weeks
later, the servants had gathered in the
kitchen of the Royal Palace and were
telling each other tall tales for amusement. One of the servants told the tale
of the Czar-Maid Fair:*]

"In a distant clime, my brothers,
Flows an ocean like no others;
And it washes foreign shores,
And it's sailed by blackamoors;

From true Christian soil, however,
Noblemen nor peasants never
Sailed those pagan waters—though
Merchants who have sailed and know,
Tell about a maiden fair
Living on that ocean there.
She's no common maiden, see—
Daughter to the moon is she,
And she's sister to the sun.
This fair maid, the stories run,
In a scarlet dress arrayed,
Sails a boat—of gold it's made;
And she wields a silver oar,
Steers that boat from shore to shore;
Gusli * in her hand, she sings
As she plucks its silver strings."
At these words, the Chamberlain
Bounded up as if insane;
To the Royal Chamber sped,
Where the Czar was still a-bed;
Bowed until he hit his head
On the floor then—whining—said:

[*"We sat round the kitchen fire
drinking to your health, O Sire, and we
heard a story of the wondrous Czar-
Maid Fair. Your groom boasted that
he knew this maid and could fetch her
if he so wished." The Czar ordered Ivan
brought before him at once. Ivan denied having boasted about the Czar-
Maid Fair, but the Czar said to him
wrathfully:*]

"If you do not bring to me
That Czar-Maid, within weeks three,

* A *gusli* is a stringed instrument similar to a
small harp.

To my Royal Chamber—now,
By my Royal Beard, I vow
(Hide yourself where e'er you please,
Under ground, or under seas)—
I'll have you impaled, my man.
Off, you scum!" In tears, Ivan
To the hayloft made his way,
Where his little Humpback lay.

[*Ivanushka told his friend that he
was ordered to bring the Czar-Maid.
Humpback reminded him once more
that he had rejected his advice and now
had to pay the price. But he promised
to help him and urged him to do as follows:*]

"Now go to the Czar, Ivan,
Say: 'To catch the Czar-Maid, Sire,
Two large cloths I will require
And a tent of gold brocade
And a dinner-service, made
All of gold from overseas—
Sweetmeats, too, her taste to please.' "

[*Ivan did as he was told. The Czar
ordered that Ivan's demands be fulfilled.
Calling him now a brave young man,
the Czar said: "Godspeed to you, Ivan."
Dawn had scarcely begun to peep when
Ivan climbed upon his horse's back, and
to the rising sun they sped—off to seek
the Czar-Maid Fair.*]

Seven days they rode, I swear;
When the eighth day dawned, they stood
In a dark and dense green wood.
Humpback stopped and then said he:

"There's the pathway to the sea.
There it is the whole year round
This fair maiden can be found;
Only twice a year—no more—
Does she spend the day on shore;
And tomorrow, I've a notion,
We shall see her on the ocean."

After which, he galloped fast
Till he reached the sea at last;
In the distance, they could see
One white wave roll languidly.
Then Ivan dismounted. "Here,"
Said the Humpback in his ear,
"Pitch your tent of gold brocade;
Spread the cloth and service made
All of gold from overseas,
And the sweets her taste to please.
You must hide yourself, and see
That you don't act foolishly.
Yonder—see. The boat is nearing
With the Czar-Maid in it, steering.
She'll walk in the tent, but you
Let her be, what e'er you do:
Let her eat and drink her fill,
Stay outside the tent until
Gusli strains begin to play;
Then rush in without delay,
Seize the Czar-Maid—grasp her tight—
And shout for me with all your might."
Then he flew off like the wind,
Leaving our Ivan behind.

[*When the midday sun shone clear,
the Czar-Maid drew near to the shore.
She went into the tent carrying the
gusli in her hand, ate her fill, and then
began to sing a soft song. Lulled by her*

sweet voice, Ivan dozed off. Then the
Maid got into her boat and sailed
away.]

Slowly, sank the sun from sight;
Suddenly, he woke in fright.
By him furiously neighing
Stood his horse, who kicked him,
   saying:
"Sleep, my lad, sleep till tomorrow—
Sleep, and wake to grief and sorrow!
You will be impaled, not I!"
Here Ivan began to cry,
Sobbed upon his horse's mane,
Saying: "I won't sleep again.
Pardon me this once, please do!"
"Well, the Lord will pardon you."
Said his Humpback in reply:
"Maybe all's not lost; we'll try
And perhaps we'll mend things yet.
But no sleeping—don't forget!
For again at break of day
That Fair Maid will steer this way;
She will go into the tent,
On your honeyed mead intent:
Only, mind what I have said—
Otherwise, you'll lose your head."

[*Humpback disappeared once more.*
Ivan searched the shore for some flints
and rusty nails to use to rouse himself
with if he dozed off.]

It was early morning when
The Fair Maiden came again,
Beached her boat once more, and
   sped—
By the fragrant odors led—

To the dainties that were laid
In the tent of gold brocade.
And again she plucked a string,
And so sweetly did she sing,
That Ivanushka once more
Felt as sleepy as before.

[*But Ivan roused himself and seized*
the Maid by her long tresses. He called,
and his Humpback came in a flash.
Holding on tightly to the Czar-Maid
Fair, Ivan mounted his faithful horse
and sped away to the Royal Palace.]

At the Palace gates at last
They arrived: the Czar ran fast
To the Fair Czar-Maiden and
Took her by her lily hand,
And—beneath a canopy—
Led her to his throne. Then he
Fondly gazed into her eyes,
Said with honeyed voice and sighs:
"Oh, you beautiful princess!
Be Czarina! Please say yes!
When I first saw you, desire
Burned within my breast like fire!
Say but one sweet word to me!
Everything is ready, see;
And tomorrow, on my life,
We'll be wedded man and wife,
And live happy as the May."

But the Czar-Maid turned away
From the Czar with scornful eye,
And refused to make reply.
"Say but one sweet word to me!
Wherein have I grieved you, pray?
Is my love so hateful? Say."
"Lack-a-day," the Czar-Maid cried,

318

And she mournfully replied:
"To this chamber you must bring,
In three days, my signet ring
From the bottom of the sea,
If you wish to marry me."

Eagerly the Czar roared: "Hey!
Fetch Ivan at once, I say!"
And, excited, almost ran
Off himself to fetch Ivan!

When Ivan appeared, the Czar
Stroked his beard and murmured: "Ah!
Listen. Take a trip for me,
Vanya—to the ocean, see;
And the Czar-Maid's signet ring
To me from the seabed bring.
If you execute this task,
I will give you all you ask."
"But I've only just got back,
And my joints are fit to crack;
Now you've found another quest!
Can't I even have a rest?"
"Sirrah! dare you tell me tarry?
Can't you see I want to marry?"
Raged the Czar and with a roar
Stamped his foot upon the floor.
"No more arguments, I say.
Now, be off without delay!"
As Ivan turned round to go,
The Czar-Maiden murmured: "Oh!
Please to visit on your way
My green mansions, and convey
Greetings to my mother dear:
Say her daughter—do you hear?—
Asks why she concealed her rays
For these last three nights and days;
Why my handsome brother shrouds
His bright eyes in gloomy clouds,

Never sending rays of love
From the misty heights above?
Don't forget my message, now."
As Ivan made his last bow,
"I will not forget," he said—
"If it doesn't slip my head;
But, please tell me who's your brother?
And besides, who is your mother?
I don't know them, I confess."
In reply, the fair princess
Said: "The Moon—she is my mother;
And the Sun—he is my brother."
"See you're back in time, my man!"
Called the bridegroom to Ivan,
Who retired and made his way
To his Humpback in the hay.

"Why, Ivanushka, so sad?
What's the matter now, my lad?"
Said his Humpback with a neigh.
"Help me, little Humpback, pray,
For the Czar now wants to wed
That thin maiden, so he said.
And," Ivan said to his horse,
"He must send me off, of course,
On a journey to the sea—
Only gave three days to me—
And some cursèd signet ring
From the seabed I must bring!
Have to travel to the sky—
Give her compliments and love
To the Sun and Moon above;
And besides, there are a few
Questions I must ask them, too."
Said his horse, " 'Twixt you and me,
This is easy as can be;
Service, brother, lies ahead!
Now you just go off to bed;
Early in the morning, we

Will be traveling to the sea."
In the morning, fresh from rest,
Our Ivan, now warmly dressed,
Put three onions in his pack,

Climbed upon his horse's back,
And sped on his distant quest . . .
Brothers, let me have a rest!

PART THREE

Till yesterday, Makar used to follow the plow,
But look at him today—he's a Chieftain now!

Ta-ra-ri-ra, ta-ra-ray,
All the horses ran away;
But the peasants at long last
Caught them all and bound them fast.
Master Raven—croak, croak, croak—
Blows his trumpet on an oak
And amuses Christian folk:
"Once a peasant and his wife
Led a very merry life.
He was always blithe and gay,
She was merry as the May;
When he danced and when she sang,
Then with mirth the village rang."
This is but the prelude, friends,
And my tale starts when it ends.

Well, Ivan rode off to bring
Back the Czar-Maid's signet ring;
And his horse flew like the wind,
Leaving miles and leagues behind—
Twenty thousand leagues, ere night,
He covered in a single flight.

Near the sea he loudly neighed,
Saying: "We will reach a glade

In a minute, maybe more,
Leading to the ocean shore,
Where, with monster head and tail,
Lies the Monster-Marvel Whale.
These ten years he lies in pain,
Ignorant of how to gain
Pardon to this very day.
He will humbly beg and pray
That you, pardon for him gain,
When we reach the Sun's domain.
Promise him, Ivan, and see
That you do so faithfully!"

When they reached the glade, they flew
Straight toward the ocean blue.
There across it lay the Whale—
Monster head and monster tail;
He was all one mass of holes,
From his ribs grew stakes and poles,
On his tail a forest black,
And a village on his back;
Peasants on his lip drove plows,
Children danced between his brows;
Oak trees on his huge jaws grew,
Maidens there sought mushrooms, too.

With a clatter, clatter, clack,
Rode the Humpback o'er his back,
While the Monster-Marvel Whale
Eyed them as he swished his tail,
Opening his huge jaws wide,
As most bitterly he sighed:
"May God speed you, gentles two!
Whither bound, and whence are you?"
"We're the Czar-Maid's envoys from afar—
From the capital we both are."
Little Humpbacked Horse replied,
"Eastward to the Sun we ride,
To his residence of gold."
"Brothers, may I make so bold,"
Said the Whale, "to beg of you
When you reach the heavens blue,
Ask the Sun how long must I
Suffer this disgrace, and why?
For what sins—let him explain—
Must I bear this grief and pain?"
"Yes, yes, Monster Whale. All right,"
Yelled Ivan with all his might;
While the whale, with bitter cries,
Begged Ivan, between his sighs:
"Please have pity on poor me—
These ten years I've suffered, see.
Do this favor for me, do—
I will serve you some day, too!"
"Yes, yes, Monster Whale. All right!"
Yelled Ivan with all his might.
Then his horse with one leap bore
Vanya to the other shore,
Leaving clouds of dust behind
As he flew on like the wind.

Near or far, or high or low—
How they traveled, I don't know;
Nor did anybody say

If they saw them on the way—
(Tales, you know, are quickly spun,
Deeds are sooner said than done);
Only, brothers, I did hear—
Indirectly, though, I fear—
That the Humpback came to where
Earth meets sky, and it is there
Peasant maidens spinning flax
Use the clouds as distaff racks.

Bidding Mother Earth good-bye,
Vanya rode up to the sky;
Like a prince he proudly sped,
Hat askew upon his head.
"What a wonder! Oh, I say!"
Mused Ivan aloud, as they
Rode the cloudy meadows blue,
"Though our country's pretty, too,
When compared with this blue sky,
It's not worth a button. Why,
Our old Earth down there is so
Black and muddy, as you know;
Here the soil is bright and blue,
And how brilliant it is, too!"
But, my horse, what can that be
In the East? Up yonder, see—
Gleaming there so fair and high
Like a palace in the sky?"
"That's the Czar-Maid's tower you
    see—
Our Czaritsa's—that's to be,"
Neighed the Humpback in his ear;
"Every night the Sun sleeps here,
And here, every day, the Moon
Comes to take her rest at noon."

Palace portals met their sight,
Crowned in crystal, gleaming bright;

All its pillars, made of gold,
Twisted cunningly and scrolled;
On each pillar shone a star;
Round the palace near and far
Fragrant gardens, fair to see,
Spread in verdant brilliancy.
Birds of paradise were singing
In their golden cages, swinging
From the silver branches there;
And the towers tall and fair
And the palaces so pretty
Spread just like a royal city.

Through the portals then they rode,
And Ivan, dismounting, strode
To the palace with bare head—
There he saw the Moon and said:

[*"Greetings, gracious Moon, from
the Earth and from your daughter, the
Czar-Maid. I have crossed the ocean
wide to do the Czar-Maid's will. I come
before you with this message from her:
she craves to know why for three nights
and three days now you've concealed
from her your rays, and why her brother
the Sun shrouds his bright face in gloomy
clouds, never sending rays of love."*]

Here the Moon in glad surprise
Hugged Ivan and dried her eyes.
"Oh, Ivanushka Petrovich,"
Murmured gracious Moon Moonovich,
"You have brought such news today
That I don't know what to say;
How we mourned, you'll never guess,
When we lost our dear princess.
That's the reason why, you see,

I've been grieving bitterly
These three nights and these three days,
In dark clouds concealed my rays;
All this time I mourned and wept,
Never ate a crumb, nor slept;
That's why her brother shrouds
His bright eyes in gloomy clouds;
Why he sends no warming rays
To the Earth these many days,
Shedding many a bitter tear
Mourning for his sister dear.
Let me know, though—is she well?
Is she homesick for us? Tell."
"She'd be pretty, I would say,
But she's wasting right away;
She's as thin as thin can be—
Only skin and bones, you see.
When she's married, though, no doubt
She'll improve and get quite stout,
For the Czar will wed her soon."
"What? The villain!" screamed the
    Moon.
"Why—he's eighty, if a day,
And he wants to wed with May!
I declare upon my life
She will never be his wife;
See what that old nasty toad
Wants—to reap, who never sowed.
Why, he's greedy as he's vain!"
Here Ivan spoke up again:
"Please do not deny this boon
For the Whale, O gracious Moon:
O'er the ocean down below
Lies a Monster Whale, you know;
He is all one mass of holes—
From his ribs stick stakes and poles—
And, poor thing, he begged me to
Speak for him when I saw you.

Why has he deserved this pain?
How can he his pardon gain?
Will he get his freedom soon?"

[*In reply the Moon said that the
Whale was punished because thirty
ships he swallowed one morning on the
open sea. When he sets them free again,
God will forgive him and take away all
his pain. Ivan then said farewell to the
Moon, kissed her bright face three
times as he clasped her in a warm embrace, and . . .*]

Bowing low as best he knew,
Vanya climbed his Humpback true,
Whistled like a noble knight
And rode back with all his might.

[*Next day Ivan came once more to
the ocean shore. With a clatter and a
clack he rode once more over the
Whale's back. When the Monster-
Marvel Whale asked the Humpback if
he would soon get his freedom, the little horse did not reply but went to the
marketplace of the Whale Village and
announced loudly:*]

"Heed my words, O Christians true!
Mark what I am telling you—
If you wish to keep away
From a briny grave today,
Get you gone this minute. Now
Wonders will take place, I vow,
For the sea will seethe and churn
When the Whale begins to turn."
Here the peasants great and small—

True believers, one and all—
Hurried off to home and farm
Crying out in wild alarm,
Gathered all their carts and placed
All their goods on them in haste,
And with many a woeful wail
Fled from off that Monster Whale.

[*Humpback then returned to the
Whale and shouted in his ear as loudly
as he could shout:*]

"Monster-Marvel Whale, rejoice!
All this was your punishment,
For, without the Lord's consent.
Thirty ships one morning you
Swallowed on the ocean blue.
When you set them free again,
He will take away your pain;
All your wounds he will assuage,
And reward you with old age."
And when his long speech was said,
He bit his bridle, tossed his head,
Gave one leap, and lo, once more
Stood upon the distant shore.

Then the Monster Whale turned round,
Like a mighty heaving mound;
Threshed the ocean with his tail,
And a fleet of thirty sail
One by one cast from his jaws,
Sails and sailors, boats and oars.

All the ships sailed out of view,
Hid by rolling billows blue;
And the Monster-Marvel Whale
Threshed the waters with his tail,
Opened up his jaws so wide,
Lifted up his voice, and cried:

"Tell me, friends, what can I do
In return—or give to you?
Colored sea shells, do you wish?
Would you care for golden fish?
Lovely pearls? Oh, anything
You may ask for I will bring."
"No, O Whale Fish," said Ivan,
"We don't need them. If you can,
We would rather have you bring
Us the Czar-Maid's signet ring
From the bottom of the sea,
For our Czar's bride that's to be."
"To be sure, for friends like you
There is nothing I won't do;
Ere the sun sets, I will bring
The Czar-Maiden's signet ring,"
Said the whale, and sank like lead
To the very ocean bed.

[*There the Monster-Marvel Whale
thumped his tail, called the tribe of
sturgeons, and ordered them to get the
signet ring, which was hidden in a chest
lying on the bottom of the sea. In an
hour or so the sturgeons returned without the ring. They told him that only the
perch knew where the ring was, but
that the perch had left his home that
very night. Two dolphins were then dispatched to find the perch. They searched
for him from shore to shore. In all the
lakes, rivers, creeks, and bays they
looked for him. But, it was in vain.
Suddenly, from somewhere came a most
unexpected cry. It came from a little
pond. The dolphins dived below without delay. There they found the little
perch in furious battle with a little carp.
The perch, as everyone knows, is fond*

*of squabbling. The dolphins dragged
him off his foe, but he struggled furiously. He fairly begged them to let him
give the carp one more punch, but the
dolphins—holding the perch by his fins
—swam with him through the seas in
grim silence. Thus they brought him to
the whale.*]

"Traitor's son, what does this mean?
You are late. Where have you been?"
Wrathfully roared out the whale;
And the perch, all meek and pale,
Begged for pardon on his fins
And confessed to all his sins.
"Well, I'll pardon you this time
If you fulfill my royal wish,"
Said the monarch to the fish.

"I shall only be too proud,"
On his fins the perch squealed loud.
"You are always in and out
Of the oceans, and no doubt
Saw the Czar-Maid's ring?" "Yea, yea!
I can find it straightaway."
"Well, be off with you, and see
That you bring it instantly."

Then the perch, with humble tail,
Bowed and left the Royal Whale;
Railed the servants to their face,
Tried to kiss a pretty dace,
Punched a dozen sprats in play,
Ere he went upon his way.
After that he fearlessly
Dived into the briny sea
And, beneath the ocean bed,
Dug a box out with his head,
Weighing no less than a ton.
"This is easier said than done,"

Cried the perch; and gave a shout
For the herrings to come out.
Though the herrings did their best—
Pushed and crowded round the chest,
Squeaking, squealing high and low,
"Yo, heave-ho!" and "Yo, ho-ho!"
All their efforts were in vain.
They grew hoarse from cries and strain,
While that casket still stuck fast
Till the perch cried out at last:
"O, you herrings—worse than sprats!
Only fit for pickling vats!"
Then, in dudgeon, quickly made
Off to seek the sturgeons' aid.
All the sturgeons flocked around,
And without a single sound,
Raised the large jewel box
Stuck in the mud and rocks.
"Well, you fellows, just take care,"
Said the perch, "and now repair
To the Whale; while I shall go
Home and take a rest below.
My poor eyes just cannot keep
Open—they're so full of sleep . . ."
And the sturgeons, then and there,
Swam off to the Whale with care;
While the brawling vagabond
Made his way toward the pond
Whence he had been hauled away
Somewhat earlier that day.
Back to fight the carp, maybe?
I can't say; no fish told me.
But forget him—if you can—
And return to our Ivan.

[*Holding on to the casket with the
signet ring, Ivan mounted the faithful
Humpback and they sped off. Two days
had already elapsed and on the morrow*

*Ivan was to deliver the ring to the Czar.
With the dawning of the third day Ivan
made his way to the city. When the Czar
saw him coming in the distance, he ran
to meet him—so anxious was he to wed
the Czar-Maid. The Czar came before
the Maid with the casket and ring, and
said to her in a voice tender and
sweet:*]

"Dear, your ring is found. Rejoice!
Now permit me to repeat
There's no obstacle, my sweet,
To prevent us, O my life,
From becoming man and wife
In the morning; but, my dear,
Come and see, your ring is here."
"Yes, I know, I know," she said;
"Still, we cannot yet be wed."
"Why can you not be my wife?
Why? I love you more than life,
And—forgive my boldness. do—
I just long to marry you.
If you don't . . . at dawn tomorrow
I shall die of grief and sorrow!
O Czar-Maid, pity me!"
But the Czar-Maid said, said she:
"Do but look—you're old and gray;
I'm but fifteen and a day.
How can we be married, pray?
All the czars will laugh and say:
'At the twilight of his life,
Grandsire took a child to wife.' "

[*"I should like to see them try," the
angry Czar replied. And he vowed to
put to death any one who would mock
him for marrying the young princess.
Nothing would persuade the Czar-Maid*

to marry the old Czar. He assured her that when he dressed in his very best raiment he was still handsome, but the Maid replied that fine clothes will not make him less old and toothless. And she added:]

"But regain your youth anew,
And I'll gladly marry you.

"If you have no fear of pain,
You will soon be young again.
Listen, early in the morn
On the palace courtyard lawn
Let them have three cauldrons ready—
Two, on fires burning steady.
And the first one must be filled
To the brim with water chilled;
While the next, with water hot—
Have it boil there on the spot;
Then, with milk fill up the last—
Heat it till the milk boils fast.
If you wish to marry me,
Young and handsome wish to be,
First you must your robes divest,
Plunge into the milk undressed,
Next in boiling water, then
In the water cold, and when
You emerge—believe me—you
Will be young and handsome too!"

All the Czar did, was to say
That his Groom come straightaway.
"Are you sending me once more,"
Cried Ivan, "off to the shore?
No, Your Majesty—not if
I can help it—I'm still stiff
As it is—no, I won't go!"
"No," the Czar said. "No, no, no.
I intend, tomorrow morn,

That upon the courtyard lawn,
They have three huge cauldrons ready—
Two, on fires burning steady;
I will have the first one filled
To the brim, with water chilled;
In the second cauldron-pot
There'll be water, boiling hot;
While with milk I'll fill the last,
Heating it till it boils fast.
You, Ivan, must do your best—
These three cauldrons you must test:
Bathe first in the milk, my son,
Then the waters, one by one."
"Listen to his sly talk," said
Ivan, and shook his head.

[*"People scald chickens, pigs, and turkeys; but I'm no pig or turkey," he cried. And as to being boiled alive, he told the Czar not to try to get him to do any such thing.*]

"But enough, Your Majesty!
Don't you make a fool of me."
Wrathfully, the Czar's beard shook:
"What?—me argue with you? Look!
If my bidding be not done
With the rising of the sun,
I will have you drawn and quartered,
Tortured on the wheels, and slaughtered!
Off with you, you wretched plague, you!"
Shaking as though with the ague,
Vanya to the hayloft crept,
Where his little Humpback slept.
"Why, Ivanushka, so sad?
Why so downcast, my dear lad?

Has our bridegroom found another
Task for you, my little brother?"
Said his horse. Ivan, in tears,
Kissed his little horse's ears,
Held his neck in close embrace
As the tears rolled down his face.
"Woe, woe is me, my horse," sobbed he;
"The Czar will be the death of me:
Now I've got to bathe undressed,
In three cauldrons, for a test—
In the first, there's water chilled;
Next with boiling water's filled;
In the third, milk scalding hot."
"Yes, that *is* a task you've got!"
Said his horse. "For this you need
All my friendship—yes, indeed.
Your misfortunes are the price
Of refusing my advice;
Thank that evil feather for
All your woes and sorrows sore.
But, God bless you—do not cry—
We will manage, you and I.
I would perish sooner than
I'd abandon you, Ivan!
Listen, lad, tomorrow morn,
When you strip there on the lawn,
Say: 'Your Gracious Majesty!
Please to send my horse to me
So that I can say good-bye
To my horse before I die.'
Now, I know he will agree
And he'll send a groom for me.
I will wave my tail about,
In each cauldron dip my snout,
Then I'll squirt upon you twice,
Whistle long and loudly thrice;
You—be sure to look alive—
In the milk then quickly dive,
Then in waters hot and cold

Dive, just as you have been told.
Now, my lad, go say your prayers,
Sleep in peace, forget your cares."

Dawn had scarce begun to peep,
Humpback roused Ivan from sleep:
"Hey, my lad, stop snoring, do!
Up! Your duty's calling you!"
So Vanyusha scratched his head,
Yawned and scrambled out of bed,
Crossed himself and said a prayer,
Sauntered to the courtyard, where,
Near the cauldrons, in a row,
Sat the servants, high and low.
Princes, dukes and lords and pages,
Cooks and coachmen, fools and sages—
All sat and whispered with a smile
And discussed Ivan; the while
Logs were fed on to the fire
So that it should not expire.

Then the portals opened wide
And the Czar with his young bride,
Came to watch there, with the rest,
How Ivan would stand the test.
And the Czar called out, "Ivan,
Now, undress yourself, my man;
Dive and bathe without delay
In those cauldrons there, I say!"
Vanya stripped—no word said he,
And the young Czar-Maid, she
Veiled her face so young and fair,
So as not to see him bare.
Vanya climbed up to the top
Of one cauldron, . . . made a stop,
Looked inside and scratched his
    head . . .
Then the Czar, impatient, said:
"What's the matter now, Ivan?
Come on—in with you, my man!"

Said Ivan: "Your Majesty,
Please to send my horse to me
So that I can say good-bye
To my horse before I die."
Pondering over this request,
Graciously he acquiesced,
And the Czar was pleased to send
For Vanuysha's faithful friend;
And Ivan said "good-bye" to
Little Humpback, tried and true.

Humpback waved his tail about,
In each cauldron dipped his snout,
Then he squirted on him twice,
Whistled long and loudly thrice;
Vanya gave his horse one look,
Then a deep, long breath he took,
After which, as he was told,
In each pot he dived full bold.
In and out he dived, and when
He emerged—no words nor pen
Could describe him—he was so
Handsome, I should have you know!
Then he dried himself and dressed,
To the Czar-Maid bowed his best,
Glanced around with haughty air—
No prince handsomer, you'd swear.

[*What a wonder! We never heard
of anyone becoming handsome that
way,*" everyone exclaimed. *The Czar,
reassured, threw his robes off, crossed
his heart and forehead twice, dived into
the hot cauldron, and was boiled there
on the spot!*]

Here the Czar-Maid stood up, and
Called for silence with her hand;
Then, unveiling her fair face,

Thus addressed the populace:
"Listen, now! The Czar is dead—
Will you have me in his stead?
Am I pleasing in your eyes?
Speak! If so, then recognize
As the lord of all the land,
My beloved husband"—and,
Pointing to Ivan, she placed
Her fair arm around his waist.

"We are willing!" all replied;
"We would die for you!" they cried;
"For the sake of your sweet eyes,
Czar Ivan we'll recognize."

Hand in hand, the royal pair—
Czar and young Czaritsa fair—
To the holy altar sped,
And in God's church they were wed.
Cannons from the castle flashed,
Trumpets blared and cymbals crashed;
From the cellars, then and there,
Casks were rolled with vintage rare.
And all night the happy throng
Shouted out in merry song:
"Long live Czar Ivan!" they cried,
"And the Fair Czar-Maid, his bride!"

In the palace mirth held sway,
Wines like water flowed that day,
And before the groaning boards
Princes drank with Dukes and Lords.

'Twas a pleasure! I was there,
Mead and wine I drank, I swear;
Though my whiskers bathed in wine,
Nothing passed these lips of mine.

THE END

FABLES

IVAN KRYLOV

Sir Bernard Pares, the leading authority in the English-speaking world on the fables of the most famous Russian fabulist, Ivan Krylov (1768–1844), has said:

> *Krylov's fables are a treasury of the vernacular, of the mother wit, and of the morale of the Russian people. They have passed almost wholesale into proverb, and are among the favorite reading of all Russian children and grown-up children—that is to say, of all Russians; and even in his adaptations from La Fontaine and others, Krylov never for a line ceases to be original and typically Russian. This is the interest and value of his work.*

Here are three of Ivan Krylov's fables best known to Russian school-children.

THE DOG AND THE HORSE

A Dog and a Horse once served the same peasant;
Said the Dog to the Horse, in a tone quite unpleasant:
   "Your plowing and carrying are useless at best;
   "Now, *my* work is what counts," and he stuck out his chest.

"Tell me, Horse, what do you do that makes you so famous?
"You sleep while *I* guard so no thief robs and shames us.
   "In the daytime I keep the flock safely together,
   "At night I stay out in the cold, bitter weather."

   "To be sure, you *do* guard," said the Horse;
   "And on this we depend."

   "But if I did not plow," said the Horse,
   "'There'd be naught to guard, my friend."

When partners are three, and they all disagree,
    Their work won't prosper—
For all their pain, they'll get nothing but strain.

    Once a Swan, a Pike, and a Crab
    Tried to pull a loaded cab,
All harnessed together, by fin, shell, and feather.
    They pulled hard, did not flinch,
    But they gained not an inch.
        And you soon will see why:
The Swan pulled hard toward the sky,
The Crab to crawl backward did try,
The Pike made for the river nearby.

    Who was wrong and who was right, we can't judge;
    But the cab's still there—it wouldn't budge.

THE QUARTET

    A tricky Monkey,
        A Goat,
        A Donkey,
And a bandy-legged Bear:
    One day the four met
    To form a Quartet.

With notes, a viola, two fiddles, a bass,
They choose 'neath a tree a cool shady place:
    One, two, three—and together they start,
    To impress the world with their art.
They strike, saw, and pluck with much poise,
But all they produce is much noise.
    "Hold it, fellows," cries Monk,

"Wait a bit!
"This is the wrong way to sit:
"Viola must face bass, you see,
"And second fiddle should face me."

Places they change, start again—
But all that they've done is in vain!
Says the Donkey, "Listen, I have the answer:
"It will go better, I know,
"If we all sit in a row."
To try this they now decide,
Seating themselves side by side.

But they find the advice of the Donkey
No better than that of the Monkey.

Λ heated dispute then arose:
As to how they should their seats dispose.

Now, a Nightingale happens by;
With relief the players sigh,
They beg this fine musician
To their troubles to listen—
Their problem to resolve,
The question of seating to solve.

The Nightingale's answer is far from gallant:
"To be musicians, you must have talent;
"So, changing your positions won't make of you musicians."

PART IV

SHORT STORIES
SELECTIONS FROM NOVELS
PROSE POEMS

for more mature young readers—
ages twelve to fifteen and up

To The Young Reader

This section offers Russian short stories, excerpts from novels, and prose poems for the more advanced young reader. The classic stories, like those by Anton Chekhov, Ivan Turgenev, Leo Tolstoy, Vladimir Korolenko, and Maxim Gorky, have been great favorites with young and adult readers for many years. The more modern Soviet works are deservedly among the most read. As masters of the written word, most of these authors are also read in translation throughout the civilized world. These writers have regarded their calling as an art. Konstantin Paustovsky, a fellow author, spoke for them as well as for himself when he described in his book, *The Golden Rose,* the process of creating literary works.

It was long ago, perhaps in my childhood, that I heard the story of a Paris dustman who earned his bread by sweeping the small shops of artisans. At the end of the day he threw out all the refuse he collected, except the sweepings from the jewelers. These he sifted carefully for he knew that they contained gold dust from the jeweler's file. After many years, he found himself in possession of a sufficient amount of this gold dust to make a mold of it and to shape it into a golden rose.

Every minute, every chance word and glance, every thought, profound or flippant, the imperceptible beat of the human heart, and, by the same token, the fluff dropping from the poplar, the starlight gleaming in a pool, all are grains of gold dust. Over the years, we writers subconsciously collect millions of these little grains and keep them stored away until they form into a mold out of which we shape our own particular golden rose—a story, a novel, or a poem. And from these precious little particles a stream of literature is born.

Here is offered a small part of the *Russian* stream of literature.

The selections you are now going to read have been published for Russian young people of about your age. Although some of them were originally written for adults, the authors whose works have thus been taken over by the young did not object to this early appropriation, for they knew that the young reader would anyhow be heir to all their creative work when he became an adult.

Some of the novels and short stories of most of the nineteenth-century authors included in this section of the book are available in English translations and they can be found in an average American public library for adults. Biographies and autobiographies of some of these writers have also been translated and published in America. They make excellent reading, throwing much light on the work of these fine authors. Perhaps you will want to avail yourself of this rich literature as you grow older.

Russian literature mirrors the key social and political events of Russia's turbulent history. The vital literature of any country reflects in an important way its history. It reveals with special insight and feeling the strivings and aspirations of the people and speaks with understanding and compassion of their grievances and struggles. Russian authors have been even more deeply involved in their country's explosive social upheavals and the strivings of their long-suffering countrymen.

The reader of the earlier works in this section would find them more meaningful and enjoyable if he bore in mind the basic facts about the conditions of life in Russia, particularly throughout the nineteenth century and up to the Revolution of 1917. For centuries nearly all the people in this country's large population had been subject to the will and the whims of the czars. They were absolute monarchs who ruled for centuries over an oppressed populace. The Russian peasant-serf was virtually a slave! He could be bought and sold, whipped, even killed by his owner; there was no law to prevent it. Serfdom was abolished in 1861 (the same year that the Civil War for the emancipation of Negro slaves began in America), but the peasant continued to exist in dire poverty and he had few civil rights.

The industrial revolution in Russia created a working class that also had no rights. Hours of work were long, wages were very low, and safety devices in factories and mines almost unheard of. The worker had no right to protest, to organize into unions, or even to express any disapproval of the actions of his employer or of the czar.

Peasants and wage earners would be imprisoned and exiled to Siberia for many years at hard labor for any expressions or actions of protest.

There was no social welfare for the unemployed, the sick, or the aged. The majority of the Russian population was pauperized and illiterate.

And it was from these wretched sections of the population that the Russian emperors recruited vast armies to carry on an almost constant warfare with Russia's neighbors. The period of military service under the czars was twenty-five consecutive years. No veterans' aid was provided. The discharged soldier often had to become a beggar.

Russian writers took up the cause of these unhappy people, mirroring in their works, with realism and deep sympathy, their suffering and their hopes for a better future. Many of the writers were hounded, persecuted, and exiled to Siberia for being outspoken in their books about the abuses of the czarist autocracy.

More recent Russian literature, created by Soviet authors, has recorded in memorable stories, novels, and poems the bitter war the Russian people waged against Nazi Germany. Several selections from such works are included in this volume.

Despite Russia's dramatic social history, her literature is rich not only in serious writings but also in works of humor and satire, and it shines with faith in mankind and with love of life. This is true both of the earlier and the more recent writings represented in this part of the book.

The stories and excerpts in this section are arranged chronologically with respect to the period in which the events of the narratives occurred.

MUMU

IVAN TURGENEV

This fine story about a deaf-mute serf and his beloved pet is based on an incident that actually occurred on the estate of the author's widowed mother.

After he finished writing *Mumu* (in 1852), Turgenev was unable to get it published; the czar's censor suppressed it, declaring it to be too outspoken about the lot of the Russian serf. Two years later the censor received a petition from a society for the prevention of cruelty to animals claiming that the story's main theme was not the mistreated serf but his mistreated dog. On this basis the censor finally allowed it to be published. The serf, Gerasim, is, of course, the actual hero of the story.

John Galsworthy, the English author, believed *Mumu* to be the most moving story in all nineteenth-century literature.

Ivan Turgenev was born in 1818 and died in 1883.

On a street near the outskirts of Moscow, in a gray house with white pillars and a lopsided balcony, there lived some time ago, surrounded by a numerous staff of household serfs, a landowner's old widow. Her sons were in government service in St. Petersburg, her daughters were married. The old woman seldom went out and was spending her miserly, tedious old age in seclusion.

The most remarkable person among her household serfs was the *dvornik* * Gerasim, a giant of a man, six feet and five inches tall, with the build of a valiant knight—but deaf-and-dumb from birth. The widow had taken him from her village estate where he had lived by himself in a small hut, apart from his brothers. He had been regarded in her village as nearly the most punctual among the peasants in fulfilling his quota of work for his owner and in paying his taxes to her.

He was strong enough to do the work of four men—and did. It was a pleasure to watch him plow, the palms of his huge hands bearing down so hard on the handle of the plow that it seemed as if he alone was furrowing the resilient soil—without the help of plow or horse. He would flourish the scythe with such power that you would think he could, if he wanted to, slice a thicket of young trees from their roots. Over the threshing floor he wielded a seven-foot flail, the long hard muscles of his shoulders rising and falling like a lever. The dead silence in which the mute man worked lent solemn importance to his untiring labors. He was a fine young peasant, and if not for his unfortunate handicap, any peasant girl would have been glad to marry him. But the old mistress brought this Gerasim to Moscow, bought him a pair of boots, had a long peasant coat made for him for the summer and a sheepskin for the winter, put a broom and a spade into his hands, and made him a dvornik.

Gerasim hated his new life. From childhood he had been accustomed to work in the fields, to village life. Withdrawn by his affliction from his fellowmen, he had grown up mute and strong, like a tree that had

---

* A *dvornik* is a yard porter.

grown in fertile soil. Transplanted to the city, he did not understand what was happening to him; he was homesick and bewildered. The work which he was to do now seemed to him, after his hard peasant labors, more a mockery than real work. He would get through with his tasks in half of an hour and either spend the rest of the day standing in the middle of the yard gaping at the passers-by as if trying to read in their faces the meaning of his puzzling situation, or he would go off to some corner and, after flinging the broom and spade far from him, would throw himself face downward on the ground and lie there motionless for hours, like a trapped animal.

But man gets used to anything, and at last Gerasim began to get used to his new life.

He had very little to do. His duties consisted of keeping the yard clean, bringing from the river a barrel of water twice a day, chopping and fetching wood for the kitchen and house stoves, and in not letting strangers into the yard. He also kept watch at night. It must be said, however, that he fulfilled his duties with diligence. There was never any refuse in the yard, not so much as a splinter of wood. When the old cart drawn by the miserable nag given him to carry the water barrel got stuck in the mud in rainy weather, he just put his shoulder to the wheel, pushed, and not only the cart but the horse as well moved forward. When he chopped wood, the ax rang out like glass, and chips and split logs flew in all directions. And as for strangers, ever since the night when he had caught two thieves and banged their heads together—banged them so hard that it was quite unnecessary to take the men to the police station—everyone in the neighborhood began to respect him. Even in the daytime, innocent strangers going past the open gate to the courtyard, at the sight of the stern dvornik raised an arm in self-defense and shouted at him, as if he could hear them.

With the rest of the servants Gerasim's relations were not exactly friendly; they were rather terse, for they were a little afraid of him. Just the same he regarded himself as one of them. They spoke to him with signs and he understood them, obeying all orders with precision. At the same time he was aware of his rights and no one dared, for instance, to sit at his place at the table in the servants' eating quarters. On the whole, he was a strict and serious man who preferred order in everything. Even the cocks knew this and did not dare fight in front of him. If he saw them, they were in trouble—he would grab them by the legs, spin them around in a wide circle about ten times, then fling them apart.

A small storeroom over the kitchen was assigned to him as his living quarters. There he arranged things according to his own taste. He made himself a bed of oak boards and set it on four wooden blocks—a bed fit for a giant. Over a ton of weight could have been placed on it without bending it. Under this bed was his sturdy trunk. In a corner Gerasim placed an equally sturdy table and at the table a three-legged stool, so broad and solid that to test its strength he would sometimes lift it up, throw it down, and chuckle with approval. The door of this room was fastened with a huge padlock, and Gerasim always carried the key on his belt. He did not want people going into his room.

A year passed. And then Gerasim had a small adventure.

The rich old widow whose dvornik he was, a stickler for old traditions, kept a huge retinue of servants. There were in her household not only laundresses, seamstresses, carpenters, tailors and dressmakers, but even a saddler, who was also a veterinary and a doctor for the servants. There was a household doctor for the lady herself. And last but not least there was a shoemaker, a hopeless drunkard by the name of Kapiton Klimov.

Klimov saw himself as an unfortunate man whose gifts as an educated and urbane individual, unjustly destined to live in God-forsaken Moscow instead of in sophisticated St. Petersburg, were not at all appreciated. He drank, as he himself put it—speaking eloquently and pausing to smite his chest—only to drown his sorrows. And one day the mistress of the household mentioned him to her head butler, Gavrilo, a person whose yellowish eyes and duck's nose marked him as a man destined for a position of authority. The old lady deplored the depraved conduct of the shoemaker who only the day before had been found dead drunk in the street.

"Shouldn't we marry him off, Gavrilo?" she said suddenly. "What do you think? Perhaps that would bring him to his senses."

"Yes, why not marry him off, Ma'am, it's possible, Ma'am," replied Gavrilo. "Indeed, it would be a very good thing to do, Ma'am."

"Yes, but who would want to marry him?"

"Certainly, Ma'am! It is for you to say, Ma'am. After all, he may be of use to someone. Everyone is good for something."

"It seems that he likes Tatiana."

Gavrilo was about to object, but instead closed his lips tightly.

"Yes, let him marry Tatiana," decided the old lady, treating herself to a pinch of snuff. "Do as I say."

"Yes, Ma'am," said Gavrilo and took himself off.

The first thing Gavrilo did when he got back to his own room was to send his wife away and seat himself at the window to think. The unexpected order issued by his mistress apparently burdened him with a problem. After thinking for a while, he sent for the shoemaker. Kapiton appeared. But, before we relate their conversation to our reader, it will not be useless to say a few words about this Tatiana whom Kapiton was to marry, and why his mistress' order had so upset the head butler.

Tatiana, who was one of the laundresses, but so skilled and experienced that she was given only the finest linen to do, was about

twenty-eight years old, small, thin, flaxen-haired, with moles on her left cheek. A mole on the left cheek is regarded in Russia as a sign of ill luck, foretelling an unhappy life. Indeed, Tatiana could hardly boast of her fate. She had led the life of a drudge from early youth, working for two and never being shown by anyone the least sign of affection. She was always poorly dressed, and received an insignificant wage. She had no relations except for some distant uncle who had been a steward and was left behind in the village as useless, and there were some other distant relatives among the peasants—that was all. Only a few years earlier she had been considered a beauty, but her looks had very soon faded. She was meek, intimidated, indifferent to what happened to her, and mortally scared of others. She thought of nothing but finishing her work in time, never spoke to anyone, and trembled at the very mention of the name of her mistress, though the latter hardly knew her by sight.

When Gerasim arrived from the village, Tatiana nearly died of terror at the sight of his huge figure, tried desperately to keep out of his way, and lowered her eyes whenever she happened to walk past him on her way from the house to the laundry. At first Gerasim took no particular notice of Tatiana, but later he would laugh softly whenever he caught sight of her, look admiringly at her, and then he began to follow her everywhere with his eyes. Perhaps it was her shyness and timid movements that attracted him—who can say! And one day, when she was passing through the yard, one of her mistress' starched blouses held carefully between her finger tips, she felt her elbow firmly grasped. She turned and shrieked—behind her stood Gerasim. Smiling and emitting amiable grunts, he held out to her a gingerbread rooster with goldleaf tail and wings. She was about to refuse it, but he thrust it into her hand, nodded his head, left her, and looking back gave her a very friendly grunt.

From that day he gave her no peace—

wherever she went, there he was, coming to meet her, smiling, waving his hands, suddenly drawing a ribbon from under his shirt and forcing it upon her, or sweeping away the dust in front of her. The poor girl did not know how to be or what to do. Soon the whole household knew of the carryings-on of the mute dvornik. Jeers, taunts, stinging words were showered upon Tatiana. But no one dared to make fun of Gerasim—he did not like jokes, and in his presence Tatiana too was left in peace. Whether she liked it or not, he became her protector. Like all deaf-mutes, he was very observant, and he understood very well when people were laughing at either of them. At dinner one day, Tatiana's taskmistress, the head laundress, teased her until the poor girl did not know what to do and almost wept with annoyance. Gerasim rose suddenly from his seat, thrust out his heavy fist, placed it on the head of the teasing woman, and looked into her face with such threatening ferocity that she bent low over the table with fright. No one said a word. Gerasim returned to his seat and went on eating his cabbage soup.

Another time, having noticed that Kapiton—the same Kapiton about whom we just spoke—was chatting too amiably with Tatiana, Gerasim beckoned to him with his finger, led him to the coach house, grabbed a shaft standing in the corner, and threatened him with it, mildly but very meaningfully. After this no one dared to engage Tatiana in flirtatious conversation. And he got away with it all. True, the head laundress fainted away as soon as she left the dinner table the time Gerasim threatened her, and afterward managed to bring the news of Gerasim's roughness to the ears of the old mistress. But that queer old woman went into fits of laughter, to the extreme indignation of the offended laundress, made her repeat how Gerasim had bent her head with his heavy fist, and next day she sent

---

* A *ruble* is a unit of Russian currency now worth a dollar and ten cents.

Gerasim a silver ruble.* She valued him as a faithful and powerful watchman.

Gerasim himself was somewhat afraid of his mistress, but trusted in her favor and was getting ready to go to her to ask permission to marry Tatiana. He was only waiting for the new coat the head butler had promised him, so as to appear before the mistress properly attired, when suddenly the old lady took it into her head to marry Tatiana to Kapiton, the shoemaker.

The reader will now easily understand why the head butler was so disturbed after his talk with the lady of the house. "My mistress," he thought, sitting at his window, "of course, favors Gerasim. (Gavrilo had been well aware of this and had therefore himself been nice to the dvornik.) After all, he's a dumb creature. I can't very well tell the mistress that Gerasim is courting Tatiana. Besides—what sort of a husband would he make? But, on the other hand, if that devil finds out that Tatiana is to marry Kapiton, he'll tear the house down, as true as I'm alive!"

The appearance of Kapiton broke the thread of Gavrilo's reflections. The befuddled cobbler came in, clasped his hands behind his back, and leaning against the wall in a casual manner, he crossed his right leg over his left and tossed his head back to get the hair out of his eyes.

Gavrilo surveyed Kapiton, drumming on the windowsill with his fingers. Kapiton merely narrowed his pale eyes but did not lower them. He even gave a short laugh, passing his hand through his whitish locks, which stuck out in all directions. "Well, I, well, here I am! What are you staring at?"

"You're a sight!" said Gavrilo, paused, then added, "What a sight! I must say!"

The shoemaker only shrugged his shoulders. "And are *you* any better?" he thought to himself.

"Look at yourself—just look at yourself!" continued Gavrilo in the same vein. "Do you know what you look like?"

Kapiton cast a calm glance at his worn

342

and ragged jacket, his patched trousers, and a particularly careful glance rested longer on his broken boots, especially on the tip of the one on which his right foot rested so jauntily, before returning to the head butler.

"So what?"

"So what?" mimicked Gavrilo. "So what?" he repeated once more. "You resemble the devil—may God forgive me—that's just what you look like."

Kapiton blinked his small eyes.

"Curse me out, go ahead, Gavrilo Andreich," he thought to himself.

"You got drunk again," Gavrilo began, "didn't you? Well, answer me!"

"For reasons of poor health I indeed availed myself of alcoholic beverages," asserted Kapiton.

"For reasons of poor health—you don't say! The truth is that you love the stuff. And you, a man educated in St. Petersburg. . . . A lot you learned there—how to eat bread that you don't earn. . . ."

"In this, Gavrilo Andreich, my only judge is God—and no one else. Only He knows what kind of a man I am and whether I earn my bread. And as to the consideration of drunkenness—even there I

am not the one to blame but a certain friend who lied to me, tricked me, left me, that is, while I . . ."

"And you were left like a drunken fool right on the street. Oh, you drunken fool! But that is not the issue," continued the head butler. "This is what's up—the mistress," here he paused, "the mistress wishes you to marry. Do you hear? She assumes that you will come to your senses by marrying. Do you understand?"

"It's simple enough; of course I understand."

"Well, then. I think that what you need is for someone to take you in hand. That's what you really need. However, it's her business. Well? Do you agree?"

Kapiton grinned.

"Marriage is good for man, Gavrilo Andreich. And for my part, I agree with the greatest pleasure."

"Of course, what can you lose?" Gavrilo said, and to himself he thought that it must be admitted the man expresses himself well. "But," he continued aloud, "the mistress has found for you an unsuitable bride. . . ."

"What kind, if I may be allowed some curiosity?"

"Tatiana."

"Tatiana?!"

And Kapiton's eyes bulged and he moved away from the wall.

"Well, why are you so alarmed? Doesn't she suit you?"

"Why should she not suit me, Gavrilo Andreich? She's not a bad sort—a hard-working, tame wench. . . . But you know very well, Gavrilo Andreich, that that hob-goblin, that scarecrow, is after her . . ."

"I know, I know all about it," the butler interrupted, vexed at the thought of Gerasim. "But . . ."

"But, have mercy, Gavrilo Andreich, he'll kill me, he will—he'll kill me as if he were squashing a fly. He has such an arm—you know yourself what an arm he has. He's deaf, and he strikes and doesn't hear the thud. And there is no way of shaking him off. In addition he is stupid. And he is some sort of wild beast. He's deaf and a graven image, he's worse than a graven image. . . . He's a block of wood! And why should I take such chances with him? Of course, I no longer really care what happens to me. I've been through so much, I've endured everything, I'm soaked through and through with woe like an old gray pot! But just the same, I'm a human being and not just an insignificant pot."

"I know, I know, don't put it on so thick. . . . You're a weakling. What's the use of going on like this?"

"My God!" the cobbler continued with passion, "he will kill me! Poor wretch that I am! What a fate! Just think, what a fate! When I was a mite, I was beaten by my German boss, in the best years of my life I was beaten by my brothers, and finally, in the prime of my life, this is what awaits me. It's not beatings I'm afraid of, Gavrilo Andreich. If my master punishes me when we're alone, I can hold up my head after-ward, so long as he treats me with respect before others, but to be humiliated by a creature like that Gerasim . . ."

"That'll do—get out!" shouted Gavrilo,

interrupting. He was at the end of his patience.

Kapiton hurried away.

"Say, but for him would you agree?" the butler called after the shoemaker.

"I express my consent," replied Kapiton, and quickly departed. Even in extreme circumstances the cobbler's eloquence did not desert him.

Gavrilo paced the room several times.

"Perhaps by tomorrow the mistress will have forgotten about this marriage," Gavrilo then said to himself. "Why should I let it worry me? We'll manage that bully Gerasim—hand him over to the police if necessary."

The head butler's expectations were not realized. The idea of Kapiton's marriage took such a hold on the old woman's mind that she talked of little else that night to her companions, who were kept in the house especially for the purpose of relieving their mistress' insomnia. When Gavrilo went to report to her next morning, her first question was: "And how are the wedding preparation proceeding?" He, of course, replied that they were going splendidly and that Kapiton would come to pay his respects to her that very day.

The old lady was indisposed and did not detain Gavrilo to discuss the day's affairs. He returned to his quarters and called a council. The matter called for special consideration. Tatiana, of course, had offered no objection, but Kapiton announced, so that all could hear him, that he was no fool. Gerasim looked morosely at all concerned, did not leave the porch of the servants' quarters, and it seemed that he knew that something not to his advantage was being conspired. To begin with, for his own safety, Kapiton was locked up in the lumber room, and then they gave some serious thought to the situation. Of course, it was simple to resort to force, but—heaven help us!—there would be a commotion, the old lady would get upset—there would be trouble! What to do? They thought, and they thought, and finally came up with a plan.

They had often observed that Gerasim could not stand drunkards. Each time a drunkard would pass when Gerasim was sitting at the gate, he would turn away with disgust. It was decided to rehearse Tatiana in pretending to be drunk and to have her walk past Gerasim swaying and shuffling. For a long time she would not agree to this, but at last they persuaded her. What's more, she realized herself that there was no other way to get rid of her admirer. She went. Kapiton was released from his captivity— after all, the whole affair concerned him. Gerasim was at the gate, aimlessly thrusting his spade into the ground. He was being watched from all corners and from behind window blinds.

The trick worked beyond all expectations. Seeing Tatiana, Gerasim at first, as was his habit, nodded to her uttering his affectionate grunt. When he looked more closely, he dropped the spade, approached her, and put his face near hers. From fright she swayed even more and closed her eyes. He grabbed her by the arm, dragged her across the yard, pulled her into the room where the council was in session, and pushed her toward Kapiton. Tatiana nearly died of fright. Gerasim stood there for a moment, and then with a depricating gesture of the hand and a bitter laugh stumped heavily out of the room to his own place. He did not leave his room for a day and a night. The stable boy, Antipka, peeped through a chink in the wall and reported that Gerasim was sitting on the bed with his face propped on the palm of his hand, that he was quiet— only moaning now and then and swaying in grief.

When Gerasim came out of his room the next day, no special change could be seen in him. He only seemed more morose and he paid not the slightest attention to Tatiana and Kapiton. That same evening the two called on their mistress, each with a goose tucked under the arm, and in a week's time they were married. On the day of the wedding there seemed to be not the least change in Gerasim's conduct, except that he came back from the river without any water: he had somehow managed to break the barrel on the way. And toward evening, in the stable, he groomed and scrubbed the horse so zealously that the animal swayed like a blade of grass in the wind, shifting from foot to foot under Gerasim's iron fists.

All this took place in the spring. Another year passed, during which Kapiton finally succumbed to drink, and, having become absolutely worthless, was sent to a remote village with his wife. Just before their departure, Gerasim burst out of his room, went up to Tatiana, and gave her a red cotton kerchief, which he had bought for her a year ago as a keepsake. Tatiana, who had till this moment suffered all the misfortunes of her life with Kapiton in silence, suddenly burst into tears and before getting into the cart exchanged three kisses with Gerasim, in the Christian manner. He meant to accompany her to the town gates and at first walked beside the cart, but stopped suddenly, waved his hand, and set off along the shore of the river.

It was almost evening. Gerasim walked slowly, looking at the water. All of a sudden he thought he noticed something struggling to get out of the silt at the water's edge. Bending down, he saw a small puppy, white with black spots, vainly trying to scramble out of the water, slipping back again and again, and trembling all over its small, thin, wet body. Gerasim looked at the puppy, scooped it up with one hand, thrust it inside the front of his shirt, and walked with it home, taking big strides. In his tiny room he put the just-rescued pup on the bed, covered it with his heavy coat, and ran first to the stable for straw and then to the kitchen for a bowl of milk.

Carefully turning back the coat, and spreading the straw under the pup, he placed the bowl of milk on the bed. The unfortunate little creature was only three weeks old. Its eyes had only recently opened

for the first time, and one was still less open than the other. It did not know yet how to drink from a bowl and lay there trembling and blinking. Gerasim took its head gently between two fingers and pushed its nose into the milk. The puppy began to lap greedily, snorting, trembling, and choking. Gerasim sat looking at it, and all of a sudden burst out laughing. He took care of the little dog throughout the night, keeping it covered, rubbing it; and at last he fell into a light, somewhat happy sleep at its side.

No mother ever cared for her infant as Gerasim cared for his new find. At first the pup was very weak, sickly, and ugly, but gradually it began to get shapely, to grow, and to improve in appearance. Eight months later, owing to the untiring care of its rescuer, it turned into a handsome dog of a Spanish breed, with long ears, a bushy trumpet-like tail, and large expressive eyes. It was passionately attached to Gerasim, never leaving his side for a minute, and following him everywhere wagging its tail. He gave it a name—dumb people know that they can attract attention with their cowlike lowing—he called his pet Mumu. All the servants grew fond of her and also called her Mumu.

Mumu was extremely intelligent, would cuddle up to anyone, but loved only Gerasim. As for Gerasim, he loved his dog to distraction, and he didn't like anyone to pet her. Whether he was concerned for the dog, or jealous, God alone knows! Mumu would wake him every morning tugging at his clothes, would lead the old water-barrel horse—with whom she lived on terms of the deepest friendship—to Gerasim by the bridle, would trot to the river beside her master with an air of great self-importance, would watch over his brooms and spades, and would let no one come near his room. Gerasim cut a hole in the door so that the dog could come and go at will, and Mumu, feeling that she was at home nowhere but in Gerasim's room, would jump on to the bed with a satisfied look as soon as she entered

the place. She would stay awake all night but was not one to bark for no reason, like a silly dog that sits up on its hind legs and raises its head blinking and barking at the stars from mere boredom, and usually three times in succession. No! Mumu's shrill voice was never raised without reason. Only when a stranger passed close by the fence, or a suspicious noise or rustle came from somewhere or other did she bark. In a word, she was a splendid watchdog.

Mumu never went inside the big house and, when Gerasim took wood into the rooms, always stayed behind waiting for him impatiently on the steps—her ears cocked, turning her head from left to right at the slightest sound from inside.

Another year passed. Gerasim went on working as a dvornik and seemed more content with his lot, when suddenly an unusual thing happened. One fine summer day the mistress, surrounded by her companions, was pacing up and down her sitting room. She was in high spirits—laughing and joking; and her companions laughed and joked with her, though their mood was not as jolly. Her companions did not care for those sudden spurts of good humor in their mistress. In the first place, she always insisted on immediate and absolute sympathy from everyone around, and would get angry if she noticed a face not radiant with joy; and in the second place, these fits of cheerfulness usually did not last long and were followed by a grim and sour mood. That day had begun well for her: four jacks had turned up (she consulted the cards every morning), which meant that her wishes would be fulfilled, and she had enjoyed her tea very much, for which the maid received praise in words and ten kopecks * in money. And so, walking about her sitting room, a pleased smile on her withered lips, the mistress came up to the window. There was a garden planted beneath the window, and on the middle bed, under a rose bush, lay

---

* A *kopeck* is a Russian penny.

Mumu gnawing busily at a bone. The mistress saw her.

"Goodness gracious!" she exclaimed. "Whose dog is that?"

The companion, poor soul, to whom the mistress addressed the question, was all of a flutter, not knowing how to take the old lady's curiosity.

"I—d-d-on't know," she muttered. "I think it belongs to the deaf dvornik. . . ."

"Goodness gracious! What a sweet little doggie!" interrupted her mistress. "It's a cute one. Order them to bring it in. Has he had it long? How is it I never saw it before? Order them to bring it here."

The companion flew into the entry.

"You, there!" she shouted. "Bring Mumu in at once. She's in the garden."

"So they call it Mumu?" said the mistress. "A very good name."

"Yes, a very good name," the companion was quick to agree. "Hurry up with the dog."

Stepan, a great big strong fellow employed as a footman, rushed headlong into the garden and fell upon Mumu. The dog, escaping his grasp, ran with all her might to Gerasim, who was at the moment emptying a barrel, turning it in his hands as if it were no heavier than a toy drum. Stepan ran after the dog and tried to grab her as she pressed against her master's leg. But the spry little creature would not let a stranger get hold of her and slipped through his hands with many a squirm. Gerasim looked on with a proud smile. At last Stepan straightened himself with an air of annoyance and explained gruffly, by means of signs, that the mistress wished the dog brought to her. Gerasim, somewhat surprised, called Mumu, lifted her up, and handed her over to Stepan, who carried her into the sitting room and set her on the floor. The mistress began calling Mumu to her in a kindly voice. Mumu, finding herself for the first time in such magnificent surroundings, rushed in terror to the door, and when pushed back by the officious Stepan, squeezed herself, trembling, against the wall.

"Mumu, Mumu, come here, Mumu, won't you come to your mistress?" the old lady cajoled. "Come on, little silly, don't be afraid!"

"Go, go to the mistress," the servants coaxed.

But Mumu only looked around despairingly and refused to budge.

"Bring her something to eat," said the mistress. "What a silly dog! Won't go to her mistress! What is she afraid of?"

"She's not used to you yet," one of the companions said in a timid and sympathetic tone.

Stepan brought in a saucer of milk and placed it before Mumu, but the dog would not so much as sniff at it and kept trembling and looking anxiously about her.

"Queer little thing!" said the mistress, approaching her. She stooped to stroke the dog, but Mumu turned sharply, baring her teeth. The old lady quickly drew her hand back.

There was a moment of silence. Mumu uttered a low whine, as if complaining and apologizing at the same time. The old lady moved away, frowning. The dog's sudden movement had frightened her.

"Take it away!" she said in an unsteady voice. "Nasty, bad-tempered little thing!"

And turning slowly, she moved toward her study. The companions, exchanging uneasy glances, were about to follow her; but she stopped and, looking at them coldly, said, "Why are you following me? I didn't invite you, did I?" And she walked out of the room.

The companions motioned despairingly to Stepan, who picked Mumu up and flung her outside, right at the feet of the waiting Gerasim. Half an hour later, deep silence reigned throughout the house, and the old woman sat on her sofa, darker than a storm cloud.

What absurd things can at times disturb a person!

The mistress was moody for the rest of the day, would speak to no one, would not play cards, and slept badly when she went to bed. She complained that she had been given the wrong cologne, that the pillow smelled of soap; she ordered the maid to smell all the bedding—in a word, she fussed and fumed. Next morning she summoned Gavrilo earlier than usual.

"Kindly inform me," she began, when the head butler, not without a feeling of alarm, stepped into her study, "what dog was barking all night in our yard? It kept me awake!"

"Dog? What dog? . . . Do you mean the dumb man's dog?" he said in a shaking voice.

"I don't know whether it belongs to the dumb man, or to anyone else; all I know is that it kept me awake. And I don't see why we need such a lot of dogs! We have a watchdog, don't we?"

"Oh, yes, Volchok."

"Well, then, what do we want another for? It only causes disorder. And why should the dumb man want a dog? Who told him he could keep dogs on my premises? I looked out of the window yesterday and saw it lying in the garden, gnawing at some filthy thing it had brought there, right where my roses are planted."

The old lady paused for a moment.

"It must be gotten rid of this very day—do you hear me?"

"Yes, Ma'am."

"This very day! Now, go! I'll hear your report for the day later."

Gavrilo left.

As he passed through the sitting room, the butler picked up the hand bell from one table and put it on another, "for the sake of order," and blew his ducklike nose discreetly before stepping into the entry. Stepan lay asleep on the window sill in the pose of a slain warrior in a battle painting, his bare feet protruding stiffly from under his coat, which served him as a blanket. The butler shook him and gave him an order in a low voice; hearing it, Stepan replied with a short laugh, and smothered a yawn. When the butler left, Stepan jumped to his feet, pulled on his coat and boots, and went to the top of the steps leading to the yard. Five minutes had not elapsed before Gerasim appeared with a heavy load of wood on his back and the devoted Mumu at his heels. (The old lady made her servants heat her bedroom and study even during the summer months.) Standing sideways at the door, Gerasim pushed it open with his shoulder and entered with his burden, Mumu waiting for him outside as usual. Choosing the right moment, Stepan pounced upon Mumu like a kite swooping down upon a chicken, gathered her up in his arms, and—running into the street without stopping to put on his cap—leaped into the first cab which came along and drove off at a gallop. He soon found a buyer to whom he sold the dog for half a ruble, merely stipulating that it was to be kept tied up for at least a week. Then he returned. He got out of the cab, however, before he reached the house, walked around it through a lane in the back of the house and climbed over the fence into the yard. He did not dare to go in by the gate, for fear of meeting Gerasim.

But he need not have been afraid. Gerasim was nowhere to be seen in the yard. The moment he had come out of the house, he had discovered Mumu's disappearance. It had never happened before that Mumu was not waiting for him. Gerasim ran all over the place looking for her, calling to her in his own fashion. He rushed to his room, into the hayloft, ran out into the street, looking everywhere. She was lost! He asked the servants about her with desperate gestures, stooping down and holding his hand about a half of a foot above the ground, describing Mumu's shape with his hands. Some really did not know what had happened to the dog, and merely shook their heads, others knew but only chuckled for reply, while the head butler assumed a dignified air and fell to scolding the grooms. Then Gerasim rushed out of the yard and went off to continue his search.

Evening was approaching when he came back. His drawn look, weary step, and dusty clothes all showed that he had been through half the streets of Moscow. Stopping in front of the mistress' windows, with a glance toward the porch where six or seven of the servants were gathered, he turned his face away, grunting out once more: "Mumu." Mumu did not answer his call. He walked off. Everyone looked after him, but no one either smiled or spoke. The next morning the inquisitive stable boy, Antipka, was telling them in the kitchen that the dumb man had moaned all night long.

Gerasim did not leave his room the next day. The groom had to fetch the water, a task he greatly resented. The old lady asked if her orders had been carried out. Gavrilo told her that they had. The day after, Gerasim came out of his room and went to work. At dinner time he came to the table, ate his dinner, and went without bowing to any one. His face, always expressionless, as the faces of the deaf and dumb usually are, was now like a mask of stone. After dinner he went out again, but soon returned and went into the hayloft. Night came, serene and moonlit. While he was tossing on the hay, sighing deeply, Gerasim suddenly felt something tugging at his coat. He shook all over, but did not raise his head, only screwed up his eyes tighter, till he felt another, a stronger pull. He sprang up, and there was Mumu jumping and wagging her tail, a piece of rope dangling from her collar. A long-drawn sound of joy came from the speechless depths of Gerasim's breast. He caught Mumu in his arms and held her tight. The next moment she was licking his nose, his eyes, his mustache, his beard. Standing still for a few minutes to collect his thoughts, Gerasim slipped out of the hayloft and, making sure there was no one watching him, reached his room in safety.

He had already guessed that the dog could not have got lost, that she must have been taken away on the mistress' orders. The servants had explained to him by signs how Mumu had snarled at the old lady. He now made up his mind to take precautions. First he gave Mumu bread to eat, fondled her, and put her to sleep. He spent the whole night wondering how best to hide her. At last he decided to leave her in his room in the daytime, paying her occasional visits, and to take her out at night. He plugged up the hole in the door with an old coat, and as soon as it was morning, he was out as if nothing had happened, still keeping—the cunning of the simple-hearted!—the same unhappy expression on his face. The idea that Mumu might expose her presence by her squeals never crossed the mind of the unfortunate deaf man. Indeed, very soon all the servants were aware that the dumb man's dog was back and was being kept locked up in his room. But, partly out of pity both for the animal and the master, partly out of fear of the latter, no one let him see that his secret was known. The head butler scratched the back of his head and gave a shrug that seemed to say, "I'm washing my hands of the whole business—so long as the mistress doesn't find out!"

Gerasim had never worked with greater zeal than on that day. He cleaned out and scrubbed the whole yard, weeded the grass, pulled out with his own hands every paling in the low fence around the garden, to test its strength, and then hammered each one back in its place. In fact, he made such an effort that the mistress herself noticed his diligence. Twice during the day Gerasim managed to slip into his room to see his captive pet. In the evening he lay down to sleep beside her, not in the hayloft, but in his room, and only after two o'clock in the night dared to take her out for a breath of air.

Just as he was about to return after quite

a long nocturnal walk, a rustling sound could be heard from the lane close to the fence. Mumu pricked up her ears, growled, trotted up to the fence, sniffed, and burst into loud, shrill barking. Some drunkard had taken it into his head to lie down against the fence for the night. It was just then that the mistress was dropping off to sleep after a prolonged attack of "nervous upset" —she always had those attacks after too heavy a supper. "Girls, girls," she moaned. "Oh, girls!" The frightened maids rushed into her bedroom. "Oh, oh, I'm dying!" she moaned, flinging her arms about in despair. "It's that dog again! . . . Get the doctor! Quick! They want to kill me. . . . That dog, that dog! . . . Oh!" and she threw her head back, which was supposed to indicate that she was fainting.

They rushed for the doctor—that is, the household physician, Dr. Khoriton, whose total expertness consisted in wearing felt-soled boots and in his ability to feel the patient's pulse very delicately, slept fourteen hours a day, dividing the rest of his time between sighing and continuously prescribing laurel drops for his mistress. This healer came running to her bedside instantly, burned a bunch of feathers in the room, and as soon as the mistress opened her eyes, offered her the laurel drops in a small tumbler on a silver tray. The mistress swallowed the medicine, and began complaining tearfully about the dog, about Gavrilo, about her lot generally, claiming that she had been deserted by everyone in her old age, that no one had any pity for her, that they all longed for her death. In the meantime, the unfortunate Mumu went on barking, Gerasim vainly trying to get her away from the fence. "There it is again!" wailed the mistress, and once more rolled up her eyes. The doctor whispered to one of the girls; she rushed out into the hall to wake Stepan; Stepan rushed to wake Gavrilo, who, in the excitement of the moment, ordered the entire household to be roused from their sleep. Gerasim, turning, saw lights and shadows

fluttering across the window of the big house, and feeling intuitively that disaster was impending, snatched up Mumu and ran with her under his arm to his room and locked the door. A few minutes later five men tried to force the door, but feeling the strength of the bolt, gave up. Gavrilo came running up to them in a distracted state, ordered them all to stay there till morning and guard the door. Then he ran back to the servants' quarters and sent word to the mistress that the dog had, unfortunately, come back, but that it would be put to death the next day, and begged the mistress not to be angry and to calm herself. The mistress would probably not have calmed herself nearly so soon if her doctor, in his haste, had not poured forty, instead of twelve, drops of laurel water. The medicine took effect and in fifteen minutes the mistress was in a relaxed slumber. And Gerasim, pale as death, lay on his bed, holding Mumu's muzzle tight.

The mistress opened her eyes quite late the next morning. Gavrilo waited for her to wake before giving orders for an all-out assault on Gerasim's room, while he prepared himself to weather a violent storm. But there was no storm. Remaining in bed, the mistress summoned her senior companion to her bedside.

"Liubov Liubimovna," she began in a low, feeble voice. She liked to pose at times as a pathetic and abandoned martyr. It goes without saying that everyone about the house felt extremely uncomfortable at such times. "Liubov Liubimovna, you can see in what a state I am; go to Gavrilo Andreich, my darling, and speak to him: is it possible that some wretched dog means more to him than his mistress' peace—nay, than her very life? I would hate to think so," she added in tones of deep feeling. "Go my dear, do me the kindness, go and speak to Gavrilo Andreich."

Liubov Liubimovna went off to Gavrilo's room. Exactly what they said to each other remains unknown, but in a very short time a whole crowd of domestics was seen moving across the yard in the direction of Gerasim's room. Gavrilo headed the procession, for some mysterious reason holding on to his cap, although there was no wind. After him came the footmen and chefs. At the end of the parade came some skipping and grimacing urchins who did not even belong to the household. On the steps of the narrow staircase leading to Gerasim's room sat some of the "watchmen," and two others, armed with sticks, were guarding the door. The group mounted the stairway, occupying it from top to bottom. Gavrilo approached the door, banged on it with his fist, and shouted:

"Open the door!"

"There was a stifled bark, but no other answer.

"Open the door, I tell you!"

"Gavrilo Andreich," said Stepan from the bottom step, "He's deaf—he can't hear you."

Everyone laughed.

"Well, what are we to do?" asked Gavrilo from the landing.

"There is a hole in the door," answered Stepan, "poke a stick into it and wave it about."

Gavrilo stooped down.

"He's stuffed his coat or something in it."

"Just push it in, that's all."

Again there came a hollow bark.

"There she goes, giving herself away," someone from the crowd said.

Gavrilo scratched behind his ear.

"No, brother," he said at last, "go and push the coat in yourself, if you like."

"I don't mind!"

Stepan seized a stick, pushed in the coat and began to wave the end of the stick inside the hole, saying, "Come out, come out!"

He was still at it when the door was suddenly flung open, sending them all tumbling down the steps, Gavrilo first of all.

"Take care, now!" shouted Gavrilo from the yard. "Watch it!"

Gerasim stood motionless on the threshold. The crowd regathered at the foot of the stairs. Gerasim, his arms on his hips, looked down on all those puny men in their servant coats of German cut; standing there in his crimson peasant blouse he seemed a giant as he faced them. Gavrilo stepped forward.

"Take it easy, fellow," he warned. "I won't put up with any nonsense!"

Then he started to explain by signs that the mistress demanded Gerasim's dog immediately, and that there would be trouble if he did not obey her orders.

Gerasim looked at him, pointed at the dog, drew his finger across his neck, as if tightening a noose, and then looked inquiringly at the butler.

"Yes, yes," the latter answered, nodding vigorously. "Without fail."

Gerasim lowered his eyes, gave himself a shake, pointed once more at Mumu, who stood near him all the time, innocently wagging her tail, her ears cocked inquisitively. He then repeated the sign of strangling around his neck, and thumped his chest meaningful, as if to say that he would destroy Mumu himself.

"You'll cheat!" Gavrilo signaled back.

Gerasim shot him one look, smiled scornfully, thumped his chest once more, went into his room, and closed the door.

The servants exchanged glances in silence.

"What does he mean?" Gavrilo began, "now he has locked himself up again!"

"Leave him alone, Gavrilo Andreich," said Stepan. "He'll be as good as his word. That's the way he is. . . . When he gives his word, he keeps it. He's not like us. That's God's truth, it is!"

" 'Tis so," the others echoed, nodding their heads. " 'Tis true."

"All right, we'll see," said Gavrilo. "But we'll watch him, just the same. Hey, there, Yeroshka!" he shouted, addressing himself to a pale-faced fellow dressed in a brown nankeen coat, who was supposed to be a gardener. "You have nothing to do, anyway!

Get a stick and sit here. If anything happens, run for me at once!"

Taking a stick, Yeroshka planted himself on the bottom step. The crowd dispersed, only a few idlers and boys loitering, while Gavrilo went home and sent a message to his mistress through Liubov Liubimovna that her orders had been obeyed. The mistress tied her handkerchief in a knot, poured some eau-de-cologne on it, sniffed it, rubbed her temple with it, drank her tea, and—still under the influence of the laurel drops—fell asleep again.

An hour after the tumult had subsided, the door of Gerasim's room opened, and he appeared. He had put on his best coat; he was leading Mumu on a string. Yeroshka made way for him. Gerasim walked toward the gate. The boys and all those who happened to be in the yard watched him in silence. He did not once look back. Gavrilo sent Yeroshka after him to spy on him. From a distance Yeroshka saw Gerasim go

into a tavern with the dog, and waited for them to come out.

They knew Gerasim at the tavern and understood his signs. He ordered cabbage soup with meat and sat leaning his arms on the table. Mumu stood by his chair, looking serenely at him with her intelligent eyes. Her coat was smooth and glossy. It had obviously just been combed. The soup was placed before Gerasim. He crumbled some bread into it, cut the meat into small pieces, and put the plate down on the floor. Mumu began eating with her usual delicacy, her muzzle hardly touching the food. Gerasim did not take his eyes off her, and two heavy tears suddenly rolled down his cheeks. One fell on the little dog's round head, the other into the soup. He put his hand up to his face. After eating half a plateful, Mumu moved away licking her chops. Gerasim got up, paid for the food and went out, followed by the puzzled stare of the waiter. Catching sight of Gerasim, Yeroshka stepped behind

353

the corner to let him pass unobserved, then followed him.

Gerasim walked on with unhurried steps, leading Mumu by the string. When he reached the corner of the street, he stopped for a moment as if trying to make up his mind, then walked rapidly toward the river. On the way, he turned into a house where a new wing was in process of being built and came out carrying two bricks under his arm. He turned and walked along the bank of the river until he came to a place where there were two rowboats with the oars fastened to pegs. He jumped into one of them, taking Mumu with him. A lame old man came out of a shed in the corner of the vegetable plot and shouted at him. But Gerasim merely nodded and bent over the oars with such vigor that very soon, though he was rowing against the current, he had rowed the boat over two hundred yards up the river. The old man looked on for a while, scratched his back, and limped back to his shelter.

Gerasim rowed on and on. He had passed the city now. Fields, meadows, vegetable gardens, and cottages appeared on the banks. The surroundings got more and more rustic. Releasing the oars and letting his face sink on to the head of Mumu perched on the dry seat opposite him, he remained motionless, his strong hands crossed over the dog's back, while the current softly carried the boat back in the direction of the city. At last Gerasim straightened up and hurriedly, with an expression of frenzied bitterness, tied a piece of rope around the two bricks, made a loop in it, placed it around Mumu's neck, lifted her in the air, and gazed at her for the last time.

She looked back at him, with trust and without any fear, wagging her tail. Turning his face away and closing his eyes tightly, Gerasim loosened his grip. . . . He heard no sound, neither Mumu's whine as she fell, nor the heavy splash as she touched the water. To him the stormiest day was still and

soundless, stiller than the calmest night is for us. When he opened his eyes again, the wavelets were still moving over the surface of the water as if chasing one another, still splashing and playing against the side of the boat, and only far behind him, near the shore there was a spot from which the water was receding in wide circles.

No one saw Gerasim that day. He did not appear at dinner. And in the evening, when everyone had come to the supper table, Gerasim was not there.

"He's an odd one, that Gerasim," said the fat washerwoman. "To make such a fuss over a dog! Really!"

"He's back." Stepan blurted out, scooping *kasha* * with his spoon.

"Where? When?"

"Just an hour or two ago. Of course, I had to bump into him at the gate as he was leaving again. I kind of wanted to ask him about the dog, but he didn't seem to be in the proper mood. He gave me such a shove! I suppose he just meant to push me out of his way, but how it hurt!—right in the spine! Stepan chuckled and rubbed the back of his head. "Some hand he has, like a hammer! What a hand!"

Everyone laughed at Stepan, and after the meal everyone went off to bed.

And at that very moment a giant with a bag on his back and a long stick in his hand could be seen walking with an invincible determination, never halting, along the highroad. It was Gerasim. He was hurrying along, hurrying with all his might, homeward, toward his village, his birthplace.

After drowning poor Mumu Gerasim had rushed back into his room, put his few possessions together quickly, tied them in an old horsecloth, slung the bundle over his shoulder, and was off. He had carefully noted the way when they were bringing him to Moscow. The village from which his mis-

---

* *Kasha* is mush made of grain.

tress had taken him was about fifty versts *
from this road. He walked on with an indom-
itable courage, with a desperate and at the
same time elated resoluteness. He walked
on, his shirt wide open, his bare chest
thrown out, his eyes fixed hungrily and lovingly on everything before him. He hastened
on, as if he had an aged mother waiting for
him at home, calling him back to her after
he had long wandered in foreign lands,
among strangers.

It was beginning to grow dark and the
summer night would be still and warm. On
one side, where the sun had set, the sky was
still light, faintly flushed with the last reflections of the ending day; on the other, gathered the blue, gray dusk. Night was
approaching from there. The quails—there
were hundreds of them—were flying about
making a terrific din, the corn cranes were
calling to one another incessantly. Gerasim
could not hear them, he could not hear the
soft whispering of the trees as his strong legs
carried him past them. But he felt the familiar smell of the ripening rye from the dark
fields, he felt the wind as if it flew to meet
him—a messenger from his birthplace—and
he felt it caressing his face and playing in
his hair and beard. He saw the lighted road
stretching ahead, the road home, straight
as an arrow. He saw the countless stars
lighting his way, and walked on like a lion,
powerfully and boldly. When the humid red
rays of the rising sun shone upon the tireless
wayfarer, there were many versts between
him and Moscow.

Within two days he was home in his own
cottage, much to the surprise of a soldier's
wife who had been accommodated there in
his absence. After saying his prayers before
the icon, he at once went to see the village
elder. At first the elder was taken aback by

* A *verst* is a measure of distance equal to
about ⅔ mile.

Gerasim's sudden appearance; but it was
hay-mowing time, and, as Gerasim was
known to be a splendid worker, a scythe
was put into his hands immediately, and he
started mowing in his customary way, in a
way that put to shame other peasants who
watched him as his scythe rose and fell.

And in Moscow he was missed the day
after he disappeared. They went into his
room, searched it, and informed Gavrilo.
The head butler came, looked, shrugged his
shoulders, and decided that either the dumb
one ran away or that he had drowned himself together with his silly dog. The police
were alerted, and the mistress was notified.
The mistress flew into a rage, burst into
tears, gave orders that he be found at all
costs, assured everyone that she had never
insisted that the dog be destroyed, and
ended by giving Gavrilo such a scolding
that he could only shake his head for the
rest of the day as he kept saying, "Well!
well!"

At last the news of Gerasim's arrival in
the village reached Moscow. The mistress
calmed down somewhat. At first she ordered Gerasim to be brought back to the
city. Later, however, she proclaimed that
she had no use whatever for such an un-
grateful person. Anyway, she died very soon
after that and her heirs didn't care about
Gerasim one way or another.

And Gerasim lived as before, all by himself in his lonely hut. He continued to be
healthy and strong—to do the work of four
men—and was as reserved and dignified as
ever. The neighbor observed, however, that
since his return from Moscow he never kept
a dog. "Anyway," the peasants reasoned
among themselves, "of what use would a
dog be to him! You couldn't drag a thief
into his yard by force!"

Such was the fame of the giant strength
of the mute one.

HOW A MUZHIK FED
TWO OFFICIALS

MIKHAIL SALTYKOV-SCHEDRIN

The purpose to which all the works of Mikhail Saltykov-Schedrin (1826–1889) were devoted was to expose and condemn serfdom in Russia. His weapon of attack was satire; he has been regarded as the Jonathan Swift of Russian literature.

The writer came from a family of rich serf-owning landowners. His childhood was spent on a country estate, and to quote his own words he "grew up in the lap of serfdom, was fed on the milk of a serf woman, brought up by serf nurses, . . . and witnessed the horrors of the bondage of serfdom in all their grimness."

How a Muzhik Fed Two Officials is no exception to the author's dedicated purpose to condemn serfdom.

Once upon a time there were two Officials. They found themselves one day suddenly transported to an uninhabited island, as if on a magic carpet.

They had passed their whole life in a Government Department, where records were kept. They had been born there, bred there, grown old there, and as a result had not the least acquaintance with anything outside the Department, and the only words they knew were: "With assurances of the highest esteem, I am your humble servant."

But the Department was abolished, and as the services of the two Officials were no longer needed, they were dismissed. So the retired Officials moved to Podyacheskaya Street in St. Petersburg. Each had his own house, his own cook, and his pension.

Waking up on the uninhabited island, they found themselves lying under the same cover. At first, of course, they couldn't understand what had happened to them, and they spoke as if nothing unusual had taken place.

"What a peculiar dream I had last night, Your Excellency," said one Official. "It seemed to me as if I were on an uninhabited island."

Scarcely had he uttered the words, when he jumped to his feet. The other Official also jumped up.

"Good Lord, what does this mean? Where are we?" they cried in astonishment.

They felt each other to make sure that they were no longer dreaming, and finally convinced themselves of the sad reality.

Before them stretched the ocean, and behind them was a little spot of earth, beyond which the ocean stretched again. They began to weep—the first time since their Department had been shut down.

They looked at each other, and each noticed that the other was dressed in nothing but his nightshirt, with his order of rank hanging about his neck.

"We really should be having our coffee now," observed the one Official. Then he thought again of the strange situation he was in and fell to weeping again.

"What are we going to do now?" he

sobbed. "Even if we were to draw up a report, what good would it do?"

"You know what, Your Excellency," replied the other Official, "you go to the east and I will go to the west. Toward evening we will come back here again, and, perhaps, we shall have found something."

They started to determine which was the east and which was the west. They recalled that the head of their Department had once said to them, "If you want to know where the east is, then turn your face to the north, and the east will be on your right." But when they tried to find out which was the north, they turned to the right and to the left and looked around on all sides. Having spent their whole life in the Department of Records, their efforts were all in vain.

"To my mind, Your Excellency, the best thing to do would be for you to go to the right and for me to go to the left," said one Official, who had served not only in the Department of Records, but had also been teacher of penmanship in the School for Reserves, and was therefore a little bit cleverer.

No sooner said than done. The one Official went to the right. He came upon trees bearing all sorts of fruit. Gladly would he have plucked an apple, but they all hung so high that he would have had to climb up. He tried to climb, but couldn't. All he succeeded in doing was to tear his nightshirt. Then he came upon a stream. It was swarming with fish.

"Wouldn't it be wonderful if we had all this fish in Podyacheskaya Street!" he thought, and his mouth watered. Then he entered the woods and found partridges, grouse, and hares.

"Good Lord, what an abundance of food!" he cried. His hunger increased tremendously.

But he had to return to the appointed spot with empty hands. He found the other Official waiting for him.

"Well, Your Excellency, how did it go? Did you find anything?"

"Nothing but an old issue of the *Moscow Gazette*, not another thing!"

The Officials lay down to sleep again, but their empty stomachs gave them no rest. They were partly robbed of their sleep by the thought of who was now enjoying their pension, and partly by the recollection of the fruit, fish, partridges, grouse, and hares that they had seen during the day.

"Human food in its original form flies, swims, and grows on trees. Who would have thought it, Your Excellency?" said the one Official.

"To be sure," rejoined the other Official. "I, too, must admit that I had imagined that our breakfast rolls came into the world just as they appear on the table."

"From which it is to be concluded that if we want to eat a pheasant, we must catch it first, kill it, pull its feathers, and roast it. But how's that to be done?"

"Yes, how does one do that?" repeated the other Official.

They grew silent and tried again to fall asleep, but their hunger kept them wide awake. Before their eyes swarmed flocks of pheasants and ducks, herds of porklings, and they were all so juicy, done so tenderly, and garnished so deliciously with olives, capers, and pickles.

"I believe I could devour my own boots now," said the one Official.

"Gloves are not bad either, especially if they have been worn quite soft," said the other Official.

The two Officials stared at each other. In their glances gleamed an evil-boding fire, their teeth chattered, and a dull groaning came from their throats. Slowly they crept toward each other. However, the sight of the order of rank around their necks brought them to their senses.

"God save us!" they cried at the same time. "We certainly don't mean to eat each other up. How could we have come to such a pass as this? What evil genius is making sport of us?"

"We must, by all means, entertain each other to pass the time away, otherwise there will be ruin and death," said the one Official.

"You begin," said the other.

"Can you explain why it is that the sun first rises and then sets? Why isn't it the reverse?"

"Aren't you a funny man, Your Excellency! You get up first, then you go to your office and work there, and at night you lie down to sleep."

"But why can't one assume the opposite, that is, that one goes to bed, sees all kinds of dream figures, and then gets up?"

"Well, yes, certainly. But when I was still an Official, I always thought this way: 'Now it is dawn, then it will be day, then will come supper, and finally will come the time to go to bed.' "

The word "supper" recalled that occasion in the day's events, and the thought of it made both Officials sad, so that the conversation ceased.

"A doctor once told me that human beings can sustain themselves for a long time on their own juices," the one Official began again.

"What does that mean?"

"It is quite simple. You see, one's own juices generate other juices, and these in their turn still other juices, and so it goes on until finally all the juices are consumed."

"And then what happens?"

"Then food has to be taken into the system again."

"Darn it!"

No matter what subject of conversation the Officials chose, the talk invariably reverted to the subject of eating; which only increased their appetite. So they decided to give up talking altogether, and, remembering the *Moscow Gazette* that one of them had found, they picked it up and began to read it eagerly.

BANQUET GIVEN BY THE MAYOR
The table was set for one hundred persons.

The magnificence of it exceeded all expectations. The remotest provinces were represented at this feast of the gods by the costliest gifts. The golden sturgeon from Sheksna and the silver pheasant from the Caucasian woods held a rendezvous with strawberries so seldom to be had in our latitude in winter. . . .

"For God's sake, stop reading that, Your Excellency! Couldn't you find something else to read about?" cried the other Official in sheer desperation. He snatched the paper from his colleague's hands and started to read something else.

Our correspondent in Tula informs us that yesterday a sturgeon was found in the Upa (an event which even the oldest inhabitants cannot recall, and all the more remarkable since they recognized the former police captain in this sturgeon). This was made the occasion for giving a banquet in the club. The main course of the banquet was served in a large wooden platter garnished with vinegar pickles. A bunch of parsley stuck out of its mouth. Doctor P—, who acted as toastmaster, saw to it that everybody present got a piece of the sturgeon. The sauces to go with it were unusually varied and delicate . . .

"Permit me, Your Excellency, it seems to me you are not so careful either in the selection of reading matter," interrupted the first Official, who secured the *Gazette* again and started to read.

One of the oldest inhabitants of Vyatka has discovered a new and highly original recipe for fish soup. A live codfish (*lota vulgaris*) is taken and beaten with a rod until . . .

The Officials' heads drooped. Whatever their eyes fell upon had something to do with eating. Even their own thoughts were fatal. No matter how much they tried to keep their minds off beefsteak and the like, it was all in vain; their thoughts returned invariably, with irresistible force, back to that for which they were so painfully yearning.

Suddenly an inspiration came to the Official who had once taught penmanship.

"I have it!" he cried delightedly. "What do you say to this, your Excellency? What do you say to our finding a *muzhik* *?"

"A muzhik, Your Excellency? What sort of a muzhik?"

"Why a plain ordinary muzhik. A muzhik like all other muzhiks. He would get the breakfast rolls for us right away, and he could also catch partridges and fish for us."

"Hm, a muzhik. But where are we to find one if there is no muzhik here?"

"Why shouldn't there be a muzhik here? There are muzhiks everywhere. All one has to do is hunt for them. There certainly must be a muzhik hiding here somewhere so as to get out of working."

This thought so cheered the Officials that they instantly jumped up to go in search of a muzhik.

For a long while they wandered about on the island without the desired result, until finally a concentrated smell of black bread and old sheepskin assailed their nostrils and guided them in the right direction. There under a tree was a colossal muzhik lying fast asleep with his hands under his head. It was clear that to escape his duty to work he had impudently withdrawn to this island. The indignation of the Officials knew no bounds.

"What, lying asleep here, you lazybones, you!" they raged at him. "It is nothing to you that there are two Officials here who are perishing from hunger. Up, forward march, work!"

The Muzhik rose and looked at the two severe gentlemen standing in front of him. His first thought was to make his escape, but the Officials held him fast.

He had to submit to his fate. He had to work!

---

* A *muzhik* is a simple peasant of czarist Russia.

First he climbed a tree and plucked several dozen of the finest apples for the Officials. He kept a rotten one for himself. Then he turned up the earth and dug out some potatoes. Next he started a fire with two bits of wood that he rubbed against each other. Out of his own hair he made a snare and caught partridges. Over the fire, by this time burning brightly, he cooked so many kinds of food that the question arose in the Officials' minds whether they shouldn't give some to this idler.

Beholding the efforts of the Muzhik, they rejoiced in their hearts. They had already forgotten how the day before they had nearly been perishing of hunger, and all they thought of now was, "What a good thing it is to be an Official. Nothing bad can ever happen to an Official."

"Are you satisfied, gentlemen?" the lazy Muzhik asked.

"Yes, we appreciate your industry," replied the Officials.

"Then you will permit me to rest a little?"

"Go take a little rest, but first make a good strong rope."

The Muzhik gathered wild hemp stalks, put them in water, beat them and broke them, and toward evening a strong rope was ready. The Officials took it and tied the Muzhik to a tree so that he would not run away. Then they lay down to sleep.

Thus day after day passed, and the Muzhik became so skillful that he could almost cook soup for the Officials in his bare hands. The Officials had become round and well fed and happy. It cheered them that they didn't have to spend any money here and that in the meanwhile their pensions were probably accumulating in St. Petersburg.

There is no saying how long this life might have lasted. Finally, however, it began to bore the Officials. They often thought of their life in St. Petersburg, and even shed a few tears in secret.

"I wonder how it looks in Podyacheskaya Street now, Your Excellency," one of them said to the other.

"Oh, don't remind me of it, Your Excellency. I am pining away with homesickness."

"It is very nice here. There is really no fault to be found with this place, but the lamb longs for its mother sheep. I also miss my beautiful uniform."

"Yes, indeed, a uniform of the fourth class is no joke. The gold embroidery alone is enough to make one proud."

Now they began to urge the Muzhik to find some way of getting them back to Podyacheskaya Street, and—strange to say— the Muzhik even knew where Podyacheskaya Street was. He had once drunk beer and mead there. The Officials rejoiced and said, "We are Officials from Podyacheskaya Street."

The Muzhik now pondered long and heavily on how to give great pleasure to his Officials, who had been so gracious to him, the lazybones, and had not scorned his work. And he actually succeeded in constructing a boat. It was not really a boat, but still it was a vessel that would carry them across the ocean, close to Podyacheskaya Street.

"Now, take care, you dog, that you don't drown us," said the Officials, when they saw the raft rising and falling on the waves.

"Don't be afraid. We muzhiks are used to this," said the Muzhik, making all the preparations for the journey. He gathered swan's down and made a comfortable seat for his two Officials, then he crossed himself and rowed off from shore.

How frightened the Officials were on the way, how seasick they were during the storms, how they scolded the coarse Muzhik for his idleness, can neither be told nor described. The Muzhik, however, just kept rowing on and fed his Officials on herring. At last they caught sight of dear old Neva River. Soon they were in the glorious Catherine Canal, and then—oh joy!—they struck the grand Podyacheskaya Street. When their cooks saw the Officials were so well fed, round, and so happy, they rejoiced. The Officials drank coffee and ate many rolls, then put on their uniforms and drove to the Pension Bureau. How much money they collected there is another thing that can neither be told nor described. Nor was the Muzhik forgotten. The Officials sent a glass of whisky out to him and five kopecks.*

Now, Muzhik, rejoice.

---

* A *kopeck* is a Russian penny.

CHILDREN OF THE VAULTS

VLADIMIR KOROLENKO

"Man is created for happiness, as a bird is for flight," was the conviction that guided this author's adult life, inspiring his efforts to improve the life of his countrymen. In his literary work he championed the poor, the abused, and other victims of greed and injustice. But for his services to his unfortunate countrymen he was "rewarded" at the age of twenty-three with exile to Siberia. For the next forty years he was hounded by the czarist police and censors. But Korolenko kept on writing and championing good causes.

Children of the Vaults, originally published under the title, *In Bad Company,* is partly autobiographical. The author's father was a judge with a strong sense of impartiality—a rare phenomenon in those days. His family lived in a small Ukrainian town, very similar to the one in which the story is set and where the destitute were also always present. The friendship of the judge's young son with the two pauper children is authentic.

Vladimir Korolenko was born in 1853 and died in 1921. He is still widely read.

RUINS

My mother died when I was six. My father, absorbed in his grief, seemed altogether to forget my existence. He would pet my little sister Sonya at times and do what he could to make her happy, for she reminded him of Mother. But I—I grew wild, like some sapling tree in a neglected field. There was no one to care about me. Nor was there anyone to hamper my freedom.

We lived in a little town known as Kniazhe-Veno, or, as we more often called it, Kniazh-Gorodok. It was the seat of a proud but impoverished family, and very much like any other small town of the Russian southwest. It lay low on the banks of its drowsy ponds. The river spanned by the decrepit bridge took its rise in one pond and emptied into another. The town was thus bounded north and south by broad stretches of water and marshland. The ponds were going dry, and were overgrown with weeds. Tall reeds grew thickly on the marshland, billowing like the sea in every wind. There was an island in the middle of one of the ponds, and on the island an ancient castle half fallen to ruin.

I recall the dread I always felt, looking over the water to that majestic, decaying building. What gruesome tales were told of it! The island, it was said, had not always existed. It had been piled up by Turkish prisoners of war. "On human bones the old castle stands," the townsfolk whispered. Shuddering, I pictured in my childish imagination thousands of Turkish skeletons buried beneath the pond, supporting on upraised bony arms, the island, the ancient castle, and the tall Lombardy poplars that surrounded it.

That made the castle seem more awesome still, of course. Sometimes, emboldened by the bright sun and cheerful bird calls, we would venture quite close; but even on such days, as often as not, my comrades and I would be struck with sudden panic. The empty window holes looked out at us so blackly, and the deserted rooms were full of such mysterious rustlings and whisperings.

And on a stormy autumn night, when the huge poplars tossed and moaned in the gusts of wind sweeping down from beyond the pond, fear would come spreading from the ancient castle to reign over the entire town.

At one time the old castle on the island offered free asylum to all seekers, whoever they might be. All those in our town who had no place to lay their heads, who, for whatever reason, lacked means to secure even the cheapest shelter against night and foul weather—all such would find their way in the end to the island and lay down their limbs among the ruins. The expression, "He lives in the castle," had come to signify the utmost extreme of poverty. Clerks in temporary difficulties, old women without home or friends, professional tramps—the castle received and sheltered any and all with equal cordiality. And all these unfortunates tore at the remains of the ancient building, breaking away the floors and ceilings, bit by bit, for fuel, that they might heat the stoves and cook what food they could get, and manage somehow to keep body and soul together.

But a day came when dissension arose among these people sheltering in the ruins. And then old Janusz, who had once held some small post in the Count's household, somehow got himself appointed to a nominal stewardship and launched a campaign of reform. For several days there was such a din on the island and such desperate cries that one might have thought the Turkish prisoners had risen to life again. Janusz was sorting out the population of the ruins—retaining the "good Christians" and discarding the shady characters. When order was finally restored, it turned out that Janusz had settled his choice, for the most part, on the Count's former servants, or descendants of his servants and their line: blue-nosed old men in shabby coats of ancient cut and shrill, hideous old women still clinging to their old-fashioned hoods and mantuas. These people formed a close-knit aristocratic grouping, claiming the exclusive right to respectable poverty. On weekdays, their lips devoutly pursed, they would visit the homes of the more prosperous of the townspeople, to retail gossip, and complain tearfully of fate, and cadge what they might. On Sundays they would stand in long rows outside the churches, majestically accepting alms in the name of Our Lord Jesus and Our Lady, His Mother.

Attracted by the tumult that hung over the island during this "revolution," I crossed over with two or three playmates and hid among the poplars. From the shelter of the trees, we watched Janusz and his army of purple-nosed old men and hideous old women driving out the last of the castle dwellers who had been sentenced to expulsion. It was almost evening, and a light rain was sifting down from a cloud that hung low over the poplars. Like so many moles driven from their burrows, several wretched creatures ran about the island—frightened, pitiful, ashamed, holding their rags about them, attempting again and again to slip in unnoticed at one or another of the castle's openings.

In the end, however unwillingly, the poor wretches filed dejectedly across the bridge, leaving the island forever. One by one they disappeared into the dripping murk of the swiftly gathering evening.

From that evening I saw both Janusz and the castle in a different light. Meeting me near the island next day, Janusz began urging me to come and visit him. "The son of

such estimable parents," he assured me with evident satisfaction, might now approach the castle without hesitation, for he would find within its walls only the most respectable of company. Indeed, he took me by the hand and led me almost to the castle door. But I tore my hand free and ran away, my eyes full of tears. The castle had become hateful to me. I could not forget the brutality with which, having gained their victory, Janusz and his cronies had driven out their unfortunate neighbors. My heart ached at the memory of those poor wretches left without shelter.

The town had some uneasy nights after the coup on the island. Dogs barked and house doors creaked, and the good people kept going out to rattle sticks along the palings of their fences, that all might know that they were on the alert. The town knew that there were people wandering through the streets in the rainy murk, knew that these people were cold and hungry, drenched and shivering. It realized that a fierce resentment might arise in these people's hearts. And so it was on the alert, sending out its warnings. As luck would have it, night after night descended on the town in cold pouring rain and left behind it when morning came a train of low-hung, swiftly moving clouds. And a wind raged through the wetness, swaying the treetops, rattling the shutters, and reminding me as I lay in my bed that to tens of my fellow beings warmth and shelter were denied.

But spring triumphed over these last efforts of the winter to maintain its sway. The sun dried the earth. And at about this time the homeless wanderers found refuge. They had found shelter, it was said, on the hill where the old chapel stood. What sort of shelter human beings might find there no one could say. But people saw them—the queerest, the most suspicious-looking figures—approaching the town of a morning from the direction of the hills and gullies surrounding the chapel, and disappearing in the same direction as evening began to gather. The good people watched them with anxious, hostile eyes, for they stood out like grim blots against the drab background of the town, disturbing the quiet, sleepy flow of life. They were different from the aristocratic beggars of the castle, and the town would not accept them. Nor could their attitude toward the town be called anything but hostile.

It must be said that, as it often happens, there were those among the ragged, shady crowd of unfortunates who in wit and talents might have shone among the select society remaining at the castle; but, uncomfortable in that society, they preferred the more democratic company at the chapel.

The organizer and leader of this band of unfortunates was one Tiburcy Drab, the most remarkable personality of all those driven from the castle.

Tiburcy's origins were veiled in the darkest obscurity. Some said he was the bearer of an aristocratic name, which he had so disgraced that he had been forced to go into hiding. There was nothing of the aristocrat, however, in his appearance. He was a tall man, with massive, coarse but expressive features and reddish hair, close-cropped and bristling. His low forehead and somewhat protruding lower jaw and his unusual mobility of feature had something of the monkey in them. But the eyes that gleamed from under his bushy brows had a grim and stubborn look, lit by shrewdness and keen perception, by energy and intelligence.

Tiburcy's hands were rough and calloused, and he set down his big feet in heavy, peasant fashion. On these grounds most of the townsfolk refused to believe the rumors about his aristocratic birth. But how, then, explain his extraordinary learning, which nobody could deny? There was not a tavern in all the town in which Tiburcy had not edified the peasants gathered for a drink on a market day with whole orations from Cicero, or chapters from Xenophon, delivered from the top of a wine barrel. Ukrainian peasant folk are richly gifted with imagination, and they read meaning of their own into these impassioned if incomprehensible recitations. When, striking his fist upon his chest, with flashing eyes, he addressed them as *"Patres conscripti,"* * they would draw their brows together in answering frowns, commenting to one another:

"Ha! the son of evil, hear him curse!"

And when, raising his eyes to the ceiling, he launched into flowing Latin texts, his listeners would follow voice and gestures with half-frightened, half-pitying interest. It would seem to them at such times that Tiburcy's soul was wandering in some unknown land where this un-Christian tongue was spoken, and was there experiencing terrible misfortunes. His voice would roll out in such hollow, such mournful tones that the more drunken of his listeners in the corners of the room would hang their heads until their long forelocks fell over their eyes, and mumble sadly:

"Ah, but he pulls at your heartstrings, the devil!"

And the tears would brim from their eyes and run down their long, drooping mustaches.

And then, when Tiburcy sprang suddenly down from his barrel top and broke into ringing laughter, the peasants' sorrowful faces would clear and their hands would dive into their pockets in search of coins. Rejoiced by this safe conclusion of his tragic wanderings, they would embrace him

---

* *Patres conscripti* is Latin for (Roman) senators; literally it means "fathers and enrollees in the service of their country."

and offer him vodka, and coins would shower clinking into his cap.

This amazing erudition gave rise to a new legend: that Tiburcy, as a boy, had been a serf in some count's household; that he had been sent with the count's son to a Jesuit school to attend his young master there and keep his boots well polished; and that while the young nobleman idled away his years at school, the young serf had absorbed all his master's lessons.

No one knew, either, where the children came from who lived with Tiburcy, but there the fact was not to be denied. Two facts, indeed: a boy of eight or nine, tall for his age and well grown, and a little girl of about three. The boy had been with Tiburcy from his first appearance in our town. As to the little girl, she had first appeared in Tiburcy's arms on his return from an absence that lasted several months. The boy Walek —tall, slender, black-haired—sometimes wandered aimlessly about the town, silent and gloomy, his hands in his pockets. Catching his glance, the pastry women would clutch their baskets nervously. The little girl was seen only once or twice—in Tiburcy's arms. Then she disappeared, and no one knew where she might be.

There was some talk of underground vaults on the hill where the old chapel stood. This talk was widely believed. Such vaults were no rare thing in our parts, and, after all, these people must live somewhere. It was always in the direction of the chapel that they disappeared of an evening—the half-insane old beggar whom everyone called "Professor," hobbling along in his sleepy way, and Tiburcy, with his swift, energetic stride, and all the other shady characters. And, as they disappeared into the twilight, there was no one in all the town bold enough to follow them up the pitted clayey slopes. The hill, with its sunken graves, had a bad name. Blue lights were seen in the old graveyard on damp autumn nights, and the owls in the belfry screeched loud and shrill. Even our blacksmith—fearless soul—shuddered at the hooting of those accursed birds.

MY FATHER AND I

"That's no way, young man, that's no way," old Janusz from the castle often said to me, meeting me in the streets of the town among Tiburcy's listeners. And the old man would shake his gray head reproachfully.

"That's no way, young man. You're in bad society. A pity, such a pity—the son of such estimable parents!"

Yes, now that Mother was dead and my father's stern face had grown so morose, I was seldom to be found at home. Late of a summer evening I would creep in through the orchard stealthy as a wolf cub, carefully avoiding my father. I would pry open my window half hidden behind thick lilac bushes and slip quietly into my bedroom.

At the first sign of daylight, when all the household was still asleep, I would be out of doors again, cutting a dewy trail through the thick, tall grass. Soon I would be over the orchard fence and off for the pond where my comrades, just such graceless scamps as myself, would be waiting with their fishing rods. Often I would wander off by myself. I liked to watch the awakening of nature. It was a joy to me to start up a lark still lingering in his nest, or frighten a rabbit out of some furrow. The dew would be dripping from the grass tips and the meadow flowers as I made my way through the fields

to the wood outside the town. Here the trees
would make me welcome with a lazy,
drowsy whispering.

A vagabond everyone called me, and a
good-for-nothing scamp. I was so often re-
proached with the most varied of evil tend-
encies that in time I myself began to believe
these reproaches. My father believed them,
too, and tried, at times, to teach me better
ways. But these attempts were always unsuccessful. Confronted by that stern and
gloomy face with the mark of hopeless grief
upon it, I would be awed and shrink into
myself. I would stand there before him,
shifting my weight from one foot to the
other, pulling at my trouser strap, perhaps,
and keeping my eyes averted. There were
moments when something stirred within me,
when I wanted his arms around me, wanted
to be taken up onto his knees and pressed to
his heart. I would have clung to him then,

and perhaps we might have wept together—
child and stern man—for our common loss.
But he would look at me with clouded eyes
that seemed to stare over my head into the
distance, and I would shrink before his
gaze, which I could not understand.

And, gradually, the gulf that parted us
grew wider, deeper. More and more he
came to regard me as a spoiled and vicious
child, cold-hearted and selfish. It was his
duty, he knew, to make something of me,
but he could not. It was his duty to love me,
but he could find no real love for me in his
heart. And the sense of duty unfulfilled still
further estranged him from me.

From the age of six I knew the desolate
pain of loneliness.

Sonya, my sister, was only four. I loved
her with all my heart, and so did she me.
But I was regarded by all as an incorrigible
young rogue, and this built up a high wall

even between us two. Every time I began to play with Sonya in my noisy, lively way, her old nurse—always sleepy, always dozing over the feathers she was for ever picking—would come wide awake at once and carry my Sonya off into the house, glaring at me as she went.

I had become hardened to reproaches, receiving them much as I might a sudden rainstorm or a day of oppressive heat. Having heard them out in sullen silence, I would continue to do as I pleased. I would roam about the town observing everything with childish curiosity.

When I had explored every corner of the town, to the very last of its muddy alleys, my thoughts turned to the chapel on the hill. At first, like some timid creature of the woods, I tried the approaches to the hill from every side—wanting to climb it, but afraid, so bad was its reputation. Stare as I might, however, I saw nothing on the hillside but quiet graves and crumbling crosses. There was not the slightest sign of human habitation, of human activity. Everything was subdued, somehow, and peaceful—empty, abandoned. Nothing but the chapel, frowning out through its paneless windows, as though deep in melancholy thought. And I made up my mind to go up close and even look inside, to convince myself that there was nothing there but dust. Only it was rather a scary expedition to undertake alone, and, besides, I might need help. And so, among my playmates in the streets I recruited a little band of three young daredevils, bribed by the promise of cookies and apples from our orchard.

I MAKE NEW FRIENDS

We set out from town after dinner and went straight to the hill. We climbed as fast as we could, helping one another over the rough places. The sun was just beginning to sink westward. Its slanted rays softly gilded the grass in the old cemetery and the askew crosses on the graves, and reddened the few bits of glass that still remained in the windows of the chapel. It was very quiet. The hush of utter peace hung over the abandoned graveyard.

We were alone, except for the chattering sparrows and the swallows darting soundlessly in and out at the chapel windows. The old building stood sunk in melancholy among the overgrown graves, the simple crosses, and the crumbling remnants of stone tombs. Even the stone of the tombs was carpeted with green and dotted with buttercups, clover, and violets.

The door of the chapel was securely boarded up, and the windows were very high. With the help of my comrades, however, I hoped to reach a window and look in.

"Don't!" one of them cried, seizing my arm, his courage suddenly evaporated.

But another, the eldest in our little army, shouldered him out of the way with a contemptuous "Scaredy-cat!" and stooped willingly to help me.

I climbed onto his back. Then he straightened up, and I stood on his shoulders. From this elevation I could easily reach the window frame. It proved strong enough to hold me, and I swung up and perched on the sill.

"What's inside there?" my companions asked eagerly.

I did not answer. Clinging to the frame, I was looking, awed into silence by the solemn hush of the abandoned chapel. It was a narrow, lofty place, bare of all ornament. The evening sunlight, pouring freely through the open windows, cast designs of vivid gold on the plasterless old walls. I could see the inside of the barred door, the broken-down gallery, the mouldering columns, which seemed to stagger under a weight beyond their power to support. The corners were wreathed in cobwebs and sunk in that somehow different sort of darkness that fills the corners of all such old buildings. It seemed much farther from my window to the floor than to the grass outside. I had the feeling of one peering down into a deep pit. Dimly, I could make out several queerly-shaped objects scattered about the floor, but it took me some time to guess what they might be.

My friends soon tired of waiting from below for my report, and one of them swung up beside me.

"What's that over there?" he asked curiously, pointing to a dark object lying near the altar.

"A priest's hat."

"No, it's a pail."

"What would a pail be doing there?"

"They might have kept the coal in it for the censer."

"No, it's a hat, I tell you. Go look, if you don't believe me. We can tie a belt to the window frame, and you can slide down there."

"Not me! Go ahead yourself if you want to."

"Well, I will. Don't think I'm scared."

"Go ahead, then."

Without stopping to think, I took our two belts, tied them securely together, looped one end over the window frame and gave it to my companion to hold, and by the other end swung down into the chapel. I shivered a bit when my feet touched the floor, but a glance at the friendly face looking down at me from the window restored my courage. The first step I took rang loudly through the empty chapel and echoed back from the

dark corners. Some birds darted from their shelter in the gallery and out at a big hole in the roof. All at once I saw, looking down at me from the wall beside the window by which I had entered, a stern, bearded face, crowned with a wreath of thorns. A huge crucifix hung high on the wall, reaching almost to the ceiling.

Dread came over me. My friend's eyes, up above, gleamed with breathless curiosity and sympathy.

"Will you go over and see?" he asked in a half-whisper.

"Yes," I answered, whispering too.

But at that moment came a startling interruption.

It began with the rattle of falling plaster, up on the gallery. Something stirred, sending down a shower of dust, and a great gray bulk rose heavily, with flapping wings, from one of the darkest corners. It was a huge owl, awakened by our voices. For an instant it blocked the blue patch of sky shining in at the hole in the roof, and the chapel grew darker. The next instant, it was gone.

I was seized with sudden frantic fear.

"Pull me up," I cried to my comrade, seizing hold of the belt.

"Don't worry, there you go," he said soothingly, and braced himself to pull me up into the light of day.

But all at once his face contorted with terror and, with a loud cry, he dropped out of sight outside the window. Instinctively, I looked behind me. What I saw was truly very strange, but it inspired astonishment rather than horror.

The vague object of our debate—hat, or pail? Actually, it turned out to be an earthen pot. It flashed through the air and, as I watched, disappeared under the altar.

I just glimpsed the hand that held it. It was a small hand, evidently a child's.

It is not easy to describe my feelings. I can hardly even say that I was afraid. I was not in this world at all. From I knew not where—from some other planet—I heard for a while the rapid frightened patter of two pairs of running feet. But that soon faded, and I remained alone, abandoned in this place of strange and mysterious happenings.

Time for me had ceased, and so I cannot say how long it was before I heard voices whispering under the altar.

"Why doesn't he climb out again?"

"He's scared—can't you see?"

The first voice seemed to belong to a very small child, the second, to a boy of about my age. I thought, too, that I saw dark eyes gleam at me through a crack in the altar boards.

There was a sound of something moving. The altar seemed to rock, and then, from under it, a human figure emerged.

It was a boy of about nine—taller than I, but thin as a reed. His hands were thrust into the pockets of his short, tight pants, his shirt was dirty, and his dark and curly hair hung uncombed over dark, wistful eyes.

Though he had appeared on the scene in so sudden and strange a manner, and though he now came toward me with that air of careless bravado which the boys about our market place assumed when they meant to fight—for all that, I was tremendously relieved by the sight of him. And I was still more relieved when a face appeared behind him under the altar, or rather in the trap door which the altar screened—a dirty little face, framed in fair hair, with sky-blue eyes that looked out at me with childish curiosity.

I moved forward from the wall and thrust my hands, too, into my pockets—to indicate that I was not afraid of my opponent and that I held him more or less in contempt.

We stopped, face to face, and for an instant our eyes met. He looked me silently up and down, and then demanded, "What are you doing here?"

"Nothing," I answered. "What do you care?"

He hunched a shoulder, as if about to pull his hand from his pocket and hit out at me.

"I'll show you!" he threatened.

"Just you try!" I retorted, puffing up my chest.

It was a critical moment. On the turn events now took would depend the outcome of our encounter. I stood waiting; but my opponent, still measuring me with his eyes, made no further move.

"I can show you, too," I said, but rather more peaceably.

All this while the little girl behind him had been trying to climb out at the trap door. Grasping its edges with her tiny hands, she had lifted herself several times, but each time she had fallen back again. Now, at last, she succeeded and came toddling unsteadily across the chapel. Reaching my opponent, she pressed up close to him, her arms around his waist, and turned to look at me, wondering and a little frightened.

That decided it. Clearly, he could not fight with the child clinging to him so. And I, of course, was too generous to take advantage of his handicap.

"What's your name?" he asked me, stroking the little girl's hair.

"Vasya. What's yours?"

"Walek. I know who you are. You live in the house up above the pond. You've got the hugest apples in your orchard!"

"Yes, that's true. They are the best! Would you like some?"

I pulled two apples from my pocket, the wages meant for my friends who had so shamefully deserted me and offered one to Walek and the other to the little girl. But she only clung closer to Walek, hiding her face against him. He handed the apple to her.

Then turning back to me he asked, "What did you come here for? I don't go poking in your orchard, do I?"

"Come if you like," I returned hospitably.

My answer seemed to puzzle Walek. He hesitated a moment, then said wistfully, "I'm not fit company for you."

"Why not?" I demanded, upset by his sad tone.

"Your father's the Judge."

"Well, so what?" I said. "It's me you'll be playing with, not my father."

Walek shook his head. "Tiburcy wouldn't let me," he said. And, as though the name had reminded him of something, he went on hurriedly, "Look, you seem to be a good guy, but just the same you'd better go home. There'll be trouble if Tiburcy finds you here."

I agreed that I had really best be going. The last rays of sunlight were slipping away, and it was a good distance back to town.

I got up to the window with my new friend's help, untied my belt, and looped it over the window frame so that I could jump with both ends in my hand. The next instant I was dangling in midair. Then I let go of one end, dropped to the ground, and jerked the belt free. Walek and Marusya were already outside, waiting for me.

The sun had just sunk behind the hill, and the town lay veiled in misty violet shadow. Only the tips of the poplars on the island still gleamed red-gold in the last rays of light. It seemed to me that I was in tomorrow, that a whole day, if not more, must have passed since I had come up the hill to the old cemetery.

We did not go down by the pitted slope that I had climbed. Walek knew a better way that took us through the reeds of a dried-up marsh and across a little stream by a bridge of thin boards, and then straight down to the flatland at the foot of the hill.

Here we stopped to say good-bye.

"Will you come again?" the little girl asked.

"Yes," I answered, "I surely will."

"Well, yes," Walek said slowly. "I suppose you could. Only pick a time when our people are down in the town."

"Whom do you mean by 'your people'?"

"Why, all of them. Tiburcy and the Professor, and all the rest. Though I suppose the Professor doesn't matter much."

"All right, I'll come when I see them in town. Good-bye."

And I started off. But Walek called after me, "Wait a minute! Look, you won't tell anybody that you saw us, will you?"

"I won't tell anybody," I said without hesitating.

In the days that followed I was entirely absorbed by my new friends. Going to bed at night and getting up in the morning, I thought of nothing but visiting the hill. I had only one purpose now in loitering about the streets: to make sure that all the members of what Janusz had described as "bad society" were safely in town. And if I found Tiburcy orating in his usual haunts and the other shady characters of his company poking about the marketplace, I would be off at once, on the run across the marsh and up the hill to the chapel, my pockets stuffed with apples and with whatever sweets had come my way, for I saved them all for my new friends.

Walek, undemonstrative by nature, and with grown-up ways that rather awed me, would accept these offerings simply and quietly, generally putting away his share for his sister. But Marusya—she would throw up her little hands, her blue eyes dancing with delight. Her pale cheeks would color, and she would laugh aloud. And her laughter would echo in our hearts, rewarding us for the sweets that we denied ourselves to give her.

She was a pale, puny child, much like a flower that has never known the sun. Four years old, she could not yet walk properly, but tottered along with short uncertain steps, swaying like a grass blade on her rickety little legs.

I could not help but compare her with my sister. They were about the same age, but

Sonya was so plump and round and lively. She could run so fast when she was in the mood, and she laughed so ringingly. She always wore such pretty dresses and there was always a bright red ribbon in her dark braids.

My new little friend hardly ever ran and very seldom laughed. When she did laugh, it was like the tiniest of silver bells, not to be heard more than a few steps away. Her dress was old and soiled and she had no ribbon in her braids. Her hair, though, was far thicker and longer than Sonya's. Walek, to my surprise, was very good at braiding it, and did so for her every morning.

I was very active and restless. I brought my usual animation into my play with my new friends. Never, in all likelihood, had the old chapel echoed to such shouts as mine, as I tried to stir up Walek and Marusya and draw them into play. But I was not very successful.

Walek would look from me to Marusya, and once, when I tried to make her run, he said, "Don't, she'll cry."

And, true enough, when I teased her into running off, and when she heard me running after her, she suddenly stopped and turned to face me, her little arms raised as though in defense—looked at me helplessly, like a trapped bird, and began to cry.

"You see," Walek said. "She doesn't like to play."

He sat her down in the grass, gathered some flowers, and threw them to her. She stopped crying and sat quietly picking over the flowers, whispering to the golden buttercups and lifting the bluebells to her lips. Somewhat subdued, I lay down in the grass near by, with Walek.

"What makes her that way?" I asked after a while.

"Afraid to play, you mean?" Walek returned, and he answered in a tone of absolute conviction, "Well, you see, it's all because of the gray stone."

"What gray stone?"

"The gray stone sucks the life out of her," Walek explained. He was lying on his back, looking up at the sky. "That's what Tiburcy says. And Tiburcy always knows."

I could make nothing of this puzzling explanation. But I was impressed by Walek's conviction that Tiburcy "always knew." Raising myself on my elbow, I turned to look at Marusya. She sat just as Walek had set her down, quietly picking over her flowers. The movements of her thin hands were slow and languid. The blue of her eyes, under long drooping lashes, was deepened by the pallor of her face. Surely something was sucking the life out of this queer little girl who cried when other little girls would laugh. But stone—how could stone suck life?

This puzzle held more dread for me than all the phantoms of the ancient castle. It had something to do with what was not only strange and fearful but very real. There was something shapeless, merciless, cruel, and hard as stone hanging over this little girl. In the night it must happen, I supposed.

Ruled by this feeling, I curbed my animation and tried to adapt myself, like Walek, to Marusya's quiet ways. We would settle her in the grass somewhere and run about picking flowers for her or collecting pretty stones, or catching butterflies. And sometimes we would stretch out on the grass beside her, looking up at the clouds floating high over the ragged chapel roof, and tell her stories, or perhaps simply talk.

And as the days passed, these talks strengthened our friendship, which grew steadily although we were so unlike in character. I was lively, restless, impulsive. Walek was sober, restrained, and always with a hint of sadness. He spoke of his elders in a careless way that excited my admiration.

Noticing that he spoke of Tiburcy as he might of a comrade his own age, I asked. "Isn't Tiburcy your father?"

"I suppose so," he answered slowly, as

though the question had never occurred to him.

"Does he like you?"

"Oh, yes"—and this time the answer came far more confidently. "He's always worried about me and, you know, he kisses me sometimes, and cries."

"And me, too," Marusya put in, with childish pride. "He kisses me, too, and cries."

"My father doesn't care for me," I said. "He never kisses me. He's just no good."

"No, no!" Walek exclaimed. "That isn't true. You don't understand. Tiburcy knows better. Tiburcy says the Judge is the best man in this whole town. Why, he even decided a case against a count once."

"Yes, that's true. The count was terribly angry. I heard him."

"There! And it's no simple thing to go against a count."

"Why?"

"Why?" Walek paused a moment, thinking. "Well, because a count isn't just anybody. A count does whatever he pleases, and rides in a carriage, well, and—a count

has money. He can give a judge money, and some judges would take his money and decide the case his way, against the fellow who had no money to give them."

"Yes, that's so. I heard that count shouting when he came to our house. 'I can buy you and sell you,' he said."

"And what did the Judge say?"

"And my father said to him, 'Get out of my house!' "

"There you are! That's what Tiburcy says, that the Judge has the courage to throw a man out even if he's rich."

Again and again, I turned this conversation over in my mind. Walek had shown me my father from a point of view from which it had never occurred to me to think of him. Walek's words had touched a chord of filial pride deep in my heart. It was pleasant to hear my father praised, the more so that the praise came from Tiburcy, who "always knew." But at the same time I ached with an anguished love, mingled with the bitter certainty that my father had never loved me, would never love me, as Tiburcy loved his children.

THE GRAY STONE

And so the days slipped by until suddenly the members of the "bad society" stopped coming to town. Dejectedly, I wandered through the streets, on the watch for their appearance, ready at the first sight of them to hurry up the hill. But they did not come, and I grew terribly lonely. It had become a real necessity to me to be with Walek and Marusya. At last one day, as I wandered aimlessly along the dusty street, Walek overtook me and laid his hand on my shoulder.

"Why don't you come around any more?" he asked.

"I was afraid to. Your people don't come to town."

"Oh, so that's it! They're all away. You can come if you want to. I thought it was something else."

"What else?"

"I thought you were tired of us."

"No, no! Let's go right away," I cried hastily. "I've even got some apples with me."

When I spoke of the apples Walek swung quickly toward me, as though about to say something. But he did not say anything. He only looked at me, in the strangest way.

Then, seeing my questioning glance, he shrugged.

"I was just thinking," he said. "Look, you go ahead, and I'll catch up with you on the hill. I've got some things to do in town."

I walked slowly, looking back every now and then for Walek. But I got all the way up the hill, and approached the chapel, and still he had not come into sight. I looked about me. What was I to do? Clearly, I had best wait for Walek. And while I waited, I wandered idly about among the graves, trying to make out the half-obliterated inscriptions on the moss-grown stones. After a while I came upon a big stone tomb, roofless and with crumbling walls. Its roof, torn off perhaps by some storm wind, lay on the ground near by. Its door was boarded up. Driven by curiosity, I propped an old cross against the wall, climbed up on it, and looked inside. The tomb was empty. But there was a window cut into its floor, a real window, with glass panes. And through these panes I glimpsed black emptiness.

While I perched there on the wall, wondering at this strange window, Walek came running up the hill, tired and out of breath. He had a loaf of bread in his hand and something bulged under his shirt. His face was streaming with sweat.

"Ho!" he cried, when he saw where I was. "So that's where you are! Wouldn't Tiburcy be mad if he caught you there! Well, it's too late to do anything about it now. You're a good guy, I know. You won't tell anyone where we live. Come on in."

"In where?" I asked.

"You'll see in a minute. Follow me."

Parting the branches, he ducked in among the bushes along the chapel wall and disappeared. I followed. A few steps brought me out into a bare small space, entirely concealed by vegetation. The ground here was hard and trampled. Between the two bird-cherry tree trunks yawned a large opening in the ground, with earth steps leading down. Walek started down the steps and motioned to me to come along. In a few seconds we were in pitch darkness underground, and Walek took my hand to guide me. For a while we followed a damp, narrow passageway, then suddenly, after a sharp turn to the right, came into a roomy vault.

I stopped short in the entrance, amazed by the strange sight that met my eyes. Two shafts of light poured down into the vault, dazzling in the underground darkness. The light came in through windows in the ceiling. One of these I had already seen from above, in the floor of the tomb. The other, evidently, was arranged in the same manner. The sunlight could not reach these windows directly. It was reflected down to them from the crumbling walls of the tombs. Pouring down through the damp air of the vault, it struck the stone slabs that made the floor and, thrown back from them, cast dull gleams into every corner. The walls, too, were stone. Massive columns, rising heavily from the floor, sent out stone arches to every side. These joined overhead in a vaulted ceiling. Under each of the windows, a human figure sat on the floor. One was the old Professor.

Under the other window sat Marusya, picking over a heap of flowers, as she always liked to do. The light fell on her fair head, on all her tiny figure. Yet, somehow, she hardly stood out at all against the background of gray stone—just a queer, dimly outlined little shadow that seemed on the verge of fading into nothing. When a cloud floated between the windows and the sun, blocking the light, the walls of the vault would disappear entirely into darkness, only to appear again—when the cloud passed— in their cold, hard reality, joining together in heavy arches over the tiny, childish figure. I remembered Walek's talk of the "gray stone" that sucked the life out of Marusya, and a superstitious dread crept into my heart. I seemed to feel an invisible, stony stare—greedy, penetrating, boring into me as well as Marusya.

"Walek!" Marusya cried joyfully as her brother came in.

And when she caught sight of me, her eyes began to sparkle.

I gave her my apples and Walek broke his white bread loaf in two and gave half to Marusya and the other half to the Professor.

I could not stand still. I felt uncomfortable with the glare of the gray stone upon me.

"Let's get out of here," I said, pulling at Walek's sleeve. "Get her out too."

We went out together into the daylight. Walek seemed more dejected than usual and less inclined to talk.

TIBURCY APPEARS ON THE SCENE

I came to the chapel again the following day. We set about the construction of an intricate trap for sparrows for which I had brought along a supply of string. We gave the end of the string to Marusya; and every time an incautious sparrow, attracted by our bait, hopped carelessly into the trap, she would jerk the string and capture it, and then let it go.

Toward noon, however, the sky clouded over. Thunder rolled cheerily and then the rain came pouring down. I very much disliked the thought of going underground. But remembering that, after all, Walek and Marusya lived there all the time, I conquered my aversion and went inside with them. The vault was dark and very quiet. But we could hear the thunder rolling up above, like a huge cart rumbling over cobblestones. For a while we all sat listening to the earth resounding to the downpour. The sound of falling, splashing water and the constant pealing of the thunder teased our nerves, giving rise to an animation that demanded action.

"Let's play blind-man's-buff," I proposed.

I was blind man. Marusya toddled about the stone floor on her feeble little legs, bubbling over with her pitiful, silvery laughter, and I pretended that I could not catch her. Suddenly I bumped into somebody's wet legs, and immediately the somebody seized me by my own leg, and swung me up by it. My head swung down, and the kerchief fell from my eyes.

It was Tiburcy, wet and angry, holding me up by the leg and rolling his eyes in the most frightful way—and all the more frightful that I saw him upside down.

"What's the meaning of this?" he demanded sternly of Walek. "You have good times here, I can see. And pleasant company."

"Let me go!" I screamed, surprised that I could utter a sound at all in such an extraordinary position.

But Tiburcy only grasped my leg the tighter.

"Well?" he demanded, still staring angrily at Walek.

But Walek, in this predicament, found nothing better to do than to stuff two fingers into his mouth, as though in proof that there was nothing he could say in reply. I noticed, however, that he was watching me with no little sympathy as I swung miserably in space, like a human pendulum.

Tiburcy lifted me higher, so that he could look into my face.

"Ha! His Honor, the Judge, if my eyes don't deceive me! And to what do we owe the honor of this visit?"

"Let me go!" I repeated loudly. "Let me

go this minute!" And, unconsciously, I tried to stamp my foot—which only made me swing more violently than ever.

Tiburcy laughed aloud.

"Aha! His Honor is pleased to be angry! Well, but you don't know me yet. Tiburcy —that's my name. And I'm going to hang you up over the fire and roast you, just like a little pig."

Walek's frightened eyes seemed to confirm the likelihood of so sad a fate for me. At this point, however, Marusya came to my rescue.

"Don't be scared, Vasya, don't be scared," she said, coming right up to Tiburcy. "He never roasts little boys over the fire. He just made it up."

With a sudden movement, Tiburcy righted me up and set me on my feet. I was so dizzy that I almost fell, but he steadied me, and then, sitting down on a block of wood, set me between his knees.

"How did you get in here?" he demanded. "Has this been going on long?"

As I did not answer, he turned to Walek.

"You tell me, then."

"Six days or so."

Tiburcy seemed rather pleased than otherwise by this answer.

"Six whole days!" he exclaimed, turning me around so that he could see my face. "Six days is quite a long time. And haven't you told anyone, in all that time, where you go visiting?"

"No, I haven't."

"Honestly?"

"Honestly."

"Good for you! Then it may be hoped that you won't tell in the future either. As a matter of fact, I've always thought you a

fine boy, seeing you about town. A real tramp, judge or no judge. And will you be judging us some day—eh?"

His tone was quite good-natured now. But I still considered myself insulted and therefore answered sulkily:

"I'm no judge, I'm Vasya."

"That makes no difference. Being Vasya is no hindrance to being a judge, and if you're not one now, you may be one later. That's the way the world has always gone. Look at us: I'm Tiburcy, and there is my boy, Walek. I'm a beggar and he's a beggar. I steal at times from hunger and he'll probably steal too. And your father is my judge. Well, and some day you'll be Walek's judge."

"That's not true," I returned sullenly. "I won't ever be a judge over Walek."

"Don't be so sure of that," this queer man said slowly, speaking to me in the tone he might have used to a grown man. Then he continued.

"You don't understand me, of course. You're only a youngster, after all. And so I'll put it to you in this way: if a time ever comes when Walek here is brought up before you to be judged, remember that when the two of you were still young fools and played together—that even then you took your road in whole clothes and with all the food you could eat, and Walek took his in rags and with an empty belly. Well, and for the time being"—his tone changed sharply —"for the time being, remember this: if you let out a word of what you've seen here to that Judge of yours, yes, or to so much as a bird that flies past you in the fields, why, my name won't be Tiburcy Drab if I don't hang you up by your feet in the fireplace here and make smoked ham of you. That's clear to you, I hope."

"I won't say anything to anybody. I . . . May I keep coming here?"

"Come if you like, on one condition —what I've already told you about smoked ham. See you don't forget it!"

Evening was gathering when I started down the hill that day, deep in thought, my brain in a pitiful muddle.

Coming through the orchard in the darkness, I bumped suddenly into my father. He was pacing gloomily up and down, as his habit was, with the usual strange, befogged look in his eyes. When I tried to slip past, he laid his hand on my shoulder.

"Where have you been?"

"Just . . . walking."

He looked at me intently and seemed about to say something, but then his eyes clouded over again, and with a shrug he strode on down the path. The meaning of that shrug—even then, it seems to me, I understood it: "Ah, what does it matter? *She,* his mother isn't here to care."

I had lied to him—for the first time, perhaps, in all my life.

I had always been afraid of my father. Now I feared him all the more, for now I carried within me a whole world of questions and experiences, vague and troublesome. Could he possibly understand me? Could I admit anything to him without treachery to my friends? I trembled at the thought that he might some day learn of my acquaintances, of this "bad society." But I could not betray Walek and Marusya. Had I betrayed them and broken my word to them, I could never have looked them in the eyes again for shame.

376

AUTUMN

Autumn approached. Harvesting set in, and the trees began to yellow. And our Marusya began to ail.

She complained of no aches or pains. But she grew thinner and thinner, paler and paler. Her eyes darkened and seemed bigger than before. And it was only by an effort that she could raise her drooping eyelids.

With every visit to the hill I found Marusya worse and worse. She did not go out of doors at all now, and the gray stone—the dark wordless monster of the vaults—pursued its fearful work uninterrupted, sucking the life from her tiny frame. Most of the time she lay in bed, and Walek and I did everything we could think of to amuse her, to evoke the faint, silvery music of her laugh.

Now that I was so much with the "bad society," Marusya's smile had grown almost as dear to me as my own sister's. And there was no one here to keep reproaching me with my wickedness, no ever-grumbling nurse. Here I was needed. My coming always brought a flush of pleasure to Marusya's cheeks. Walek threw his arms around me like a brother, and even Tiburcy, at times, would watch us with a strange look in his eyes and a glint of something that might have been tears.

In the meantime I could feel the gathering of a storm at home. Slipping through the orchard as usual, one morning, I was stopped by the sight of my father, and with him old Janusz from the castle. The old man was telling my father something, bow-ing and scraping at every other word. My father listened glumly, and as he listened a sharp furrow of angry impatience cut across his forehead. Then he threw out his arm, as though to brush Janusz from his way.

"Be off with you, old scandalmonger that you are!" he said.

But the old man—blinking strangely, his hat in his hands—only scurried up the path a few steps, and again blocked the way. My father's eyes flashed with anger. Janusz spoke so quietly that I could not make out a word. My father's brusque responses, though, reached me sharp and clear, like the lash of a whip.

"I don't believe a word of it. . . . What have you got against those people? Where are your proofs? . . . I take no word-of-mouth reports, and if you make a written report, you're obliged to bring proof. . . . Be still! That's my affair. . . . I won't hear another word."

In the end, my father brushed Janusz aside so decisively that he dared not annoy him further. When Janusz left, my father turned down one of the side paths, and I ran on to the gate.

I had a great dislike for the old owl from the castle, and this encounter made my heart heavy with foreboding. I was certain that the conversation I had overheard concerned my friends—and perhaps myself as well. Tiburcy, when I told him about it, made a terrible face.

"Eh, youngster, but that's unpleasant news! The cursed old hyena!"

THE DOLL

Marusya grew worse. Her great eyes darkened and looked out unmoving, indifferent at all our efforts to amuse her. For many days now we had not heard her laugh. I began bringing her my toys, but even these would occupy her only for the briefest time. And I decided to appeal to my sister, Sonya.

Sonya had a big doll, with bright pink cheeks and wonderful flaxen hair, the gift of our dead mother. I laid the greatest hopes on that doll. And so I called Sonya away from the nurse, down one of the far paths in our orchard, and asked her to give me the doll for a time. At first she only hugged her treasure the tighter. But I begged so earnestly, described to her so vividly the poor, sick child who had never had any toys of her own, that she gave it to me willingly and promised to play with other toys for two or three days, and say nothing to anyone about it.

The effect produced by the dainty doll exceeded all my expectations. Marusya, drooping like a flower in the autumn, came suddenly back to life—or so it seemed to me. How she hugged me, and how she laughed and talked with her new playmate! The doll achieved almost a miracle. Confined to her bed for so many days, Marusya got up again and walked about leading her flaxen-haired daughter by the hand.

But for me the doll was the cause of many an anxious moment. First of all, there was old Janusz. I passed him in the street when I started for the hill with the doll under my jacket, and he looked after me and shook his head. Then, a day or two later, our old nurse noticed that the doll was missing and began to search for it in every corner of the house. My father knew nothing of this as yet. But Janusz came and talked to him again. And though he was sent packing with even greater anger than before, my father stopped me on my way to the gate that day and ordered me to stay at home. Next day, too, the order was repeated. It was only four days later, by getting up very early, that I managed to climb the fence and run off before my father woke.

Things were bad on the hill. Marusya was in bed again and worse than ever. Her face was strangely flushed, her fair hair spread in confusion over her pillow. She knew no one at all. Beside her lay the doll, with its rosy cheeks and bright expressionless eyes.

I explained the situation to Walek, and we decided that the doll must be taken home—the more so that Marusya was in no state to notice its disappearance. But we were mistaken. Half-conscious as she was, she opened her eyes when I drew the doll away, and stared vacantly before her, as though she did not see me or understand what was going on. And then, suddenly, she began to cry, very softly, but so plaintively, and with a look of such poignant grief on her thin face through the mask of delirium, that I was frightened and quickly put the doll back in her arms. She smiled and hugged it. And I realized that I had been about to deprive my little friend of the last joy of her brief life.

Coming home that day, I met Janusz again in the gateway. Indoors, I found Sonya with her eyes full of tears, and the old nurse threw me an angry, annihilating glance. She muttered something under her breath with her sunken, withered lips.

My father asked me where I had been. I made my usual answer. He listened gravely, but made no comment. He ordered me once more not to leave the house without his permission. The order was very firmly put.

A few days later I was summoned to my father in his study. I went in and stopped timidly just inside the door. Through the window opposite the melancholy autumn sun was looking in. My father was in his armchair, before my mother's portrait. For some time he did not move, or turn his face to me. I could hear the rapid beating of my heart.

At last he turned. I looked up at him, and quickly dropped my eyes. His face was terrifying. Perhaps half a minute passed, during which I could feel his heavy, unmoving, crushing gaze.

"Did you take your sister's doll?"

I started, so sharply, so distinctly did the words descend upon me.

"Yes," I answered, just audibly.

"Didn't you know that it was a gift from Mother, that you ought to treasure her memory? And so—you stole it!"

"No," I said, lifting my head.

"Dare you deny it?" he cried, starting to his feet. "You stole it, and took it away somewhere. Where did you take it? Speak up!"

He strode across the room to me and laid a heavy hand on my shoulder. With an effort, I raised my head and looked up at him. His face was white, his eyes blazing with anger. I shrank from his look.

"Well, then! Speak up!"

His hand weighed still more heavily on my shoulder.

"I . . . I won't tell," I answered, very low.

"Yes, you will!" he said with strange distinctness. Now his voice held a threatening note.

"I won't tell," I whispered, lower still.

"And I say you will! You will!"

His voice faltered, as though he had to force the words out with painful effort. I could feel his hand trembling on my shoulder. I hung my head lower and lower. Tears filled my eyes, overflowed, and dropped to the floor. But still I repeated, barely audibly:

"I won't tell. I'll never, never tell you, not for anything."

In those moments, I proved myself my father's son. Not by the most fearful torments could he have got any other answer from me. In response to his threats, my heart swelled with a deep sense of injury—the injury, not as yet clearly understood, of a neglected child—and of poignant love for those who had taken me in so warmly, out there in the ruined chapel.

My father drew a heavy breath. I could feel my body shrinking in his grasp. Bitter tears ran, stinging, down my cheeks. I waited.

He was terribly hot-tempered, I knew. And I knew he was now boiling over with fury. What would he do to me? Even in that dreadful moment I loved my father, and I felt that he was on the verge of some act of wrathful violence that would shatter my love for him beyond repair. I was not afraid any more, not in the least. I stood waiting, as I remember, wishing for an end of it all. If that was how it was to be, why let it. And all the better. Yes, all the better.

Again my father drew a heavy breath. Perhaps he had conquered his fury. To this day, I do not know. Just at that moment a harsh voice came suddenly in at the open window.

"Ha! My poor young friend!"

Tiburcy! But, though I felt my father's hand on my shoulder quiver at this interruption, it never occurred to me that Tiburcy's coming might stand between my father and myself, might avert that which I considered inevitable.

Tiburcy came quickly into the house and paused in the doorway to the study. His sharp, lynx eyes took in the situation immediately.

"Ha! I find my young friend in quite a predicament!"

My father met the intruder with a stare of

morose surprise, but Tiburcy held his stare with undisturbed calm. He was serious now, with no sign of buffoonery. The melancholy in his eyes seemed deeped than usual.

"Your Honor!" he said quietly. "You're a just man. Let the child go. He's been in bad society, true, but—God's my witness—he's done nothing evil. And if he's befriended my poor little ragamuffins, why, I swear to it, you can have me hanged before I'll let him suffer for it. Here's your doll, youngster."

He undid the bundle he was carrying, and there the doll was.

My father's hand relaxed its grip on my shoulder. His face showed his amazement.

"What does all this mean?" he demanded.

"Let the boy go," Tiburcy repeated, and his broad hand gently stroked my bowed head. "You'll get nothing out of him by threats, whereas I'll gladly tell you all you want to know. Shall we go into some other room, Your Honor?"

My father, still staring at Tiburcy amazedly, agreed. They went out of the room together, and I remained alone, overwhelmed by a torrent of emotions that filled my heart to overflowing. At that moment, I knew nothing of what went on around me. There was nothing in the world but a little boy, in whose heart two very differing emotions, wrath and love, had been stirred so violently that everything had clouded over. I was that little boy, and, as I remember it, I was rather sorry for myself. Yes, and there were the voices—two voices, sounding through the shut door in muffled, but animated talk.

I was still standing where they had left me when the door opened and they both came in. Again I felt a hand on my head. I started. It was my father's hand, gently stroking my hair.

Tiburcy lifted me and sat me down on his lap—in my father's presence!

"Come to the hill," he said. "Your father will let you come to say good-bye to my little girl. She . . . she's dead."

Tiburcy's voice shook, and his eyes blinked strangely. But he got up at once, set me down on the floor, threw back his shoulders, and went quickly out of the room.

I looked up questioningly at my father. It was a different man who stood before me now, and in him I sensed the warmth, the kinship I had so vainly sought before. He stood looking at me in his usual thoughtful way, only now there was a hint of surprise in his eyes, and what seemed to be a question. It was as though the storm that had just passed over us both had swept a dense fog from my father's soul, as though only now had he begun to see me once more as his son.

Taking his hand trustfully, I said, "I didn't steal it, truly. Sonya gave it to me herself, for a few days."

"Yes," he answered slowly, "I know. I've been in the wrong, my boy, and I can only hope that some day you'll try to forget it—won't you?"

Eagerly I seized his hand and kissed it. Never again, I knew now, would he turn on me that dreadful look of a few minutes ago. And love, so long restrained, came flooding hotly into my heart.

I was not afraid of him now.

"May I go to the hill right away?" I asked, recalling Tiburcy's parting words.

"Yes, yes. Go say good-bye, my boy," he said gently, still with that hint of question in his voice. "Though—wait one minute. Do wait, my boy, just a minute more."

He went out into his bedroom and returned a moment later with some money, which he thrust into my hand.

"Give this to . . . Tiburcy. Tell him that I humbly beg him—will you remember? That I humbly beg him—to take this money. In your name. Will you remember? Yes, and tell him"—my father seemed to hesitate—"tell him that if he knows a man here named . . . Fedorovich, he might warn this Fedorovich that it would be best for him to leave our town. And now go, my boy, go quickly."

Only on the hillside did I catch up with Tiburcy. Clumsily, panting for breath, I did my father's errand.

"Father . . . humbly begs . . ."

And I pressed the money into his hand.

I did not look into his face. He took the money, and received the message concerning Fedorovich in gloomy silence.

Marusya lay on a bench in a dark corner of the vault.

"Dead"—to a child, the word in itself has not much meaning. It was only now at the sight of that lifeless form that realization came, and I choked with bitter tears. She lay there so grave and sad—my tiny friend, with such a wistful look on her little face. Her eyes were shut. They were a little sunken, and the blue shadows under them were darker than before. Her lips were parted in an expression of childish sadness, as though in response to our sorrow.

The Professor stood beside her, shaking his head apathetically. In another corner of the vault, someone was at work with an ax, making a coffin out of old boards torn from the chapel roof. Others were decking Marusya in autumn flowers. Walek was asleep. In his sleep, he quivered nervously. From time to time, he drew a deep, sobbing breath.

Soon after the events I have described the members of the "bad society" dispersed.

Tiburcy and Walek disappeared, and no one could say where they had gone, just as none could say where they had come from when they appeared in our town.

Sonya and I often visited Marusya's grave, and sometimes, too, our father would come with us. We liked to sit here on the hill in the shade of a gently whispering birch tree with the town gleaming mistily far below. We read books together here, and thought together, and confided to one another our earliest thoughts and dreams, and hopes and plans of our high-aspiring youth, our hearts overflowing with life and hope.

Anton Chekhov (1860–1904) is famous throughout the civilized world for his realistic short stories and plays depicting Russian life and human nature. Although a sworn realist, Chekhov is always compassionate in his writings. However, he often leavened his affection for his fellowmen with a wry sense of humor.

Chekhov was fond of children, took an interest in their developing literature, and wrote stories about them and for them. Here are two such stories.

THE BOYS

"Volodya has arrived!" cried someone in the courtyard.

"Volodichka is here!" shrieked Natalya the servant girl, rushing into the dining room.

The whole Karolev family ran to the window, for they had been expecting their Volodya for hours. At the front porch stood a wide sleigh with its troika of white horses enveloped in a mist of steam. The sleigh was empty because Volodya was already standing in the entry, untying his *bashlik* * with red, frost-bitten fingers. His school uniform, overcoat, cap, galoshes, and the hair on his temples were all silvery with frost, and from his head to his feet he exuded such a wholesome fragrance of cold that looking at him one felt a pleasant shiver and wanted to say "br-r-r." His mother and aunt rushed to kiss and embrace him. Natalya got down on her knees and began pulling off his felt boots. His sisters shrieked, doors creaked and

---

* A *bashlik* is a hood with two long ends, which are wound around the neck like a muffler.

banged on every side, and his father came running into the hall in his shirt sleeves, waving a pair of scissors and crying in alarm:

"What has happened? We expected you yesterday! Did you have a good trip? For heaven's sake, give him a chance to greet his own father! I *am* his father, after all!"

"Bow—wow—wow!" the large black dog, My Lord, barked in a bass voice, flailing his tail against the walls and furniture.

Everything mingled into one great, happy clamor that lasted several minutes. When the first outburst of joy had subsided, the family noticed that besides Volodya, there was still another small person in the hall. He was wrapped in scarfs and shawls and bashliks covered with frost and was standing motionless in the shadow of his huge fox-skin coat.

"Volodya, who is that?" whispered Volodya's mother.

"Good gracious!" Volodya exclaimed. "Let me present my friend Chechevitsin. I brought him from school to stay with us."

"We are delighted! Make yourself at home!" cried the father gaily. "Excuse me for not having my coat on! Allow me!—Natalya, help Mr. Chechevitsin take off his things! For heaven's sake, get that dog away! This noise is unbearable!"

Within a few minutes Volodya and his friend were sitting in the dining room drinking tea, dazed by the noisy reception and still pink-cheeked from the cold. The winter sun, piercing the frost patterns and snow on the windowpanes, trembled on the shiny samovar and bathed its pure rays in the rinsing cup under the spigot. The room was warm, and the boys felt heat and cold wrestling inside their bodies, neither wanting to give in to the other.

"Well, Christmas will soon be here!" Volodya's father said in a singsong voice, rolling a cigarette with dark russet tobacco. "Has it seemed long since your mother cried as she saw you off last summer? Time flies, my son! Old age comes before one has time to heave a sigh. Mr. Chechevitsin, go on, help yourself! We don't stand on ceremony here!"

Volodya's three sisters, Katya, Sonya, and Masha, the oldest of whom was eleven, sat around the table with their eyes fixed on their new acquaintance. Chechevitsin was the same age and size as Volodya, but he was neither as plump nor as fair, but swarthy and thin, and his face was covered with freckles. His hair was bristly, his eyes were like slits, and his lips were thick. He was quite unprepossessing, and, had it not been for his school uniform, he might have been taken for the son of a cook. He was morose and silent, and never once smiled. The girls immediately made up their minds that he must be a very wise and learned person. He seemed to be reflecting and was so preoccupied with his own thoughts that he started when spoken to and asked to have the remark or question repeated.

The girls noticed that Volodya, who was usually so talkative and jolly, seldom spoke now and never smiled, and on the whole did not seem to be glad to be at home. He addressed his sisters only once at tea, and even then his comment was strange. He pointed to the samovar and said, "In California they drink gin instead of tea."

He, too, seemed to be busy with thoughts of his own, and to judge from the glances he occasionally exchanged with his friend Chechevitsin, their thoughts were identical.

After tea the whole family went into the nursery, and Papa and the girls sat down at the table and continued some work which they had been doing when they were interrupted by the arrival of the boys. They were making Christmas tree flowers and ornaments out of colored paper. It was an exciting and noisy occupation. Each new flower was greeted by the girls with screams of rapture, of terror almost, as if it had dropped from the sky; and Papa, too, was delighted, but every now and then he would throw down the scissors, complaining angrily that they were dull.

Mamma came running into the nursery with a worried face and asked, "Who has taken my scissors? Have you taken my scissors again, Ivan?"

"Good heavens, I'm not even allowed to have a pair of scissors!" said Papa in a tearful voice, throwing himself back in his chair with the air of a much-abused man. But the next moment he was in rapture again over something or other.

On former holidays Volodya had always helped with the making of the Christmas tree decorations, and had run out into the yard to watch the coachman and the shepherd heaping up a mound of snow, but this time neither he nor Chechevitsin took any notice of the colored paper, nor did they once visit the stables. Instead they sat by a window whispering together, and then opened an atlas and concentrated on studying a map.

"First, we must go to Perm," whispered Chechevitsin. "Then to Tyumen, then to

Tomsk, and then—then to Kamchatka. From there the *Samoyeds* * will take us across the Behring Strait in their canoes, and then—we'll be in America! There are a great many fierce animals there."

"And where is California?" asked Volodya.

"California is farther down. Once we get to America, California will be just around the corner. We can make our living by hunting and highway robbery."

Chechevitsin avoided his friend's sisters and when he met them, looked at them askance. After evening tea he was left alone with the girls for five minutes. To remain silent would have been awkward, so he coughed morosely, rubbed the back of his right hand with the palm of his left, looked severely at Katya, and asked:

"Have you read Mayne Reid?"

"No, I haven't—but tell me, can you skate?"

Chechevitsin became lost in thought once more and did not answer her question. He only blew out his cheeks and heaved a sigh as if he were very hot. Once more he raised his eyes to Katya's face.

"When a herd of buffalo stomp across the pampas," he said, "the whole earth trembles and the frightened mustangs kick and neigh."

Chechevitsin smiled wistfully and added, "And Indians attack trains, too. But worst of all are the mosquitoes and the termites."

"What are they?"

"Termites look something like ants, only they have wings. They bite dreadfully. Do you know who I am?"

"You are Mr. Chechevitsin!"

"No, I am Montezuma Hawk-Claw, the invincible chieftain."

Masha, the youngest of the girls, looked first at him and then out of the window into the garden, where night was already falling, and said doubtfully:

Samoyeds is the name of a tribe of Siberian Eskimos living in the Russian far north.

"We had Chechevitsa (lentils) yesterday."

The absolutely unintelligible remarks of Chechevitsin, his constant whispering with Volodya, and the fact that Volodya never played now and was always absorbed in thought—all this seemed to the girls to be both strange and mysterious. Katya and Sonya, the two oldest ones, began to spy on the boys, and when Volodya and his friend went to bed that evening, they crept to the door of their room and listened to the conversation. Oh! what they heard! The boys made plans to run away to America in search of gold! They were all prepared and had obtained a pistol, two knives, some dried bread, a magnifying glass for lighting fires, a compass, and four rubles. The girls heard that the boys would have to walk several thousand miles, fight on the way with savages and tigers, and that they would then find gold and ivory, slay their enemies, turn pirates, drink gin, and at last marry beautiful wives and settle down and cultivate a plantation. Volodya and Chechevitsin both talked at once and kept interrupting each other with excitement. Chechevitsin called himself "Montezuma Hawk-Claw," and Volodya he called "my Paleface Brother."

"Be sure you don't tell Mamma!" said Katya to Sonya as they went back to bed. "Volodya will bring us gold and ivory from America, but if you tell Mamma she won't let him go!"

Chechevitsin spent the day before Christmas Eve studying a map of Asia and taking notes, while Volodya, his face looking tired and puffy as if it had been stung by a bee, roamed about the house, refusing all food. He stopped once in front of the icon in the nursery and crossed himself, saying, "O Lord, forgive me, a miserable sinner! O Lord, take care of my poor, unfortunate mother!"

Toward evening he burst into tears. When he said good night he kissed his father and mother and sisters over and over again. Katya and Sonya realized the reason for his behavior, but Masha, the youngest, understood nothing at all. Only when her eye fell upon Chechevitsin did she grow pensive and sigh.

"Nurse says that when Lent comes we must eat peas and Chechevitsa," she said.

Early on Christmas Eve, Katya and Sonya slipped quietly out of bed and went to the boys' room to watch them run away to America. They crept up to their door.

"So you won't go?" asked Chechevitsin angrily. "Answer me—you won't go?"

"Oh, dear God!" wailed Volodya, weeping softly. "How can I go? I'm so sorry for Mamma!"

"Paleface Brother, I beg you to go! You promised you would. You told me yourself how nice it would be. Now, when everything is all set, you get scared!"

"I-I'm not afraid. I-I'm sorry for Mamma."

"Answer me—are you going or not?"

"I'll go, only—only wait a while, I want to stay home a little while longer!"

"If that is the case, I am going by myself!" Chechevitsin said with decision. "I can get along splendidly without you. I want to hunt and fight tigers! If you won't go, return my pistol!"

Volodya began to cry so bitterly that his sisters could not endure it and began to sob softly.

"Then you won't go?" demanded Chechevitsin again.

"I-I'll go."

"Then get dressed!"

And to keep up Volodya's spirits, Chechevitsin began singing the praises of America, roaring like a tiger, and whistling like a steamboat. He also scolded, but promised to give Volodya all the ivory and gold they would find.

And this thin, dark boy with his bristling hair and his freckles seemed to the girls to be an extraordinary and wonderful person.

He was a hero, a fearless man who could roar so well that, through the closed door, one could really mistake him for a tiger or a lion.

When the girls were dressing next morning in their own room, Katya said tearfully, "Oh, I'm so scared!"

All was quiet until the family sat down to dinner at two o'clock, and then it suddenly appeared that the boys were not in the house. Inquiries were made in the servants' quarters, at the stables, and in the village, but they could not be found. At tea time they were still missing, and when the family had to sit down to supper without them, Mamma was terribly worried and even crying. That night another search was made in the village and men were sent down to the river with lanterns.

Next morning a policeman arrived and went into the dining room to fill out a missing-persons report. Mamma was crying.

Suddenly—lo and behold!—a sleigh pulled up at the front door with a mist of steam rising from its three white horses.

"Volodya has arrived!" cried someone in the courtyard.

"Volodichka is here!" shrieked Natalya the servant girl rushing into the dining room.

My Lord barked, "Bow—wow—wow!" in his bass voice.

It seemed that the boys had been stopped in the town, where they had gone around the shopping area asking where they could buy gunpowder. As he came into the house, Volodya burst into tears and threw his arms around his mother's neck. The girls trembled with terror at the thought of what would happen next, for they heard Papa call Volodya and Chechevitsin into his study and begin talking to them. Mamma wept and joined them.

"Do you think it was right?" Papa asked in a scolding tone. "Do you think such a thing is permissible? What if they find out about this at school—if they do, you will certainly be expelled. You ought to be ashamed of yourself, Master Chechevitsin! You're a bad boy. You're a trouble-maker and your parents ought to punish you. Do you think it was right to run away? And pray tell, where did you spend the night?"

"At the railway station," answered Chechevitsin proudly.

Volodya was put to bed, and a towel soaked in vinegar was placed on his head. A telegram was dispatched and the following day a lady arrived, Chechevitsin's mother, who took her son away.

As Chechevitsin departed, his face looked arrogant and stern. He said not a word as he took leave of the girls, but in a notebook of Katya's he wrote these words for remembrance:

Montezuma Hawk-Claw.

VAN'KA

Van'ka Zhukov, a boy of nine who had been apprenticed to the shoemaker Alykhin three months ago, was staying up that Christmas Eve. Waiting until his master and mistress, together with their workmen, had gone to midnight service, he took from his master's cupboard an inkwell and a penholder with a rusty penpoint, and spreading out a crumpled piece of paper, began to write. Before tracing the first word he looked around uneasily at the doors and the windows, glanced at the dark icon,* on both sides of which stretched shelves full of lasts, and heaved a broken sigh. The sheet of paper lay on a bench, and he knelt in front of it. He began to write:

Dear Grandfather, Konstantin Makarich! I am writing you a letter. I send you Christmas greetings and pray that God Almighty bestow upon you all His blessings. I have neither a father nor a mommie—you are the only one left to me in this world.

Van'ka raised his eyes to the dark window, in which the light of his candle was reflected, and clearly imagined his grandfather, Konstantin Makarich, night watchman to the Zhivarev family. He was a short, slight, uncommonly spry oldster of about sixty-five, with a perpetually smiling face and the bleary eyes of a drunkard. By day he slept in the servants' kitchen or joked with the cook; at night, wrapped in a large sheepskin, he would walk the rounds on his master's estate, tapping with his little mallet. The dogs, Kashtanka and Eel, the latter given that name because of his long black body, would follow him with their heads lowered. This Eel was exceptionally polite and gentle. He would gaze up as lovingly at strangers as he did at people he knew. But underneath his politeness and docility there lurked a most cunning duplicity. He was not trusted. No one knew better than Eel how to sneak up and snap at a person's shins, or how to get into the storage room, or how to steal a hen from a peasant. Not once had his hind legs been nearly pulled off, twice was he about to be hanged, every week he was beaten severely, but he always bounced back.

* An *icon* is a sacred image of Jesus, Mary, or a saint.

At this moment, no doubt, Grandfather would be standing at the gate, screwing up his eyes at the red windows of the village church, stamping his felt boots, and playing the buffoon with the servants. His little mallet would be tied to his belt. He would be beating his arms for warmth, shrugging his shoulders with the cold, and with an old man's chuckle, pinching first the maid, then the cook.

"How about a pinch of my snuff," he would be saying, offering the women his snuff box.

They would be taking a sniff of his snuff and sneezing. Grandfather would be indescribably delighted, laughing hilariously, and yelling, "Come on, knock it off, it has turned into an icicle!"

They would be giving the dogs some snuff, too. Kashtanka would sneeze, shake her head, and—offended—walk away. But Eel was too well mannered to sneeze, and would only wag his tail. And the weather must be magnificent—the air still, fresh, and transparent; the night dark, but the entire village visible with its snow-covered roofs, the smoke streaming upward out of the chimneys, the trees covered with silvery frost, and the snowdrifts. The whole sky must be seeded with winking stars and the Milky Way must stand out so clearly, as if it had been scrubbed for the holidays and rinsed in snow.

Van'ka sighed, dipped his pen, and went on with the letter:

Yesterday, I got a beating. The master dragged me out into the yard by the hair and hit me with his strap because while I was rocking their baby in the cradle, I unexpectedly fell asleep. And last week, the mistress told me to clean a herring and I began with the tail, and she grabbed the herring and pushed its head into my face. The workmen make fun of me, send me to the tavern for vodka, and make me steal the master's cucumbers for them; and the master hits me for it with whatever he can lay his hands on. And there is nothing to eat. In the morning they give me a piece of bread, for dinner I get some mush, and for supper, again bread, but as for tea or soup, they gobble it all up themselves. They make me sleep on the porch and when their baby cries, I don't get to sleep at all, but have to rock the cradle. Dear Grandpa, show divine mercy, take me back home to the village, this is more than I can stand. I bow down at your feet and will pray to God for you forever. . . . Take me away from here or I'll die.

Van'ka's chin trembled; he wiped his eyes with his grimy fist and gave a sob, then continued:

I'll crush your snuff for you, I'll pray for you, and if I do anything bad, wallop me all you want. And if you feel that I must have some work, then I'll beg the steward for Christ's sake to let me clean his boots, or I'll be a shepherd boy instead of Fed'ka. Dear Grandpa, it is impossible to remain alive here—only death awaits me. I'd run away and return to the village on foot, but I have no boots and I'm afraid I'll freeze. When I grow up, I'll repay you and will provide food for you and will not let anyone mistreat you, and when you die, I'll pray for the peace of your soul, just as for Mommie's. Moscow is a big city, all the houses belong to gentlefolk and there are many horses, but there are no sheep and the dogs aren't mean. Once I saw a nice store; in the window fishing hooks were for sale, already with the line and for different kinds of fish, very good ones; there was even one hook that could hold a forty-pound catfish. And I've seen shops where they sell guns of all kinds, like the master's guns at home, and I'll bet they are a hundred rubles each. And in the meat stores there are woodcocks, trout, and hares, but the clerks don't tell you where they shoot them.

Dear Grandpa, when they have a Christmas tree at the master's house with treats, get a gilded walnut and keep it for me in the little green trunk. Ask the young lady, Olga Ignatyevna, say it is for Van'ka.

Van'ka gave a tremulous sigh and again stared at the window. He remembered how his grandfather had always gone into the forest to get the Christmas tree for his master's family and had taken Van'ka with him. Those were happy times! Grandfather crackled and the frost crackled and, listening to those two, Van'ka crackled too. Before chopping down the fir tree, Grandfather would smoke his pipe and laugh at the freezing Van'ka. The young fir trees, covered with hoar frost, stood motionless, waiting to see which of them would be struck down. A hare flew like an arrow over the snowdrifts. Wherever did he come from? The grandfather couldn't refrain from shouting, "Get'im, get'im! The short-tailed devil!"

Grandfather would drag the chopped-down Christmas tree into the master's house and there they would set to work decorating it. The young lady of the house, Olga Ignatyevna, Van'ka's favorite, would be in charge. When Van'ka's mother was alive and a servant in the big house, the young lady used to give him candy and, not having much else to do, taught him to read and write, count up to a hundred, and even to dance a quadrille. When his mother died, Van'ka had been moved to the servants' kitchen to be with his grandfather, and from the kitchen he was sent off to Moscow, to the shoemaker Alykhin.

Van'ka continued with the letter.

Come and get me, dear Grandpa, in Christ's name. I beg you, take me away from here. Have pity on me, a miserable orphan. Here everyone hits me, and I'm awfully hungry, and I'm so homesick I can't even tell you how, and I keep crying. The other day the master struck me so hard on the head that I fell down and could hardly come to again. Wretched is my life, worse than any dog's. I send my greetings to Alyona, to one-eyed Egorka, and to the coachman, and don't forget, don't give away my harmonica to anyone. I remain your grandson, Ivan Zhukov. Dear grandfather, come for me.

Van'ka folded the letter and put it into an envelope he had bought the day before for a kopeck.* After thinking for a moment, he dipped his pen and wrote the address:

To Grandfather in the village

Then he scratched the back of his head, thought a little and added: *Konstantin Makarich.* Glad that he had been able to write without interference, he put on his cap and without putting on his little winter jacket, ran out into the street as he was, in his shirt.

The clerks at the butcher's, whom he had consulted the day before, told him that letters were put in mailboxes and from there were carried to all parts of the world in mail carts with drunken drivers and ringing bells. Van'ka now ran to the nearest mailbox and pushed his precious letter through the slit.

An hour later, lulled by sweet hopes, he was sound asleep. He dreamed of the stove. On it sat his grandfather swinging his bare legs and reading the letter to the cooks.

Eel stood by the stove wagging his tail.

---

* A *kopeck* is a Russian penny.

TALES OF ITALY

MAXIM GORKY

In these tales the Russian writer Maxim Gorky (1868–1936) sketches scenes from life in the Italy he knew. Gorky's participation in the Russian Revolution of 1905, and the publication of his anti-czarist novel, *Mother,* made it impossible for him to remain in his native country without facing imprisonment and exile to Siberia. Moreover, his health had been severely undermined by years of poverty and overwork. In 1906 he went to southern Italy for a cure. It was there, in the period between 1906 and 1913, that he wrote the *Tales of Italy.*

There is a freshness and a newness in all the twenty-eight stories and sketches of the book, reflecting the author's delight in what he saw and experienced in that sunny land. For Gorky, who had lived all his life in the cold, harsh climate of Russia and in the atmosphere of her tragic struggle against reaction, found Italy full of color, zest, and promise.

There are children in a number of the street scenes of his tales. Gorky wrote about them not only because they were a colorful feature of Italian street life, or a confirmation of the Italian's love for children; for Gorky children were always a symbol of the future for which their fathers were sacrificing and striving. The "heralds of spring," he called them.

It was hard to choose only the two tales given here, because every one of the twenty-eight is as fine.

PEPE

Pepe is ten. He is as frail, slender, and quick as a lizard. His motley rags hang from his narrow shoulders, and the skin, blackened by sun and dirt, shows through innumerable tears.

He looks like a dried-up blade of grass which the sea breeze blows hither and thither. From sunrise to sunset Pepe leaps from stone to stone on the island and often one can hear his tireless little voice pouring forth:

> Italy the Beautiful,
> Italy my own!

Everything interests him: the flowers that grow in riotous profusion over the good earth, the lizards that dart among the purple boulders, the birds amid the chiselled perfection of the olive-tree leaves and the malachite tracery of the vines, the fish in the dark gardens at the sea bottom, and the foreigners on the narrow, crooked streets of the town—the fat German with the sword-scarred face, the Englishman who reminds one of an actor in the role of a misanthrope, the American who tries in vain to look like an Englishman, and the inimitable Frenchman as noisy as a rattle.

"What a face!" Pepe remarks to his playmates, with his keen eyes on the German, who is so puffed out with importance that his very hair seems to stand on end. "Why, he's got a face as big as my belly!"

Pepe doesn't like Germans for he shares the ideas and sentiments of the streets, the squares, and the dark little saloons where the townsfolk drink wine, play cards, read the papers, and discuss politics.

Here is the morose Englishman, striding along on his scissor-like legs. Pepe runs in front of him humming something like a funeral dirge or just a mournful ditty:

> My friend has died,
> My wife is sad . . .
> And I do not know
> What ails her.

Pepe's playmates trail along behind, convulsed with laughter, and they scurry like mice to hide in the bushes or behind walls whenever the foreigner glances at them calmly with his faded eyes.

One could tell a host of amusing stories about Pepe.

One day some signora sent him to her friend with a basket of apples from her garden.

"I will give you a soldo *!" she said. "You can well use it."

Pepe readily picked up the basket, balanced it on his head, and set off. Not until evening did he return for the soldo.

"You were in no great hurry," the woman remarked.

"Ah, dear signora, but I am so tired!" Pepe replied with a sigh. "You see, there were more than ten of them!"

"Why, of course, there were more than ten! It was a full basket!"

"Not apples, signora, boys."

"But what about the apples?"

---

* A *soldo* is an Italian copper coin.

"First the boys, signora: Michele, Giovanni . . ."

The woman grew very angry. She seized Pepe by the shoulder and shook him. "Answer me, did you deliver the apples?" she cried.

"I carried them all the way to the square, signora! Listen to what a good boy I was. At first I paid no attention to the boys' teasing. Let them compare me to a donkey, I told myself. I will endure it out of respect for the signora—for you, signora. But when they began to poke fun at my mother, I decided I had had enough. I put the basket down and you ought to have seen, good signora, how neatly I aimed at those devils with your apples. You would have enjoyed it!"

"They stole my fruit!" cried the woman.

Pepe heaved a mournful sigh.

"Oh, no," he said, "the apples that missed were smashed against the wall, but the rest we ate after I had beaten my enemies and made peace with them."

The woman loosed a flood of abuse on Pepe's small shaven head. He listened attentively and humbly, clicking his tongue now and then in admiration of some particularly choice expression. "Oho, that's a beauty! What language!"

And when at last her anger had spent itself and she left him, he shouted after her:

"You wouldn't have felt that way if you had seen how beautifully I smacked the filthy heads of those good-for-nothings with those wonderful apples of yours. If only you could have seen it, why you'd give me two soldi instead of one!"

The silly woman did not understand the modest pride of the victor. She merely shook her fist at him.

Pepe's sister, who was much older but not smarter than he, went to work as housemaid in a villa owned by a rich American. Her appearance changed at once; she became neat and tidy, her cheeks became rosy, and she began to bloom and ripen like a pear in August.

"Do you really eat every day?" Pepe once asked her.

"Twice and three times a day, if I wish," she replied proudly.

"See you don't wear out your teeth," he advised.

"Is your master very wealthy?" he inquired after a pause.

"Oh, yes, I believe he is richer than the king!"

"You can't fool me! How many pairs of trousers has he got?"

"It's hard to say."

"Ten?"

"More, perhaps . . ."

"Then bring me a pair, not too long in the leg, but the warmest you can find," said Pepe.

"What for?"

"Well, just look at mine!"

There was indeed not much to see, for little enough remained of Pepe's trousers.

"Yes," his sister agreed, "you can use some clothes! But won't he think we have stolen them?"

"Don't think that folks are more stupid than we are!" Pepe reassured her. "When you take a little from someone who has a lot, that isn't stealing, it's just sharing."

"You're talking nonsense," his sister said, but Pepe soon persuaded her. And when she came into the kitchen with a good pair of light-gray trousers that were, of course, far too large for Pepe, he knew at once how to take care of that difficulty.

"Give me a knife!" he said.

Together they quickly changed the American's trousers into a very comfortable garment for the boy. The result of their efforts was a somewhat loose, baggy sack reaching to the shoulders and held up by bits of string tied around the neck. The trouser pockets served as sleeves.

They might have turned out an even better and more comfortable costume had the wife of the owner of the trousers not interrupted their labors. She came into the kitchen and let loose a flood of very ugly words in many languages, all pronounced equally badly.

Pepe could do nothing to check the flood. He frowned, pressed his hand to his heart, clutched despairingly at his head, and sighed loudly, but the woman did not calm down until her husband appeared on the scene.

"What's up?" he asked.

Whereupon Pepe spoke up. "Signor, I am greatly astonished by the commotion your signora has raised. In fact I am somewhat offended for your sake. As far as I can see she thinks that we have spoiled the trousers, but I assure you that they are just right for me! She seems to think that I have taken your very last pair of trousers and that you cannot afford to buy yourself another pair."

The American, who had listened calmly to the speech, now remarked, "And I think, young man, that I ought to call the police."

"Really?" Pepe queried in amazement, "what for?"

"To take you to jail . . ."

Pepe was extremely hurt. In fact he was ready to weep, but he swallowed his tears and said with great dignity:

"If, signor, it gives you pleasure to send people to jail, that is your affair! But I would not do that if I had many pairs of trousers and *you* had none! I would give you two, perhaps even three pairs, although it is impossible to wear three pairs of trousers at once! Especially in hot weather."

The American burst out laughing. Then he offered Pepe some chocolate and gave him a coin.

Pepe bit at the coin and thanked the donor. "Thank you, signor! The coin is genuine, I presume?"

But Pepe was at his best when he stood alone somewhere among the rocks, pensively examining their cracks as if reading the dark history of rock life. At such moments his vivid eyes were wide with wonder, his slender hands were laced behind his back, and his head, slightly bent, would sway a little from side to side like a flower in the breeze. And under his breath he softly hummed a tune, for he was forever singing.

It was good also to watch him looking at flowers, at the wisteria blossoms that poured in purple profusion over the walls. He stood as taut as a violin string, as if he was listening to the soft tremor of the silken petals stirred by the breath of the sea breeze.

As he looked he sang: "Fiorino . . . Fiorno . . ."

And from afar, like the sound of some huge tambourine, came the muffled sigh of the sea. Butterflies chased one another over the flowers. Pepe raised his head and followed their flight, blinking in the sunlight, his lips parted in a smile tinged with envy and sadness, yet the generous smile of a superior being on earth.

"Shoo!" he cried, clapping his hands to frighten an emerald lizard.

And when the sea is as placid as a mirror and the rocks are bare of the white lacy spume of the tide, Pepe, seated on a stone, gazes with his bright eyes into the transparent water, where among the reddish seaweed the fish glide smoothly, the shrimps dart back and forth, and the crab crawls along sideways. And in the stillness the clear voice of the boy pours gently forth over the azure waters.

"Sea, oh Sea . . ."

Adults often shake their heads disapprovingly at Pepe, saying, "That one will be an anarchist!"

But kinder folk, possessed of greater discernment, are of a different opinion.

"Pepe will be our poet," they say.

And Pasqualino, the cabinet-maker, an old man with a head seemed cast in silver and a face like those etched on ancient Roman coins—stout and respected Pasqualino—has his own opinion.

"Our children will be far better than we, and their lives will be better too!"

Many folk believe him.

CHILDREN OF PARMA

On the little square in front of the railway station in Genoa, a large crowd had gathered—workingmen mostly, but there were also well-fed, well-dressed people. In front of the crowd stood members of the city council, and above their heads waved the heavy and intricately embroidered silk banner of the city, with the many-colored banners of the workers' organizations beside it. The golden tassels, fringes, and cords glittered, the tips of the flagpoles shone, the silk rustled, and a low hum like a choir singing sotto voce * rose from the festive crowd.

_____
* _Sotto voce_ means softly or in an undertone.

Above, on its tall pedestal, stood the statue of Christopher Columbus, the dreamer who had endured so much for his beliefs and who had won because he believed. Today too he looked down at the people and his marble lips seemed to be saying: "Only those who strongly believe can win."

The musicians had laid their instruments around the pedestal at Columbus' feet, and their brass glittered like gold in the sun.

The semicircle of the station building spread its heavy marble wings as if wishing to embrace the waiting crowd. From the harbor came the heavy breathing of the steamships, the muffled churning of a propeller in the water, the clanging of chains, whistling and shouting. But the square was still and hot under the blazing sun. On the balconies and at the windows of houses women stood with flowers in their hands, and beside them were children looking like flowers in their holiday clothes.

As the locomotive rolled whistling into the station, the crowd stirred and several crushed hats flew into the air like so many dark birds. The musicians took up their trumpets, and a few grave, elderly men spruced themselves, stepped quickly forward, and turning to face the crowd, spoke excitedly, gesturing to the right and left.

Slowly the crowd parted, clearing a wide passage to the street.

Whom have these people come to meet? The children from Parma!

There was a strike on in Parma. The employers would not yield, and the striking workers were now in such dire straits—without money or food—that they had decided to send their children to Genoa to save them from starvation.

From behind the columns of the station building there now appeared a neat procession of little people, half-naked and looking in their ragged clothes like some strange shaggy little animals. They walked hand in hand, five abreast—small, dusty, and tired. Their faces were serious, but their eyes shone brightly, and when the musicians struck up the Garibaldi * hymn a smile of pleasure brightened those drawn, hunger-pinched faces.

The crowd welcomed the children with a deafening shout, banners dipped before them, the brass trumpets blared out, stunning and dazzling them. Somewhat taken aback by this reception, they shrank back for a moment and then suddenly drew themselves up so that they looked taller, and from

---

* *Garibaldi* was an Italian patriot who helped unify his country; he lived from 1807 to 1882.

hundreds of throats there rose a single shout:

"Viva Italia!"—"Long live Italy!"

"Long live young Parma!" thundered the crowd in response, rushing toward the children.

"Evviva Garibaldi!" shouted the children, as in a gray wedge they cut into the crowd and were engulfed by it.

From the hotel windows and from the roofs of houses handkerchiefs fluttered like white birds, and a shower of flowers and gay, lively shouts poured down on the heads of the crowd below.

Everything took on a holiday appearance, everything sprang to life, even the gray marble seemed to blossom out in daubs of bright color.

The banners waved in the breeze, caps and flowers flew into the air, small grimy paws stretched out in greeting sought to catch the flowers.

Nearly all the children were snatched up; some of them sat perched on the shoulders of the grownups, others were pressed against the broad chests of stern, bewhiskered men; the music was barely audible above the hubbub of shouting and laughter.

Women darted in and out of the crowd, picking up the remaining newcomers and shouting to one another:

"Will you take two, Annita?"

"Yes, and you?"

"Don't forget to take one for lame Margaret . . ."

A feeling of happy excitement reigned, and there were beaming faces and moist kind eyes on all sides. And already some of the strikers' children were munching bread.

"No one thought of this in our time!" remarked an old man with a beaklike nose and a black cigar between his teeth.

"And how simple it is!" someone else added.

"Yes. Simple and sensible," the man with the cigar said.

The old man removed the cigar from his

mouth, glanced at its tip, and sighed as he shook off the ash. Then noticing nearby two little Parma children—brothers obviously—he assumed a fierce expression and, as the boys looked on gravely, he pushed his hat down over his eyes, spread out his arms, and suddenly squatted down and crowed like a rooster. The boys roared with laughter, stamping their bare soles on the cobbles. The man rose, straightened his hat, and walked off unsteadily, feeling that he had done his good deed for the day.

A tall man with powerful bare arms, wearing a leather apron, carried a little girl of six on his shoulder, a gray mousey little thing.

"See what I mean?" he remarked to the woman who walked beside him leading a small boy with flaming red hair, "If this sort of thing takes root . . . it won't be easy to get the better of us, eh?"

And with a deep laugh of triumph he threw the little girl up into the blue air, crying: "Evviva Parma-a!"

The people gradually dispersed, carrying the children or leading them by the hand, until the square was empty of all save a group of jolly porters, and the noble figure of the man who discovered the New World.

And the happy shouts of the people going forward to a new life echoed through the streets.

THE FIRST SONG

SEMYON E. ROSENFELD

The First Song is an absorbing short novel about a boy who loves music and the cello, and dreams of some day becoming a talented cellist. But the circumstances in czarist Russia at the beginning of the twentieth century were such that a poor boy wanting, no matter how desperately, to become a musician faced nearly insurmountable obstacles. The hero experiences many frustrations but he also has many adventures as he earns a living and pursues his musical goal in the teeming Black Sea port of Odessa, a city that is also a musical center.

Here the first three chapters of the book are given, as well as an excerpt from a later dramatic development. The story is told by its hero, Kolya.

It is interesting to note that *The First Song* reveals a number of close similarities to *Johnny Tremain* by the Ameircan author, Esther Forbes. *Johnny Tremain* has been translated into Russian and published in the Soviet Union. Soviet children read it avidly. It is also a story about a talented boy (apprenticed to a silversmith), who also tries to make his way in a port city (Boston) on the eve of a revolution (the American Revolution), and by doing so gets involved in the underground activities of revolutionaries (the Colonial rebels). *The First Song* was published many years before the American story.

My father had recently been transferred to a job in Odessa. On a clear sunny morning at the end of September, my mother, my brother, and I went to the docks and boarded the same ship on which the opera company had left our town a month ago. Father had left several days before our departure. Ours was a freight ship. Usually it carried coal and iron from Mariopol to Odessa; * from Odessa to Mariopol it carried roof tiles and other merchandise. Despite this the ship was clean and comfortable, and it was interesting and lively on its decks. But when the propeller began to turn, and when the green water was stirred up noisily into spraying foam, forming a long white pathway in the wake of the moving ship, and as I saw the familiar shore slowly disappear from sight, I felt very sad.

I had spent most of my life here in Mariopol. In the summer I would almost live on the beach, baking myself on the hot light-yellow sand, and when I was overcome with the heat, I would throw myself into the green transparent water of the Azov Sea, swim and dive. Here, also, only several versts ** from the city, on the Kalka—a river associated with many legends about the fighting between the Russians and the

---

* Both cities are seaports in the south of Russia —Odessa on the Black Sea, Mariopol on the Azov Sea.

** A *verst* is a measure of distance about two-thirds of a mile.

invading Mongols, centuries ago—we boys would often make our way across in an old flat-bottomed rowboat. Tall reeds grew thickly on the opposite shore—this was almost the beginning of the Don Cossack Region. On this spot we had made a momentous decision: to explore this land of the Cossacks for buried Tartar * treasure, hoping to find a cauldron of gold, a trunkful of daggers, and a chest full of ornamented saddles and harness. Yes, I was leaving behind me a great deal, and my spirit was heavy.

But the captain was soon shouting into the loudspeaker, to the men down in the engine room, "Full speed ahead!" and the ship, gathering momentum, quickly left my city behind us. Its outlines became dimmer and dimmer and soon disappeared altogether as the blue sky merged imperceptibly with the green sea.

Gradually my sad thoughts left me. Many other ships passed us, ships carrying nothing but coal—the white ship *Emerance,* followed by the heavy black one called *Pyotr Karpov,* then an unusually long one, the *Maria Regger,* and the fat, clumsy one, *Taras Bulba.* Our boat, the *Pyotr Regger,* courteously saluted them all with her flag, and they answered our greeting properly, and all this was new and interesting to me. Cupping our hands into an improvised telescope, my brother and I scanned the sea and the one who was the first to spot a ship, no bigger than a dot on the far horizon, felt very superior to the other.

The weather, although it was already autumn, was dry and clear. It was as warm as in summer. The calm water was a smooth blue-green. The gold of the sun was mirrored in it, forming an endlessly long, fiery-gold stripe across the immensity of the sea, and its million sparkles were blinding.

Everything on board ship was unfamiliar and fascinating. I felt an uncontrollable desire to touch everything with my hands, to

---

* Mongols were also called *Tartars.*

feel the shape of every strange object and to examine it. The gear that rested in the prow and in the stern, the large coils of thick hemp rope, the heavy chains that stretched along the sides of the ship from the captain's bridge to the helm—all were intriguing. Nor could we ignore the tremendous windlass. The signal lanterns were fascinating, too, with their bright colors and their beautifully shaped glass—green, white, and red; and within reach was a box with a large assortment of the flags of all countries.

But most interesting of all was the engine room.

With great curiosity we looked down below through the open hatchway and saw the large engines breathing heavy steam and the thick steel pistons, covered with heavy oil, going up and down with a slow and steady rhythm. To know that these engines activized the enormous ship's propeller, which was turning so lightly in the water and making the ship move forward so steadily, made one regard all this machinery with respect, as one would a very strong and competent person.

A man in a striped sailor's jersey often looked up at us from below. His face was almost black, but his eyes stood out sharply from this blackness like two white circles and seemed to shine like lanterns in the darkness. He often wiped his hands on a piece of sackcloth and looked up, smiling at us and showing a row of snow-white teeth. He sang some tune, but the racket of the engines drowned out his voice.

As the sun was setting, a cool breeze suddenly passed over the washed deck, and the ripples on the sea looked like many-colored dabs of paint as they reflected the colors of the setting sun in the water, which was now becoming noticeably darker. The seamen now gathered on the stern from all parts of the boat.

The stoker, whose acquaintance we had already made, was among them. Now his face was not at all black—he had washed it. And his eyes were now not white—the color they seemed to be before—but light gray, and friendly. He was wearing a clean sailor's blouse and a muffler made of sackcloth. In his hands he held an accordion. At first he tinkered with it for quite a time—loosening this, tightening that, and checking various parts. Then, resting for a minute, as if to gather strength, he began to sing, lowering his head to the left, nearly touching the accordion with it, as if afraid to miss a single sound. He played a sentimental song, keeping his eyes closed, and one saw only his dark lashes. When he finished playing the waltz, he opened his eyes, lifted his head, and smiled in a self-conscious way. The sea breeze blew against his heavy locks of hair and this made his face look even more pleasant and friendly. But again he hid his face, lowering his head to the accordion, and played something unfamiliar, wonderfully warm and sad.

The other seamen stood or sat around him. A little farther away some passengers had made themselves comfortable on coils of cable, and still farther away, on a reclining deck chair sat the captain's assistant, and near him stood the fat engineer. Everyone listened attentively and with obvious pleasure—some even with rapture. I too was absorbed in Egor's singing, and I watched the fingers of his coarsened hands run lightly over the keys and drank in the slightly hoarse music of the old accordion.

A blue twilight soon enveloped us. Green, red, and white lights appeared on the stern, and on the bridge. The sea became even darker and soon looked like a gigantic pool of ink in which played the reflections of the colored lights of the lanterns and the yellow-blue stars. The breeze became chillier and was now blowing up our sleeves.

Twice my mother had sent someone to get me to go down for supper and to put on a jacket. But I couldn't even think of it. How could one go away when Egor was playing?

Annoyed with my stubborness, Mother came herself to get me, but she too stayed on and listened with enjoyment. Then she got too chilled, went away, and sent my brother with my coat and cap.

Egor played on for a long time. His skillful hands, completely invisible now in the darkness, continued to draw wonderful melodies from the accordion.

He interrupted his playing suddenly, rose, and said in a pleasant, light tenor voice, "Well, enough! Must get some sleep. Have to work tonight."

Closing the accordion carefully, fastening it with a leather strap and throwing it over his shoulder, he made his way among the piles of rope, explaining: "Too much carousing today and carousing on the morrow, and a kopeck for bread you'll have to borrow." Egor, as I soon found out, liked to talk in proverbs.

He started down to the f'o'c'sle and I followed him.

"Egor, may I come with you?"

"Why not? Welcome to our tent!"

The f'o'c'sle was poorly lighted and was filled with the stale smoke of cheap tobacco. There was an odor of coal dust, tobacco, whisky, and dark bread. Someone was snoring with a startlingly different, rolling snore. Someone else was lying awake on a cot and was almost invisible in the semi-darkness and the smoke haze of the crowded cabin.

Egor wrapped his instrument in a large flowered peasant kerchief and put it away in a green trunk with iron fastenings. Then he took a guitar from the wall, sat down at the table and began to loosen the tuning pegs, to fix its strings, and to adjust other things with his quick hands. But no sooner did I begin to question him about what he was doing with the guitar than my older brother came and announced that unless I went up to supper at once, Mother would send a seaman for me.

"Don't worry, Kolya," my new acquaintance said to me. "Come again tomorrow and I'll show you something else. There are many days of this trip left to us and luckily, tomorrow is Saturday."

Reluctantly I left Egor and consoled myself with the thought that tomorrow I would see him again, and would then, without fail, ask him to teach me to play the accordion.

But next morning I managed to see Egor only through the hatchway. It was forbidden for passengers to go to the engine room, and for some reason Egor worked all day even after his night shift.

We soon came to the end of the Azov Sea and entered the Kerchinsky Strait, and after passing one more floating beacon, we were on the Black Sea. But I experienced a great disappointment now—this sea was not at all black. And no one was able to explain why it was called black. I thought even the Azov was darker. However, when I found out that the Black Sea was bigger and deeper, and that its water was bitter and salty and never froze over, while the water of the Azov Sea was sweet and fresh and froze over for several months in the year, I unwillingly felt respect for its vastness and depth. Fantasy now took over, and I imagined that our ship had entered the ocean and was carrying us to unknown distant shores. Any minute now I expected the captain to look through his telescope and excitedly announce that he had spied the barely visible outline of the new land; and the ship's passengers and crew, crowding at the rails, would avidly watch the silhouettes of the blue mountains emerge from the foggy horizon.

But one of the seamen mercilessly ruined my daydream. In passing he said casually, "Look, this is my place of birth. Feodosya—a golden city!"

We were passing the shores of the Crimea.

The ship moved on keeping closer to the shore, as if the captain was intent on showing us the many splendid places of the Crimea.

We passed Alushta! . . . Yalta! . . . and Alupka!

We could see not only the white houses, the tall cypresses, the winding ribbons of the roads near the shoreline, but even the dark figures of the people on the beaches. We passed white yachts with billowing sails, sturdy fishing boats, small rowboats used by vacationers, and solitary swimmers.

It all looked like a scene from a fairy tale set in an azure kingdom. The light-blue transparent water, strong smell of sea salt, and the faint scent of flowers and sunbaked earth, the serene, cloudless sky—this was indeed an azure fairyland.

But soon we left the Crimea behind us. The shore disappeared. We were aware only of the boundless sea, the blue horizon, the soft warm air, and the gay dolphins emerging now and then from the water. They followed the ship and, seeming determined to entertain the passengers, they performed nimble and graceful leaps, making a semicircle high in the air then quickly diving into the waves like urchins.

The ponderous, noisy engine made the ship shudder as it sped along, cutting a turbulent wake edged with white foam.

I waited impatiently for the evening when Egor would appear again on deck with his accordion. But it was a long time till evening, an unbearably long time. Stealthily, so that no one would notice me, I went down to the engine room. It was almost dark in the long, narrow passageway. I proceeded feeling my way along the wall with my hands. I was somewhat scared and worried —what if Egor should get angry? With every step it became hotter. The air was as hot as in an overheated bathhouse. I put my head through a narrow opening and a stream of scorching air hit me.

I saw something that looked like the enormous jaw of a monstrous iron beast. Its mouth was full of flames and red hot embers, and in front of it stood Egor. I recognized him at once although he was half naked and his face was invisible in the smoke.

Bending over he would scoop up large pieces of coal with a wide shovel and throw them into the furnace, which hissed, smoked, and flamed up as Egor fed it shovelful after shovelful. I could hardly breathe in this impossible heat. I began to choke and felt as if my clothes were on fire. I quickly retreated and ran back to the deck.

There, after the heat of the furnace room, despite the blazing sun, it seemed as cool as under a sea wave. I relished the spaciousness, the fresh air, and the ease with which I could now breathe. And it made me sad to think of poor Egor spending days and nights in that inferno below.

That evening, when Egor came up to the deck, I ran over to him and asked, "How can you stand it down there?"

"Well, what can you do?" was his reply. "Do what work there is, to live; eat what they give. . . . Otherwise, death will get you, all right."

"But, can't you find other work?"

"There is no way to escape from it. It's all right," he laughed. "It will be easier in the next world."

As on the previous day, when his work shift was over Egor settled himself in his customary place on deck amidst the large piles of cables, put his accordion on his knees, and began to tune it. Then, after pausing in thought for a few moments, he lowered his head to the instrument, stretched its bellows, listening closely to the drawn-out chord. The many-voiced chord of the accordion seemed to me very beautiful, and I was ready to listen to it forever.

Egor played on. And again a crowd of passengers and crew gathered around him. Getting up suddenly, he said, "I didn't sleep last night and was on duty all day . . . have to catch a few winks." And he went below.

In the morning a large white city appeared on the horizon. Odessa. A little later a tall white lighthouse came into view unexpectedly, as if it sprang out of the water, and from the lighthouse to the shore a semicircular breakwater opened its passageway to us. We entered its wide gates and the ship glided noiselessly through the glass-smooth surface of the water, cautiously nearing the pier.

I didn't manage to see Egor again. As soon as the ship docked my father came up the gangplank and led us ashore. I kept looking up for as long as I could, keeping my eye on the opening to the engine room, but no one appeared from there.

The driver soon finished putting our things into the horse-drawn carriage. My brother and I climbed up and sat on a narrow bench facing my parents sitting in the wide seats of the phaeton, which smelled of leather and the stable. In another minute we would be on our way and still there was no sign of Egor. The driver pulled on the reins, turned the carriage toward the city, and the ship disappeared from view.

I couldn't put Egor and his music out of my mind.

That first night in my new home in Odessa, I couldn't sleep. I kept thinking of the ship and felt as if I was still on it! I heard the shudder of the hull, the thud of the engine, and the sound of the accordion.

Then, suddenly an idea struck me—after all, the ship was still in port! In an instant I decided to go down to the harbor next day and find Egor.

Very early next morning, the moment my father left for work, I got up quietly, dressed, and slipped out of the house. I soon turned down a street leading to the Nikolayevsky Boulevard and reached the wide steep stairway leading down to the harbor. I skipped down two steps at a time, glancing back now and then at the statue of Cardinal Richelieu overlooking the stairway, to see what progress I was making down the seemingly endless number of stairs.

The pier, stretching along the entire length of the harbor, was lined with shops; behind them were the wharfs, moorings, stone jetties; and a short distance out in the bay were rows of ships and boats of all shapes and colors. They were moored and their flags of many countries fluttered in the breeze, making one think of mysterious distant lands.

I crossed over to the mounds of coal at the refueling dock and wended my way through the narrow walks to the wharf from which we left yesterday for the city. These walks were crisscrossed with steel cables and hemp hawsers with which the ships and boats were moored to the iron bitts, and were cluttered with unused gangplanks. Lines of stevedores manually loading and unloading Russian and foreign ships moved along slowly. But I dodged all this and hurried on to the large warehouses storing Marseille tiles, near which a ship was being loaded.

There it was!

I recognized it even from a distance—the high hull with the familiar inscription in silver letters—*Pyotr Regger*.

I went up the gangplank, red-yellow from the dust of the tiles, and found myself on the deck. I went stealthily down the ramp leading to the engine room. It was unusually quiet down there. The engines were silent, the pistons were still. I ran down the steep steps to the fo'c'sle. There was no one there. I was about to return to the deck when I heard Egor's voice:

"Hey, Kolya, where are you off to?"

In a small cabin, dimly lit by a kerosene lamp, Egor was working over the small parts of a disassembled machine. He didn't look as black as usual, but his face had dark smears on it and his hands were covered with machine oil.

"How did you get here?" he asked, putting aside his work. "How did you find your way to the ship?"

I didn't say anything for what seemed quite a long time; then I explained with embarrassment: "I wanted to ask you. . . . Teach me how to play. . . ."

"So, that's it! You don't give up so easily! You know, there's a proverb: 'Learn when your bones aren't yet stiff.' OK, let's go while the crocodile—I mean the captain—is still out on the town. Let's have a lesson."

He showed me how to work the keys on the accordion. He did this unhurriedly. He picked out some chords, slowly drawing out every one, patiently explaining what he was doing. He made me repeat the chords. Then he offered me his seat, placed the heavy instrument on my knees, and said:

"Now, go to it, pick out some simple song. Go on, begin . . . 'Oh, the endless plains . . .'"

He sang the melody in a low tenor voice, helping me pick out the tune. This was hard, almost impossible. I lost the melody, couldn't find the right keys, forgot to stretch the bellows, or, stretching them, I couldn't manage at the same time to press the keys.

I was about to give up, but Egor wouldn't hear of it.

"Go on, keep trying. Don't be easily discouraged."

After many attempts and failures, I finally managed to play a few decent sounds, and, to my delight, I heard the beginning of the familiar song. I repeated the tune many times, and when Egor left for a few minutes for the deck to see if the machinist was coming, I began to sing to my own accompaniment and was amazed how good my voice sounded as it blended with the sounds of the accordion. I kept repeating the refrain, "Oh, the e-en-nd-less plains . . ."

Egor returned and praised my progress.

"You can't graft talent onto your skin—if you weren't born with it. But any one can see that you have some! As water is to a ship, you might say, talent is to a musician."

His eyes beamed, his white teeth glistened, locks of hair fell across his forehead. He was handsome, despite the greasy black smears on his face, the worn rag around his neck, and the dirty sweatshirt he wore.

"Come, let me play something for you now, before we say good-bye. The crocodile will soon be back."

He picked up the instrument carefully, sat down, and, as usual, lowered his head to the accordion as he played something very moving; he played it very softly as if only to himself.

Then he stopped for a minute, not raising his head, and after thinking briefly about something, resumed his playing. The chords poured forth and the music sounded like a huge chorus. I thought Egor played beautifully and wondered how he learned to play so well.

Once more Egor passed the accordion to me. With impatience I felt the keys, picked out another song, much faster than the first one, and began to sing. The melody came all at once, as if without my bidding, and my voice followed it freely.

I was happy and proud—my fingers were playing a real tune, they were making real music. Within a few minutes I had sung the entire melody, and each time I played the refrain with greater assurance.

"Good boy, Kolya, well done!" Egor exclaimed. "You'll amount to something one day, mark my word. You have, my young friend, the soul of a minstrel."

And, pausing for a moment, he continued: "If someone will take an interest in you, you'll be an artist! Only, my young friend, you have to study; without studying, nothing will come of it. I know that from my own experience. As the saying goes: 'To avoid failure, start learning in your youth!' "

All of a sudden he stood up.

"The crocodile has come back, I hear his voice. Have to go now. My friend, we'll not see each other so soon again. Tomorrow we sail with some tiles for Sochi, Pati, Batum. Then we go to Mariopol with coal, and only

then will we be back here. If you'll write down your address, when we land here again, I'll drop by to see you."

Walking me to the pier, he said: "The accordion is all right. You can learn a bit on it. But it isn't for you. You should play the viola or even that—how do you call it? It's like a viola, only about four times as large and it rests on the floor when it is played."

"Do you mean the cello?"

"Yes, that's it, that's for you! I'd gladly play one myself, it sounds so good. But it isn't for the likes of me, lacking talent."

I protested, "You'd play the cello better than anyone!"

"Kolya, my boy, you're a good kid!"

I insisted.

"It's true. I mean it. If only you took lessons . . ."

Egor broke into a boisterous laugh. "If only I took what? And with whose money, if you please? The English King's, I suppose! What's more, I'm almost illiterate—went to primary school for three months and that was the end of my education. After that I had to go to the city with my father, to work there. I read syllable by syllable and write with a child's scrawl." He kept laughing, then went on to say, "You flatter me. 'Take lessons,' you say. 'The bear would buy some honey if he had the money.' Talent is not enough when the pocket is empty."

Then Egor raised his hands, examined his fingers attentively; they were dark, rough, and massive. "Such hooks are good for pulling barges, not for plucking cello strings!"

I liked his proverbs and the way he chose his words generally. I could have listened to him longer, but I had to go.

Egor led me across the railroad tracks and offered his strong hand. "Well, good-bye, Kolya! In two weeks or so I'll come to see you; I'll bring you a treat. But don't forget what I told you: music is for you. It is in your head, in your heart, in your fingers."

Then he left, and I ran along the now familiar route to the city, to my new home, and in my ears without pause sounded "Oh, the endless plains . . ."

Kolya and Egor became good friends although they did not see each other often. When Egor's ship would dock in Odessa, he would pay Kolya a visit. Once he brought him a mandolin, and several months later he surprised his young friend with a gift of his favorite instrument—a cello!

Kolya worked hard at different jobs, but earned so little that there was nothing left for cello lessons. He tried again and again to obtain free instruction but was repeatedly disappointed. However, he never gave up hope—some day, somehow, he knew he would become a musician. But how?!

In the meantime, his attention was diverted to other things. The year 1905 was one of great social unrest in all of Russia. There were uprisings and strikes also in the busy seaport city of Odessa. The seamen, who had had no choice but to work very long exhausting hours for small wages, while subjected to much abuse, rose in protest. They struck! Many of them were arrested. All opposition to employers and to the czar and his government was cruelly suppressed, for democracy was hated and feared by those in power. Egor joined the seamen's strike and soon fell into the hands of the police. Kolya wanted to help his imprisoned friend and walked to the town where Egor was jailed, pawned his cello, and bought the things that Egor needed badly. Then he continued to earn money by singing in taverns and on streets, accompanying himself on the mandolin which Egor had given him. For striking, Egor was sentenced to eight years of hard labor.

Kolya continues his story:

The day of Egor's departure for Siberia came.

How lucky that I was able the day before to get him some of the things he would need so badly for the long, hard journey. Egor's silent acquaintance, "The Beard," had waited for me not far from the jail. Together we went to the store, bought a sack and filled it with sugar, tea, salted pork, soap, tobacco, and biscuits. The Beard gave me ten rubles for Egor. I delivered the things and the money at the prison and got a receipt for them and also for a pair of felt boots which the same savior, the taciturn Beard, had brought for Egor.

There was a crowd of the convicts' relatives and friends at the prison gates. The guards and the police kept dispersing them gruffly, but they would regather in small groups and resume their long, gloomy vigil. They were waiting for a glimpse of their kin about to be sent off to some God-forsaken Siberian prison center.

I recognized in the crowd the woman with the hollow cheeks and tired eyes, whose husband had gone out on strike and had been sentenced to eight years at hard labor. I also saw the short woman with the puffy face and faded brows, who had complained that her husband "had only hung around with those good-for-nothing workers' groups," but he had been sentenced to ten years. Here was also the old man with the reddish-gray, matted beard and red, teary eyes: his oldest son got eight years and his younger one the full twelve. He stood at the side of the old woman whose son— "quiet, gentle, and obedient"—got six years.

They had all been standing around near the prison since the night before, but only now, late in the evening of the second day, were they about to see their dear ones. Pushing the crowd to some distance from the gates, the guards herded the convicts into the prison yard in two lines. The space between the prisoners and their relatives was lit by smoking torches held by the police. Suddenly the air was filled with the clanking of irons and out into the lighted space, four abreast, came the shadowy figures of the prisoners, chained together at their feet and hands. By fours they formed a long column and were surrounded on all sides by soldiers with bared swords. The column moved forward slowly. From a side street came about twenty mounted Cossacks who quickly formed a second ring around the convicts.

The crowd broke up and walked alongside the column as close as the two rings of soldiers and Cossacks would allow, and they looked into the faces of the prisoners, trying to find their own. But from such a distance the prisoners, who were dressed alike and all with unshaven, bearded faces, were not recognizable in the dim light of the torches.

I also moved along with the column and ran from one end of it to the other looking intently at every face, but, like the rest, I couldn't find the one I was looking for.

I began to wonder if Egor was there at all? Perhaps he was left behind to be sent off with the next group of convicts.

Then, before realizing what I was doing, I shouted with all my might into the semidarkness:

"Egor, are you there?"

"Here! little brother, here!" I heard the reply in Egor's familiar voice. "So long! Take care of yourself!"

"Be quiet, youngster," an old man said, nudging me in the back. "Be quiet, or they'll beat him up because he answered you."

I was seized by fear. Could it be that for such a thing they would beat a wonderful person like Egor?

I gritted my teeth and continued to move alongside the column.

In this fashion the unusual procession continued to the very ship, piercing the night's blackness with the smoky light of the torches and breaking the soft silence of the sleeping city with the cruel music of the irons.

On the pier the police, after allowing the column of prisoners to pass, held back their relatives and friends. The chained convicts went up the narrow gangplank in two's. They soon disappeared into the hold of the ship, together with their guards.

I stood around watching what would happen next. I saw the late passengers rush up the gangplank and managed to slip on board with them.

The ship didn't pull away until late in the night. But the dark, motionless, silent mass of the prisoners' kin remained on the pier to the end.

A hushed stillness reigned on deck, in the passageways, and in the common cabin of the third class. It was broken now and then by someone's moan, by the heavy snoring of an old man, or the crying of a baby.

At the stern, about twenty feet from the opening to the hold into which the prisoners had been herded, the guard called out to anyone approaching: "Halt! It is forbidden to come closer!"

A dim brown light shone from the few lanterns inside the hold. There, in its foul-smelling depths usually filled with crates, barrels, sacks, iron, and tiles, now suffered in its airless darkness hundreds of men, tired unto death.

Among them was Egor.

I saw clearly in my mind his shaven head, sallow face, sunken eyes. I saw the heavy chains on his sore legs, the handcuffs that tied him to his fellow prisoner. I saw him lying there on the filthy boards of the ship's floor—there, on the very bottom of the ship.

I felt such pity for my friend that I could barely hold back the tears. I wanted to console him, to send him a kind word, to raise his spirits with some reassuring act.

But how was I to do this?

I took up my mandolin and began to sing softly the song he loved, which he had taught me so patiently long ago.

I wasn't sure that Egor could hear my low singing and the soft sounds of the mandolin. I moved closer to the opening to the hold and sang more loudly. With each word I increased the volume. I wanted to make sure that Egor heard me.

But the hold was not so close and its bottom was deep down. I stole up still closer, leaned forward, stretched my neck, and sang in full voice:

"Oh, eagle, don't fly so close to earth,
Cossack don't walk so close to the shore. . ."

My song was interrupted by a rough shout from the guard.

"Beat it, you singing scum!"

Much else happened to Kolya and Egor. Both continued to struggle against great odds and both were sustained by courage and hope. Kolya became a composer—of songs of protest—but he continued to dream of someday becoming a cellist.

THE COTTAGE IN THE STEPPE

VALENTIN KATAEV

The Cottage in the Steppe is the second in a widely read series of four Soviet novels for young readers by this leading author. They have been published in two volumes, under the general title of *Waves of the Black Sea* (1935–1961).

The background for these four novels is the revolutionary movement in the southern part of Russia, with the city of Odessa, a Black Sea port, as its center. The story is about two friends, boys who witness the cataclysmic events of the period, and who are drawn into them as they grow up. The events are the Revolution of 1905 and its aftermath, the Revolution of 1917, and the Civil War that followed the birth of the Soviet Republic.

Petya is the son of a teacher; Gavrik is the son of a fisherman. The two boys, as well as the other characters, are flesh-and-blood people who react with the complexity of human beings to the unusual circumstances that face them, including political circumstances. There are humor and satire—as well as drama—in the telling of the story, and it rings with the true-to-life quality of autobiography.

The Cottage in the Steppe begins in the year 1910 with the death of the great humanitarian, the world-renowned Russian author, Leo Tolstoy, and ends two years later. The death of Tolstoy sets off a chain of events that permanently changes the lives of Petya and his family and brings them ever closer to the dangerous activities of the local underground groups, led by Gavrik's brother.

Petya is a very busy boy as he keeps up with his demanding studies, helps his father eke out an existence as a fruit farmer in the steppe, assists revolutionaries, and tutors Gavrik in Latin.

The first chapters of the novel are given here.

THE DEATH OF TOLSTOY

Gusts of wind from the sea brought rain and tore the umbrellas from people's hands. The streets were dim gray, and Petya's heart felt just as dreary as that morning.

Even before he reached the familiar corner he saw a small crowd gathered around the newsstand. Stacks of overdue papers had just been dropped off and were being snatched up eagerly. The unfolded pages fluttered in the wind and were instantly spotted by the rain. Some of the men in the crowd removed their hats, and a woman sobbed loudly, dabbing a handkerchief at her eyes.

"So he is dead," Petya thought. He was near enough now to see the wide black border of mourning around the pages and a dark portrait of Leo Tolstoy with his familiar white beard.

Petya was thirteen and, like all young boys, he was terrified by thoughts of death. Whenever someone he knew died, Petya's heart would be gripped by fear, and he would recover slowly, as after a serious illness. Now, however, his fear of death was of an entirely different nature. Tolstoy had not been an acquaintance of theirs. Furthermore, Petya could not conceive of the great man as living the life of an ordinary mortal. Leo Tolstoy was a famous writer, just like Pushkin, Gogol, or Turgenev. In the boy's imagination he was a phenomenon, not a human being. And now this phenomenon was on his deathbed at Astopovo Station,* and the whole world waited with deep grief for the announcement of his death. Petya was caught up in the universal anticipation of an event that seemed incredible and impossible, where the immortal known as "Leo Tolstoy" was concerned. And now that the event had become a reality, Petya was so crushed by the news that he stood motionless, leaning against the wet trunk of an acacia tree.

It was just as mournful and depressing at his school as in the streets. The boys were quiet, there was no running up and down the stairs, and they spoke in whispers as in church at a requiem mass. During recesses they sat around in silence on the window sills. The older boys of the seventh and eighth grades gathered in small groups on the landings and near the cloakroom where they furtively rustled the pages of newspapers, since it was against the rules to bring them to school. Lessons dragged on with maddening monotony. The inspector or one of the assistant principals would look in through the panes of the classroom door, their faces bearing an identical expression

_____
* Leo Tolstoy died at the age of eighty-two, while on a journey.

of cold vigilance. Petya felt that this familiar world of the high school, with the official uniforms and frock coats of the teachers, the light-blue stiff collars of the ushers, the silent corridors where the tiled floor resounded to the click of the inspector's heels, the faint odor of incense near the carved oaken doors of the school chapel on the upper floor, the occasional jangling of a telephone in the office downstairs, and the tinkling of test tubes in the physics laboratory—this was a world utterly remote from the great and terrible thing that Petya knew was taking place beyond the walls of the school, in the city, in Russia, throughout the world.

Petya would look out of the window from time to time, but could see only the familiar uninteresting scene of the streets leading to the railway station. He saw the wet roof of the court building, a beautiful structure with a statue of the blind Themis in front. Beyond was the cupola of the St. Panteleimon Church, the Alexandrovsky district fire tower, and in the distance the damp, gloomy haze of the workers' quarter with its factory chimneys and warehouses, and with a certain leaden darkness on the horizon. After lessons had ended for the day, Petya found himself in the street.

An early twilight descended on the city. Oil lamps lit up the shop windows, throwing sickly yellow streaks of light on the wet pavements. The ghostly elongated shadows of passers-by flitted through the mist. Suddenly there was a sound of singing. Row after row of people with their arms linked were rounding the corner. A hatless student marched in front, pressing a black-framed portrait of Leo Tolstoy to his chest. The damp wind ruffled his fair hair. "You fell a victim in the fight," the student was singing in a defiant tenor above the discordant voices of the crowd.

Both the student and the procession of singing people had suddenly and with great force brought back to Petya a long-forgotten time and street. Then, as now, the pavement had glittered in the mist, and along it marched a crowd of students—mostly men and a few women wearing tiny karakul * hats—and factory workers in high boots. They had sung "You fell a victim." A scrap of red bunting had bobbed over the heads of the crowd. That had been in 1905.** As if to complete the picture, Petya now heard the clickety-clack of horseshoes striking sparks on the wet granite cobbles. A Cossack patrol galloped out of a side street. Their peakless caps were cocked at a rakish angle, and short carbines dangled behind their shoulders. A whip cut the air near Petya and the strong odor of horses' sweat filled his nostrils. In an instant everything was a whirling, shouting, running mass. The Cossacks were dispersing the marchers.

Petya held his cap with both hands as he jumped out of the way. He bumped into something hot. It turned over. He saw that it was a brazier outside the greengrocer's. The hot coals scattered and mixed with the smoking chestnuts. There was no one in the street now.

For days Tolstoy's death was the sole topic of conversation in Russia. Extra editions of the newspapers told the story of Tolstoy's departure from his home in Yasnaya Polyana. Hundreds of telegrams date-lined Astapovo Station described the last hours and minutes of the great writer. The tiny, unknown Astapovo Station became as world-famous as Yasnaya Polyana, and the name of the obscure stationmaster Ozolin, who had taken the dying man into his house, was on everybody's lips. Together with the names of Countess Sofya Andreyevna Tolstoy and Chertkov,† these new names, Astapovo and Ozolin, which accompanied Tolstoy to his grave, were just as frightening to

Petya as the black lettering on the white ribbons of the funeral wreaths.

Petya noted with surprise that this death, which everyone regarded as a "tragedy," apparently had something to do with the government, the Holy Synod, and the police. Whenever he saw the bishop's carriage with a monk sitting on the box next to the coachman, or the clattering *drozhki* * of the chief of police, he was certain that both the bishop and the chief of police were rushing somewhere on urgent business connected with the death of Tolstoy.

Petya had never before seen his father in such a state of mind; he was not just upset, but, rather, exalted and inspired. His usually kind, frank face suddenly became sterner and younger. The hair above his high, classic forehead was combed back student fashion. But the aged, red-rimmed eyes full of tears behind his pince-nez conveyed such grief that Petya's heart ached with pity for him.

Vasily Petrovich came in and put down two stacks of tightly bound exercise books on the table. Before changing into the old jacket he wore about the house, he took a handkerchief from the back pocket of his frock coat with its frayed silk lapels and wiped his wet face and beard thoroughly. Then he said decisively: "Come on, boys, wash your hands and we'll eat! "

Petya sensed his father's mood. He realized that Vasily Petrovich was taking Tolstoy's death badly, that for him Tolstoy was not only an adored writer, he was much more than that: almost the moral center of his life. All this the boy felt keenly, but could not put his feelings into words.

Petya had always responded quickly to his father's moods, and now he was deeply upset. He grew quiet, and his bright inquiring eyes never once left his father's face.

Pavlik, who had recently turned eight and had just become a schoolboy, was oblivious to all that was taking place. He was

---

* *Karakul* is the loosely curled, usually black fur made out of the fleece of newborn lambs.
** This refers to the days preceding the Revolution of 1905.
† *Countess Sofya Andreyevna* was Tolstoy's wife; *Chertkov* was a close friend and associate.

---

* A *drozhki* is an uncovered carriage.

completely absorbed in the affairs of his class and his first impressions of school.

"During our writing lesson today we caused an incident!" he said, pronouncing the difficult word with obvious pleasure. "Old Skeleton ordered Kolya Shapozhnikov to leave the room although he wasn't to blame. Then we all booed with our mouths closed until Skeleton banged so hard on the desk that the inkwell bounced up to the ceiling! "

"Quiet! You should be ashamed of yourself," his father said with a pained look. Suddenly, he burst out, "Heartless brats! You should be whipped! How could you mock an unfortunate, sick teacher whose days are almost numbered? How could you be so brutal?" Then, apparently trying to comment on the matter that had been worrying him all those days, he went on: "Don't you realize that the world cannot live on hate? Hate is contrary to Christianity and to plain common sense. And this at a time when they are laying to rest a man who, perhaps, is the last true Christian on earth."

Father's eyes became redder still. Suddenly he smiled wanly and put his hands on his sons' shoulders. Gazing at each in turn he said:

"Promise me that you will never torture your fellow creatures."

"I never have," Petya said softly.

Pavlik screwed up his face and pressed his close-cropped head against his father's frock coat which smelled singed and faintly of moth balls.

"Daddy, I'll never do it again. We didn't know what we were doing," he said, wiping his eyes with his fist and sniffling.

SKELETON

"It's terrible, say what you like, it's terrible," Auntie said at dinner. She put down the ladle and pressed her fingers to her temples. "You can think what you like about Tolstoy—personally, I look on him as the greatest of writers—but all his nonresistance and vegetarianism are ridiculous, and as for the Russian government, its attitude in the matter is abominable. We are disgraced in the eyes of the whole world! As big a disgrace as Port Arthur or Bloody Sunday." *

---

* In 1904 the Russians were badly beaten by the Japanese in the Battle of Port Arthur.

On *Bloody Sunday,* January 22, 1905, the czar's forces fired on workers who were peacefully marching to the St. Petersburg Palace to petition for reforms; it was the first bloodshed of the emergent Revolution—70 were killed and 240 wounded; the demonstrators were led by a priest, Father Gapon.

"I beg you to—" Father said anxiously.

"No, please don't stop me. We have a dull-witted czar and a dull-witted government! I'm ashamed of being a Russian."

"Stop, I beg you!" Father shouted. His chin jutted forward and his beard shook slightly. "His Majesty's person is sacred. He is above criticism. I won't permit it. Especially in front of the children."

"I'm sorry, I won't do it again," Auntie promised.

"Then let's drop the subject."

"There's just one thing I can't understand, and that is how an intelligent, kindhearted man like you, who loves Tolstoy, can honestly regard as sacred a man who has covered Russia with gallows and who—"

"For God's sake!" Father groaned, "let's not discuss politics. You are an expert at turning any conversation into a political discussion! Can't we talk without getting mixed up in politics?"

"My dear Vasily Petrovich, you still haven't realized that everything in our lives is politics. The government is politics. The church is politics. The schools are politics. Tolstoy is politics."

"How can you talk like that?"

"How can I?"

"Blasphemy! Tolstoy is not politics."

"That's exactly what he is!"

And for a long time, while Petya and Pavlik were doing their homework in the next room, they could hear the excited voices of Father and Auntie, interrupting each other.

Then Father's: "Stop, I beg you! The children can hear us."

Pavlik and Petya were sitting quietly at Father's desk, beside the bronze oil lamp with the green glass lampshade.

Pavlik had finished his homework and was busy putting together his new writing set of which he was still very proud. He was pasting a stencil on his pencil box, patiently rolling up the top layer of wet paper with his finger. A multicolored bouquet of flowers bound with light blue ribbons could be seen through it. He heard the voices in the dining room, but did not pay any attention to them; his mind was full of the scene that had taken place during the writing lesson earlier in the day. The "incident," which at first sight seemed such a daring and funny prank, now appeared in another light altogether. Pavlik could not banish the horrible scene from his mind.

There, at the blackboard, stood the teacher, old Skeleton. He was in the last stages of consumption and was ghastly thin. His blue frock coat hung loosely about his shoulders. It was too long, old, and very worn, but there were new gold buttons on it. The front of his starched shirt bulged on his sunken chest and a skinny neck protruded from the wide greasy collar. Skeleton stood stock-still for a moment or two, challenging the class with his dark eyes. Then he turned swiftly to the blackboard, picked up a piece of chalk with his thin, transparent fingers, and began tracing the letters.

In the ominous quiet they could hear the scratching of the chalk on the slate: a light, delicate touch when he outlined a feathery curlicue and a loud screech as he drew an amazingly straight line at a slant. Skeleton would crouch and then suddenly straighten again, just like a puppet. He'd cock his head to one side, utterly oblivious to his surroundings, and either sing out "stro-o-ke" in a high thin voice, or "line" in a deep rasping one.

"Stroke, line. Stroke, line."

Suddenly a voice from the last row, still higher and as fine as a hair, mimicked, "Stro-o-ke." Skeleton's back twitched, as if he had been stabbed, but he pretended he hadn't heard. He continued writing, but the chalk was already crumbling in his emaciated fingers, and his large shoulder blades jerked painfully beneath the threadbare frock coat.

"Stroke, line. Stroke, line," he sang out and his neck and large ears became crimson.

"Stro-o-oke! Stro-o-oke! Stro-o-oke!" mimicked someone in the last row. All of a sudden Skeleton spun round, walked rapidly down the aisle and grabbed the first boy he could lay hands on. He yanked him up from his desk, dragged him to the door, and threw him out of the classroom. Then he banged the door so hard that the panes rattled and dry putty fell all over the floor.

Skeleton walked back to the blackboard with heavy steps. He was wheezing loudly as he picked up the chalk and was about to continue the lesson. Just then he heard the hum of steady, barely audible booing. Startled, he froze into immobility. His knees trembled visibly. His cuffs and baggy blue trousers trembled too. His black sunken eyes glared at the boys with undisguised hatred. But he had no way of finding out the culprits. They were all booing steadily, monotonously, and imperceptibly. The whole class was booing, but no one could be accused of it. Then a tortured scream of pain and rage broke from his lips. He was jerking like a puppet as he hurled the chalk at the blackboard. It broke into bits. Skeleton stamped his foot. His eyes became bloodshot. His thin hair was plastered to his damp forehead. His neck twitched convulsively and he tore open his collar. He rushed over to his desk, hurled the chair aside, flung the class register against the wall, and began pounding the desk with his fists. He no longer heard his own voice as he shouted, "Devils! Devils!" The inkpot bounced up and down, and the purple liquid stained his loosened shirt front, his bony hands, and damp forehead.

The scene ended when Skeleton, suddenly becoming limp, sat down on the window sill, rested his head against the frame, and was seized with a terrible coughing spell. His deeply sunken temples, almost black eye sockets, and bared yellow teeth made his face look like the skull of a skeleton. Were it not for the sweat streaming down his forehead, one could have easily taken him for a corpse.

That was the picture Pavlik could not banish from his mind. The boy felt terribly upset; however, his mental state in no way interfered with the job at hand. He bestowed special care on pasting the picture, for he did not want to make a hole in the wet paper and spoil the bouquet and light-blue ribbons that looked so bright in the light of the lamp.

Petya, meanwhile, was absent-mindedly leafing through a thick notebook. There were emblems scratched in on the black oilskin cover—an anchor, a heart pierced with an arrow, and several mysterious initials. He was listening attentively to Father and Auntie arguing in the dining room. Some words were repeated more often than others; they were: "freedom of thought," "popular government," "constitution," and, finally, that burning word—"revolution."

"Mark my words, it will all end in another revolution," Auntie said.

"You're an anarchist!" Father shouted shrilly.

"I'm a Russian patriot!"

"Russian patriots have faith in their czar and their government!"

"Have you faith in them?"

"Yes, I have!"

Then Petya heard Tolstoy mentioned once more.

"Then why did this czar and this government in whom you have such faith excommunicate Tolstoy and ban his books?"

"To err is human. They look on Tolstoy as a politician, almost a revolutionary, but Tolstoy is simply the world's greatest writer and the pride of Russia. He is above all your parties and revolutions. I'll prove that in my speech."

"Do you think the authorities will allow you to say that?"

"I don't need permission to say in public that Leo Tolstoy is a great Russian writer."

"That's what *you* think."

"I don't think it—I am absolutely sure!"

"You're an idealist. You don't know the kind of country you're living in. I beg you not to do that! They'll destroy you! Take my word for it."

WHAT IS A RED?!

Petya woke up in the middle of the night and saw Vasily Petrovich sitting at his desk in his shirtsleeves. Petya was used to seeing his father correct exercise books at night. This time, however, Father was doing something else. The stacks of exercise books were lying untouched, and he was writing something rapidly in his fine hand. Little fat volumes of an old edition of Tolstoy's works were scattered about the desk.

"Daddy, what are you writing?"

"Go to sleep, son," Vasily Petrovich said. He walked over to the bed, kissed Petya, and made the sign of the cross over him.

The boy turned his pillow, laid his head on the cool side, and fell asleep again.

Before he dozed off he heard the rapid scratching of a pen, the faint clinking of the little icon at the head of his bed, saw his father's dark head next to the green lampshade, the warm glow of the candle flame in the corner beneath the big icon, and the dry palm branch that cast a mysterious shadow on the wallpaper, bringing to mind, as always, the branch of Palestine, the poor sons of Solim, and the wonderful soothing music of Lermontov's poem:

Peace and silence all around,
On the earth and in the sky. . . .

Next morning, while Vasily Petrovich was busy washing, combing his hair, and fastening a black tie to a starched collar, Petya had a chance to see what his father had been writing during the night.

An ancient homemade exercise book sewn together with coarse thread lay on the desk. Petya recognized it immediately. Its usual place was in Father's bureau, next to the other family relics: the yellowed wedding candles, a spray of orange blossom, his dead mother's white kid gloves and little bead bag, her tiny mother-of-pearl opera glasses, some dried leaves of a wild pear tree that grew on Lermontov's grave, and a collection of odds and ends, which in Petya's view were just junk, but to Vasily Petrovich very precious.

Petya had leafed through the exercise book once before. Half of it was taken up with a speech Vasily Petrovich had written

on the hundredth anniversary of Pushkin's birth; there had not been anything in the other half. The boy now saw that a new speech filled up this yellowed half of the book. It was written in the same fine hand, and its subject was Tolstoy's death. This is how it began:

"A great Russian writer is dead. Our literary sun has set."

Vasily Petrovich put on a pair of new cuffs and his best hollow-gold cuff links, carefully folded the exercise book in two and put it in his side pocket. Petya watched his father drink a quick glass of tea and then proceed to the hall where he put on his heavy coat with the frayed velvet collar. The boy noticed that his fingers were trembling and his pince-nez was shaking on his nose. For some reason, Petya suddenly felt terribly sorry for his father. He went over to him and brushed against his coatsleeve, as he used to do when he was a very small boy.

"Never mind, we'll show them yet!" Father said and patted his son's back.

"I still advise you against it," Auntie said solemnly as she looked into the hall.

"You're wrong," Vasily Petrovich replied in a soft tremulous voice. He put on his wide-brimmed black hat and went out quickly.

"God grant that I am wrong!" Auntie sighed. "Come on, boys, stop wasting time or you'll be late for school," she added and went over to help Pavlik, her favorite, buckle his satchel on his back, as he had not yet mastered the fairly simple procedure.

The day passed—a short and, at the same time, an interminably long and dreary November day, full of vague feelings of expectation, furtive rumor, and endless repetition of the same agonizing words: "Chertkov," "Sofya Andreyevna," "Astapovo," "Ozolin."

It was the day of Tolstoy's funeral.

Petya had spent all his life on the southern sea coast, in the Novorossiisk steppe region, and had never seen a forest. But now he had a very clear mental picture of

Yasnaya Polyana, of woods fringing an overgrown ravine. In his mind's eye Petya saw the black trunks of the ancient, leafless lindens, and the plain pine coffin containing the withered old body of Leo Tolstoy being lowered into the grave, without priest or choir boys attending. And overhead the boy could see the ominous clouds and flocks of crows.

As usual, Father returned from his classes when the lamp had been lit in the dining room. He was excited, happy, and deeply moved. When Auntie, not without anxiety, asked him whether he had delivered his speech and what the reaction had been, Vasily Petrovich could not restrain the proud smile that flashed radiantly beneath his pince-nez.

"You could have heard a pin drop," he said taking his handkerchief out of his back pocket and wiping his damp beard. "I never expected the young rascals to respond so eagerly and seriously. And that goes for the young ladies too. I repeated it for the seventh grade of the Marynsky School."

"Were you actually given permission to do so?"

"I didn't ask anyone's permission. Why should I? I hold that the literature teacher is fully entitled to discuss with his class the personality of any famous Russian writer, especially when the writer in question happens to be Tolstoy. What is more, I believe that it is my duty to do so."

"You're so reckless."

Later in the evening some young people, strangers to the family, dropped in: two students in very old, faded caps, and a young woman who also seemed to be a student. One of the youths sported a crooked pince-nez on a black ribbon, wore top boots, smoked a cigarette and emitted the smoke through his nostrils; the young woman had on a short jacket and kept pressing her little chapped hands to her bosom. For some reason or other they were reluctant to come into the rooms and remained in the hall talking with Vasily Petrovich for a long time. The deep, rumbling bass seemed to belong to the student with the pince-nez, and the pleading, lisping voice of the young woman kept repeating the same phrase over and over again at regular intervals: "We feel certain that as a progressive and noble-minded person and public figure, you won't refuse the student body this humble request."

The third visitor kept wiping his wet shoes shyly on the door mat and blowing his nose discreetly.

It turned out that news of Vasily Petrovich's talk had somehow reached the Higher Courses for Women and the Medical School of the Imperial University in Odessa, and the student delegation had come to express their solidarity and also to request him to repeat his lecture to a Social-Democratic student circle. Vasily Petrovich, while flattered, was unpleasantly surprised. He thanked the young people but categorically refused to address the Social-Democratic circle. He told them that he had never belonged to any party and had no intention of ever joining one; and he added that he would regard any attempt to turn Tolstoy's death into something political as a mark of disrespect toward the great writer, as Tolstoy's abhorence of all political parties and his negative attitude to politics generally were common knowledge.

"If that's the case, then please excuse us," the young lady said dryly. "We are greatly disappointed in you. Comrades, let's go."

The young people departed with dignity, leaving behind the odor of cheap tobacco and wet footprints on the doorstep.

"What an astonishing thing!" Vasily Petrovich said as he strode up and down the dining room, wiping his pince-nez on the lining of his house jacket. "It's really astonishing how people always find an excuse to talk politics!"

"I warned you," Auntie said. "And I'm afraid the consequences will be serious."

Auntie's premonition turned out to be correct, although the results were not as immediate as she had expected. At least a month went by before the trouble began. Actually, the approaching events cast a few shadows before them. However, they seemed so vague that the Bachei family paid little attention to them.

"Daddy, what's a 'red'?" Pavlik asked unexpectedly, as was his habit, at dinner one day, his naive eyes fixed on Father.

"Really, now!" Vasily Petrovich said. He was in excellent spirits. "It's a somewhat strange question. I'd say that red means . . . well—not blue, yellow, not brown, h'm, and so on."

"I know that. But I'm talking about people; are there red people?"

"Oh, so that's what you mean! Of course there are. Take the North American Indians, for example, the so-called redskins."

"They haven't got to that yet in their primary class," Petya said haughtily. "They're still infants."

Pavlik ignored the insult. He kept his eyes on Father and asked: "Daddy, does that mean you're an Indian?"

"Basically, no." Father laughed so loudly and boisterously that the pince-nez fell off his nose and nearly landed in his soup.

"Then why did Fedya Pshenichnikov say you were a red?"

"Oho! That's interesting. Who is this Fedya Pshenichnikov?"

"He's in my class. His father is senior clerk in the Governor's office in Odessa."

"Well! If that's the case, then perhaps your Fedya knows best. However, I think you can see for yourself that I'm not red; the only time I ever get red is during severe frost."

"I don't like it," Auntie commented.

Not long afterward a certain Krylevich, the bookkeeper of the mutual aid society at the boys' school where Vasily Petrovich taught, dropped in one evening to see him about some savings bank matters. When they had disposed of this, Krylevich, whom Vasily Petrovich had always found to be an unpleasant person, remained for tea. He stayed for an hour and a half, was incredibly boring, and kept turning the conversation to Tolstoy, praising Vasily for his courage, and begging him for his notes, saying he wanted to read them at home. Father refused, and his refusal upset Krylevich.

Standing in front of the mirror in the hall, putting on his flat, greasy cap with the cockade of the Ministry of Education, he said with a sugary smile: "I'm sorry you don't want to give me the pleasure, really sorry. Your modesty is worse than pride."

His visit left a nasty aftertaste.

There were other minor happenings of the same order; for instance, some of their acquaintances would greet Vasily in the street with exaggerated politeness, while others, on the contrary, were unusually curt and made no attempt to conceal their disapproval.

Then, just before Christmas, the storm broke.

A HEAVY BLOW

Pavlik, who had just been "let out" for the holidays, was walking up and down in front of the house in his overlong winter topcoat —meant to last several seasons—and his new galoshes, which made such a pleasant crunching sound and left such first-rate dotted prints with an oval trade mark in the middle on the fresh December snow. His report card for the second quarter was in his bag. His marks were excellent, there were no unpleasant reprimands and he even had "excellent" for attention, diligence, and behavior, which, to tell the truth, was overdoing it a bit. But, thanks to his innocent chocolate-brown crystal-clear eyes, Pavlik had the happy knack of always landing on his feet.

The boy's mood fit the holiday season, and only one tiny little worm of anxiety wriggled down in the deep recesses of his soul.

The trouble was that today, after the last lesson, the class, throwing caution to the winds, had organized another "incident." This time they took revenge on the doorman who had refused to let them out before the bell rang. The boys got together and tossed somebody's galosh into the cast-iron stove that stood next to the cloakroom, with the result that a column of acrid smoke rose up, and the doorman had to flood the stove with water. At that moment the bell rang, and the class scattered in a body. Now Pavlik was worried that the inspector might get to know about their prank, and that it would lead to serious complications. This was the sole blot in his feeling of pure joy at the thought of the holidays ahead.

Suddenly Pavlik saw what he feared most. A messenger was coming down the street and heading straight for him; he wore a cap with a blue band and his coat was trimmed with a lambskin collar. He was carrying a large cardboard-bound register under his arm. The messenger walked up leisurely to the gate, looked at the triangular lamp with the house number underneath it, and stopped. Pavlik's heart sank.

"Where do the Bacheis live?" the messenger asked.

Pavlik realized that his end had come. There could be no doubt that this was an official note to his father concerning the be-

havior of Pavel Bachei, primary-class pupil —in other words, the most dreadful fate that could befall a schoolboy.

"What is it? Do they want Father?" Pavlik asked with a sickly smile. He did not recognize his own voice and blushed a deep crimson as he added, "You can give it to me; I'll deliver it and you won't have to climb the stairs!"

"I must have his signature," the messenger said sternly, curling his big mustache.

"Second floor, number four," Pavlik whispered and felt hot, choked, nauseous, and scared to death.

It never dawned on the boy that the messenger was a stranger. And in any case, this being his first year at school, he could not possibly know all its personnel.

The moment the front door closed after the messenger the light went out for Pavlik. The world with all its beauty and freshness no longer existed for him. It had vanished in an instant. The crimson winter sun was setting beyond the blue-tinted snow-covered Kulikovo Field and the station; the bells of the frozen cab horse around the corner tinkled as musically as ever; the pots of hot cranberry jelly, set out on the balconies to cool, were steaming as usual; the coat of delicate pale-blue snow on the balcony railings and the steam curling over the pots seemed as cranberry-red as the cooling jelly itself; the street, full of the holiday spirit, was as gay and as lively as ever.

But Pavlik no longer noticed any of this. At first he made up his mind that he would never go home again; he would roam the streets until he died of hunger or froze to death. Then, after he had walked around the side streets, he took a sacred vow to change his whole way of life and never, never take part in any "incidents" again; moreover, he would be a model pupil, the best-behaved boy not only in Odessa, but in all Russia, and thus earn Father's and Auntie's forgiveness. Then he began to feel sorry for himself, for his ruined life, and even started to cry, smearing the tears all over his face. In the end pangs of hunger drove him home, and, utterly exhausted with suffering, he appeared on the threshold after the lamps had been lit. Pavlik was ready to confess and repent when he suddenly noticed that the whole family was in a state of great excitement. The excitement, apparently, had nothing at all to do with the person of Pavlik, as no one paid the slightest attention to him when he came in.

The dining room table had not been cleared. Father was striding from room to room, his shoes squeaking loudly and his coattails flying. There were red spots on his face.

"I told you. I warned you," Auntie kept repeating, as she swung back and forth on the swivel stool in front of the piano with its wax-spotted silver candlesticks.

Petya was breathing on the window pane and etching with his finger the words, "Dear sir, Dear sir."

It turned out that the messenger had been from the office of the Education Department and had nothing to do with Pavlik's school at all. He had delivered a message to Councillor Bachei, requesting him to appear the following day "to explain the circumstances which prompted him to deliver an unauthorized speech to his students on the occasion of Count Tolstoy's death."

When Vasily Petrovich returned from the Education Department next day, he sat down in the rocker in his frock coat and folded his arms behind his head. The moment Petya saw his pale forehead and trembling jaw, he knew something terrible had happened.

Father was reclining on the wicker back of the chair and rocking nervously, shoving off with the toe of his squeaking shoe.

"Vasily Petrovich, for God's sake, tell me what happened!" Auntie said finally, her kind eyes wide with fright.

"Please, leave me alone!" Father said with an effort, and his jaw twitched more violently.

His pince-nez had slid down, and Petya saw two tiny pink dents on the bridge of his nose which gave his face the appearance of helpless suffering. The boy recalled that he had had this same look when Mother had died and lay in a white coffin covered with hyacinths; then, too, Father had rocked back and forth nervously, arms folded behind his head, his eyes filled with tears. Petya walked over to Father, put his arms around his shoulders, which bore faint traces of dandruff, and hugged him.

"Daddy, don't!" he said gently.

Father shook the boy's arms off, jumped up, and gesticulated so violently that his starched cuffs popped out with a snap.

"In the name of Our Lord Jesus Christ— leave me alone!" he shouted in an agonized voice and fled into the room that was both his study and bedroom and the boys' room as well.

He took off his jacket and shoes, lay down and turned his face to the wall.

At the sight of Father lying huddled up, of his white socks and the blue steel buckle on the crumpled back of his waistcoat, Petya broke down and began to cry, wiping his tears on his sleeve.

What actually had taken place at the Education Department? To begin with, Vasily Petrovich had spent a long and uncomfortable time sitting alone in the cold, officially sumptuous waiting room on a gilded blue velvet chair, the kind usually seen in museums or theater lobbies. Then a dandified official in the uniform of the Ministry of Education appeared, his figure reflected in the parquet floor, and informed Vasily Petrovich that His Excellency would see him.

His Excellency was sitting behind an enormous writing desk. He was hunchbacked and, like most hunchbacks, was very short, so that nothing could be seen of him above the massive malachite desk set with two bronze malachite candelabra, except a proud, malicious head, iron gray and closely cropped, propped up by a high starched collar and white tie. He was wearing his formal civil service dresscoat with decorations.

"Why did you take the liberty of appearing here without your uniform?" His Excellency demanded, without offering the caller a seat or getting up himself.

Vasily Petrovich was taken aback, but when he tried to picture his old uniform with the rows of holes where Petya had once yanked the buttons off together with the cloth, he smiled good-naturedly, to his own surprise, and even waved his hands somewhat humorously.

"I would request you not to act the clown. Don't wave your arms about: you are in an office, not on the stage."

"My dear sir!" Vasily Petrovich said as the blood rushed to his face.

"Silence!" barked the official in the best departmental manner, as he crashed his fist down on a pile of papers. "I am a member of the Privy Council, 'Your Excellency' to you, not 'my dear sir'! Be good enough to remember where you are and sta-a-and at ATTENTION! I summoned you to present you with an alternative," he continued, pronouncing the word "alternative" with evident relish, "to present you with an alternative: either publicly recant your baleful errors in the presence of the School Inspector and the students at one of the next lessons, and explain the demoralizing effects of Count Tolstoy's teachings on Russian society, or hand in your resignation. Should you refuse to do so, you will be discharged under Article 3, with no explanation and with all the unfortunate consequences as far as you are concerned. I will not tolerate antigovernment propaganda in my district. I will mercilessly and unhesitatingly suppress every instance of it."

"Allow me, Your Excellency!" Vasily Petrovich said in a trembling voice. "Leo Tolstoy, our famous man of letters, is the pride and glory of all Russia. I don't understand. What have politics got to do with it?"

"First of all, Count Tolstoy is an apostate, excommunicated from the Orthodox Church by the Holy Synod. He is a man who dared to encroach upon the most sacred principles of the Russian Empire and its fundamental laws. If you cannot grasp this, then government service is not the place for you!" *

"I regard that as an insult," Vasily Petrovich said with great difficulty, as he felt his jaw begin to tremble.

"Get out!" roared the official, rising.

Vasily Petrovich left the office with his knees shaking, a shaking that he could not control either on the marble staircase, where in two white niches there were two gypsum busts of the czar and the czarina in a pearl tiara, or in the cloakroom, where a massive attendant threw his coat to him over the counter, or even later, in the cab, a luxury the Bachei family indulged in only on very special occasions.

And so here he was, lying on the bed with his feet tucked up under him, deeply insulted, powerless, humiliated, and overwhelmed by the misfortune that had befallen not only him personally but, as he now realized, his whole family as well. To be discharged under Article 3 with no grounds stated meant more than the black list and social ostracism; it signified in all probability an administrative exile, that is, utter ruin, poverty, and the end of the family. There was only one way out—a public recantation.

By nature Vasily Petrovich was neither hero nor martyr. He was an ordinary, kind-hearted, intelligent man, a decent, honest intellectual, the kind known as an "idealist," and a "pure soul." As a university

---

* Petya's father was a teacher of literature at a government school.

man, tradition would not allow him to retreat. In his opinion a "bargain with one's conscience" was the extreme of moral degradation. But nevertheless, he wavered. The pit they had dug for him so ruthlessly would not bear thinking about. He realized that there was no way out, although he tried to think of one.

Vasily Petrovich was so disheartened that he even decided to petition the Emperor and sent for ten kopeks' worth of the best "ministerial" stationery from the shop around the corner. He still adhered to his belief that the czar, the Lord's Anointed, was just and upright.

Perhaps he would actually have written to him, had it not been for the fact that at this juncture Auntie took a hand in the matter. She told the cook on no account to go for any "ministerial" stationery, and addressing herself to Vasily Petrovich, said: "My God, what an innocent you are! Don't you understand that the czar is at the head of the whole bunch?"

Vasily Petrovich blinked in confusion and kept repeating, "But what's to be done, Tatyana Ivanovna? Tell me, what can I do?"

Auntie, however, had no advice to offer. She retreated to her little room next to the kitchen, sat down at her dressing table, and pressed a crumpled lace handkerchief to her red nose.

REQUIEM

It was Christmas Eve, the twenty-fourth of December, a day that had a special meaning for the Bachei family. It was the day of Mother's patron saint. Every year on that day they visited the cemetery to offer up a mass for the dead. They set out today too. There was a blizzard blowing and the blinding whiteness hurt their eyes. The snowdrifts at the cemetery blended with the white of the sky. Fine, powdery snow crystals fell on the black iron railings and crosses. The wind whistled through old metal wreaths with porcelain flowers. Petya stood knee-deep in the fresh snow. He had taken off his cap, but still had on a hood. He was praying diligently, trying to visualize his dead mother, but could recall only insignificant details: a hat with a feather in it, a veil, the hem of a wide silk dress with a fringe on it. Two kind eyes were smiling at him through the dotted veil tied under her chin. That was all Petya could remember. There was a faint trace of a long past grief that time had healed, the fear of his own death, and the gold letters of Mother's name on the white marble slab from which the sexton had carelessly brushed the snow just before they had arrived. Next to it was Grandma's grave, and there was a vacant place between the two graves where, as Vasily Petrovich was wont to say, he would one day be laid at rest between his mother and his wife, the two women he had loved so faithfully and steadfastly.

Petya crossed himself and bowed at the proper moments; he kept thinking about his mother, and, at the same time, observed the priest, the psalm-reader, Father, Pavlik, and Auntie. Pavlik was fidgeting all the time; the turned-up hood irritated his ears and he kept tugging at it. Auntie was weeping into her muff quietly. Father stood with eyes fixed on the tombstone, his folded hands held humbly before him and his graying head bent low. Petya knew Father was thinking about Mother. But he had no idea of the terrible conflict raging within him. Especially now did Vasily Petrovich miss her, her love, and her moral support. He thought of the day when he, an eager young man, had read to her his essay on Pushkin, of how they had both discussed it long and heatedly, of the glorious morning when he had put on his new uniform and was standing in the hall ready to set out to read his essay, and she had handed him his freshly pressed handkerchief, still warm from the hot iron, kissed him fondly, and crossed him with her thin fingers; and afterward, when he had returned home in triumph, they had had a hearty dinner and little Petya, whom they were training to be an independent young man, had smeared his porridge all over his fat cheeks and kept repeating, "Daddy! Eat!" his black eyes sparkling. How long ago, and yet, how close it all seemed! Now Vasily Petrovich had to decide his fate alone.

For the first time in his life he understood clearly something that he either could not or refused to understand before: that it was impossible in Russia to be an honest and independent person if one held a government job. One had to be a docile czarist official, with no views of one's own, and obey the orders of other officials—one's superiors—unquestioningly, no matter how unjust or even criminal they might be. But worst of all, as far as Vasily Petrovich was concerned, was the fact that the one responsible for this state of affairs was none other than the Russian czar himself, the Anointed of the Lord, in whose sanctity and infallibility Vasily Petrovich had trusted so deeply and implicitly.

Now that this trust had been shaken, Vasily turned wholeheartedly to religion.

He offered up prayers for his dead wife and implored divine help and guidance. But his prayers no longer brought him consolation. He crossed himself, bowed low, and yet somehow or other he seemed to see the priest and psalm-reader, who were rushing through the service, in a new and different light. Their words and actions no longer created the religious atmosphere of former years, but, instead, seemed crude, unnatural, as if Vasily Petrovich himself was not praying, but only observing two shamans performing some rite. That which formerly had moved him deeply was now bereft of its poetry.

The priest, in a mourning chasuble of brocade with a silver cross embroidered on the back, his short arms wrapped in the dark sleeves of a protruding tunic, was chanting the beautiful words of the requiem as he deftly swung the censer to and fro, making the hot coals glow like rubies. Purple smoke poured from it, turned gray quickly and melted in the wind, leaving the air heavy with incense.

The psalm-reader had an enormous mustache and his winter overcoat was exactly like Vasily Petrovich's, even to the frayed velvet collar. His bulging eyes were reverently half closed, and his voice rose and fell as he quickly echoed the priest's singing. Both priest and psalm-reader made a pretense of not hurrying, although Vasily Petrovich could see they were rushing the service, as they had to officiate at other graves where they were eagerly awaited and whence impatient relatives were already signaling to them. Their relief was evident when they finally reached the last part and put all their energy behind the words "the tears at the grave turn to singing," etc.; after which the Bachei family kissed the cold silver cross, and while the psalm-reader was hurriedly wrapping it up in his stole, Vasily Petrovich shook the priest's hand and awkwardly pressed two silver rubles into his palm. The priest said, "I thank you!" and added, "I hear that you're having trouble with the Education Department. Have faith in the Lord, perhaps there is a way out. Good-bye for the present. Dreadful weather, isn't it? A regular blizzard."

Vasily Petrovich had caught a faint trace of insult in those words. Petya saw his face turn red. Suddenly there flashed into Vasily Petrovich's mind the Education Department official scolding and his own humiliating fear, and once again the feeling of pride, which until then he had tried so hard to subordinate to Christian humility, welled up in him. At that moment he decided that not for anything in the world would he surrender, and if necessary he would suffer all the consequences for the sake of Truth.

However, once they had returned home from the cemetery and he had calmed down a little, his former doubts returned: Had he the right to jeopardize his family?

Meanwhile, the school holidays pursued their usual course, the only difference being that this time they were not as jolly or as carefree as in previous years.

Tedious and tiresome as usual was the waiting for nightfall on Christmas Eve; appetizing smells drifted in from the kitchen while they awaited the appearance of the first star in the window—the signal to light the lamps and sit down to dinner and Christmas pudding. They had the usual Christmas party next day, and carol singers came in carrying a star hung with tinsel and a round paper icon in the center. Blue diamonds of moonlight glittered festively and mysteriously on the frosted window panes, and on New Year's Eve there was apple pie with a new silver coin hidden in it for good luck. The regimental bands played as usual in the clear, frosty noonday for the Twelfth-Day parade on Cathedral Square.

The holidays were coming to an end. Some kind of decision had to be made. Vasily Petrovich became despondent, and his depression affected the boys. Auntie alone tried to keep up the holiday spirit. She put on a new silk dress, and all her favorite rings were brought out to adorn her slender fingers; she smelled of "Coeur de Jeanette" perfume, and she would sit at the piano, open a large folio, and play Madame Vyaltseva's repertoire of waltzes, polkas, and gipsy serenades. On Twelfth-Day Eve she decided to have the traditional fortune-telling. They poured cold water into a basin and dropped melted paraffin into it, as they had no wax, and then interpreted the various shapes it froze into; in the kitchen they burned balls of crumpled paper and then told the meaning of the shadows cast by them on the freshly whitewashed wall. But there was something strained in all this.

THE RESIGNATION

Late at night, the last night of the school holidays, Petya, who was drowsing off to sleep, again heard Father and Auntie talking heatedly in the dining room.

"You cannot and you must not do such a thing!" Auntie was saying in an excited voice.

"What then?" Father asked, and there was a sharp click as he cracked his knuckles. "What shall I do? How shall we live? Have I the right to do this? What a tragedy that Zhenya is no longer with us!"

"Believe me, if Zhenya were here now, she would never let you grovel before these officials!"

Petya soon fell asleep and did not hear

any more, but an astonishing thing happened the next morning: for the first time in his life Vasily Petrovich did not put on his frock coat and did not go to his classes. Instead, the cook was sent to the shop for "ministerial" stationery, and Vasily Petrovich wrote out his resignation in his clear flowing hand, unadorned by flourishes or curlicues.

His resignation was accepted coldly. However, there was no further unpleasantness; apparently, it was not in the interests of the Education Department to have the story spread around. And so, Vasily Petrovich found himself out of a job, the most terrible thing that could happen to a family man with no other means of support except his salary.

Vasily Petrovich had put aside a little money a long time ago; he had dreamed of going abroad with his wife, and then, after her death, with his boys. Now that dream evaporated. This money, together with what he would get from the mutual aid society, would see the family through the next year, if they lived frugally. But it was still a mystery how they were to exist after that, especially as another question arose: How were Petya and Pavlik to continue at the school? As the sons of a teacher they had been exempt from tuition fees; now, however, he would have to pay out of their meager budget a sum that was beyond his means.

But worst of all, where Vasily Petrovich was concerned, was his enforced idleness, for he had been used to work all his life. He did not know what to do with himself and hung around the house for days on end in his old jacket, forgetting to go to the barber, looking older every day, and making frequent visits to the cemetery, where he spent long hours at his wife's grave.

Pavlik, still too young to be touched by the terrible thing that had befallen them, continued his former carefree existence. But Petya understood everything. The thought that he would have to leave school, remove the cockade from his cap, and wear his uniform with hooks instead of shiny metal buttons, as was the case with boys who had been expelled or had not matriculated, made him blush with shame. Things were aggravated by an ominous change in the attitude of the teachers and some of his classmates.

In short, the New Year could not have begun worse. Petya was most unhappy and was amazed to see that Auntie, far from being upset or downhearted, gave the impression of everything being fine. There was a look of determination in her eyes, which implied that she was going to save the family at all costs.

Her plan was as follows: she would serve tasty, nourishing, and inexpensive home-cooked meals to working intellectuals, which, in her opinion, would yield enough to keep the family in food. In order to add to the income, Auntie decided to move into the dining room, move the cook into the kitchen, and rent out the two rooms, thus vacated, with board.

Father winced painfully at the mere thought of his home being turned into an "eating house," but as there was no other way out, he gave in.

"Do whatever you think best," he said.

That was Auntie's green light. "To let" notices that could be read clearly from the street were posted on the windows of the two rooms. On the gatepost they nailed a little board that said: "Dinners served." It had been done artistically in oils by Petya, and depicted a steaming tureen with the inscription mentioning single, working intellectuals. Auntie believed that this would impart a social, political, and even an opposition note to their commercial undertaking. She began to buy new kitchen utensils and put in a stock of the best and freshest foods; she had a new calico dress and snow-white apron made for Dunyasha, the maid, and spent most of her time studying the Molokhovets Cookery Book, that bible of every well-to-do home. She copied the most useful recipes into a special notebook and made up tasty and nourishing menus.

Never before had the Bachei family eaten so well—or, rather feasted so. After a month's time they had all put on weight, including Father, a fact that seemed strangely at variance with his status of a man persecuted by the government.

All would have gone well, perhaps even brilliantly, had it not been for the lack of customers. One might have thought that all the working intellectuals had agreed never to dine again.

True, the first few days brought some customers. Two well-dressed bearded gentlemen with sunken cheeks and a fanatical glitter in their eyes called, discovered that there were no vegetarian dishes on the menu, and stamped out without bothering to say good-bye.

Then a brash orderly in a peakless cap, serving in the Modlinsky Regiment, came in at the back door and asked for two portions of cabbage soup for his officer. Auntie explained that there was no cabbage soup on the menu, but that there was *soupe printanière*. That, said the soldier, was quite all right with him, provided there was plenty of bread to go with it, as his gentleman had lost all his money at cards and has been sitting in his quarters with a bad cold and nothing hot in his stomach for nearly two days. Auntie gave him two portions of *soupe printanière* and plenty of bread on credit, and the orderly scurried down the stairs on his short, thick legs in worndown boots, leaving the heavy odor of an infantry barracks in the kitchen. Two days later he appeared again; this time he carried off two portions of bouillon and meat patties—also on credit— and promised to pay as soon as his gentleman won back his money; apparently, his gentleman never did, because the soldier disappeared for good.

No one else came to dine.

As far as letting the two rooms was con-cerned, things were not much better. The very day they put the little cards in the window a newlywed couple made inquiries: he was a young army surgeon, and everything he had on was new and resplendent; she was a plump, dimpled blonde with a beauty mark over her Cupid's-bow lips, wearing a squirrel-lined cloak and pert bonnet, and carrying a tiny muff on a cord. They seemed to be the personification of happiness. Their new, twenty-four carat gold wedding rings shone so dazzlingly, they were surrounded by such a fragrant aroma of scented soap, cold cream, brilliantine, hair tonic, and Brokar perfume—the mixture of which seemed to Petya the very essence of newly-weddedness—that the Bachei flat with its old wallpaper and poorly-waxed floors suddenly appeared to be small, shabby, and dark.

While the young couple was looking over the rooms, the husband never once let go of his wife's arm, as if he were afraid she'd run off somewhere; the wife, in turn, pressed close to him as she looked around in horror and exclaimed in a loud singsong voice, "Dahling, it's a bahn! It's a real bahn! It smells like a kitchen! No, no, it's not at all what we're looking for!"

They left hurriedly. The army surgeon's silver spurs tinkled delicately, and the young wife raised her skirts squeamishly and stepped gingerly as if afraid to soil her tiny new shoes. It was only after the downstairs door had banged behind them that Petya realized the strange foreign word "bahn" was just plain "barn," and he felt so hurt he could have cried. Auntie's ears were still burning long after they had gone.

No one else came to see the rooms. And so Auntie's plans failed. The specter of poverty again rose up before the Bachei family. Despair banished all hopes. Who knows what the outcome would have been, if salvation had not come one fine day—out of the blue, as it always does. . . .

ALIEN BLOOD

MIKHAIL SHOLOKHOV

This is one of the *Tales from the Don,* a collection of short stories published at the beginning of Sholokhov's writing career, about forty years ago. It is regarded as one of his best. This Soviet writer has been awarded the Nobel Prize in Literature for 1965 for his novels, *Quiet Flows the Don* and *The Don Flows Down to the Sea.* These novels, as well as all the stories in *Tales from the Don,* are about the Cossacks of the Don River region and the violent years during and immediately after the Revolution of 1917.

The first snow fell early that year, in the beginning of November. The wind blew up from the Don at night, rustling the tall bleached-red steppe grass, sweeping the shaggy snowdrifts into smooth waves of down, and licking bare the hillocks edging the roads.

The night enveloped the village in a dusk-like green quietude. And beyond its homesteads dozed the overgrown, unplowed steppe.

At midnight a wolf howled on the steep riverbank, village dogs responded, and old Gavrila woke up. He sat up, dropped his legs down over the edge of the stove,* and, leaning against the chimney wall, he coughed and coughed, spat, then reached for his tobacco pouch.

Every night the old man would wake before dawn, would smoke, cough, force the phlegm hoarsely from his lungs, and between fits of coughing his thoughts followed their customary, well-trodden path. He thought of only one thing—his son, lost in the war without a trace.

He had been an only son, the first and the last. Gavrila had toiled for him, never allowing his hands to be idle. Then the time

had come to see him off to do battle against the Reds. The old man had taken two pairs of bullocks to market and with the money he got for them bought a military service horse from a Kalmik. It wasn't a mere horse, but a veritable tearing steppe storm! Then Gavrila got out a saddle from the family chest and his grandfather's bridle inlaid with silver. Before the parting, the old man said to his son:

"Well, Pyotr, I've fixed you up proper, haven't I? Even an officer wouldn't be ashamed to be outfitted like this. Go and serve as your father has done, don't disgrace your Cossack army and the Quiet Don. Your grandfathers and great-grandfathers all served the czar, and you must do likewise!"

The old man gazed now at the window shimmering with the green reflections of moonlight, listened to the wind rolling along outside and, awaiting the impossible, remembered the days that had passed and would never return.

The Cossacks had gathered in Gavrila's hut to send off the recruits. They had thundered out, under the reed-thatched roof of his house, an old Cossack song:

> Fighting, we never violate battle order,
> And we obey but one command
> Of our elders, our commanders—
> With saber, bayonet, and gun.

---

* In peasant huts in old Russia, an alcove over the kitchen stove served as a place for sleeping.

Gavrila remembered Pyotr as he had sat at the table, tipsy, his face shadowed with a bluish pallor, drinking his last glass, the "stirrup" glass, his eyes narrowed with weariness. But he had later sat firmly on his horse, and, after adjusting his Cossack hat, had leaned down to pick up a handful of earth from his ancestral land before departing. But where lay he now? What earth, in what stranger's land, was now warming him?

The old man coughed a persistent, dry cough, the bellows of his chest wheezing and ringing out in various tones, and between coughs he leaned his stooped back against the chimney wall as his thoughts moved along their customary, well-trodden path.

He had seen his son off. Within a month the Reds had come. They had invaded the long-established Cossack way of life as enemies, turning the old man's existence inside out, like an empty pocket. Pyotr was then fighting on the other side of the front, near the Donetz, where he had won a sergeant's stripes through his zeal in battle, while old Gavrila trained, tended, and nursed a dull hatred for the Reds as he had formerly trained, tended, and nursed his love for his towheaded young son.

To spite the Reds, Gavrila wore his traditional, baggy Cossack trousers, with the crimson stripe sewn on along the side of the trouser leg with black stitches, a symbol of Cossack independence. He wore his Cossack peasant overcoat with its orange braid, showing that he had served in a guards regiment, and still displaying the marks of a quartermaster's stripes. He hung on his chest all the medals and crosses he had received for his service to the monarch "in faith and in truth," and on Sundays, on his way to church, he wore his sheepskin wide open so that everyone could see these decorations.

The chairman of the village Soviet,* meeting him one day, said casually:

"Take those trinkets off, old man. They are not allowed now."

The old man flared like gunpowder:

"Tell me, did you hang them on me that you think you have the right to tell me to remove them?"

"Those who pinned them on you have probably long since been feeding the worms."

"So, let them. But I'll not take them off. Would you pull them off the dead?"

"What makes you say that! Here, I feel sorry for you and give you good advice, and you. . . . You can sleep in them for all I care. But watch out for the dogs, they'll go for your pants; they're no longer used to all that fancy trimming and won't recognize it for what it is."

That insult was as bitter as wormwood in bloom. Gavrila took off the decorations, but the feeling of injury grew in his soul, and flourished into something akin to hatred.

With his son vanished, there was no posterity to work for. Gavrila had allowed the shed to tumble down, the cattle had knocked down the fence, the rafters of the sheep shed had rotted after the storm had loosened its doors. In the empty stalls of the stable the mice now kept house, and the mower went rusty lying outside under the eaves of the shed.

The Cossacks had taken his horses with them when they fled from the Reds, and the Reds took whatever was left, giving him in exchange a shaggy-legged and long-eared animal whom the Makhno men ** later, in

---

* A *soviet* is a council or body of delegates. In the Soviet Union, it is any of the various governing councils, local, intermediate, and national, elected by and representing the people.

** *Makhno men* were bands of Cossacks fighting and marauding during the Civil War that followed the Revolution of 1917, under the leadership of the notorious Cossack bandit, Makhno.

the autumn, "bought" at first sight, giving old Gavrila in payment a pair of English puttees.

"We'll pass them on to you," the Makhno machine gunner had said with a wink. "Grow rich on this treasure, old man."

Everything Gavrila had accumulated over the years had gone up in smoke. His hands went limp and refused to work. But in the spring, when the barren steppe lay underfoot, humble and spent, the earth beckoned to the old man, called to him at night with an insistent, inaudible call. Unable to resist it, he harnessed the bullocks to the plow and set off to furrow the steppe with the steel, to sow the insatiable womb of the black earth with vigorous southern wheat.

The Cossacks kept coming home from the sea and from overseas, but none of them had seen Pyotr. They had served with him in the same regiments, in many different regions—Russia is vast!—but the men who had been recruited with Pyotr from the village had all fallen in battle against a Red detachment somewhere in the Kuban.*

Gavrila seldom spoke to his wife about their son. At night he would hear her cry into her pillow.

"What's wrong, old woman?" he would ask, groaning.

She'd be silent for a few moments, then would say:

"The stove must be smoking, it's given me a headache."

He pretended not to know what really bothered her, and suggested:

"Maybe you should drink some brine from the pickled cucumbers. Should I go down to the cellar to get you some?"

"No, go back to sleep. It'll pass."

And once more silence spread in the hut like an invisible cobweb. And the moon peered brazenly through the window, staring at their grief, as if taking pleasure in the mother's longing.

They kept waiting and hoping that their son would return. Gavrila sent away some sheepskins to be prepared, and said to his wife:

"You and I can get by with what we have, but when Pyotr comes back, what will he wear? Winter will be upon us soon, he'll need a sheepskin."

They made a sheepskin jacket to fit Pyotr's size and put it away in the family chest. They had a pair of work boots made for him which he would wear when tending the cattle. The old man brushed his blue woolen uniform thoroughly and scattered tobacco on it to keep the moths away, wanting to keep it in good condition to wear when Pyotr came back. And he slaughtered a lamb and made a hat of lamb's wool for his son. He hung the hat on a nail. Whenever he entered the hut, his eyes would rest on it and give him the feeling that any moment his son would come out of the best room and ask with a smile:

"Well, Father, is it cold enough outside for you?"

A couple of days later he had gone out at dusk to bring in the cattle. He raked some hay into the manger and was about to draw water from the well when he realized that he had forgotten his mitts in the house. He went to the hut, opened the door, and saw his wife kneeling at the bench, clasping to her breast the lamb's wool hat that Pyotr had never worn, and rocking it as one rocks a baby.

Gavrila saw red. He rushed at her like a beast, knocked her down, and roared hoarsely:

"Let go of it, you idiot, let go! What do you think you are doing?"

He tore the hat from her hands, threw it into the chest, and fastened the lock on it. He noticed that from that day the old

---

* The *Kuban* is a fertile region, several hundred miles in area, in southern Russia.

woman developed a tic in her left eye and her mouth became twisted.

The days and the weeks flowed by, the water flowed in the autumn Don, a transparent green, and always rushing.

That day the edges of the Don froze. A gaggle of wild geese flew over the village. In the evening a neighbor's son came over and, crossing himself hastily before the icon,* said:

"Have you had a good day?"

"Thank God."

"Have you heard the news, Grandfather? Prokhor Likhovidov has returned from Turkey. He served in the same regiment as your Pyotr."

Gavrila hurried off to Prokhor's, losing his breath from coughing and the rapid walking. Prokhor was not at home; he had gone to his brother's village and had said he would return the following morning.

Gavrila didn't sleep at all that night. He lay there on the stove, wearing himself out with sleeplessness.

He got up before it was light, lit the floating wick, and sat down to sew some felt boots. The morning, weakly pale, spread a sickly light at dawn. The moon faded in the middle of the sky, strengthless to reach the clouds, there to bury itself for the day.

Just before breakfast Gavrila happened to glance through the window, and said, speaking for no reason in a whisper:

"There comes Prokhor."

Prokhor came in. He didn't look like a Cossack but like a foreigner. He had on squeaking English shoes, and his coat of foreign cut hung on him like a sack; it had evidently been taken off foreign shoulders.

"So you're still hail and well, Gavrila Vasilich!"

"Praise be to God, soldier! Come in and sit down."

---

*An *icon*, in the Orthodox Eastern Church, is a sacred image of Jesus, Mary, or a saint.

Prokhor removed his cap, greeted the old woman, and sat down on the bench close to the entrance.

"Some weather we're having! All that snow! It's impossible to get through!"

"Yes, we've had early snow. Other years at this time the cattle were still in the pasture, feeding on green fodder."

There was an uncomfortable silence for a minute. Seeming calm, Gavrila said in a firm voice:

"You've aged in foreign parts, young man!"

"There wasn't anything there to make one younger, Gavrila Vasilich!" Prokhor said with a rueful smile.

The old woman stammered:

"Our Pyotr . . . you've . . ."

"Be quiet, woman!" Gavrila shouted angrily. "Let the man thaw out from the frost, you'll hear all in good time, you'll find out . . ."

And turning to his guest, he asked:

"Tell me, Prokhor Ignatich, how did life treat you out there?"

"There's nothing to boast about. I managed to drag myself home like a cur who had been beaten, but thank God for even that much."

"You don't say! That means you had a rough time with the Turks?"

"We had to fight plenty to keep alive." Prokhor drummed on the table with his fingers. "But you look older, too, Gavrila Vasilich, your hair is sprinkled with gray How's life under the Soviet regime?"

"I'm waiting for my son to come back . . . to provide for us old folk," Gavrila said, forcing a smile.

Prokhor quickly turned his eyes away. Gavrila noticed this and asked bluntly and in a sharp voice:

"Tell us, where is Pyotr?"

"Haven't you heard?"

"We've heard all kinds of things," Gavrila interrupted him tersely.

Prokhor knotted the dirty fringe of the

tablecloth with his fingers and didn't answer for a while.

"It was in January, I think. Yes, it was in January. There were about a hundred of us, quartered just outside Novorossiisk.* It's a city near the sea. Well, we were just quartered there . . ."

"Tell me, was he killed?" Gavrila said, leaning forward and speaking in a low whisper.

Prokhor sat there, eyes lowered, as if he hadn't heard the question.

"We were stationed there, and the Reds broke through, from the hills, and joined up with the other forces. Our commander—his name was Sesin—sent out your Pyotr with a reconnaisance group—he was in charge of it—and that's when it happened, you understand . . ."

Near the stove an iron kettle fell to the floor with a crash, and the old woman, her arms stretched out in front of her, stumbled toward the bed, uttering a cry of anguish.

"Don't howl!!" Gavrila barked threateningly and, leaning on his elbows on the table, looked steadily at Prokhor as he said slowly and wearily, "Go on, tell us the rest."

"They sabered him," Prokhor shouted, turning pale. He stood up and groped on the table for his cap. "They sabered him to death. The reconnaisance had stopped near a forest to give the horses a rest . . . he had loosened the saddle girth . . . and the Reds came out of the forest." The words stuck in his throat, he kneaded his cap with trembling hands. "Pyotr grabbed the saddle bow, but the saddle slipped under the horse's belly. His horse was a fiery one, it couldn't stand the touch of the saddle there, it took off. . . . Pyotr was left behind. . . . And that's all there is to tell."

"And suppose I don't believe a word of this?" Gavrila said sharply, articulating each word distinctly.

Without looking around Prokhor hurried toward the door.

"Suit yourself, Gavrila Vasilich, but I sincerely . . . I've told you the truth . . . the naked truth . . . I saw it with my own eyes . . ."

"What if I don't wish to believe it?" Gavrila said hoarsely, turning livid. His eyes filled with blood and flashed with tears. Tearing his shirt at the collar, he advanced on the quailing Prokhor, his hairy chest bared, groaning and thrusting forward his sweating head: "My only son killed?! Our breadwinnner?! My Pet'ka?* You are lying, you scoundrel! Do you hear?! You are lying! I don't believe you!"

But that night, throwing his sheepskin over his shoulder, Gavrila went out into the yard, walked over the crunching snow to the barn, and stood outside near a cornstack.

The wind blew from the steppe, carrying fine snow. Darkness, black and hostile, had settled over the naked cherry trees.

"Little son!" Gavrila called out under his breath. He waited for a while and, without moving, without turning his head, called out once more: "Pyotr! My little son!"

Then he threw himself on the snow, where it was trampled down around the stack, and closed his eyes, overcome with grief.

There was talk in the village of grain requisitioning, and of the Whites advancing from the lower reaches of the Don. The news was whispered about in the village and at the meetings of the Executive Committee,** but old Gavrila never set foot on the rickety porch of the building where the committee met, for he had no use for it. But because of this he missed much of what was going on. He was astounded, therefore,

_____

* *Novorossiisk* is a city in the southeastern part of the Soviet Union, on the Black Sea.

* *Pet'ka* is a familiar and endearing nickname for Pyotr.

** The Executive Committee of the village Soviet.

when, one Sunday after mass, the chairman appeared with three other men in short yellow jackets, carrying rifles.

The chairman shook hands with Gavrila and at once blurted out, like a punch on the back of the head:

"Come on, confess, old man, you've got grain."

"Well, what do you think?—that we're fed by the Holy Spirit?"

"Don't get smart, tell us right off: where is the grain?"

"In the granary, where else?"

"Take us there."

"Permit me to ask, what business do you have with my grain?"

A robust, towheaded man, evidently the chief of the group, tapped his heels in the hardened snow, and answered:

"We're here to take surplus grain for the government. Food requisitioning. Have you heard about it, old man?"

"What if I refuse to give it?" Gavrila said hoarsely, bursting with fury.

"If you refuse, we'll take it ourselves."

The three men held a whispered consultation with their chief, then went to the granary and climbed into the bins of cleaned, dark-golden wheat, loosening clumps of snow that dropped into the grain from their boots. Lighting a cigarette, the chairman said:

"We'll leave you enough for seed and for food, and take the rest."

With the experienced eye of a farmer, he estimated the quantity of grain in the bins and, turning to Gavrila, asked:

"How many dessiatines * do you plan to sow?"

"I'll sow the devil's bald spot—that's what I'll sow!" Gavrila hissed, coughing and grimacing convulsively. "Take it all, and be damned! You robbers! It's all yours!"

"What's come over you, are you going out of your mind, or what?" the chairman

---

* A *dessiatine* is a Russian unit of land measure equal to 2.7 acres.

shouted, waving his mitt at the old man.

"May you choke on someone else's goods! May you burst!"

The towheaded man pulled a melting icicle from his mustache, shot an intelligent, amused glance sidelong at the upset Gavrila, and said with a calm smile:

"Take it easy, Dad! Yelling won't help you. Why yelp as though someone has stepped on your tail?" And, frowning, he continued in a changed tone: "Don't let your tongue wag! If it's too long, tie it to your teeth. For this kind of attitude . . ." and without finishing what he was going to say, he added, less sternly: "Take that grain down to the collection point today."

Perhaps the old man was scared, but he certainly calmed down at the sharp and sure words of the towheaded man, as if he realized that shouting was really of no use. He waved his hand in disgust and went off toward his porch. He was barely halfway across his yard, when a wild shout made him start:

"Where is that food-requisitioning detachment?"

Gavrila swung around and saw a horseman reining in his prancing horse on the other side of the fence. A presentiment that something horrible was about to happen made the old man's knees shake. Before he could open his mouth, the horseman, seeing the others near the granary, abruptly checked his steed, and with almost an imperceptible motion of the hand, removed the rifle from his shoulder.

A shot rang out, and in the silence that followed could be heard clearly the rifle bolt being pulled back and the cartridge case being released with a buzzing sound.

The petrifying moment passed. Pressing close to the doorpost, the towheaded man drew his revolver slowly with a shaking hand, squatted down and rushed like a hare across the yard to the barn. One of the other three men of the detachment dropped to his knee and sent a bullet from his rifle into the black fur cap of the horseman on the other side of the fence. The yard rang with the sound of firing. Gavrila lifted his numb feet with difficulty out of the snow and trudged heavily to the porch. Looking back, he saw the three men of the detachment rush toward the barn, getting stuck in the snowdrifts while other horsemen poured in through the wide-open gate.

The leading rider, mounted on a bay stallion and wearing a Kuban * fur hat, bent low over his saddle bow and brandished his sword above his head. Before Gavrila's eyes the streamers of the rider's white cowl flickered like a swan's wings, and the snow sprayed by the horse's hoofs splashed into his face.

Leaning helplessly against the carved porch railing, Gavrila first saw the bay stallion gather speed and fly over the fence, then turn around on its hind hoofs near the stack of barley straw. Then he watched the man from the Kuban, hanging right out of the saddle, swing his saber from left to right and right to left, slashing at the food collector who was trying to crawl out of reach.

From the barn he could hear scuffling, a mixed hubbub, and then someone's prolonged, sobbing wail. A minute later a single shot split the air. The doves, who had been frightened by the first shot and had regathered on the roof of the granary, now scattered into the air like violet-colored shrapnel. The horsemen dismounted at the barn.

Incessantly the church bells rang out merrily over the village. Pasha, the village idiot, had gone up into the belfry and, following his own dull-witted thinking, had seized the cables of all the bells, so that instead of sounding the alarm he was ringing out a jolly Eastertide dance.

The man from the Kuban drove over to Gavrila. His white cowl was down around

---

* Kuban peasants were owners of fertile land, and rich. They were the most hostile in the region toward the new, Soviet regime.

his shoulders, his hot, sweaty face was twitching.

"Have you got any oats?" he shouted.

Dazed by all he had just seen, unable to move his paralyzed tongue, Gavrila moved with difficulty away from the porch railing.

"Have you gone deaf, you old devil? I say, any oats? Bring out a sack."

Before they had time to lead their horses to the trough now filled with fodder, another horseman galloped into the yard.

"Mount your horses! Red infantry is coming down the hill!"

Swearing, the Kuban bridled his still-steaming stallion, grabbed up a handful of snow and rubbed hard against the cuff of his sleeve, smeared with blood.

All five of them rode out of the yard. As the last one passed outside the gate, Gavrila recognized the light-haired chairman's yellow, blood-stained jacket rolled up and stuck between the saddlestraps.

There was shooting until the oncoming evening. The village then settled into a humbled silence, like a whipped dog. The shadows were turning blue when Gavrila finally made himself go to the barn. He entered through the wide-open wicket gate and saw the chairman lying across a rack, head down, caught by a bullet. His hanging arms looked as though they were reaching for his cap which was lying to the side, on the floor. And not far from the cornstack, the other three men of the detachment lay in a row, stripped to their underwear. Looking at them Gavrila no longer felt in his heart, touched with horror, the rage that had nested in it earlier that day.

It seemed to him unreal, a bad dream, that in his barn, where ordinarily the neighbor's goats played robbers, pulling out large tufts of straw, there should now lie sabered corpses.

The towheaded one lay with his head twisted oddly to one side and, except for that head pressed so hard against the snow,

429

one would have thought he had lain down to rest, so relaxed were his stretched legs.

Gavrila bent over this one, looked into his darkened face, and shook with pity. What he saw was a mere youngster, not more than nineteen—not the tough food commissar with the piercing eyes. Under the yellow fuzz of his mustache, around his lips, the frost had stiffened a dejected smile, but there was a small frown, deep and fierce, across his forehead.

With no seeming purpose in mind, the old man put his hand on the bared chest of the dead man and drew back in astonishment, for through the surface chill his palm felt a faint warmth.

The old woman cried out and crossed herself, and fell back against the stove when she saw Gavrila, straining and groaning, carry in the stiff, blood-covered body on his back.

He laid it on the bench, washed it with cold water, and rubbed the legs, arms, and chest with a rough woolen sock, until he was sweating with the effort. He put his ear against the cold chest and, listening carefully, heard the weak, slow beating of the heart.

Four days the wounded youth lay in the best room, his face saffron yellow, like a corpse's. The cut across his forehead and cheek turned into a livid scar, the quilt rose and fell as, wheezing and gurgling, the tensed chest drew in air.

Every day Gavrila put his gnarled finger into the unconscious youth's mouth, carefully parted his lips and clenched teeth with the end of a knife, and the old woman poured warmed milk and broth made from lamb bones down through a reed.

In the morning of the fifth day a flush spread over his face, and by midday his face was flaming like a whitethorn bush burnt by frost. A chill shook his whole body, and under his shirt a cold, clammy sweat covered his skin. From that day he began to mutter in delirium and would strain to jump out of the bed. Gavrila and his wife took turns sitting with him day and night.

In the long winter nights, when the east wind blew hard from the Don, disturbing the blackened sky, and low clouds hung over the village, Gavrila sat at the bedside of the delirious man, leaning his head on his hands, listening to his ravings in an unfamiliar dialect. He looked long at the swarthy triangle of suntan on the sick man's chest, at the faint-blue lids of his closed eyes, circled by dark-blue horseshoes, and when his drawn-out moans flowed from the bloodless lips, mingled with incoherent commands and frightful oaths, his face disfigured with fury and pain, hot tears welled up in Gavrila's eyes. He felt unexpected pity.

Gavrila saw how with every day, with every sleepless night, his wife grew paler and more withered, sitting there at the wounded man's bedside. He noticed also the tears on her wrinkled cheeks, and understood, or, more likely, felt with his heart, that her pent-up love for Pyotr, her dead son, had spread like a flame over this motionless, death-kissed son of an unknown mother.

One day, unexpectedly, a commander passing through the village paid them a call. Leaving his horse at the gate with the orderly, he ran up the steps of the porch, his sword and spurs rattling. He took off his cap in the best room and stood silently at the bed for a long time. Faint shadows passed over the wounded man's face, and from his lips, parched with fever, a small stream of blood trickled. The commander shook his prematurely gray head, and his face clouded with sadness. Looking past Gavrila's eyes, he said:

"Take care of the comrade, father!"

"We'll take care of him," Gavrila said firmly.

The days and the weeks passed. Twelfth Night came and went. On the sixteenth day of his illness, the towheaded man opened his eyes for the first time, and Gavrila heard a voice as thin as a spider's thread, and creaking:

"Is that you, old man?"

"It's me."

"They nearly finished me off, didn't they?"

"Christ forbid!"

Gavrila thought he detected an expression of good-natured mockery in the young man's vague eyes.

"And my pals?"

"Those . . . they were buried on the square."

He silently ran his fingers over the quilt and turned his glance away to the unpainted beams of the ceiling.

"By what name should we call you?" Gavrila asked.

Wearily the young man lowered his blue-veined eyelids, and whispered:

"Nikolai."

"But we'll call you Pyotr . . . we had a son . . . Pyotr . . ." Gavrila explained.

He thought for a moment, then was about to ask another question, but hearing the even, nasal breathing of the patient, he tiptoed away from the bed, balancing himself by extending his arms.

Life returned to the towheaded youth slowly, as if unwillingly. In the second month he was barely able to lift his head from the pillow. Bed sores appeared on his back.

With every day Gavrila realized with a kind of panic that he was growing attached to the new Pyotr, as to a blood relation, while the image of the first, flesh of his flesh, was fading and growing dim, like the reflection of the setting sun on the mica window of the hut. He forced himself to feel the former longing and pain, but these emotions receded ever further, and as a result Gavrila felt ashamed and uneasy. He would go out into the yard, putter about for hours, and then, remembering that his wife was sitting incessantly at Pyotr's bed, he experienced a

pang of jealousy. He then returned to the hut, hung around at the head of the bed, tried to adjust the pillow case with his awkward fingers, and, noticing his wife's annoyed glance, moved away humbly, sat down on the bench, and quieted down.

The old woman fed Pyotr on groundhog fat and on an extract from healing herbs gathered in the spring, in their May bloom. With the help of this, or because youth won out over the injury, Pyotr's wounds began to heal, and color appeared in his rounded cheeks. Only his right arm, mutilated near the shoulder, mended poorly; evidently it had finished its work for good.

During the second week of Lent, Pyotr sat up in bed for the first time without anyone's help and, surprised at his own strength, smiled for a long time in disbelief.

That night in the kitchen, a whisper came from on top of the stove:

"Are you asleep, old woman?"

"Why do you want to know?"

"He's getting back on his feet, our Pyotr. Tomorrow get out Pyotr's trousers from the chest. Get all the things ready. He has nothing to wear."

"I've already thought of it myself. I got them out the other day."

"Aren't you a smart one! Did you get out the sheepskin, too?"

"What do you think? He can't go around in his underwear, can he?"

Gavrila was restless for a while, then dozed off, but woke again, remembered something, raised his head triumphantly, and said:

"And the hat? I bet you forgot the hat, you old goose!"

"Stop pestering me. You must have passed it forty times—it has been hanging on that nail since yesterday."

Gavrila coughed with disappointment and was silent.

The early spring was already quickening the Don. The ice over it darkened as though eaten away by worms, and swelled. The hillocks were bared of snow. The snow receded from the steppe into the hollows and gullies. The Don basin was filled with sunlit floodwater. The wind spread generously the bitter scent of blossoming wormwood.

It was getting near the end of March.

"I'll get out of bed today, Father!"

Although all the Red Army men who crossed Gavrila's threshhold, seeing his white hair, called him "father," he felt that this time there was a warm note in the word. Did it just seem so to him, or did Pyotr actually add a son's gentle tone to the word? Gavrila wasn't sure, but he flushed, coughed, and, concealing his embarrassed joy, muttered:

"You've lain there three months. It's time to get up, Petya!"

Pyotr walked out on the porch, moving his legs stiffly, and almost choked with the gulp of air the wind forced into his lungs. Gavrila held him up from the back, while the old woman fussed around the porch, wiping away the customary tears with the edge of the curtain.

As he walked past the granary, the foster son, Pyotr, asked:

"Did you deliver the grain that time?"

"I did," Gavrila answered curtly.

"Well, you did the right thing, Father!"

And once more the word "father" warmed Gavrila's heart.

Every day now Pyotr walked about outside, limping and leaning on a crutch. And from everywhere—from the barn, from the shed—Gavrila followed his new son with an uneasy, watchful glance. If only he didn't stumble and fall!

They didn't talk much to each other, but their relationship grew into an easy and loving one.

Some days after Pyotr went outdoors for the first time, as Gavrila was settling down for the night on the stove, he asked:

"Where are you from, son?"

"From the Urals."

"Of peasant stock?"

"No, workers."

"What kind? Some handicraft or other, such as bootmakers or coopers?"

"No, Father, I worked in a factory, in an iron foundry. Ever since I was a kid."

"Then how did you happen to become a food collector?"

"I had been assigned by the army."

"Then you must have been some kind of officer?"

"Yes, I was."

It was hard to put the next question, but he had led up to it:

"That means you're a party man?"

"Yes, I am," Pyotr answered with an open smile.

Somehow, because of that smile the unfamiliar word no longer seemed frightening to Gavrila.

The old woman, who had been waiting her chance, asked with liveliness:

"Have you got any family, Pet'ka dear?"

"Not a speck. I am as alone as the moon."

"Your parents must have died, then."

"When I was quite small, about seven, my father was killed in a drunken brawl, and my mother disappeared somewhere . . ."

"You mean she abandoned you, poor little one . . ."

"She went off with some contractor, and I grew up around the factory."

Gavrila sat up, let his feet hang down from the stove, and after a thoughtful silence, said clearly and slowly:

"Why, then, son, since you have no parents, stay with us. We had a son once; we've named you after him, Pyotr. We had him and he grew up, but now there are just the two of us left, rattling around here. While you've been with us, we've suffered with you plenty, maybe that's why we've grown so fond of you. Although you have alien blood, our hearts bleed for you, as if you were our own flesh and blood. Stay. We'll all get our food from the land. The soil here, on the Don, is fertile and the land bountiful.

We'll set you up, then marry you off. I've had my day, so you can take over the farm now. All I ask is that you respect our old age and that you don't refuse us a crust of bread before we die. Don't abandon us old folks, Pyotr."

A cricket chirped behind the stove, loudly and monotonously.

The shutters groaned with the wind.

"My old woman and I have already looked around for a bride," Gavrila said, winking with forced gaiety, but his lips twisted into a pitiful smile.

Pyotr gazed persistently down at his feet and drummed on the bench with the fingers of his left hand. The noise was irritating and sharp.

He was obviously thinking over his reply.

And, having decided, he stopped his drumming and said:

"I'll gladly remain with you, Father. Only, as you know, I'm not much of a worker, my right arm, my provider, refuses to heal, damn it! But, I'll do my best, I'll give it all I've got. I'll stay with you through the summer, then we'll see."

"After that, maybe you'll stay on for good," Gavrila added.

The spinning wheel, worked by the treadle under the old woman's foot, buzzed merrily, and purred away as it wound the wool thread onto the spindle.

Whether it was humming a lullaby, or whether it was holding out a promise of an abundant life with its measured, lulling clatter—who knows?

THE EAGLETS

N. NADEZHDINA

There is a large children's park in Leningrad which had been given to them as a gift from the city's adults. After World War II, Leningrad sculptors and architects erected a monument in this park—a monument dedicated to the city's child-heroes, boys and girls who had given their lives to help save their besieged city and invaded country from the brutal German enemy.

Leningrad was under siege for 900 days—from September, 1941, to January, 1944. The Germans intended to conquer the city by starving and freezing its inhabitants. But the enemy didn't count on the endurance and courage of the citizens of Leningrad, old and young.

Another "monument" was later dedicated to the young heroes: It was a book written by several authors and given the title *The Eaglets*. It contains sixteen true stories about as many boys and girls who chose to join the partisans to carry on the struggle in the enemy rear. These boys and girls were about as old as the young reader of this part of the anthology.

They had died for their city and for their country, but they are still alive in the memories of their families, friends, and fellow countrymen who remember them with love and gratitude.

The Hard Road is the story of Lara, one of the sixteen Eaglets.

THE HARD ROAD

It had become strangely quiet in the house. No one sang there now, and no one practiced ballet steps in the hallway or clattered down the stairs to rescue the cat who had fallen into the hands of some boys in the street. Lara was gone.

Her grandmother had left to visit her son Rodion, in the village of Pechenevo, and had taken her granddaughter with her. Lara had begun to feel homesick even before the departure. Putting her curly head against her mother's arm and looking up at her with brown eyes that resembled ripe chestnuts, the girl had said:

"Mother, why must we go to Uncle Rodion's? Maybe he doesn't even want us to stay with him the whole summer."

"What makes you think that you won't be welcome?"

"I heard you say to Grandmother that he's very stingy. Stingy people don't like guests. Please, I don't want to go there."

But they had gone just the same. Lara's mother had seen them off at the railway station.

The next day was Sunday. The mother was tidying their room. She opened the chest of drawers to examine the linen. A

cool, fresh smell came from the neat stack of heavily starched sheets. On top of another pile lay a man's shirt. Sighing deeply, she hid the shirt at the very bottom of it.

She knew it upset Lara to see her father's things. When he was killed in the war with Finland, his little daughter was heartbroken. They had been great friends.

When Lara was seven and had started attending school, she was too active a child to sit still all day at her desk. And the trouble had soon started.

"I hate school! I hate ABC's! Why do I have to learn the alphabet?"

"So that you'll learn how to read; no one can read without knowing the alphabet."

"Soon there will be books 'that talk.' I'm not going to school any more." Lara was obstinate.

She had given in one day only because her mother cried. She was a girl who couldn't stand to see another person's tears.

A few months later, her mother was obliged to write notes to the librarians:

"I request that you do not allow my daughter, Larissa Mikheyenko, pupil of the 106th School, to check out any more books. She belongs to three libraries and reads day and night."

There was no likelihood, however, that this summer, at Uncle Rodion's, Lara would read nights. Her uncle would not permit her to have the light on that long, for light cost money. But, it was just as well, her mother decided, Lara should get a lot of rest after her winter's illness, so that she would be strong enough to continue with her ballet lessons next fall.

And Lara's mother stood there in the quiet room, imagining a day in the future when a curtain would part and on the stage would appear a young ballerina, willowy and almost weightless, twirling in the limelight like a white moth. She could even hear the music.

"Don't you hear me, Tatyana Andreevna?"

Lara's mother started, and returned from her dream of the future to the present.

"Can you hear me?" the neighbor was shouting from her doorway. "They just announced over the radio that the fascists are attacking us. It's war!"

"Larochka!" was all that her mother could utter.

The train taking Lara and her grandmother to the country was already far away.

That evening all the shades were drawn. Not one light could be seen in the whole city. There were antiaircraft guns on the rooftops of the tallest buildings, shooting at the enemy planes. Several times that night the people of Leningrad were awakened by the voice of the radio announcer:

"Citizens! Air raid! Air raid!"

The bombings frightened Lara's mother badly, but she did not leave the city. She kept hoping that her daughter would return to her. Maybe they'll come back tomorrow or the day after, or by Thursday at the latest. But even by the end of Thursday Lara and the grandmother hadn't come back. Friday evening she found in the mailbox a letter written on a piece of notebook paper. It was from Lara.

"Dearest Mommie! I love you very much and miss you terribly, but the railroad has been bombed. It's impossible to get through. I'd come on foot, but it would be too much for Grandmother, and I can't leave her behind."

"I can't leave her behind," her mother

repeated the words in a whisper. "I knew you'd say that. But what about me, how can I live without you, my darling? . . ."

Then there were more alerts in the night. And again the mother would go to work next morning and return home in the evening and look for a letter. But there were no more letters from Lara.

In her only letter Lara had said not a word about her uncle. This was not an oversight—she did not want to worry her mother. Uncle Rodion had not welcomed his visitors. The grandmother had put her arms around her son, but he had looked over her head at his niece and had said:

"You lost no time in coming and even brought the kid with you."

He was even more glum when the family sat down to a meal. Whenever Lara reached for a slice of bread she met with a look from her uncle that seemed to measure the amount of food she was eating.

"Let's go away from here, let's go home," Lara pleaded with her grandmother. But the grandmother was afraid to risk a trip back to the city. The Germans were bombing many roads.

Soon there was no more passenger travel at all.

The news from the front was bad. Our armies were retreating. When a military unit was passing through Pechenevo, Lara asked one of the soldiers to take along a note to her mother.

"What's the good of that?" Uncle Rodion said. "Now you mother can't send through more money from Leningrad for your keep."

Money for her keep—that was all that interested him at a time like this! And a few days later, when all the money they had brought with them from the city was used up, Uncle Rodion told them that they would have to move into the small bathhouse, a "black" hut given that name because its stove didn't have a chimney and the room would fill up with black smoke whenever a fire was made. He planned to move them into the bathhouse after dark so that the neighbors wouldn't notice it.

He didn't know that it would be light as day that evening. On the other side of the wood, a collective farm had been bombed by the fascists and was in flames. The conflagration had spread over a wide area, and the sky over Uncle Rodion's place was bright orange. The dew on the grass glistened like broken glass.

It hurt the eyes to look at the blinding fire. Lara sat down on the little porch of the bathhouse and buried her head on her knees. Never before in her life had she felt so scared and so lonely.

She heard the sound of the garden gate and lifted her head. Along the path quickly came two towheaded girls; one was tall and thin as a stalk, the other was short and round, like the fairy-tale doughnut. Lara knew the tall girl, Raya, but she had never seen the "doughnut."

The girls stopped near a bush just short of the porch and whispered to each other, casting sidelong glances at Lara.

"You tell her . . ."

"No, you. You brought it for her, you tell her."

At last the short round girl made up her mind. "Here, this is for you," she said, offering Lara a small earthen pot of hot milk. "I guess you had nothing for supper."

"But . . . why give this to me? We don't even know each other."

"This is Frosya," Raya introduced the short girl. "Her other name is Kondrunenko. . . . If you want us to, we can stay with you for a while. Do you want us to?"

"Yes, I do. Very much!"

The porch was narrow and the three girls had to squeeze together as they sat on the top step. But from the touch of their shoulders, and from the pot of steaming milk which Lara was hugging to her, a wave of wonderful warmth flowed over her. She knew that she now had friends.

Lara fell asleep late that night and woke late the next day. Her grandmother had gone somewhere. She had to find her right away if they were to go together, as Raya had suggested, to the Village Soviet.* Yesterday, Raya had said, "Our government takes care of old people and children."

When Lara located her grandmother, she said to her, "Let's go to the Village Soviet, Granny. They will take care of us."

"No one will take care of us now," the old woman said bitterly. "The German is master of the village now. There is no one to turn to now."

Lara knew that her grandmother always told the truth, but this time she couldn't believe her. She waved her off and ran out just as she was, uncombed and unwashed, to prove to herself that her grandmother was wrong. "It's our own soldiers who had

_____
* The *Village Soviet* is a council that governs the affairs of a village.

come to the village and not the Germans— it can't be the Germans," she said to herself as she ran.

Then suddenly she heard a shout:
"Tsurik! Get back!"

A soldier was standing in front of her, but not a Russian soldier. Everything about this one was odd—his short tunic, the voice in which he was repeating his "tsurik!"

This word must mean "not allowed." But why not? How can it be forbidden to walk in your own village?

"Tsurik!" the German threatened, raising his automatic rifle.

So that's how it was! Up to now Lara had lived as free as a bird. And now, whichever way she went another such soldier would appear and would go on tsuriking at her with the same German voice.

She glanced around, as if looking for safety. Only now did she notice that on the opposite side of the street there was a crowd

of villagers. Among them were Raya and Frosya. Lara ran across to join them.

Everyone was staring at a German car standing near the village well. A circle of German soldiers was guarding it. Inside this circle, in front of the German officer, a man in civilian clothes stood dismally. It was Uncle Rodion.

Lara at once forgot all about how he had chased her out of his home. How can you think of getting even with a person who has fallen into the hands of the enemy! "Poor Uncle Rodion!" Lara said to herself, and then she cried out:

"They've taken him! They've taken my uncle!"

"Be quiet," Raya whispered. "He sold himself to the Germans, the viper. They've made him our village elder."

Uncle Rodion turned his head in their direction and listened to the girls' whispering and so did the German officer.

The officer noticed how Lara's hair caught the sunlight and the curls at her temples that seemed to have sparks in them.

"Gut-looker!" the German said, pointing at her. "Gut-looker!"

Lara drew back, turned, and fled across the orchard. She was so pale when she reached their little hut that her grandmother exclaimed on seeing her, "Dear heart! you're as white as a sheet!"

"Grandma, it's true! The fascists have taken the village. Their leader pointed his finger at me. He said, "Gut-looker, gut-looker."

"The swine!" the grandmother said and angrily poked with a stick at the fire she was making. "Put coal dust and ashes on your face and make yourself a bit ugly. No, don't do it now, let the cinders cool off a bit."

But Lara was already bending over the fire. The stick with which the old woman was moving the coals caught at something red. It was not an ember but a burnt piece of red cloth. Lara looked furiously at her grandmother:

"You . . . you . . . how could you!"

"I'm scared for you, darling. I thought they would drag you off—the fascists hate red . . . so I threw your Pioneer * tie into the fire and burned it. . . . Come on, don't stand there saying nothing—scold me at least, say something . . . it will make me feel better."

Lara remained silent, her eyes wide open and looking off into the distance. She saw somewhere far, far away, her Pioneer Club parading to the beat of a drum along the streets of Leningrad. Their emblem fluttered over the children's heads, vivid like fire, scarlet as the dawn, and of the same color as her country's flag and the same red as the ties around the children's necks. If she could only be with them now and tell them: "Listen, fellow Pioneers, have you heard what misfortune has befallen your Lara? The fascists have taken her grandmother's village. Your Lara no longer has her Pioneer tie. But I beg you, friends, to consider Larissa Mikheyenko a Pioneer just the same. . . . I'm in deep trouble. . . . But I'll be true to my Pioneer pledge. . . . 'I, a young Pioneer of the Soviet Union, in the presence of my comrades, pledge to love my Soviet country . . .'"

"What are you whispering?" the grandmother asked guiltily. "Are you still very angry with me?"

Two autumns had passed since that day, and two winters. They had been years of slavery, grief, and hunger.

Refugees wandered through the village. They had come from places where life had become impossible. They knocked at the window panes and begged piteously.

---

* The *Pioneers* is a countrywide organization of Soviet boys and girls nine to fifteen years of age. Its ideals are patriotism, international friendship, diligence in study, neatness, courtesy, love of nature, conservation, and loyalty to the Soviet system.

"Give a crust of bread, good people! Help a homeless one!"

"You ought to beg, too," Lara's grandmother would say. "We, too, are homeless and have nothing."

"Don't you remember, Granny, that Pioneers don't beg," Lara would answer, and add, "I'm not hungry."

She said this out of pride. At night she would have long dreams about the most delicious meal in the world—dark bread, warm, just out of the oven, with a slightly burned crust making a crunchy sound as she chewed it.

Once, passing her uncle's house, Lara saw, sitting on a mound, a German soldier who had evidently come from the enemy headquarters in the neighboring town of Timonovo, to see the elder on some official business. Not finding Uncle Rodion at home and feeling bored, he had spread in front of him the plunder he had gathered on his way through the village. Before him lay a roast chicken, a piece of pork, and a loaf of village bread.

Lara stopped and stood there as if petrified. The smell of the bread tickled her nostrils, and she felt dizzy with hunger. She thought she might faint.

Thinking that Lara was the village elder's daughter, the soldier cut off a small slice of the bread and offered it to her. She shook her head, turned sharply, and walked away. She would rather die of hunger than take bread from the hand of the enemy.

She hated the fascists and had vowed never to give in to them. In the village square she had witnessed a few days ago the hanging of the old teacher, Nikolai Maksimovich. He had known that he might pay with his life if they found a radio in his home, but he had continued to tune in Moscow, for he could not live without knowing the fate of his country. For this the Germans hanged him. The fascists burned whole villages and their inhabitants when they found out that the villagers had helped the partisans.* The partisans were active all over the region, particularly on the other side of Lake Yazno. They gave the enemy no rest. They attacked German garrisons, set fire to supply depots, and blew up bridges.

Whenever Lara heard people mention the partisans, her eyes would sparkle. They were real heroes! If only she could help them in some way!

Another spring came. The footpaths were beginning to dry. The trees were enveloped in greenness so light and gentle, like green mist that would disappear at the slightest breath of wind.

Lara's grandmother asked her to look for young nettles. Maybe they could be cooked.

She went along the village streets examining every blade of new grass peeping out from behind the fences. At the well she heard two women talking about something they had overheard in Timonovo. The Germans were planning to go to the forest on bicycles to look for the partisan camp, and Uncle Rodion would show them the way.

"And when are they going?" Lara joined the conversation. She had turned very pale; her dark eyes seemed quite black, so white was her face.

"How do we know!" one of the women answered crossly. "You live on the elder's estate, it's easier for you to find out."

Lara thought hard. That evening, as she was going to bed, she said to her grandmother, "Granny, I want to ask you to do me a favor. Tomorrow, please go away somewhere for the whole day."

Next morning three German cyclists arrived at the home of Uncle Rodion, now the elder of the village of Pechenevo. They leaned their bicycles against a mound and entered the house.

The windows were closed and no one saw

_____
* The *partisans* were civilian guerrilla fighters, usually active behind the enemy lines.

439

what refreshments Uncle Rodion offered his guests. Evidently the Germans were pleased with them since they left their host in a merry mood and came out laughing. But when they looked at their bicycles, their merriment disappeared like smoke. Someone had punctured the tires. The trip through the woods had to be postponed.

The Germans yelled that the village elder should be hanged for hiding partisans on his premises. The scared elder bowed and scraped and swore that he was hiding no one and that there were no partisans on his place. The tires were cut by an outsider, he assured them.

The house was searched and so was the bathhouse, where they found no one. They searched every bush. But no traces of the criminal were revealed, although Uncle Rodion noticed a piece from a broken bottle in the grass and saw that it was covered with blood. But he pretended to have seen nothing. He felt he had already had enough to cope with that day.

At last the Germans started back, dragging their useless bicycles. When they were out of sight, Uncle Rodion approached the bathhouse and again looked through the window.

He saw a jelly jar with a small bouquet of field flowers and a light-blue ribbon on the floor, but the owner of the ribbon was nowhere to be seen. Where could that good-for-nothing girl be?

Suddenly he heard a creaking sound under the eaves of the roof. A small attic window opened and a pair of sneakers fell to the ground. Uncle Rodion hid around the corner.

He heard the sound of bare feet against the logs of the house. Someone was coming down the wall. Someone jumped down to the ground. Hurried steps, and from around the corner appeared Lara. Her right hand was wrapped in a kerchief. There was a scarlet stain on the cloth.

Seeing her uncle, Lara screamed. Her first thought was to hide her wounded hand behind her back, but she changed her mind. Let her uncle see that she is not afraid.

"How did you cut your hand?" Uncle Rodion snapped. "Not, by any chance, with the piece of glass with which you cut the tires? Eh?"

The girl said not a word. But her shining, fearless eyes gave the answer: "Yes, I did it. And I would do it again. I dare you to betray me."

"What are you trying to do? Are you trying to send me to my grave?" her uncle hissed. "Do you think you can commit acts of sabotage on my place? You just wait! I'll send you off so far that you'll never again trouble me!"

A few days later the villagers were told to assemble. A German read off a list of names of girls who were to appear at a detention camp in Pustoshka. From this camp the young people were going to be sent off to Germany as slave labor. The list included Raya and Frosya. But the youngest on this list was the fourteen-year-old Larissa Mikheyenko—Uncle Rodion had seen to that.

During the last evening her grandmother clung to Lara. She kept smoothing her hair, took her hand and held it hard as if afraid that if she let go of it, they would take her granddaughter at once.

"Sit near me, let me look at you for the last time. What are those tyrants going to think of next? Now they are dragging children into slavery! Ragged, hungry . . . . There is nothing to give them to take along."

"I don't need anything, Granny."

"Why not? What have you taken into your head to do, my pet?"

"Nothing. It's just that Frosya's mother said she would get together some things for her and for me."

This was the first time that Lara had lied to her grandmother about something important. The three friends had decided: They vowed not to be the slaves of fascists. They planned to run away into the Yazno forest and try to find the partisan camp to which Frosya's brother, Petya, had gone.

They were to meet that evening at Frosya's place. Lara had promised to come as soon as her grandmother was asleep.

But the grandmother could not fall asleep for a long time. She kept swaying while whispering her prayers, and it seemed to Lara that it wasn't her grandmother's prayers that she was hearing, but the rustling of the grass in the breeze.

Finishing her prayers, the grandmother kept turning restlessly on her cot and from time to time called to Lara.

"Are you here, my dove?"

"I'm here, Granny, I'm here with you."

Then the old woman's breathing became easier and even. She was asleep. Lara rose quietly from her cot. She could not see her grandmother's face in the dark, just the white kerchief which she wound around her head for the night. To this patch of sad whiteness, Lara now waved good-bye:

"Farewell, dear Granny."

The three girls walked all night long through woods, fields, and swamps. They passed villages on the windward side so that the enemy's bloodhounds would not pick up their scent.

When it began to dawn, the refugees again turned into the woods. Now they could take a chance and rest. They spread their jackets under some birch trees and lay down in a row. The ground was still chilly from the night's cold, but the tops of the birches were already golden with dawn, and on a golden branch a bird twittered, welcoming the new day.

Orderly Andrei found the acting commander of the Intelligence Service Brigade, Kotliarov, in the espionage shack.

"Pavel Konstantinovich, you are wanted at staff headquarters. Reinforcements have arrived. What a joke!"

"Why a joke?" Kotliarov asked.

"Why? They're just girls. It amounts to nothing. They must have been playing marbles while waiting to be brought here. Don't you think it's a joke?"

And Andrei roared with laughter.

The staff headquarters was on the edge of the village of Krivitsa, in a light spacious cottage. The morning sun shone in through the window, and on a spot yellow with sunshine stood three girls—two towheaded and one dark-haired. The latter wore a dress that was too short for her, made from blue polished cotton.

"That was once a grandmother's skirt," thought the acting commander. "The girl grows fast but there are no new clothes to be gotten for her."

"Just look at them," the commander said irritably. "They want to join the intelligence service; they say that they know the district well. I have told them ten times that we are a secret service organization not a kindergarten, but they insist: 'We'll be partisans, no matter what.' I can't make them understand a thing. Why don't you try."

Just then the door flew open and Karpenko, the commander of another detachment, entered.

"What's happening at Orekhovo?" he asked, sitting down on the bench alongside of the brigade commander. "What are we waiting for? For the Germans to slaughter all the cows?"

The Germans had seized all the cattle from the inhabitants of several villages. Karpenko had been assigned the task of seizing the cattle from the enemy. But to do this, information was needed as to where the sentries were stationed and where the ammunition was stored.

"Orekhovo is evidently well guarded," Kotliarov said. "It is impossible for a partisan to get through. They'll nab him. And they are keeping track of every person who is now in the village. A stranger will be recognized as such and seized at once. The worst of it is that we don't have a single contact there."

"My aunt lives in Orekhovo . . . ," Raya said humbly.

"A smart woman, your aunt!" Karpenko said, overjoyed by this bit of news. "She knows the right place to live."

"To Orekhovo, you must go in pairs, not just by yourself. One isn't enough," said Kotliarov. "And you must have a ready answer when they ask you what made you decide to visit your aunt just now."

"So, we'll say that we came for seeds," Lara said quickly. "Everyone is sowing now."

"Not bad! She's the youngest, but thinks right on her feet!" Kotliarov said to himself. He looked at the brigade commander and the commander nodded his head in assent.

Never had the head of intelligence been so worried. The sun was setting, but the girls had not yet returned. What kept them? Did they forget the password? To return to the partisan camp, thought Yazno, they had to say the password to the sentry.

"I went out to reconnoiter," Kotliarov later recounted to his commander, "and hiding behind trees and bushes got down the hill to the edge of the lake. At sunset a wind began to blow from the water, and I caught the sound of oars . . ."

Then a barge appeared. Kotliarov could make out the thin figures of two girls standing on it, clinging to each other. He met them as they landed.

"Strange characters!" the bargeman said, "I asked them: 'Where have you been, girls,' and they answered: 'It's a military secret.' "

"They answered properly!" Kostliarov said with a smile, and led the girls onto the shore.

He expected them to start their report right away, but they kept silent, looking back at the bargeman. When he was out of sight, they stopped and squatted down. With a twig, Lara drew a long line in the sand, while Raya opened a kerchief and spilled its contents on the ground—pea, bean, beet, and other seeds.

"What do you know . . . ," Kostliarov muttered. "They're waiting for them at headquarters and they play games. Have they forgotten it wasn't for seeds that they had been sent to Orekhovo!"

But parallel to the first line, Lara drew another, to make a path. On both sides of this path the girl drew small squares. Kostliarov now realized that the path was the village street and the squares represented homes.

"Watch: the seeds will be the German sentries," Lara said as she placed one at the end of the line. "The sentries are stationed here and here and here. The pumpkin seed is the cannon; it is here, behind this house, and the beans—watch where I place them —they are the machine guns . . ."

The clash with the Germans was fierce, but the partisans won. They got all the cattle away from the enemy and seized ammunition and prisoners as well.

Now they could rest for a while. But first Kostliarov went to the espionage shed, to thank the girls for the service they had rendered the brigade.

It was still in the shack. Some had not yet returned from their assignments. Others lay asleep on the floor. Right near the door, on a pile of grass lay Lara and Raya. It looked as if Lara was having a happy dream, she was smiling in her sleep. Her lips moved, and Kostliarov heard this "spy," who had obtained for him such valuable information, saying in her dream: "Mommie."

Strange things began to happen in the villages of the Pustoshkino region. There were rumors about three girls who had appeared in Mogilnoe one evening.

"Dear Auntie, let us sleep the night here! We are orphans, refugees!" they had pleaded.

One of the villagers took pity on them and allowed them to sleep in her hut. The orphans seemed to be full of energy. All evening they ran about the village, playing hide-and-seek and other games with the local children.

Next morning, when the woman got up, she found the window open and the orphans gone. She thought, surely they had fled with the last of the flour. No, the orphans hadn't touched a thing. Then, why, for heaven's sake, did they steal out of the house through the window? A mystery!

Things were even more mysterious in another village. There, three girls offered to watch the cows and asked little for their services. They wore rag shoes and carried staffs as shepherds always do. They watched the cows well, but were afraid of the bull. Then one day the cows came home without their shepherds. The beasts walked over the cucumber and cabbage patches, some knocked down fences.

"Where were the shepherds? What were they thinking of?"

But there was no trace of them.

That same summer, in the village of Luga, the family Kravtsov lost its baby nurse. They had been very satisfied with her. She was a well-behaved and well-educated girl. "The child needs oxygen," she would say. Well, the parents weren't going to argue about it: if the baby needed oxygen, oxygen it should have, and they allowed the brown-eyed young nurse to stay out all day with the infant.

Within three days the girl disappeared. She left without a word. Why? They didn't treat her badly.

Two more days passed and the Kravtsov family was awakened by shots in the night. The partisans had attacked the German garrison. But it didn't even occur to the Kravtsov's that the same girl who thought so highly of oxygen had shown the partisans the way.

So, to help the partisans, Lara and her friends were obliged to hire themselves out as shepherds, babies' nurses, and even pretend to be cuckoos.

Before a planned attack on a motorized German unit, the girls were assigned the task of finding out what motorized equipment was passing along a certain road. Near the village of Efimovo stood an old oak tree. Lara and Raya climbed into this tree. The partisans, waiting in the rear, listened carefully to the sound of the cuckoo.

"Cuckoo, cuckoo!"

When the bird sang its cuckoo loudly and slowly, it meant that supply trucks were passing along the road. The passing motorcycles the birds signalled with a thin, rapid call. And the number of times the cuckoos repeated their call indicated the number of vehicles moving along at one time.

When they heard the shots of the partisans the birds fell silent. They had fulfilled their task, and there was no further need for cuckooing.

A beggar girl walked along the village street. The breeze played with her curly brown hair. She was barefoot and her feet were covered with dust.

"A crust of bread, kind people," her childish voice sounded at the open windows.

Now Lara wasn't ashamed to beg because she did it to outwit the enemy.

The beggar girl entered the village of Pustoshka. There, near the railroad station, lived old man Vanya Guliayev. From his window he could see the station as if it were right on the palm of his hand. He kept track of the German trains that stopped at Pustoshka, and of what supplies they brought. And whatever grandfather Vanya knew the partisans would also know. This knowledge would be relayed to them by the beggar girl.

In the village of Yeltsy she had another grandfather Vanya, whose other name was Smoryg. On the way to the village of Chernetsovo, the little beggar often stopped at his hut. The information which this grand-father Vanya and Lara obtained helped the partisans destroy the German garrison at Chernetsovo.

It was very early in the morning when everyone in the village was still asleep except the housewives who had got up to milk the cows. The morning had barely begun and the sky was not yet blue, but whitish, as if it had been covered with a thin layer of cream.

It was that early, and on that particular morning when from the window of one of the cottages in Timonovo two girls jumped to the ground and fled. They were Lara and Raya.

The evening before the two girl partisans were detained by a German sentry. They had been brought by him to a house well known to Raya. Before the war this house was a village library for children. The Germans had given it to the wife of a former *kulak*.* The woman had met the girls with a mean smile.

"What do we have here?" she had said to them. "Not Raya from Pechenevo? And you have even brought a friend! I suppose you've come for some books that you have not yet had a chance to read. Well, this is no longer a library, thank God! This is now *my* house."

The sentry had left, leaving the detained girls under the surveillance of the woman until next morning. She watched the girls all night, but in the morning, thinking them fast asleep, she went out to milk her cow, locking the door. The girls had only pretended to be asleep. Raya knew that there was a window in the adjoining room, looking out onto the vegetable garden. It was

through this window that the two girls escaped. They ran across the garden and orchard and threw themselves into the nearby stream.

Lara was the first one to get to the opposite shore, and, extending her hand to Raya, she helped her into a thicket of reeds. Not a sound came from the house from which they had just fled.

"She's still milking," Lara said. "While they don't yet know that we've gone, let's hurry and get farther away from here."

"We don't have time to get far enough away," Raya said, shaking her head. "If we could only get to Pechenevo safely, Mother would hide us somehow."

Raya's mother had had a premonition of misfortune. She had slept badly that night and had risen earlier than usual. In the morning, just after dawn, she went to the field to look at the grain. No matter how sad and worried she felt, the sight of growing grain consoled her. Suddenly, two wet and muddy girls sprang from the rye like a pair of quail.

"Mother! Hide us!" Raya's teeth chattered from cold and from fear. "They're after us, Mother! Hide us!"

"Where, my child? Where can one hide from those demons? God! if I could only think of a place! In the cellar, maybe? . . ." The three of them ran to the cellar.

In the winter, potatoes were stored there. Now it was empty. In the semidarkness you could see four white posts, which propped the heavy stove installed in the kitchen above. The girls barely managed to hide behind these posts when they heard steps on the house porch.

"It's a mistake!" they heard Raya's mother say. "I took my girl to the detention camp in Pastushko. I know nothing else about her. No one came here today."

The sound of boots came closer and closer to the cellar. The door was thrown back with a loud thud.

"Here his neck one can break," a coarse voice said. "Old woman, give us a ladder."

---

* The word *kulak* literally means "fist." When used to refer to a certain category of peasant, it means a rich, landowning peasant employing farm labor; the land was taken away from such peasants during the establishment of collective farming in Soviet Russia.

Raya's mother answered that she didn't have a stepladder. "If you need to go down, you can jump," she added.

"It is you who jump, we from here can see," said the same voice.

Two German soldiers leaned over the hatch of the cellar, and a yellow ray from a pocket lantern glided over the cellar floor. It shone into the beady eyes of a huge eagle owl. Slowly, resting on every object, the moving yellow spot surveyed the walls. Then it swept the ceiling, next it fell to the floor again and began to steal up the posts.

Lara saw it rest on Raya's head and light up her hair, then like a sheet of lightning, it flashed between the posts. The girls did not betray their presence with a single motion.

The door was banged closed. Again it was pitch dark and quiet in the cellar. The girls reached out and hugged each other hard.

That evening, Lara's grandmother sat alone at her window thinking about her granddaughter. "Where is she now, my little dove? Far, far away . . ." The grandmother didn't know how near Lara was, nor how dangerous it would be for them to see each other. In those very moments, Lara and her friend were leaving Pechenevo. Again the courageous girl was on the hard road, where danger threatened constantly. But the little partisan was helping her country in its mortal struggle with the enemy. And Lara knew that as long as her heart kept on beating, she would not leave that road.

THE BOY AND THE OFFICER

A. BUSYREV

This true story was published in a Leningrad children's magazine, *Koster* (*Campfire*), in 1942, during the long and bitter siege by the Nazis. Despite daily air raids, famine, and intense cold, life was sustained in the embattled city. Schools, libraries, theaters, concert halls, and movies were kept open, and even this children's magazine continued to be published. A Soviet child copied out this story for me from the magazine—which I borrowed from a Moscow library—so that American children could also read about the Russian boy who is the story's hero.

The wind had piled up huge snowdrifts, making level the road connecting the villages with the meadows and covering the wide main street of the deserted village with a deep layer of snow. The village was in a region that had recently been a battleground. Many had joined the Red Army, hundreds had joined the partisans to carry on guerrilla warfare in the enemy's rear. When the Germans occupied these villages, life came to a standstill. The few remaining villagers withdrew into their homes. Even the Germans called this region on the outskirts of Leningrad a partisan stronghold.

It was in the early spring of 1942. Snorting and puffing, a German car moved slowly along the road. At the edge of the village the car got hopelessly stuck in a deep gully made invisible by the snow. A German officer crawled out and, accompanied by several soldiers, walked toward the village.

Advancing with difficulty through the deep snow, the officer plodded along the middle of the street, surveying with the eye of a ferret every yard and barn. This place was dangerous. He had been informed that only yesterday there was still a partisan detachment in this village. But where had they

disappeared to? How could they now be detected and destroyed?

Suddenly the officer saw a boy coming in his direction. Wearing knee-high felt boots and lifting his feet adroitly from the snow, the boy walked quickly through the drifts. A book was carefully tucked under his arm.

"Surely, the boy knows about the partisans and where they had hid," the German officer decided.

"Seize him!" he ordered.

The cross-examination started in the yard of one of the huts. The officer seated himself on the porch while two of the soldiers held the boy by the shoulders. The boy's cap had slid back, exposing his tow-colored head of hair. Gazing swiftly about him, the boy rested his eyes on the officer's face, then on the soldiers, and last on his book that had dropped to the ground and was lying pressed into the snow by the soldiers' boots. It was Jules Verne's *The Fifteen-Year-Old Captain*.

In a wooden voice the officer shouted his first question. He repeated it. Then he asked a second, a third. The boy stared at the large, red face of the German and, obviously frightened, kept moistening his lips. He remained silent.

This exasperated the officer. He gritted his teeth, making the muscles swell at his temples. He rose, stamped his boot a number of times, then again repeated his questions.

But the boy said not a word. The officer lowered his head for an instant, looked with rage at the prisoner, cursed, and then motioned to the soldiers.

The joints of the soldiers' fists snapped as they struck and blood streamed from the boy's nose and mouth, a bruise closed one of his eyes. His cap flew off his head, and a tuft of his hair scattered like yellow down in the wind. The boy remained silent, spitting blood and wiping his tears with his fist.

The officer stepped off the porch. He tried to feign a smile, bared his teeth, took from his pocket a square of chocolate, and offered it to his captive.

Then the boy spoke up, shouting into the officer's face:

"I don't barter my country."

Next day the partisans found near the barn the corpse of the shot boy. A large crowd gathered. The people took turns in passing the newly-dug grave. The last one to say her farewell was the dead boy's former teacher, now a guerilla fighter with this partisan detachment. Removing her rifle from her shoulder, she addressed the mourners.

"A fascist bullet pierced the loving heart of the little patriot, Tolya Nilov," she said, her voice ringing with emotion in the still, icy air. "These brutes learned nothing from him about the partisans. But they learned, once more, how strong is our people's love for their country. There will come a day when the children of Leningrad and the children all over our land will sing songs about Tolya's love for his native land." Then, turning to the grave, she added, barely able to control her voice, "We vow over your grave to avenge the executioners who are robbing our children of their happiness and life."

THE STORY OF A REAL MAN

BORIS POLEVOY

This is a splendidly written fictionalized story about a war hero. Boris Polevoy (1908———), like so many Soviet authors for young people, had been a journalist before World War II and later became a war correspondent. The book gives a firsthand account of the misfortunes and the feats of a real Russian war hero, Aleksei Mareyev. His name is only slightly changed in the story—to Mereyev.

Early in the war with the Nazis, in the winter of 1941, this Soviet fighter pilot was shot down. For eighteen days, his legs shattered, he crawled through the enemy rear to safety. His frozen legs had to be amputated. Mustering all his willpower and physical strength, he doggedly trained himself to use artificial limbs and to regain his flying skill. Back in the ranks, he fought till the end of the war.

The story paints a broad canvas of the bitter conflict and of the astounding fortitude and courage of this man and of the Soviet people at war. Mereyev symbolizes the "secret war potential of the Soviet nation"—a phrase later used repeatedly by the beaten Nazi leaders in their attempt to explain their defeat at the hands of the Russians.

The excerpt given here tells what happened on the eighteenth day of the wounded flyer's ordeal in the desolate, frigid forest in territory occupied by the enemy.

THE EIGHTEENTH DAY IN THE FOREST

He found it extremely hard to crawl. His arms trembled and gave way, unable to bear the weight of his body. Several times his face hit the melting snow. It seemed as though the earth had enormously increased its force of gravity, it was impossible to resist it. Aleksei wanted very much to lie down and rest for at least half an hour, but the determination to press on amounted to a frenzy today; and so he crawled and crawled, fell, raised himself, crawled again, conscious of neither pain nor hunger, seeing nothing, hearing nothing except the sound of artillery and machine-gun fire.

When his arms ceased to support him, he tried to crawl on his elbows, but this proved to be too strenuous, so he lay down and, using his elbows as levers, tried to roll. He found he could do that. Rolling over and over was easier than crawling and did not call for much exertion. But it made him dizzy, and every now and again he lost consciousness. He had to stop often, sit up, and wait until the earth, the forest, and the sky had stopped whirling round.

The trees began to thin out and here and there were open spaces where the trees had been felled. The trails of winter roads appeared. Aleksei was no longer thinking of whether he would reach his own people, but he was determined to go on rolling as long as he had the strength to move. When he lost consciousness from the frightful strain to which all his weakened muscles were subjected, his arms and his whole body continued automatically to make these complicated movements, and he kept rolling on in the snow—toward the sound of gunfire—eastward.

Aleksei did not remember how he spent that night, or whether he made much progress next morning. Everything was submerged in the gloom of semiconsciousness. He only had a vague recollection of the obstacles he encountered in his path: the golden trunk of a felled pine tree from which dripped amber-colored resin, a stack of logs, sawdust and shavings that were lying about everywhere, and a tree stump clearly showing the yearly rings at the crosscut.

An unusual sound brought him out of his state of semi-oblivion, restored him to consciousness, and roused him to sit up and look around. He found himself in a big forest clearing that was flooded with sunlight and strewn with felled and as yet undressed trees and logs. Standing apart were neat stacks of firewood. The midday sun was high in the sky, the strong smell of resin, of heated conifers, and of snow dampness pervaded the air; and high above the as yet unthawed earth a lark was singing, pouring all its soul into its simple melody.

Filled with a sensation of indefinable danger, Aleksei cast his eyes around the clearing. It was fresh, it did not look as if it were abandoned. The trees had been felled only recently, for the branches on the undressed trees were still fresh and green, the honeylike resin still oozed from the cuts, and a fresh smell emanated from the chips and raw bark that lay around everywhere. Hence, the clearing lived. Perhaps the Germans were preparing logs here for their dugouts and emplacements? In that case he had better clear out as quickly as possible, for the lumbermen might turn up at any moment. But his body felt petrified, fettered by dull, heavy pain, and he had not the strength to move.

Should he crawl on? The instinct that he had cultivated during these days of life in the forest put him on the alert. He did not see but felt that somebody was closely and relentlessly watching him. Who was it? Quiet reigned in the forest, the lark was singing in the sky above the clearing, the hollow pecking of a woodpecker was heard and the tomtits darting among the dropping branches of the felled trees angrily twittered to each other. But in spite of all, Aleksei felt with every fiber of his body that he was being watched.

A branch cracked. He looked around, and among the gray clumps of young pine trees whose curly tops were swaying in the wind he saw several branches that seemed to be acting independently—they did not sway in unison with the rest. And it seemed to him that he heard low, agitated whispers coming from there—the whispers of human beings. He felt a cold shiver run down his spine.

He quickly drew his pistol from the inside pocket of his pilot's suit. The pistol had already grown rusty and he had to use both hands to cock it. The click seemed to startle somebody hidden among the pines. Several of the tree tops swayed heavily, as if somebody had pushed against them, but soon everything was quiet again.

"What is it, a man or an animal?" Aleksei asked himself, and it seemed to him that he heard somebody in the clump of trees also asking: "Is it a man?" Was it his imagination, or did he really hear somebody in the clump speak Russian? Why, yes, Russian! And because it was Russian he was suddenly overcome with such mad joy that, not stopping to think whether it was a friend or foe, he emitted a triumphant yell, sprang to his feet, rushed toward the spot the voice had come from and at once collapsed as if he had been felled, dropping his pistol in the snow.

Collapsing after an unsuccessful attempt to get up again, Aleksei lost consciousness, but the sense of imminent danger quickly brought him round. No doubt there were people hiding in the pines, watching and whispering to each other.

He raised himself up on his arms, picked his pistol up from the snow, keeping it out of sight, close to the ground, and began to watch. Danger had completely drawn him out of his state of coma. His mind was working with precision. Who were these people? Perhaps lumbermen whom the Germans had forced to come here to prepare firewood? Perhaps they were Russians who, like himself, were surrounded and were now trying to get through the German lines to their own people? Or, perhaps, peasants living in the vicinity? After all, he did hear somebody exclaim distinctly, "A man!"

The pistol trembled in his hand that was numb from crawling; but he was prepared to fight and make good use of the remaining three bullets.

Just at that moment an excited childish voice called from the clump of trees.

"Hey! Who are you? Doitch? Fershteh?" *

These strange words put Aleksei on the alert, but it was undoubtedly a Russian who called, and undoubtedly a child.

"What are you doing here?" another childish voice inquired.

"And who are *you?*" retorted Aleksei and stopped, amazed at the faintness and feebleness of his voice.

This question must have caused a sensation among the trees, for whoever were there held a long whispered consultation, accompanied, evidently, with excited gesticulations, for the branches swayed wildly.

"Stop kidding, you can't fool us! I can tell a German miles away. Are you Doitch?"

"Who are *you?*" Aleksei asked.

"What do you want to know for? *Nicht fershteh. . . .*" *

"I am Russian."

"You are lying. Like hell you are! You are a fascist!"

"I am Russian, Russian! An airman. The Germans shot me down."

Aleksei cast all caution to the winds now. He was convinced that his own people were behind those trees—Russians, Soviet people. They did not believe him. That was natural. War teaches one to be cautious. And now, for the first time since he started out on his journey, he felt absolutely done in; he felt that he could not move either hand or foot, neither move nor defend himself. Tears rolled down the dark hollows of his cheeks.

"Look, he's crying!" came a voice from behind the trees. "Hey, you! Why are you crying?"

"I am a Russian, a Russian like you, an airman."

"From what airfield?"

"But who are *you?*"

"What do you want to know for? Answer!"

"From the Monchalov airfield. Why don't you help me? Come out! What the hell. . . ."

There was another, more animated, whispered consultation behind the trees. Aleksei distinctly heard the words, "D'you hear? He says he's from the Monchalov airfield. . . . Perhaps he's telling the truth. . . . And he's crying. . . ."

Then came a shout: "Hey, you, airman! Chuck your gun! Drop it, I tell you, or we won't come out! We'll run away!"

Aleksei threw his pistol away. The branches parted, and two boys, alert, like a couple of inquisitive tomtits ready to dart off in an instant, cautiously, hand in hand,

* The boy asked in German, "Are you German? Do you understand [Russian]?"

* The boy is saying, "I don't understand."

approached Aleksei. The older one, a thin, blue-eyed lad with flaxen hair, held an ax. The younger one, a red-haired, freckle-faced little fellow, his eyes shining with irrepressible curiosity, followed a step behind the first.

"He's crying," he whispered. "He is really crying. And skinny! Look how skinny he is!"

The older boy, still holding the ax, approached Aleksei, kicked the pistol farther away with his huge felt boot—it was probably his father's.

"You are an airman, you say. Have you got any papers? Let's see!"

"Who is here, our people or Germans?" Aleksei asked in a whisper, smiling in spite of himself.

"How do I know, living here in the forest? Nobody reports to me," answered the older boy cagily.

Aleksei had no alternative but to put his hand in his tunic pocket and take out his identity card. The sight of the red officer's card with the star on the cover had a magical effect on the youngsters. It was as if their childhood, which they had lost during the German occupation, was suddenly returned to them by the appearance of one of their own beloved Soviet airmen.

"Yes, yes, our people are here. They've been here for three days."

"Why are you so skinny?" The younger boy asked.

". . . Our men gave them such a licking! There was a terrible big fight here! And an awful lot of them were killed. Awful!"

". . . And didn't they run! It was funny to see them. One of them harnessed a horse to a washtub and rode off in it. Two of them —they were wounded—held on to a horse's tail and another rode on its back, like a baron. You should have seen them! . . . How did they shoot you down?"

After chattering for a while, the youngsters got busy. They said that they lived about five kilometers away. Aleksei was so weak that he could not even turn over to lie more comfortably on his back. The sleigh, which the boys had brought to get brushwood at the "German lumber camp," as they called the clearing, was too small to take Aleksei; and besides, he would have been too heavy for them to haul over the untrodden snow. The older boy, whose name was Seryonka, told his brother Fed'ka to run to the village as fast as he could for help, while he remained to guard Aleksei from the Germans—as he explained, but actually because, in his heart, he did not trust him. "You can never tell," he thought to himself. "These fascists are a sly bunch— they can pretend to be dying and even get Soviet Army papers." But gradually his fears were dispelled and he began to talk freely.

Aleksei now lay dozing on a soft bed of pine needles, with half-closed eyes, listening absent-mindedly to the boy's chatter. Only a few disjointed words reached his mind through the haze of restful languor that had at once spread over his whole body; and although he did not grasp what these words meant, the sounds of his native language gave him keen pleasure. Only later did he hear the story of the disaster that befell the inhabitants of the village of Plavni.

The Germans had arrived in this forest and lake region as far back as October. There had been no fighting in the immediate vicinity of Plavni. About thirty kilometers to the west of the village, the German columns, headed by a powerful tank vanguard, after wiping out a Soviet Army unit that had made a stand at a hastily built defense line, moved around Plavni, which was hidden near a lake away from the road, and rolled on eastward. They were in a hurry to reach Bologoye, the big railway junction, capture it, and thus disconnect the western and northwestern fronts. Here at the far approaches to this town, all through the summer and autumn, the inhabitants of Kalinin Region—townspeople, peasants, women, the aged and children, people of all ages and all professions—had toiled night and day, in the rain, in the heat, suffering from the cold dampness from the marsh and bad drinking water, digging and building defense lines. The fortifications ran from south to north for hundreds of kilometers, through forest and marsh, round the shores of lakes, and along the banks of small rivers and streams.

Great were the sufferings of the builders, but their labor was not in vain. The Germans broke through some of the defense lines in their stride, but were checked at the last one. The fighting changed to positional warfare. The Germans failed to break through to Bologoye; they had to shift the weight of their attack farther south, and on this sector to pass to the defensive.

The peasants of Plavni, who supplemented the usually meager crops they raised on their sandy, clayey soil with successful fishing in the forest lakes, were already rejoicing that the war had passed them by. In obedience to the orders of the Germans, they renamed the chairman of their collective farm village "elder," but continued to carry on as a collective farm, in the hope that the fascists would not for ever trample on Soviet soil and that they would be able to live quietly in their remote haven until the storm blew over. But the Germans in field-gray uniforms were followed by others in black uniforms with skull and crossbones on their forage caps. The inhabitants of Plavni were ordered, on pain of severe penalties, to provide, within twenty-four hours, fifteen volunteers for slave work in Germany. The volunteers were to muster in the building at the end of the village that served as the collective farm office and fish shed, and to have with them a change of underclothing, a spoon, knife and fork and a ten days' supply of provisions. But nobody turned up at the appointed hour. It must be said that, taught by experience, the black-clad Germans evidently had not had much hope that anyone would turn up. To teach the village a lesson,

they seized the chairman of the collective farm, that is, the village "elder," Veronika Grigorievna, the elderly teacher of the kindergarten, two collective-farm team leaders, and ten other peasants they chanced to lay their hands on, and shot them. They gave orders that the bodies should not be buried and said that they would treat the whole village in the same way if the volunteers failed to turn up at the appointed place next day.

Again nobody turned up. Next morning, when the Hitlerites from the *SS Sonderkommando* went through the village, they found every house deserted. Not a soul was in the place, neither young nor old. Abandoning their homes, their land, all the belongings they had accumulated by years of toil, and almost all their cattle, the people had vanished under cover of the night fogs that are prevalent in those parts, without leaving a trace. The entire village, down to the last man, went off to an old clearing, deep in the forest, eighteen kilometers away. After making dugouts for their habitation, the men went to join the partisans,* while the women and children remained to rough it until the spring. The *Sonderkommando* burnt the recalcitrant village to the ground, as they did most of the villages in this district, which they called a dead zone.

"My father was the chairman of the collective farm, 'village elder' they called him," said Seryonka, and his words reached Aleksei's mind as if they came from the other side of a wall. "They killed him. And they killed my big brother. He was a cripple. He had only one arm. He had his arm crushed on the threshing floor and had to have it cut off. Sixteen they killed. . . . I saw it myself. The Germans made us all come and look. My father yelled and swore at them. 'You'll weep tears of blood for this!' he told them."

Aleksei felt a strange sensation sweeping

---

* Civilians fighting in the enemy rear as guerrillas were called *partisans*.

452

through him as he listened to this fair-haired boy with the large, sad, tired eyes. He seemed to be floating in a dense mist. Unconquerable weariness bound his whole body, which had been subjected to such superhuman strain. He was unable to move a finger, and he simply could not believe that he had been on the move only two hours before.

"So you live in the forest?" he asked the boy in an almost inaudible voice, releasing himself with difficulty from the fetters of sleep.

"Yes, of course! There are three of us now. Fed'ka, Mother and I. I had a sister, Niushka her name was. She died in the winter. She got all swelled up and died. And my little brother, he died too. So there are three of us. . . . The Germans aren't coming back, are they? What do you think? Grandfather, my mother's father, that is—he's our chairman now—he says they won't; he says: 'The dead don't come back from the graveyard.' But Mother, she's frightened. She wants to run away. They may come back again, she says. . . . Look! There's Grandad and Fed'ka."

At the edge of the clearing stood red-haired Fed'ka, pointing to Aleksei; and with him was a tall, round-shouldered old man in a ragged, light-brown homespun coat tied at the waist with cord and wearing a high, German officer's peaked cap.

This was Grandad Mikhail, as the boys called him. He had the benevolent face of St. Nicholas as depicted in the simple village icons, the clear, bright eyes of a child and a soft, thin, floating beard which was quite silvery. He wrapped Aleksei in an old sheepskin coat, which was all in multicolored patches.

And as he lifted and rolled his light emaciated body, he kept on saying with naive surprise: "Poor, poor lad! Why, you're wasted away to nothing! Heavens, you're nothing but a skeleton! The things this war is doing to people!"

As carefully as if he were handling a newborn babe, he laid Aleksei on the sleigh, tied him down with a rope, thought for a moment, took off his coat, rolled it up and put it under Aleksei's head. Then, going in front of the sleigh, he harnessed himself to a small horse collar made of sackcloth, and handing a trace to each of the boys, he said, "God, be with us!" and the three of them hauled the sleigh over the thawing snow, which clung to the runners, creaked, and gave way under the feet.

DAREDEVILS

ALEKSEI TOLSTOY

This was in the northwestern direction.

We were lying stretched out on the sweet-smelling grass, in a dense hazel grove. The signaller's post was well concealed; the sky, a pallid blue from the sultry heat, was empty. It was so hot that one could almost hear the leaves crackle. Somewhere nearby was an anthill and Lieutenant Zhabin, every now and then, brushed an ant from his cheek. Chewing a stalk of grass he was in no hurry to begin his story.

"The German soldier is forbidden to use his brains, it's a function that's considered harmful among the fascists," he said. "His brain is not adapted to grasping things at a glance—why, by the time he wakes up . . . Well, it was just these seconds that enabled us to pull it off. . . . We were in a pretty bad fix, there's no doubt about that. Looking back at it now—why, the very thought is enough to make a cold shiver run down your spine. . . . Our men, of course, have plenty of guts. Take signaller Petrov—judging by his looks, nobody would ever say that he had that kind of nerve. He's too good looking for a man—dreamy eyes, a sort of mist in them—he sends his girl a postcard every day. The men are always teasing him: 'Petrov, what are you—flesh and blood, or spirit? You're at the front, man—wake up!' 'Quit it, you fellows,' he would reply. 'Nobody has yet caught me napping in an emergency.' "

"Comrade Zhabin, but how did you manage to remain with twenty-five Red Army men for so many days behind the fascist lines and come through without a scratch?" asked the man with a notebook on his knee.

Zhabin turned over on his side and continued his story.

"I have a driver who's real smart. I asked him one day: 'What made you start chauffering, Shmelkov? You should have been at a university, in the physics and mathematics department.' 'Just happened,' he replied, 'sort of slipped into the job when I was still a kid.' You want to know how we got stranded behind the German lines? Well, you see, I was ordered to concentrate all our equipment in the village 'P' and maintain contact with headquarters until the very last minute.

"The result was that I found myself surrounded. Toward dusk two trucks—they were packed full with fascists who didn't suspect a thing—came clattering into Dubki. We let the Germans go by as calmly as you please, peppered them from the flanks with machine guns and when they started scrambling out of the trucks, we gave them a taste of our bayonets. The Germans don't like that. Some of them managed to get away. Their officer dived into the bulrushes. He sat there in the water, only the tip of his nose showing. We found very important documents in his dispatch case.

"We got the engines of those German trucks started and all twenty-five of us hopped in, with Petrov and myself in the leading car and Shmelkov at the wheel. The sky was covered with clouds, not a single star could be seen, there was no moon yet. We kept on behind the German lines, going parallel with the front. An hour went by, two hours—we didn't meet a soul. To the west of us was the glow of fire; to the east, firing and big explosions. The fires and the booming of the guns helped us to get our bearings.

"Ahead of us should be a familiar village.

We pulled up and Petrov jumped out.

" 'Permit me to reconnoitre,' said he.

"Well, I thought, this is where the man's come to life and clean forgotten about his girl. 'Go ahead.' He crammed his pockets with hand grenades and off he went. He slipped away as quickly and soundlessly as a lizard. About forty minutes later came a rustling in the bushes and there he was, standing near the driver's cabin of the truck.

" 'There's a column of fascist cars in the village,' he reported.

"Well, I thought—that's mighty unpleasant. But it was the only road we could take —to the right and left of us lay swamps and there was no sense in our turning back.

" 'Get in, boys, we'll get through,' Shmelkov said reassuringly.

"Our steel helmets could pass as German in the dark, it was impossible to make out our badges. The only thing likely to give us away was our bayonets, typical Russian bayonets. I ordered the men to hold their rifles on their knees.

"Shortly after we saw three blue lights— the German 'stop signal' at the head of a motor transport column. Shmelkov dimmed our headlights; we could then see seven-ton trucks loaded with cases, and a black swastika on a white disk painted on the radiators. On one side of the road were three officers; they were looking in our direction, flashing electric pocket lamps. Shmelkov switched on the headlights to full; the officers pulled wry faces, shaded their eyes with their hands, while we, as calmly as you please, drove past that motor transport column, turning our heads away so as not to expose the Red Stars on our helmets. We stepped on the gas, passed through a tiny village—a nice snug little place with silent huts hidden amidst blossoming apple and cherry trees; at another time it must have been wonderful to live there. The village was deserted; the inhabitants had fled.

"In an open car near the tiny wooden church sat a German officer with a wizened face and flabby Adam's apple; he was studying a map by the light of a pocket lamp. I just managed to grasp Petrov's arm—he was on the point of leaning out of the cabin and letting fly with a hand grenade.

"That officer, apparently, must have smelt a rat. We had left the village behind us when a twenty horsepower motorcycle with a machine-gunner in the sidecar overtook us. This time Petrov let fly with his hand grenade and he did it so skillfully that the machine-gunner went flying out of his sidecar in our direction for about six feet just as though he was in a hurry to tell us something; the driver, together with the motorcycle, crashed headlong into the ditch.

"We sped on in the dark with lights off. The glow of a big fire on the horizon cast a lurid glare on the black underbrush ahead of us. We came near a small river with a wooden bridge. We slowed down. We heard a gruff order in German. We sat silently, our rifles and hand grenades on the ready. Coming toward us were the dim figures of two sentries. One of them stopped, the other came right up to the driver's cabin and looked in, his nose pressed against the window. We looked each other in the eye. Suddenly he nodded to me, nodded to me and whispered in broken Russian, 'Rus, bridge no go, there fascist will shoot.'

"For about five kilometers we cut across the meadow along the river bank, listening to the croaking of the frogs. We got onto a road and again we saw blue lights, heard the clanking of iron tanks in motion, and the leading tank was about thirty yards from us.

" 'Lie flat,' I said to the men, 'and for heaven's sake keep your rear ends out of sight.'

"We kept to the roadside. We drove on at a leisurely pace respectfully giving the right of way to the heavy black tanks with the swastika painted on a white disk looking for all the world like an eye. The fascist presume that that skull and crossbones of theirs on the tabs of their tunics, their black tanks and screaming bombs are enough to cause panicky fear in their enemies. Maybe . . . They ought to know. Some savages put on masks with fangs and horns when they are on the warpath, also for the purpose of arousing terror. . . .

"After those tanks came anti-aircraft guns, gasoline tank cars and trucks. It was as plain as pie—if we didn't look out we'd get it! We had to get away to another road. But how? Just try—we'd immediately arouse suspicion.

"To our right we caught sight of a birch alley. Shmelkov took the situation in at a glance and turned into it; whitewashed tree trunks flashed by and we drove right into the yard of a *sovkhoz* * garage.

"Shmelkov swung the car around and began to back it as though intending to refuel. Several German soldiers came running up to open the doors of the garage. It's a good thing Hitler didn't teach them to use their brains and use them quickly. Shmelkov, our second truck right behind us, swung around, and, with the lights off, went racing down the birch tree alley. Behind us we heard a yell and some shots but we were already on the road where that same column of tanks and trucks was moving. We drove on like people who had every right to do who had just refueled, sped past the tanks, and turned off the road into a field of tall corn.

"At dawn we reached a small wood and here our supply of fuel gave out. We hid the trucks and sat down to have a bite. Suddenly, Petrov, a biscuit between his teeth, cocked his head, jumped to his feet and dived into the bracken—something had squeaked there—and back he came dragging a youngster of about nine by the arm, close-cropped, snub-nosed, with eyes flashing fire.

" 'What you doin? Can't you see I'm one of us. Lemme go,' the youngster cried. 'I took you for fascists.'

" 'What are you doing here, spitfire?'

---

* A *sovkhoz* is a collective farm.

" 'I'm a scout. I'm working for Grandpa Oksen.'

"It turned out that this youngster, and five other young ragamuffins like him, had remained behind in the hamlet together with eighty-year-old Grandpa Oksen. The men and women, taking their children and livestock with them, had made for the marshy woodlands and were doing a bit of guerilla fighting from there. Grandpa Oksen's homestead served as their headquarters. The six boys snooped about the district all day long, they weren't afraid even to go right up to the Germans, snivelling as if they were begging for a crust, nosing around, prying into things, and in the evening they brought whatever information they had to the old man at the homestead. The partisans * would make their way there at night and the old man assigned them their various jobs: in such-and-such a place the staff of some unit was quartered—it had to be wiped out; in another place a consignment of gasoline had been delivered; a tank unit had just arrived, which had to be blown up.

"That boy was really bright. Before the sun was up he had led us to the other end of the woods—and did he crawl! The young devil wriggled just like a lizard through the grass, we could hardly manage to keep up with him. Only Petrov was his equal. There, on the fringe of the woods, were fuelling tanks and five fighter planes.

"We settled that job in next to no time. When the shots fired by my snipers rang out and the German sentries who had been pacing up and down near their trenches in order to keep awake went sprawling onto the ground, we jumped out from behind the bushes: 'Hurrah!' This cheer of ours always has a bad effect on the nerves of the Germans, a thing that can't be said about their screaming bombs on our men's nerves. The fascists came tumbling out from their dugouts—some of them put their hands up

---

* The *partisans* were civilians who remained behind the lines and conducted guerrilla warfare against the enemy.

at once, others went scurrying around as if they were out of their minds, firing at random from their automatic rifles. We dragged one flier out of a fighter plane by his parachute straps. We set fire to the tank cars and planes and went back into the woods.

"'I'll be running along,' the boy said to us. 'So long. I'll tell Grandpa. He was planning to send a large group to this airport.'

"We stayed where we were the whole day. We heard tanks going by. They combed the woods with their machine guns, but we were well under cover. We decided to make our way at night along the Dvina, on the lookout for a weak point. The fascists don't have a solid front. They advance headlong, in narrow wedges, and—well—with a bit of brains one can always slip through.

"We set out that night, marching in deployed order with machine guns on the flanks. The town 'D' was burning in the distance. It was one mass of flames, the columns of fire reached almost to the clouds. The fascists are fond of this kind of illumination, they prefer it to the movies. Planes circled over the burning city, firing on those who were trying to get away, driving the old folk, men, women, and children back into the flames.

"But enough of that. . . . We were furious, simply itching to get at them. We stopped a passenger car with three officers in it and, before popping them off, made them turn their ugly mugs in the direction of 'D' so that the sight of it would seem less amusing to them than the movies. We cut a heap of communication lines, attacked a motor transport column of twelve tanks, wiped out the convoy, let the gasoline out and set fire to the tanks. We weren't any too pleased after we'd done that: the conflagration was too bright. We got in the way of three tanks that were crawling along at a leisurely pace and were really sorry we had no bottles with liquid fuel with us. Nevertheless, Petrov and two hand-grenade

dischargers collected from the men quite a supply of hand grenades, dashed ahead, took cover on the roadside, and let fly with bundles of hand grenades—each at his own particular target. The leading tank reared, the other two were crippled, they could do nothing but fire at random into the darkness.

"And so we went on all night long, over fields and through woods, until we reached a hamlet the Germans apparently had not been in yet. We looked into one house, then into another, the shutters were up and there was not a sign of life in the yards; suddenly, on one of the huts, on the thatched roof, a cock began to crow, heralding the dawn. Looking around we saw a stocky, bald-headed old man and a shrivelled old woman standing on the porch, awaiting death.

"'Dad,' she says, 'they look like our own.'

"She began blessing us and kissing us in turn. But we—we were in no mood to go kissing with the old lady, we were as hungry as hunters. The old man brought out a loaf of bread, cut it up, and handed out thick slices, which the woman spread with honey: 'Eat, my dears, eat,' she repeated over and over again. 'Eat. . . .'

"To spend the day there would have been dangerous. The old man got into his clothes, put on his sheepskin hat, and led us through the marshy woods to a village where the partisan detachment had its hospital. The whole village came running out to greet us, the women invited us into their huts. We couldn't, after all, offend the good people; we had to accept their hospitality: the wayfarer is lean and dusty; according to the good old custom he has to be washed and fed and taken care of. The women helped us get our things off, tended to our blisters, bathed them, gave us clean socks, and treated us to everything they had in their ovens.

"Petrov, I noticed, was his old sentimental self again, the same old faraway, soft look in his eyes. . . . The peasants tried to talk us into staying behind, to join forces with their partisan unit. . . . And wouldn't we have liked to! . . . But, after all, duty is duty. . . ."

Lieutenant Zhabin sprang lightly to his feet. "Enemy planes!" He snapped out an order. The tall grass in the hazel grove came to life. Five fascist bombers could be seen flying at a high altitude. In less than three minutes after the signaller's post had notified the airport, a unit of our fighter planes appeared in the sky. Like tight strings they sang, threatening powerfully, as they climbed up heading for the bombers. And the heavy fascist machines dipping their wings, started to turn back. But it was too late. The faint rat-tat-tat of machine-gun bursts could be heard from the pallid-blue sky. The fighter planes were hot on their tracks. One of the bombers reeled, then nose-dived toward the ground, leaving a trail of smoke after it.

Prose Poems

There are splendid writers who do not turn to writing poetry, although they respond to their world with poetic sensitivity and intensity. Some of the work of such authors is neither prose nor poetry, in the usual sense of the words. Writing such as this is best called prose-poetry; it is written in free-verse rhythm and expresses an idea or tells of an experience in a highly imaginative and impressive way, and with great beauty of language.

The prose poems by Ivan Turgenev (1818–1883) were called prose poems by the author. Those of Leo Tolstoy (1828–1910) and Mikhail Prishvin (1873–1954) read like prose poems and have been regarded as such by literary critics.

All the prose poems offered here have appeared in Soviet anthologies for young readers.

THE VILLAGE

IVAN TURGENEV

It is the last day of June. For thousands of miles around stretches Russia, my homeland.

The sky is an even blue. There is only one small cloud in it; first it sails off, then melts away. It is windless, balmy, and the air is like tepid milk.

Larks trill, full-throated pigeons coo, swallows dart about in silence, horses snort as they crop the grass, dogs do not bark but stand about gently wagging their tails.

There is the fragrance of smoke and grass, with a trace of tar and a trace of leather. The hemp has bloomed and emits its sharp but pleasant scent.

Nearby is a deep gully with sloping sides. Heavy-crowned willows with streaked trunks stand on each side. A stream flows through the gully, and the pebbles in its bed seem to quiver under the transparent surface of the water. In the distance, where earth and sky meet, the blue ribbon of a long river is visible. To one side of the gully stand neat little barns and small sheds with tightly shut doors. On the other side are a few peasant huts built of pine, with plank roofs. On each roof is a high pole supporting a bird house. Above every porch hangs a small iron horse with an iron mane. The crooked windowpanes reflect all the colors of the rainbow. Vases of flowers are painted on the outside shutters. A neat little bench stands at every hut. Nearby, on low mounds of earth lie cats curled up in balls, pricking up their small, transparent ears. A cool, dark hallway is visible from each high stoop.

I am lying at the edge of the gully on a horse blanket, and around me are piles of newly mown hay, so fragrant as to make me feel almost dizzy. The smart peasants have spread the hay around their huts to give it another chance to dry in the sun before storing it in the barns. How wonderful it will be to sleep on it!

Children peep out from under piles of the hay, the hens search for flies and beetles in it, a puppy with a white muzzle is cavorting in the tangled blades of the long, dry grass.

Fair-haired young men in low-belted clean shirts and heavy, high, trimmed boots lean against the carts, laughing and passing the time of day.

A young, round-faced woman looks out of the window. She smiles, sometimes at their words, sometimes at the children frolicking in the hay.

Another young woman, strong-armed and tall, is drawing a dripping pail from the well. The pail sways on the rope, letting fall large sparkling drops.

My hostess stands before me, an old woman in a checked linen skirt and well-polished shoes. Round her thin, swarthy neck she wears three strands of large glass beads. Her gray head is covered with a yellow kerchief, dotted with red, which she has tied low over her forehead, almost down to her dimming eyes.

But those old eyes are smiling warmly. In fact, all of her wrinkled face is smiling. She is probably seventy, this old woman, but she is still worth looking at. She must have been a beauty in her time!

In the sun-tanned fingers of her right hand she holds a pitcher of cold creamy milk, fresh out of the cellar; the sides of the pitcher are covered with drops of dew, like glass beads. On the palm of her left hand lies a slice of bread, still warm. "Eat, stranger and guest," she says, "may it do you good!"

A cock suddenly crows and beats its wings, and as though in reply comes the slow bleating of a calf from the barn.

Oh, the contentment, the serenity, and the abundance of the spacious Russian countryside. Oh, quietude and bliss!

A SEA VOYAGE

IVAN TURGENEV

I was sailing from Hamburg to London on a small steamer. There were two of us passengers on board—myself and a little monkey, a female of the species *ouistititi*. A Hamburg merchant was sending her as a gift to his English business partner.

The monkey was tied by a light chain to one of the benches on the deck, and she rushed about uttering plaintive birdlike cries.

Every time I passed her she would stretch out her small cold black hand and gaze at me with her sad, almost-human eyes. I sometimes held her hand and she would stop crying and racing about.

There was a dead calm. The sea spread out around us like a motionless leaden cloth. It didn't seem large, for thick fog lay over it, obscuring even the tips of the masts. The sun hung low, a dull red spot, but toward evening all the mist took fire and glowed strangely and mysteriously.

Long, straight folds, like the folds of some heavy, shimmering cloth, extended from the prow of the steamer and grew ever wider, wrinkling as they widened, and as they moved off they smoothed out, quivered, and finally disappeared. The churned foam curled under the monotonously stamping wheel. Milky white and hissing faintly, the foam broke into snakelike streams, which mingled before they too disappeared into the mist.

A small bell at the stern rang incessantly, with a sound as plaintive as the cry of the little monkey.

Now and then a seal would emerge, turn a sharp somersault, and disappear under the scarcely disturbed surface of the water.

The captain, a taciturn man with a weather-marked sullen face, smoked a short pipe and spat glumly into the smooth sea.

To all my questions he replied with an abrupt grunt. I was forced to turn to my one fellow passenger, the monkey.

I sat down near her. She stopped wailing and again offered me her hand.

We were both enveloped by the hushed dampness of the fog, and, sunk in the same reverie, we remained side by side as though we were kin.

I smile now when I think of that voyage, but at the time my feelings were different.

We are all children of one mother, of Nature, and I was pleased that the poor little beast grew so confidently calm and pressed against me as to one of her own.

THE SPARROW

IVAN TURGENEV

I was returning from a day's hunting and was walking toward the house along an alley in my garden. My dog was running ahead of me.

Suddenly she slowed her pace and began to advance stealthily, as though she had caught scent of game.

I looked down the path and saw a young sparrow with a streak of yellow near its beak and a bit of puff on its head. It had fallen out of the nest. (A strong wind was swaying the birch trees.) The tiny bird sat there trying helplessly to use its barely-grown wings.

My dog was stealing up to the infant sparrow when, abruptly, an old black-chested bird fell like a stone right in front of the dog's face, and with all its feathers standing on end, misshapen, uttering a desperate and pitiful chirp, it hopped once and then again in the direction of the dog's open jaw.

The bird had thrown itself in front of the dog to shield its young one, but its own small body was trembling with terror, its little voice was frenzied and hoarse, and it was numb with fright—it was sacrificing itself!

What a huge monster the dog must have seemed to the mother sparrow! Nevertheless, it could not bear to stay on its high, safe perch in the tree. A force stronger than its will to remain alive made it hurl itself to the rescue.

My Treasure, the dog, stopped still and then backed up. Evidently he, too, recognized that force. . . .

I hastened to call off the puzzled dog and went on my way, awed.

Yes, do not laugh. I was awed by that small, heroic bird—by its impulse of love.

Love, I felt more than ever, is stronger than death and the fear of death. Only through love is life sustained and nourished.

THE DEW ON THE GRASS

LEO TOLSTOY

When on a sunny morning you walk through the meadow toward the forest, you will see jewels scattered over the grass. All these jewels glisten in the sun and flash in many colors—yellow and red and blue. When you get nearer and look closer, you will see that the gems are drops of dew that have gathered in the blades of grass and reflect the rays of the sun.

The inside of each blade is mossy, and downy like velvet, and the dewdrops roll over the blades of grass without wetting them.

When you happen to tear off a blade with a dewdrop in it, the drop will roll off like a tiny ball of light. Or, perhaps you will tear off the little cupful, carefully raise it to your lips and drink up the dewdrop. You are likely to think it the most delicious drink there is.

462

THE SWANS

LEO TOLSTOY

It was autumn. A flight of swans was moving across the sky toward warm lands. The swans soared high over the sea. In the full moon they could see the black-blue water below. They had been flying day and night. All of them were tired, but they did not stop and kept on beating their wings. At the head of the flight were the older and stronger swans, behind them the younger and weaker ones. A very young swan came last. All of his strength had been spent. He kept working his wings but could no longer keep himself in the air. Spreading his wings wide, he began to come down, getting nearer and nearer to the water. His friends flew on and soon looked like white specks in the moonlit sky.

The young swan alighted on the water and noiselessly folded his wings. The waves rocked him. The flying swans now looked like a white streak in the sky. The faint sound of the beating of their wings could be heard in the stillness. When they were completely out of sight, the young swan closed his eyes, turned his neck to the side and rested his head against his wing. He did not stir, but the waves lifted him as they came up and lowered him as they receded.

Before dawn a light wind began to stir the water. It splashed against the swan's white breast. He opened his eyes. The rising sun was spreading a pink blush over the east and the moon and stars looked pale. The young swan sighed, stretched his neck, and—fluttering his wings, dipping their tips in the water—rose higher and higher and flew alone over the undulating sea.

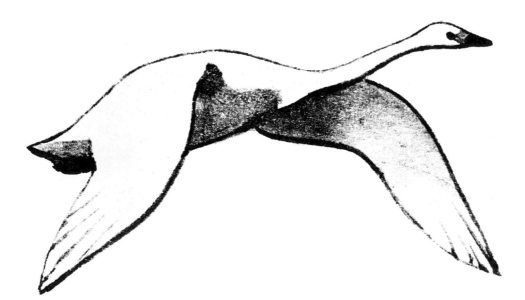

SPRING OF LIGHT

MIKHAIL PRISHVIN

To those who observe nature from day to day, the coming of spring is announced first of all by more light. The countryfolk then say that the bear is turning over in his lair; the sun smiles ever friendlier and, though more frosts are ahead, the gipsy sells his sheepskin.

January, February, and early March all belong to the spring of light. The ice seems to break up in the sky, and there is a great scurrying of airy floes up there; and you can see it best in a large town, watching it in the spaces between the heavy masses of stone buildings. He is a happy man who can meet the early spring of light in town and then go to the country, closer to nature, to meet the spring of water, the spring of woods and grass, and even—who can tell?—the spring of man.

When after a hard winter the spring of light comes into its brilliant own, people living close to the soil are stirred and keep asking themselves: What will the spring be like this year? And every year it is different from what it was the year before, and no spring is ever like another.

This year the spring of light lingered too long, and its dazzling snows were almost unbearable to the eye.

"It'll come all at once," everybody said.

No, a new spring is never like the old one, and that is what makes living so good—the thrilling expectation of something new every year.

CUMULUS CLOUDS—HERALDS OF SPRING

MIKHAIL PRISHVIN

Overnight an enormous snowdrift formed in front of our house—all smooth and gleaming like the unruffled breast of a swan. It was with some difficulty that I opened the door, against which last night's snow had piled up. Then I began to dig a trench, shoveling away the fluffy new snow and slicing through the thick caked layers underneath.

I was not sorry to destroy the drift, for up there amid the airy floes there sailed a cloud so unlike the clouds of winter; it was huge and warm, smooth and gleaming—also like the unruffled breast of a swan.

464

I stood there leaning on the spade thrust deep in the snow, my heart brimming with love—for whom I could not tell.

Two crows were somersaulting over the purple forest.

Why, that's whom I love so dearly—those birds. On a bleak winter day when the frost is so severe that the sun seems crucified on dazzling pillars, when man and beast have hidden away and most birds fall dead on the wing, when I trudge along, uncertain whether I shall ever get home, it is that bird, the crow, alone that keeps me company, flying high over the desolate whiteness, its frostbitten wing scraping the wind.

And now the crows are in a love frenzy, hurtling themselves against each other.

Crows turning somersaults—what a happy sight! A melody rings in my heart, a song without words about the blue of the skies with a warm cloud, like a great white bird with a swanlike breast, unsullied and unruffled, floating across the spring-flooded spaces.

LAND!

MIKHAIL PRISHVIN

There had been no frost for three days, and the thick mist had secretly done its work on the snow.

"Come out, Dad!" my son Petya called. "Listen to those buntings."

I came out and listened. It was good to hear their singing, and the breeze was soft and warm. The road had grown all rusty and humpbacked.

It was as though somebody had been trying hard to catch up with the spring and had at last succeeded and touched her, arresting her heedless progress and making her pause for thought. The cocks were crowing all around us and the woods loomed blue in the mist.

Petya stood peering into the milky wisps and suddenly noticed something dark way off in the field.

"Look, the earth is showing!"

He ran into the house and I heard him shouting to his mother and brother: "Come and have a look. Quick, the earth is showing!"

Even Mother came out, and shielding her eyes, asked, "Where?"

Petya ran a few steps and stood pointing at the snowy distance like Columbus:

"Land!"

THE THAW

SERGEI AKSAKOV

Sergei Aksakov (1791–1859) is best known for his remarkable book of childhood—his own—*The Childhood Years of Bagrov's Grandson,* in which he speaks with great insight, knowledge, and love about the seasons and other delights of nature. The author had been a sickly youngster and the family moved to the country to help him get stronger. A local peasant was hired to occupy himself with the boy; this peasant was a born naturalist, and the two wandered over the countryside, with the old man disclosing to his young master the wonders of the outdoors.

Referring to Aksakov's nature writing, the famous Russian novelist Nikolai Gogol once wrote to him: "Your birds and fishes are more alive than my men and women!"

Here is an excerpt from *The Childhood Years of Bagrov's Grandson.*

One of the greatest pleasures of the Russian people is to observe a river in the spring thaw.

"The river has stirred . . ." The news spreads by word of mouth, and the whole village, from its babes to its grandfathers, pours out to the riverbank, no matter what the weather. There they remain for a long, long time—a colorful crowd standing against the white and the gray of ground and sky, admiring every stirring of the ice as they make predictions and utter gay exclamations.

At this time of the year the stirring river is a magnificient, strange, and amazing sight.

For nearly half of the year it had not existed. It had been an extension of the snowdrifts and of the paths cut through them. People would walk, ride, and gallop over the river as they would over dry ground, and they would almost forget that the river was there, under them. Then, suddenly, a wide streak in this motionless, snow-covered expanse stirs, separates from the rest of the thick, hard surface and moves on—it moves with everything that happens to be on it at the time, with piles of all kinds of objects, with the cattle that happened to stray over its frozen surface, and at times even with the people who were making the crossing.

Calmly and majestically, beginning with a dull, menacing, crashing noise, the endless snow-covered ice serpent moves. Soon it begins to crack and break up into blue-white boulders of ice which turn on their side, rise up, and clash with one another like mounted warriors. They crash, whirl around, and move on.

Gradually the boulders get small, begin to sink, and then disappear in the water. The river has moved on in its course!

The churned water, freed from a half year's imprisonment, slowly stretches toward the shores, floods them, and pours over the meadows.

INDEXES

INDEX OF AUTHORS

Page numbers in italics refer to editorial comments or discussions; other page numbers refer to selections.

INDEX OF ILLUSTRATORS

The woodcuts in the part-title pages are by the noted book illustrator, Vladimir Favorsky.